ACTS

NCCS | New Covenant Commentary Series

The New Covenant Commentary Series (NCCS) is designed for ministers and students who require a commentary that interacts with the text and context of each New Testament book and pays specific attention to the impact of the text upon the faith and praxis of contemporary faith communities.

The NCCS has a number of distinguishing features. First, the contributors come from a diverse array of backgrounds in regards to their Christian denominations and countries of origin. Unlike many commentary series that tout themselves as international the NCCS can truly boast of a genuinely international cast of contributors with authors drawn from every continent of the world (except Antarctica) including countries such as the United States, Puerto Rico, Australia, the United Kingdom, Kenya, India, Singapore, and Korea. We intend the NCCS to engage in the task of biblical interpretation and theological reflection from the perspective of the global church. Second, the volumes in this series are not verse-by-verse commentaries, but they focus on larger units of text in order to explicate and interpret the story in the text as opposed to some often atomistic approaches. Third, a further aim of these volumes is to provide an occasion for authors to reflect on how the New Testament impacts the life, faith, ministry, and witness of the New Covenant Community today. This occurs periodically under the heading of "Fusing the Horizons and Forming the Community." Here authors provide windows into community formation (how the text shapes the mission and character of the believing community) and ministerial formation (how the text shapes the ministry of Christian leaders).

It is our hope that these volumes will represent serious engagements with the New Testament writings, done in the context of faith, in service of the church, and for the glorification of God.

Series Editors:
Michael F. Bird (Ridley College, Melbourne, Australia)
Craig Keener (Asbury Theological Seminary, Wilmore, KY, USA)

Titles in this series:
Romans Craig Keener
Ephesians Lynn Cohick
Colossians and Philemon Michael F. Bird
Revelation Gordon Fee
John Jey Kanagaraj
1 Timothy Aída Besançon Spencer
2 Timothy and Titus Aída Besançon Spencer
Mark Kim Huat Tan
Jude and 2 Peter Andrew Mbuvi
1–2 Thessalonians Nijay Gupta

1 Corinthians B. J. Oropeza
Luke Diane G. Chen

Forthcoming titles:
Galatians Jarvis Williams
James Pablo Jimenez
1–3 John Sam Ngewa
Matthew Jason Hood
Philippians Linda Belleville
Hebrews Cynthia Westfall
2 Corinthians Ayodeji Adewuya

ACTS

A New Covenant Commentary

Part II: Chapters 13–28

Youngmo Cho
Hyung Dae Park

CASCADE *Books* · Eugene, Oregon

ACTS
Part II: Chapters 13–28

New Covenant Commentary Series

Cascade Books
An Imprint of Wipf and Stock Publishers
199 W. 8th Ave., Suite 3
Eugene, OR 97401

www.wipfandstock.com

PAPERBACK ISBN: 978-1-5326-1884-0

HARDCOVER ISBN: 978-1-4982-4466-4

EBOOK ISBN: 978-1-4982-4465-7

Cataloging-in-Publication data:

Names: Cho, Youngmo. | Park, Hyung Dae.
Title: Acts : part II : chapters 13–28. / Youngmo Cho and Hyung Dae Park.
Description: Eugene, OR : Cascade Books, 2019. | Series: New Covenant Com-
      mentary Series. | Includes bibliographical references and index.
Identifiers: ISBN 978-1-5326-1884-0 (paperback) | ISBN 978-1-4982-4466-4
      (hardcover) | ISBN 978-1-4982-4465-7 (ebook)
Subjects: LCSH: Bible. Acts, XIII–XXVIII—Commentaries.
Classification: LCC BS2625.3 A22 2019 (print) | LCC BS2625.3 (ebook)

Manufactured in the U.S.A.

Contents

Preface

For this piece of work, the two Koreans, Youngmo Cho and Hyung Dae Park, met for the first time of their lives. They were excited about ex-egeting the Acts of the Apostles in a language foreign to them, anxious somewhat due to the importance and difficulties of this work. They concentrated on this labor for more than seven years. In the meantime, they noticed that they were quite distinct in their studies; Cho wrote *Spirit and Kingdom in the Writings of Luke and Paul: An Attempt to Reconcile These Concepts* (Paternoster, 2005) as his doctoral work, but Park did *Finding Herem?: A Study of Luke-Acts in the Light of Herem* (T. & T. Clark International, 2007). Further, Cho has been discipled in Pentecostal churches while Park in Presbyterian churches. Remarkably, as the duet agreed in unison, Cho is a kind and meticulous person like Barnabas, but Park is strict and hasty to some extent like Paul.

Nonetheless, the differences of these two writers made this composition more dynamic; Cho undertook composing the introduction and the sections from "The Beginnings" (ch. 1) to "Peter's Deliverance and Herod's Death" (ch. 12), and Park compiled the preface and the sections from "Mission to Cyprus and Pisidian Antioch" (ch. 13) to "Paul's Ministry in Malta and Rome" (ch. 28); Park fused the horizons in the sense of the community whereas Cho did it in terms of the spiritual, supernatural, and persevering perspectives; Cho's writing flows smoothly, yet Park's prose may strike readers as more abrupt. Understanding these backgrounds could be helpful in benefiting from this book.

Cho and Park have many mentors, friends, colleagues, and acquaintances, too many to be listed here altogether, otherwise the readers would confuse this short preface with an encyclopedia. Even so, there are people we as the writers would like to thank through this page. Craig Keener and Michael Bird, the editors who had waited for our final manuscripts for almost a decade and having had to tolerate the writers' few, well several, reports of postponements, and Brian Palmer, an editorial administrative assistant for the publisher who was patient with receiving the manuscripts. At the same time, to Cho's other half, Grace (Gyunhee), and their daughter and son, Naan and Hajune, and to Park's better half, Sarah (Kang Nye), and their five children, Ju Eun (Park's proofreader), Jusung David, Juhee Joy, Ju Yun Samuella, and Juha Grace, we each express our heartfelt gratitude for their love and togetherness.

Our efforts should be melted away in the support, advice, endurance, comforts, and love of others; so Hallelujah, may the Lord only be glorified. Amen.

Abbreviations

ABD	*Anchor Bible Dictionary*
AJPS	*Asian Journal of Pentecostal Studies*
ASB	*Austin Seminary Bulletin*
ATANT	Abhandlungen zur Theologie des Alten und Neuen Testaments
ATR	*Anglican Theological Review*
BBR	*Bulletin for Biblical Research*
BDAG	Walter Bauer, F. W. Danker, W. F. Arndt, and F. W. Gingrich. *A Greek-English Lexicon of the New Testament and Other Early Christian Literature.* 3rd ed. Chicago: University of Chicago Press, 2000.
BETS	*Bulletin of the Evangelical Theological Society*
Bib	*Biblica*
BR	*Biblical Research*
BSac	*Bibliotheca Sacra*
BST	Bible Speaks Today
BT	*Black Theology*
CB	*Christian Bioethics*
CBQ	*Catholic Biblical Quarterly*
DDD	K. van der Toorn, B. Becking, and P. W. van der Horst, eds. *Dictionary of Deities and Demons in the Bible.* Grand Rapids: Eerdmans, 1999.
CJ	*Concordia Journal*
DNTB	*Dictionary of New Testament Background*

DPL	G. F. Hawthorne and R. P. Martin, eds. *Dictionary of Paul and His Letters.* Downers Grove, IL: IVP, 1993.
CTJ	*Calvin Theological Journal*
CTM	*Currents in Theology and Mission*
EBD	*Easton's Bible Dictionary*
ECNT	Exegetical Commentary on the New Testament
ED	*Eerdmans Dictionary of the Bible*
ESV	English Standard Version
ExpTim	*Expository Times*
GNB	Good News Bible
HUCA	*Hebrew Union College Annual*
IBMR	*International Bulletin of Missionary Research*
ICC	International Critical Commentary
Int	*Interpretation*
ISBE	James Orr, et al., eds. *The International Standard Bible Encyclopedia.* 5 vols. Grand Rapids: Eerdmans, 1939.
ISBE^R	G. W. Bromiley, ed. *The International Standard Bible Encyclopedia.* 4 vols. Grand Rapids: Eerdmans, 1979–1988.
JBL	*Journal of Biblical Literature*
JES	*Journal of Ecumenical Studies*
JP	*Journal for Preachers*
JPT	*Journal of Pentecostal Theology*
JPTSS	JPT Supplement Series
JSJ	*Journal for the Study of Judaism in the Persian, Hellenistic, and Roman Periods*
JSNT	*Journal for the Study of the New Testament*
JSNTSup	JSNT Supplement Series

JSOT	*Journal for the Study of the Old Testament*
JSOTSup	JSOT Supplement Series
JSPSup	Journal for the Study of the Pseudepigrapha: Supplement Series
JTS	*Journal of Theological Studies*
KJV	King James Version
LEH	*A Greek-English Lexicon of the Septuagint*, second edition
L&N	J. P. Louw and E. A. Nida, eds. *Greek-English Lexicon of the New Testament: Based on Semantic Domains.* 2nd ed. New York: United Bible Societies, 1989.
LNTS	Library of New Testament Studies
LTQ	*Lexington Theological Quarterly*
LSJ	H. G. Liddell, R. Scott, and H. S. Jones. *A Greek-English Lexicon.* 9th ed. with revised supplement. Oxford: Oxford University Press, 1940.
LXX	Septuagint
NAC	New American Commentary
NASB	New American Standard Bible
*NBD*³	J. D. Douglas, N. Hillyer, and D. R. W. Wood, eds. *New Bible Dictionary.* 3rd ed. Leicester: InterVarsity, 1996.
NET	New English Translation
NICNT	New International Commentary on the New Testament
NIV	New Testament Version
NIVAC	NIV Application Commentary
NKJV	New King James Version
NLT	New Jerusalem Bible
NovT	*Novum Testamentum*

NPNF1	*Nicene and Post-Nicene Fathers*, Series 1
NPNF2	*Nicene and Post-Nicene Fathers*, Series 2
NRSV	New Revised Standard Version
NT	New Testament
MT	*Modern Theology*
OT	Old Testament
PDBS	*Pocket Dictionary of Biblical Studies*
PDSNTG	Matthew S. DeMoss. *Pocket Dictionary for the Study of New Testament Greek*. Downers Grove, IL: InterVarsity, 2001.
PEQ	*Palestine Exploration Quarterly*
Presb	*Presbyterion*
PRS	*Perspectives in Religious Studies*
QDAP	*Quarterly of the Department of Antiquities in Palestine*
RevExp	*Review and Expositor*
RQ	*Restoration Quarterly*
RSR	*Religious Studies Review*
RTR	*Reformed Theological Review*
SBLDS	Society of Biblical Literature Dissertation Series
SBLMS	Society of Biblical Literature Monograph Series
S&I	*Scripture and Interpretation*
SM	*Svensk missionstidskrift*
SP	Sacra Pagina Series
Thayer	Joseph Henry Thayer. *Greek-English Lexicon of the New Testament: Being Grimm's Wilke's Clavis Novi Testamenti*. Translated, revised, and enlarged. Grand Rapids: Zondervan, 1970 [1962].
TJ	*Trinity Journal*
TNIV	Today's New International Version

TWOT	*Theological Wordbook of the Old Testament*
TynBul	*Tyndale Bulletin*
UBS4	*United Bible Society Greek New Testament, Fourth Edition*
Wor	*Worship*
WTJ	*Westminster Theological Journal*
WUNT	Wissenschaftliche Untersuchungen zum Neuen Testament
WW	*Word and World*

ANCIENT SOURCES

1QS	*Rule of the Community*
1QSa	*Rule of the Congregation*
1–2 Macc	1–2 Maccabees
2 Esd	2 Esdras
3–4 Macc	3–4 Maccabees
4Q381	Non-Canonical Psalms
Augustine	
Conf.	*Confessionum libri XIII (Confessions)*
Spir. et Litt.	*De spiritu et littera (The Spirit and the Letter)*
CD	Cairo Genizah copy of the *Damascus Document*
Did.	*Didache*
Dio Cassius	
History	*Roman History*
Epiphanius	
Haer.	*Panarion Haereses*
Eusebius	
Hist. eccl.	*Historia Ecclesiastica*
Herodotus	
Hist.	*Histories*
Hippolytus	

Ref.	*Refutatio Omnium Haeresium*

Irenaeus
Adv. Haer.	*Adversus Haereses*

John Chrysostom
Hom. Act.	*Homiliae in Acta apostolorum*

Josephus
Ant.	*Jewish Antiquities*
J.W.	*Jewish War*
Life	*The Life*

Jub.	*Jubilees*

Justin Martyr
1 Apol.	*First Apology*

Mishnah (*m.*)
ʾAbot	*ʾAbot*
Ber.	*Berakhot*
Mak.	*Makkot*
Naz.	*Nazir*

Ovid
Metam.	*Metamorphoses*

Philo
Cher.	*On the Cherubim*
Legat.	*Legatio ad Gaium*
Moses	*On the Life of Moses*
Prob.	*Quod omnis probus liber sit*

Plutarch
Pom.	*Pompey*

Pss. Sol.	*Psalms of Solomon*

Sib. Or.	*Sibylline Oracles*

Sir	*Sirach*

Strabo
Geogr.	*Geographica (Geography)*

Suetonius
Claud.	*Divus Claudius*

Tacitus
  Ann.   *The Annals*

Tertullian
  Marc.   *Adversus Marcionem*

T. Levi   *Testament of Levi*

Tob   Tobit

ACTS 13

Mission to Cyprus and Pisidian Antioch[1]

Barnabas and Paul, along with John Mark, returned from Jerusalem to Syrian Antioch (Acts 12:25); after providing emergency aid to the brothers in Judea, the Antioch church received an important mission from the Holy Spirit (13:1–2). There is a place shift from Jerusalem to Antioch in Syria. The birth of the Antioch church is introduced in 11:19–26, then her growth in 11:27–30. Now, the situation at the house of Mary, the mother of John Mark (12:12–15), induces the Antioch church's leading status instead of the Jerusalem church. Even though John Mark accompanied Barnabas and Paul (13:5b), his companionship lasted only within Cyprus[2] (13:13b): this fact may resultantly justify the Lord's singling out the Antioch church for further missionary work rather than the Jerusalem church.

The first missionary journey might have occurred around 45–47 CE. There are two pivot points to discern this period: (1) the famine previously stated in 11:28 and (2) the proconsulship of Sergius Paul(l)us. The famine may refer to the one "under the procurators Cuspius Fadus and Tiberius Julius Alexander, i.e., between AD 44 and 48" as inferred from what Josephus said.[3] And Sergius Paulus is thought to have held his proconsulship around "AD 46–48."[4] Even though these two periods can be fixed, opinions divide in terms of the time "when Barnabas and Paul had gone through the whole island" (13:6). Some, who seem to ponder more thoroughly, conclude that they arrived at Salamis in 45 CE;[5] others,

---

1. "Πισιδίαν is an adj. here: Pisidian Antioch was so called because it was near Pisidia" (Bruce 1990: 300).

2. See comments on 11:20–21.

3. Bruce 1990: 276. See *Ant.* 20.101 and comments on 11:28.

4. Hill 1940: 255. So also Bruce 1990: 297, etc. Lake and Cadbury 1933: V: 455 conjecture, "Sergius Paulus, if the name be reported correctly, must have been Proconsul of Cyprus between the years 40 and 50, and probably within a year or two, one way or the other, of AD 45."

5. See Hill 1940: 247; Schnabel 2012: 548; Unger 1960: 229; etc.

who calculate their journey within Cyprus to be even shorter, speculate that they started their mission in Cyprus after 46 CE.[6] Meanwhile, Campbell suggests that this mission could have begun "late in the winter or very early in the spring of 37 CE" since Paulus's proconsulship could have been under Tiberius (reigned 14–37 CE) or Gaius (reigned 37–41 CE).[7] However, compelling evidence needs to be provided for his proposal to be accepted widely. Hence, to wrap up, the mission in Cyprus could have taken place around 45–46 CE, "at the commencement of the navigation season (the first week in March),"[8] and the mission in Pisidian Antioch around 46–47 CE.

Between 45 and 46 CE, Barnabas and Paul went to "the largest island in the Mediterranean (being a good deal smaller than Sicily and Sardinia)." Cyprus "has an area, according to the official figures, of 3584 square miles," and "its greatest length, from W.S.W. to E.N.E. (i.e., from Paphos harbour or C. Drepanum to C. St Andreas), is 138 miles; its greatest breadth, from N. to S. (i.e., from C. Kormakiti to C. Gata), 60 miles."[9] This island became a Roman province after the death of Cleopatra, a Ptolemaic queen of Egypt in 30 BCE: "When in 27 BC the provinces came to be divided between Emperor and Senate, it was at first imperial—perhaps in combination with Cilicia. In 22 BC it was returned to the Senate, to be governed henceforward by an ex-praetor with the title of proconsul, on whose staff were a legatus and a quaestor."[10] Hill, the writer of an exhaustive book on the history of Cyprus, introduces this island as a land compelling especially to the ruler who had illusions of imperial grandeur in the East because there was a saying that "he who would become and remain a great power in the East must hold Cyprus in his hand. This is proved by the history of the world during the last three and a half millennia, from the time of Thutmes III of Egypt to the days of Queen Victoria."[11] The mission to Cyprus can be illuminated with respect

6. Fitzmyer 1998: 502 considers the time span for "Paul's Mission I as AD 46–49," and Bruce 1990: 92 sees it as approximately 47–48 CE.

7. Campbell 2005: 13, 24.

8. According to Unger 1960: 229, "It is highly probable that the two pioneer missionaries started at the commencement of the navigation season (the first week in March) since their destination was the 130-mile trip southwest to Salamis on the east coast of the island."

9. Hill 1940: 1–2.

10. Hill 1940: 211, 230.

11. Hill 1940: 1, quoted from a German archaeologist writing, "Gustav Hirschfeld, in the *Deutsche Rundschau*, XXIII, 1880, p. 270."

to this position of Cyprus in the East. Evangelizing the whole population of the island, particularly Paulus the proconsul, sounds like a good starting point for the Roman mission.

As for Pisidian Antioch that was evangelized in the next one or two years, the city "was governed by Rome, everyone born in the city automatically had Roman citizenship (and the rights thereof), and the land was exempt from certain taxes," after becoming a Roman colony (in 25 BCE). "These [ex-soldiers] settlers of Antioch were veterans of the Alauda Legion—'the Lark'—a legion raised in Gaul by Julius Cæsar, which bore on its standards the regimental badge of a skylark."[12] It is worth being called "Little Rome" for her advantages.[13] When Barnabas and Paul arrived in the city, Pisidian Antioch belonged to Galatia because Provincia Galatia had already "stretched from Pontus on the Black Sea to Pamphylia on the Mediterranean."[14] It is right administratively for the people in Pisidian Antioch to be called "Galatians" (Gal 3:1).[15] Paul's first speech in Acts was to the Galatians; his long and unique speech to the Jews and the Godfearers is carefully introduced in Acts 13:16b–41.

12. Morton 1937 [1936]: 211. In his trip in the 1930s, he saw "the broken arches of a Roman aqueduct stand on a bleak hill," which was the unique evidence of Pisidian Antioch, so he concludes: "The more I explored the ruined cities of Asia Minor, the more truly I realized that the history of man in his country was writ literally in water" (Morton 1937 [1936]: 214–15).

13. Rothschild 2012: 347–49. His insistence that "this *inclusio* from 'Little Rome' in chapter 13 to 'Big Rome' in chapter 28 is emphasized in a number of different ways in Acts" can be agreeable, but his "denouement of the South Galatian Hypothesis" is still unstable. Rothschild 2012: 340–45 suggests five evidences to support Galatia just as a literary desideratum: "(1) stereotypes; (2) lack of detail; (3) historical inaccuracies; (4) brisk narrative pace; and (5) link between Cyprus and Antioch." However, his arguments are very subjective. In Acts, the Pisidian Antioch narrative is not short in length, and has Paul's unique speech to the Jews. John Mark's return to Jerusalem may be caused by an unexpected route. As Pervo 2009: 320 makes clear: "The route taken by Barnabas and Paul is difficult to comprehend. The normal way for those who set out from Syria to visit Derbe, etc., would be overland from Antioch." Further, the journey from Paphos to Perga should be "quite a direct route," according to Campbell 2000: 601.

14. Bruce 1982: 5. This evidence supports "the South Galatian hypothesis."

15. In regard to the province of Galatia, see R. K. Shrenk, "Roman Galatia," *ANRW* II.7.2, 954–63.

Inexplicably, in Acts 13:9 Saul (*Saulos*) is introduced as Paul (*Paulos*), "the Roman name of Saul."[16] Paul in Latin "means 'small' or 'little.'"[17] As Ramsay says, Paul doubtlessly "replied to the questions of Sergius Paulus, by designating himself as a Roman, born at Tarsus, and named Paul."[18] Nevertheless, the change of his name could represent the change of his mindset "from the proud 'big man' who persecuted the church, to the servant of 'little' David's messianic offspring," as McDonough explains.[19] Further, the location of this report could be signaling an invasion of the Word. The gospel will stretch greatly and deeply into the Roman region from Palestine and its northern neighbor, which had been for a long time a battlefield between Parthia and Rome. If we settle on Gilbert's insistence that "Luke-Acts presents Jesus and the church as existing in competition with Rome and its leaders over the claim of universal authority,"[20] we can identify their missions to Cyprus and the "Little Rome" as the process of the good news storming into the heart of Rome.

Barnabas and Saul Separated (13:1–3)

In the Antioch church "existing at that [contemporary] time,"[21] there were prophets and teachers. The Greek conjunctions (*te . . . kai*) indicate that

16. Lake and Cadbury 1933: IV: 145 confirms "Paul was the Roman name of Saul" and concludes, "It is possible, therefore, that in Paul's case the name Παῦλος has nothing to do with his Roman citizenship or with the familiar Latin cognomen Paul(l)us."

17. McDonough 2006: 390.

18. Ramsay 1975 [1897]: 83.

19. McDonough 2006: 391 also gives attention to this fact: "This [Acts 13:21] is the only time in the entire NT that (the OT) Saul appears. It seems unusual that this sole occurrence should come just after the Apostle's name change in 13:9." This idea started with Augustine, who said, "Accordingly Paul, who, although he was formerly called Saul, chose this new designation, for no other reason, as it seems to me, than because he would show himself *little*—the 'least of the apostles'—contends with much courage and earnestness against the proud and arrogant" (italics original; *Spir. et litt.* 12; *NPNF*1 5:87). Augustine also connects Paul's name change with "in testimony of so great a victory" (*Conf.* 8.4; *NPNF*1 1:120). In regard to church fathers' opinions on Paul's name change, see Lake and Cadbury 1933: IV: 145–46.

20. Gilbert 2002: 525.

21. Culy and Parsons 2003: 243. They think the present participle (*ousan*) connotes "existing at that time." This kind of the present participle can be found in Acts 5:17. The article + the participle of (*eimi*) + noun formula occurs in 2 Chr 13:9; Jer 5:7; 2 Macc 2:24; 9:26; 15:20; and 4 Macc 5:24 in the LXX. These usages show that in this formula the participle of (*eimi*) refers to "existence."

there were two groups, one composed of Barnabas, Simeon, and Lucius,[22] and the other of Manaen and Saul.[23] Seeing the first three as prophets and the last two as teachers seems to be too simple an analysis because, for example, both Barnabas and Saul could be identified as a prophetic figure as well as a teacher.[24] There are three possible reasons behind this division of groups. To begin with, the order of arrival to Antioch could be one reason; the first group came earlier than the second. Barnabas was a man of Cyprus, Lucius was a Cyrenian, and Simeon called Niger could have been an African. They fit in with the **men of Cyprus and Cyrene** (Acts 11:20) who were the first evangelists in the city. As for Saul and Manaen, they form the latter group: Saul came later with Barnabas, who went from the city to Tarsus to fetch his companion (11:25–26), and Manaen, who was not a part of the first group, but of the high status, must had been able to become one of the leaders of the church later on. Second, the provinces they came from could have been the grounds for this division. The first group could have come from the more Latinized provinces and the second group from the less Latinized provinces. No doubt Paul was born in Tarsus in Cilicia. Nevertheless, he was brought up in Jerusalem (22:3), so he could have been classified as the same group with Manaen. Third, the groups could have been arranged by the social position of its members. The second group may have had a better social rank,[25] since Paul had Roman citizenship (22:25) and it is likely that Manaen had it as well. We are also told that Manaen was "brought up" with Herod Antipas the tetrarch of Galilee and "may have held an influential position at the court of Herod Antipas."[26]

When these leaders in the churches of Antioch were worshiping the Lord while fasting, the Holy Spirit spoke to them: **Indeed separate for me Barnabas and Saul for the sake of the ministry of which I have called them** (Acts 13:2). The Holy Spirit's direct speech is rarely found in

22. Cf. "Paul's Companion" section in the introduction.

23. Contra Barrett 1994: 602–3.

24. See Peterson 2009: 374; also the name Barnabas can be defined as a "son (aramaic *bar*) of prophecy (hebrew *nabi*)" (*DPL*, 66). According to Witherington 1998: 391, "Perhaps it is best to understand the list to refer to those who were both teachers and prophets, both informing and inspiring, being themselves informed and inspired."

25. Witherington 1998: 393 talks about "persons of some social standing" in relation to Manaen.

26. Schnabel 2012: 554.

the Second Temple Jewish literature,[27] but in Acts, it can be spotted in this verse and also in 8:29; 10:19–20; 20:23; and 21:11.[28] The church leaders confronted a commandment, a critical task that would not have been easy for the church to carry out because Barnabas and Saul were already very influential and productive leaders in the Antioch church (11:26).

Nevertheless, the leaders, after fasting and praying, laid their hands on Barnabas and Saul and finally let go of these two missionaries (Acts 13:3). Barnabas had previously been sent by the Jerusalem church (11:22), thus was already a missionary. As for Saul, although not sent by a church but led by the Holy Spirit, he can also be titled a missionary for his compelled missions "in Damascus, Nabatea, and Cilicia before coming to Antioch (cf. 7:58; 9:20–22, 30; 11:25–26)."[29] Hence, considering that they had already been teaching and undertaking pastoral works in Antioch as missionaries, the act of laying hands on them could be "the gesture of ordination," as New observes;[30] but other than that, it can have the meaning of "identification" based on these two reasons: (1) Barnabas and Paul had already been missionaries so it was not necessary for them to be ordained; (2) according to the OT, laying hands on offerings indicates "identification of the offering with the one who laid hands on the offering."[31] In the OT times, ordinations had been performed along with offering sacrifices (Exod 29:10, 15, 19; Lev 8:14, 18, 22) or by offering people as an elevation offering (i.e., the Levites; Num 8:10, 12) or in connection with the Spirit (i.e., Joshua; Num 27:18–23; Deut 34:9).

Barnabas and Saul were not sent by the church leaders, but were released[32] by them. Afterward, they are introduced as those sent out by the Holy Spirit (Acts 13:4a). Even in 14:26, the church of Antioch is described as the place where they were "handed over to the grace of God." Therefore, the church should not, of course could not, take control of them, except to keep them separate. Then, the Holy Spirit, the grace of God, and Jesus the Lord will guide them to places prepared for them at the appointed times and lead them to do their ministry.

---

27. Cf. 1QS IV 6–7; 4Q504 1–2 V, 16; 1 QS IX, 2–5; 4Q504 4, 4–5; Philo's *On the Life of Joseph*, 110–15.

28. In detail, see Park 2013B: 315–48.

29. Schnabel 2012: 554.

30. Lake and Cadbury 1933: 138.

31. See Lev 1:4; 3:2, 8, 13; 4:4, 15, 24, 29, 33; 16:21; 2 Chr 29:23.

32. This word sometimes has the meaning of "divorce" in Matt 1:19, 5:31, etc. (see BDAG 118).

Mission in Cyprus (13:4–12)

Being sent out by the Holy Spirit, they [Barnabas and Paul] went down to Seleucia [23 km on foot from Antioch], **and thence they sailed to Cyprus; when they arrived at Salamis** [from Seleucia 209 km by ship], **they proclaimed the Word of God in the synagogues of the Jews** (Acts 13:4–5a). Seleucia was the port of Antioch in Syria, "founded by Seleucus Nicator (founder of the Seleucid dynasty) in 301 BC."[33] Salamis "is now filled with sand"[34] but had "possessed a good harbor and was the most populous and flourishing town of Cyprus in the Hellenic and Rom[an] periods, carrying on a vigorous trade with the ports of Cilicia and Syria."[35] Along these lines, Hill holds that there "must have been a considerable Jewish population in cities like Salamis ever since Ptolemaic times" starting from Ptolemy I, Soter (323–285 BCE).[36] Due to the number of Jewish residents, there must have been three or four synagogues at the very least. Despite the presence of the Jewish congregations, it is astonishing to find that there was no conflict when the Word of God was proclaimed: after they left Cyprus, there were always conflicts between the missionaries and the Jews in synagogues. Barnabas could have been an obstruction for any possible sparks to fly in Cyprus, either because the Jews were familiar with him since his hometown was Salamis, and/or because his presentation of the gospel was not strong enough to come into conflict with the Jews. As for Paul in most occasions, there were conflicts (see 13:45; 14:19).

Barnabas and Paul had gone through the whole island from Salamis to Paphos (Acts 13:6a) following "a circular road" which "ran round the island, keeping generally near the coast."[37] The climate summarized by Hill implies the condition they had to endure while traveling Cyprus: "The climate of Cyprus has had from antiquity an unenviable reputation for excessive heat, which is liable to inconvenience the conduct of anything, from war to excavations. . . . As in most Mediterranean lands, there is a very dry summer and a rainy winter season, with its maximum

33. Bruce 1988: 246n12.

34. Hill 1940: 11–12.

35. *ISBE* 4:2662. So this city "was the most important city on Cyprus in ancient days, even under Roman rule, when Paphos was made the administrative center for the island (*ca.* 200 BC)" (*ISBE* 4:284).

36. Hill 1940: 241. In detail, see Hill 1940: 241–42n4.

37. Hill 1940: 236.

in December."[38] In any season it must have been difficult to go around Cyprus because of the heat or rain.

The tenacious two emissaries finally arrived at the last mission point in Cyprus, Paphos, where the proconsul of Cyprus lodged. Legend has it that "Pygmalion, in his artistic frenzy, fell madly in love with a statue created by his own hands, to which Aphrodite gave the breath of life. Of this union, Paphos was born."[39] It is also said that "upon the altar of Aphrodite at Paphos, according to ancient legend, rain never fell."[40] "Paphos had been increasing in importance under the Ptolemies" perhaps because of not only "its fame as a religious centre" but also as "the silting-up of the harbour of Salamis."[41] Even in terms of the calendar systems employed in Cyprus, we can notice a distinctive feature of Paphos: "the new Roman calendar was introduced in Paphos, while Salamis went on in the old way [the Egyptian calendar]."[42]

In this congested city, Barnabas and Paul met a Jew named Bar-Jesus (Acts 13:6b). The name of this new character could imply "son of Jesus [Christ]" but he is more likely and should be introduced as the "son of Joshua."[43] Had it been the former, Luke would have made his membership of the church more obvious by including terms such as "brother" or "disciple." However, this was not the case; rather, three seldom used terms were jotted down in this one verse to offer a few, yet broad arrays of Bar-Jesus: "*magos*," "Jewish false prophet," and "Elymas." We will take a closer look at each term.

Magos is employed in the NT only for the "wise men" in Matt 2:1, 7, 16 (2x) and for this Bar-Jesus. If the term indicates a magician in general,[44] he would have been "a person skilled in the use of incantations with the goal of influencing or controlling transcendent powers to overcome

---

38. Hill 1940: 13.

39. Beza 1934: 93, who had "lectured for a long time at King's College on popular literature" and journeyed to Palestine, Syria, Cyprus, and Mount Sinai about eighty years ago.

40. Hill 1940: 13.

41. Hill 1940: 232.

42. Hill 1940: 236.

43. See Bruce 1990: 296; contra Strelan 2004: 74–76.

44. According to the Greeks' categories, magicians belonged to a second respected rank, viz. *magia*, which "was a Persian loan word and referred primarily to astrology and divination" (Walz 2004: 169).

public or private problems."[45] Otherwise, he might have been one of "those who had ideas and customs that were foreign to traditional Greek views and customs" or to "a religious adviser" like Simon[46] who, as a Cypriot Jew by birth, persuaded Drusilla to marry Felix the procurator of Judea, while pretending to be a *magos* (*Ant.* 20.142). Therefore, Bar-Jesus may not have been just a general magician but a counselor, in that he performed the function of persuading the proconsul (Acts 13:7–8), and in that his defeat by Paul resulted in the proconsul's conversion (13:11–12).

Further, Bar-Jesus was a Jewish false prophet (Acts 13:6b). A Jewish counselor beside the proconsul in Cyprus was not an atypical scene to be found at that time because there was a large Jewish community in Cyprus. In the LXX the "false prophets"[47] are identified with their actions and words. They practiced deceit, especially, for dishonest gain (Jer 6:13). Hananiah, a typical example of false prophets,[48] proclaimed that the Lord of hosts had broken the yoke of the king of Babylon (28:2 [35:1, LXX]), and was criticized for making people believe in lies (28:15 [35:15, LXX]). This notion of false prophets is spoken of in Matt 7:15–16 and 24:24–26. The fruits, namely the products of their actions, will be the criteria for discerning false prophets (7:15–16); people should not believe in their words (24:24–26). On the basis of this interpretation of false prophets, we may conclude that Luke portrays Bar-Jesus as a Jew who gained dishonest profits and benefits from the proconsul by using the Scripture falsely. According to Strelan, "This man interprets the way of the Lord wrongly, and so his authority is questionable," and these two expressions, "making crooked the straight paths of the Lord" and "an enemy of all righteousness," indicate "Bar Jesus' magical practices and his financial profit from such practices."[49]

Bar-Jesus is also explained in terms of Elymas (Acts 13:8). In regard to Elymas, it is generally admitted that "no one knows what it means";[50] Elymas is neither a Greek name nor a translation of Bar-Jesus.[51] The most literal and feasible meaning could be "a transliteration of the Arabic *alim*

---

45. Schnabel 2012: 557. So also Bruce 1990: 962.

46. Strelan 2004: 66. He prefers to the former.

47. *Pseudoprophēts* appears in Jer 6:13; 33:7–8 [26:7–8], 11 [26:11], 16 [26:16]; 34:9 [27:9]; 35:1 [28:1]; 36:1 [29:1], 8 [29:8]; Zech 13:2.

48. See Strelan 2004: 70.

49. Strelan 2004: 71–72.

50. Fitzmyer 1998: 502.

51. See Witherington 1998: 401 and Bruce 1990: 297.

(plus ending), which means 'wise,'"[52] surely translating *magos* and indicating that he is a man (considered) wise enough to consult the proconsul.

With the descriptions so far, we are left with several conclusions. First, Bar-Jesus does not mean "son of Jesus" but "son of Joshua." Second, he did not belong to a Christian community but certainly to a Jewish one. Third, his true vocation was to provide wealthy people with advice or divination by using magical methods and possibly the Scriptures. If he were to use the Scriptures and the name of YHWH, it would have been in order to give his words the highest authority. In fact, however, he was not guided nor controlled by the Lord and His words.

This Jewish magician Bar-Jesus opposed Barnabas and Saul and tried to twist the truth to turn the proconsul away from the faith, when Sergius Paulus summoned them and sought to hear the Word of God (Acts 13:7–8). Then, the first conflict between the missionaries and the Jews occurred: Paul, filled with the Holy Spirit, identified Bar-Jesus as **filled with all deceit and unscrupulousness**, as **son of the devil**, and as the **enemy of all righteousness ceaselessly making crooked**[53] **the straight paths of the Lord** (13:10); and he revealed that the hand of the Lord was upon him so he would be **blind so as not to see the sun for a while** (13:11a). And Paul's prophecy came true at that very instant: mist and darkness came over the magician; thus, the advisor had to find a guide (13:11b). As a result, the proconsul, an intelligent man (13:7), was astonished at the teaching of the Lord[54] and believed (13:12).

Bar-Jesus advised and practiced divinations in order to gain economic and social benefits; however, what Barnabas and Paul did was for earning nothing material but for helping the proconsul to be saved. They did not stay in Paphos. Rather, they left the place right after the proconsul believed in the gospel. Hence, Paul's victory over Bar-Jesus was partly based on his correct interpretation of the Bible, and on his mission strategy and lifestyle, even though it was mainly and thoroughly based on the Lord who was with him.

---

52. Witherington 1998: 140. Bruce 1990: 297 explains it well: "Elymas is more probably a word of Semitic origin, akin to Arab. *'ali*m*, 'wise,' 'learned,' which Luke explains by adding ὁ μάγος, 'for so his name (Elymas) is translated.'" So also Schnabel 2012: 557n18.

53. *Diasterphōn* can be "the complementary participle" (Wallace 1996: 646).

54. Culy and Parsons 2003: 249 regard *tou kuriou* as an objective genitive, but this can be seen as a subjective genitive.

Mission in Pisidian Antioch (13:13–52)[55]

Paul and his companions,[56] Barnabas and John Mark, set sail from Paphos and went into Perga (265 km by ship and 21 km on foot from Paphos) in Pamphylia (Acts 13:13a). They might have passed Magydus, a small port at the mouth of Aksu (at that time the Cestrus river).[57] Attaleia, as Campbell argues, "would have been an especially good and largely natural harbour, and also well placed for sheltering and victualling coastal traffic traveling in east-west directions," but it "would not have been the obvious landing point for a ship sailing from Cyprus to Perge—from coast to coast about 175 miles—and hence approaching the area from a south-easterly or easterly direction."[58] So it is highly possible that at this Magydus, John Mark backed out of their companionship, blighting the prospects of further mission as a team.[59] Afterward, John Mark could have gone to Attaleia and then to Jerusalem (13:13b; cf. 15:38), while the other two headed for Perga.

Even though John Mark disappointed Barnabas and Paul, they went on from Perga and came to Antioch in Pisidia. Ramsay infers from Paul's "physical infirmity" in Gal 4:13 that "Paul had a serious illness in Pamphylia," explaining the circumstances "by 'the sudden plunge into the enervating atmosphere of Pamphylia' after the fatigue and hardship of a journey on foot through Cyprus, accompanied by the constant excitement of missionary work, culminating in the intense nervous strain of the supreme effort at Paphos."[60] Ramsay's "the intense nervous strain of the supreme effort at Paphos" should refer to John Mark's departure. In spite of a great loss of companionship, the two exhausted evangelists finished the journey from Perga to Pisidian Antioch, which could not have

55. Paul's speech in Pisidian Antioch is a part of Park 2016: 49–100.

56. *Oi peri Paulon* may show that at this point Paul started to lead the mission. Maybe John Mark left the team because he could not stand the change in leadership.

57. Campbell 2000: 598–99.

58. Campbell 2000: 599–600. According to his calculations, it is about 13–14 miles from Magydus to Perga and about 12 miles from Perga to Attaleia.

59 Schnabel 2012: 573 understands the situation as follows: "After arriving at Perge, John Mark left Paul and Barnabas and returned to Jerusalem to his mother, Mary." However, 15:38 makes it clear that John Mark left them in Pamphylia, not at Perga. In addition, 13:13 shows the contrast between Paul's companions, who went into Perga, and John Mark, who returned to Jerusalem. So John Mark must not have entered Perga in the first place.

60. Ramsay 1975 [1897]: 93.

been easy either emotionally or physically. As Clow suggests, "The St Paul trail is a 500km 25-day way-marked footpath from Perge, to Antioch in Pisidia, now Yalvaç."[61] This long and difficult journey of five hundred kilometers might have caused John Mark to run away from the journey (cf. Mark 14:51–52).

Fusing the Horizons: The Negative Metamorphosis of the Jerusalem Church[62]

The church of Jerusalem is sometimes thought of as an ideal model for all the churches. That seems true until the appointment of the seven deacons (Acts 1:4—6:7a); in Acts we can read her change in a negative direction, and as time goes, in 6:7b—12:24, more in 12:25—19:20, and much more in 19:21—28:31, the smell of her decaying grows stronger. The backsliding of the Jerusalem church will be focused on four topics (members, functions, thoughts, and actions) and dealt with in accordance with each period, starting with "Jerusalem" (1:4; 6:7; 12:25; 19:21) and ending with "the progress of the Word" (6:7a; 12:24; 19:20; 28:31). As each period passes (1:4—6:7a; 6:7—12:24; 12:25—19:20; 19:21—28:31), the nausea spreads wide; and so does the Word.

To begin with, the church of Jerusalem's membership differed in each period. People such as Galileans (Acts 2:7), devout Diaspora Jews (2:5; 6:1), proselytes (2:11), and the Jews in Judea (4:4; 6:1) were the members in the first period. Over 8,120 members in total attended the church, people of various races and from different places; and there were also twelve apostles and seven deacons. In the second period, there were many changes. While most of the previous members scattered, the apostles remained (8:1) and many priests joined (6:7b). Her earlier members such as Barnabas (9:27; cf. 4:36) might have come back; yet, a new group of **the circumcised believers** was found in her community (11:2). Also, there was a big shift in leadership due to the delegation of leadership (8:14; cf. 12:17), mission journeys (11:2,) and martyrdom (7:60; 12:2). And more of higher rank, namely the Pharisees and elders (15:4, 6, 22), joined during the next period. Then in the fourth, tens of thousands of Jews, as described by the Jerusalem church leaders, James, and all the elders (21:18), all **who have**

61. Clow 2013: 4.

62. The main idea of this theme comes from Park 2010B: 107–32.

believed and all zealous for the law (21:20), were her members. The ethnic and cultural diversity in the membership of the Jerusalem church had decreased; as the gap was bridged, uniformity was established. In addition, leadership was exercised by the apostles, but later by the elders.

Second, the function of the Jerusalem church changed its focus. Primarily, she focused only on evangelism and succor (cf. Acts 2:42–47; 4:31–35; 5:42; 6:1). However, as the period changed, her evangelism transformed to judgment (11:2–3) and negligence (12:13–17), while those previously providing financial aid now became beneficiaries rather benefactors (11:30). No reports are made on evangelism or any type of succor during the third; then in the last period, the church issued an ultimatum to Paul for purification and payment (21:23–24), and "Jerusalem" is announced to have handed Paul over to the Romans (28:17). This was a dramatic alteration to a primitive state, yet not like their earlier stage. Jerusalem was a place where the Holy Spirit came down (1:4, 12), and now it was where Paul was handed over (28:17).

Third, the main focus in the thought of the Jerusalem church had also moved. God and His Word (Acts 1:15–22; 3:16; 4:19–20; 6:2, 4) and the salvation of everyone (2:23, 39; 4:24–30) were the center of her thought; and she maintained a fearless witness (5:41). In the second period, however, fear and doubt had seeped into her community (9:26). In the third, her rights and claims were her main concerns (15:1, 5). Finally, the period of self-interest, God and His Word and her mission were replaced by cold structures of herself (21:23–24); secularized were her thoughts and faith.

Fourth, naturally, her actions differed radically. In the first period, she picked out Matthias to fulfill the Scripture (Acts 1:16, 26); she shared good things with others (2:46–47; 3:6; 4:32, 34–37; 6:1); her members were put in prison (4:3; 5:18), stood trial (4:5–21; 5:21, 26–41), and were beaten (5:40). In the second one, only were James martyred and Peter imprisoned. In the third one, these kinds of actions are not found in the Jerusalem church at all. In the fourth one, there are only vows and purification (21:23–24; cf. 23:12–14). Her soul mate "persecution" was now only an acquaintance.

Among the many believers in these four periods of downfall, John Mark was there. His return to Jerusalem (Acts 13:13) can be viewed in relation to this historical context above. He was the heir of the house where the Holy Spirit had come down on the day of Pentecost (2:1–2; 12:12), but he failed to finish his job as an assistant during the first missionary journey (13:5).

For sure it is no accident that the mission of the Antioch church turned up together with John Mark's story. The church of Antioch succeeded in responding positively to Agabus's prophecy by sending their financial aid to the church of Jerusalem (11:28–30); however, an heir of the Jerusalem church was unable to fulfill the mission given by the Holy Spirit. His inability to handle the Holy Spirit's mission seems to warrant the replacement of the Jerusalem church by the Antioch one.

John Mark was not the only one. Other individuals and even communities also took a 180-degree turn backward. To avoid following the steps of that regular routine of regression, one needs to face toward a road of the Word and Truth and to be in the Way, in order to keep their qualities and, in fact, to improve them. Acts could be the right book to show how it can be done. It depicts how Peter and Paul came closer to the Way and kept their qualities as the Lord's servants. If anyone or any Christian community is devoted only to evangelism and succor and rejoices to be persecuted, that person or community must be in the first period. If they long to escape persecution with fear, they could be in the next period. If they focus on their safety rather than the gospel, they might be in the third. If they force others' sacrifice for the sake of their own well-being, they may be in the fourth period. We need to discern our stage, the period we are residing in, and repent our negative metamorphosis.

First Stage (13:14–43)

As soon as they arrived in Pisidian Antioch, they entered into the synagogue on the Sabbath day and sat down (Acts 13:14).[63] Following the Jews' practice certainly was not the only motivation for their participation; they had to resume the activity for evangelism. A synagogue service in general is composed of, first, "the *Shema'* ('Hear, O Israel: the Lord is our God; the Lord is one')" and then the "prayers (conducted by one of the leaders of the congregation)" and subsequently, the law and the

---

63. According to Philo, people sat down at the synagogue "according to their age in classes, the younger sitting under the elder, and listening with eager attention in becoming order" (*Prob.* 81).

prophets were read.[64] After the three parts of the service, Barnabas and Paul were invited as speakers by the rulers of the synagogue (13:15).

According to Philo, at first people "sit according to their age in classes. . . . Then one, indeed, takes up the holy volume and reads it, and another of the men of the greatest experience comes forward and explains what is not very intelligible, for a great many precepts are delivered in enigmatical modes of expression, and allegorically" (*Prob.* 81–82). So Paul and Barnabas should have been regarded as "men of the greatest experience." Probably due to unfamiliarity, it was asked whether there were some words of exhortation for the congregation (Acts 13:15b). Paul stood up and with a gesture delivered a speech (13:16a), not enigmatic but lucid and logical. It was not only **some words of exhortation for the people** (13:15) but also a challenging proclamation to evoke God's promise and to make the assembly settle on whether or not they would believe in Jesus and receive him as their Savior.

Paul's speech was provided for the Israelites and the God-fearers (Acts 13:16b). "The Jews" were called **sons of the family of Abraham** in 13:26. This speech can be broken down into two periods of time: the past (13:17–31) and the present (13:32–41). The former consists of Israel's ancient (13:17–22) and contemporary history (13:23–31); the latter, focusing on what the listeners should do now, is composed of the internal logic in Paul's gospel (13:32–37), as well as sounding a warning, together with two options offered to the audience (13:38–41).

> The past (13:17–31)
> Israel's ancient history (13:17–22)
> The recent history up to that time (13:23–31)
> The present (13:32–41)
> The internal logic in Paul's gospel (13:32–37)
> Promise and warning to the audience (13:38–41)[65]

---

64. Bruce 1990: 301: Then, there are "the reading of the Law (the Pentateuch) and the prophets, a sermon by any suitable member of the congregation (often taking the form of an exposition of one or both of the Scripture lessons), the whole being concluded with the priestly blessing (Num. 6:24–26)." Schnabel 2012: 574 suggests the texts read as "Deut 4:25–46 (the Torah reading) and 2 Sam 7:6–16 (the Haftara, the reading from the Prophets)." However, other texts could be suggested on the basis of the contents.

65. A different kind of structure is worthy of being quoted (Cheng 2011: 95):
13:16–25 God's great saving deeds in Israel's history (God vs. Historical Israelites)

In the section of Israel's ancient history, Paul employed ten indicative verbs: (1) The God of this people Israel *chose* our fathers (Acts 13:17a); (2) He *exalted* the people during [their] stay in the land of Egypt (13:17b); (3) with an uplifted arm[66] He *led* them out of it (13:17c); (4) and for about forty years He *put up with*[67] them in the wilderness (13:18); (5) after putting down seven nations by force in the land of Canaan, He *gave* the people their land *as an inheritance* "in the 450th year"[68] (13:19-20a); (6) after these things, He *gave* the people judges until Samuel the prophet (13:20b); (7) thence they *asked for* a king (13:21a); (8) God *gave* them Saul[69] the son of Kish, a man of the tribe of Benjamin, for forty years (13:21b); (9) and after having removed him, He *elected* David as their king (13:22a); (10) of whom He *said*, testifying, "I have found in David the son of Jesse a man after my heart, who will do all my will" (13:22b). Among these ten indicative verbs, the subject of nine is the God of Israel. The seventh solely has the Israelites as its subject, so his speech could be said to have been done "theocentrically."[70]

While describing the ancient history of his nation, Paul, like Stephen (Acts 7:9, 25-29, 35, 39-43), referred to a negative role of Israel. Even though God chose, exalted, led, put up with, and gave the Israelites an inheritance, as well as judges, the insatiable donees wanted more; they asked for a king. No doubt it was a refusal to accept the ever-giving donor as their king. In spite of their rebellion, God gave them Saul the king "as requested (*asked*)." He satisfied their demand by giving them Saul—as a king despite the absence of the term "king"—for forty years. This period is similar to that in the wilderness in 13:18. It seems that God bore

---

13:26-37 God's greatest saving deed at the present time (God's promise vs. Us)

13:38-41 The reality of God's salvation in relation to human response (You vs. Jesus).

66. Cf. "with an outstretched arm" in Exod 6:1, 6; Deut 4:34; 5:15; 6:21; 7:8; 2 Kgs 17:36; Ps 136:12 [135:12, LXX]; Jer 32:21 [39:21, LXX]; Ezek 20:33, 34; Bar 2:11.

67. In regard of a textual variation between ἐτροποφόρησεν (put up with someone's moods) and ἐτροφοφόρησεν (carry like a nurse; cf. Deut 1:31), see Bruce 1990: 304 and Cheng 2011: 97n18.

68. See Gen 15:13 (400 years), Num 14:33-34 (40 years), and Joshua 14-15 (10 years). In regard to *etesin tetrakosiois kai pentēkonta*, Bruce 1990: 304 says, "The dat. implies point of time, not duration, although the sense would have been clearer if ordinal numerals had been used ('he gave them their land as a possession in the 450th year')."

69. The meaning of "Saul" in Hebrew is "asked" (BDB 982).

70. Cheng 2011: 94, 96n15.

with Saul for forty years and then replaced him with David eventually. God elected David, and gave him His covenant. Paul combined some verses (Ps 89:20 [89:21, MT; 88:21, LXX], 1 Sam 13:14, and possibly Isa 11:1, 10 and 44:28) to form God's promise to David. First, Paul's divine oracle, **I found in David**, came from Ps 89:20. In Ps 89, which sings "our covenant-keeping God," vv. 19–29 [20–30, MT] stress "God's faithfulness to His covenant" on the basis of 2 Sam 7:5, 11–16.[71] Kim summarizes the Davidic king's position as follows:

> The motif of election and elevation is predominant in the stanza which starts from v. 20 and is intensified in the following verses where David is presented as the anointed king (v. 21), as the mighty warrior over every kind of enemy (vv. 23–24), and finally culminates in v. 28 with his exaltation to being the son of the Lord and the "highest one" ('elyôn) over the kings of the earth.[72]

Second, **the son of Jesse** [the one belonging to Jesse[73]] can be connected with "the root of Jesse" (Isa 11:1, 10), one of the "figurative expressions for great David's greater Son."[74] Third, **a man after my heart** is found in Samuel's speech to Saul (1 Sam 13:14): "The Lord has sought out *a man after his own heart* for himself; and the Lord has appointed him to be leader over His people." Last, the expression **who will do all my will** can be found in Isa 44:28 in reference to Cyrus.[75] As Schnabel suggests, Cyrus's task of rebuilding Jerusalem "can be understood in the context of Isaiah's new exodus motif: in Isaiah 40–55, a new deliverer is described who will deliver Israel from spiritual captivity" and "Cyrus is the only person whom Isaiah calls 'anointed one' (Gk. χριστός; Isa 45:1)."[76]

Hence, the section of Israel's ancient history ends in God's promise based on Ps 89:20, 1 Sam 13:14, and Isa 11:1, 10; 44:28. Just as in Ps 89:20, His promise is proclaimed with the first singular subject, "I found." David and Jesse are related both to "my heart" and to "all my will," which is

---

71. Boice 2007 [1996]: 723, 727.

72. Kim 1989: 167–68. He follows the verse system in *BHS*.

73. Robertson 2010 [1934]: 502, 780 deals with *ton tou Iessai* in terms of "genitive of relationship" and "the article only with genitive."

74. *TWOT* 185.

75. Bruce 1990: 305; so also NA28, UBS4.

76. Schnabel 2012: 577; so also Miura 2008: 181.

supported by the stories in both Samuels and the prophecies in Isaiah. This is a very particular promise proclaimed by God Himself.

The second section of a more neoteric history (Acts 13:23–31) articulates how God's promise has been fulfilled. **From the seed of this one [David], God, according to His promise, brought to Israel Jesus as the Savior, John having proclaimed before his [Jesus'] entry a baptism of repentance to all the people of Israel** (Acts 13:23–24). David was *elected* to be substituted for Saul, but Jesus *was brought* to Israel, not to be substituted for John the Baptist, but to be presented as the Savior. This is supported by the following verse (13:25): **In finishing his race,[77] John questioned the follower and answered, "Why do you suppose that I am [the Messiah]? I am not. But behold, he comes after me, the sandals of whose feet I am not worthy to loose."[78]**

After briefly connecting David with Jesus and describing the relationship between Jesus and John the Baptist (Acts 13:23–25), Paul announced Jesus' death on the cross and his resurrection (13:26–30). Paul continued his speech by calling the audience: **Brothers, sons of the family of Abraham, and those among you who fear God** (13:26a). This is different from the previous designation, **men of Israel and those who fear God** (13:16b). "Brothers, sons of the family of Abraham" is a title more general than "men of Israel." Israel is Jacob's name, so more people could be covered under the family of Abraham than just the Israelites. Before addressing Jesus' death and resurrection, Paul might have reaffirmed in his mind, thinking, "If you are Christ's, then you are Abraham's offspring" (Gal 3:29). Further, "those among you who fear God" may mean that "not all the Israelites do fear God" and that "fearing God is more essential than genealogical classification." Despite the distinct interpretations and expressions, "brothers," "sons of the family of Abraham," and "those among you who fear God," could be actually referring to the same group of people.

After addressing the audience in a new sense, meaningful in terms of the redemptive history, Paul provides "a summary of his main concern in the speech":[79] **To us has been sent the Word of this salvation** (Acts 13:26b). This "us" makes it clear that even Paul's companions themselves

---

77. John's task is described as "race" (*ton dromon*). This is Paul's term, employed just in 13:25; 20:24; and 2 Tim 4:7 in the NT.

78. Untying the sandals is "a slave's task" (Peterson 2009: 389). Even so Jesus' evaluation on John the Baptist was high (cf. Luke 7:26–28).

79. Cheng 2011: 99.

are the beneficiaries of the Word;[80] this "Word" is personified and is related to Jesus: **Those who live in Jerusalem and their rulers, without
recognizing** this Word, **fulfilled the prophets' voices that are read every
Sabbath, by condemning** the Word. **In addition, they asked Pilate to
have** him [Jesus the Word] **executed even though they found no reason
for a death sentence** (13:27–28). The Jerusalemites and the Jewish rulers'
asking reminds us of the Israelites' previous asking for a king (13:21a).
Both the Israelites and the Jerusalemites vehemently rejected their King,
God the Father (1 Sam 8:7) and now, His son (cf. Acts 13:33).

The Jerusalemites and their rulers' ignorance, condemnation, and
outlandish request against God's will ended ironically and, surprisingly,
in the accomplishment of everything that was written about Jesus (Acts
13:29a), which certainly happened because the Scriptures had been written in God's wisdom considering ups *and* downs, the righteous *and* the
sinners, the prerequisites *and* the conditions, and so on; God had already
known that His Servant would be discarded by His people (e.g., Isa 53:3).

The last actions that Paul mentioned were taking Jesus' body down
from the wood (cross) and placing it in a tomb (Acts 13:29b). In fact,
these actions had been done not by all but only by a few members of
the Jerusalemites and their rulers, Joseph of Arimathea and Nicodemus
(John 19:38–39, 40a, 42b), the two members of the Sanhedrin (Mark
15:43; Luke 23:50; John 3:1). Bruce says, "The plural subject, 'they took
him down . . . and laid him in a tomb,' may be generalizing; in the Gospels
Joseph of Arimathaea and Nicodemus (members of the Sanhedrin) are
specially mentioned in this connection (Luke 23:50–53; John 19:38–42)."[81]
However, it can be conjectured that Paul convicted people of their reluctance, which Joseph and Nicodemus had already shown. Furthermore,
on the basis of the OT allusions, related not only to Deut 21:23 but also to
Josh 8:29 and 10:27, it can be said that Jesus is described as the Canaanite
kings, who were hanged on the tree, then taken down from it, and later
placed in a tomb.[82] Hence, the procedure of taking down Jesus, the Word
of salvation, from the tree and placing him in a tomb projects the im-

80. With Peterson 2009: 390 ("Paul and Barnabas include themselves in the group
to whom this message has been sent"); *contra* Bruce 1988: 258, who thinks that "us"
refers to "the Jews and the God-fearing Gentiles."

81. Bruce 1988: 259n77.

82. For the full details of this argument, see Park 2007A: 149–51. He also mentions
that the word "taking down" occurs in 13:19 in relation to the "putting down" of the
seven nations (Park 2007A: 150).

ages of both the Israelites' inheritance on Canaan and their reluctance continually expressed among God's people.

In spite of the Israelites' negative decisions and actions, God of Israel fulfilled His promise finally by raising Jesus from the dead (Acts 13:30). This event occurred only once but was strong enough to silence all the human errors, including improper ignorance, wrong condemnation, an immoral demand, and actions due to lack of hope (13:27–28). In addition, it is supported by witnesses: **And he appeared for many days to those who had traveled with him from Galilee to Jerusalem; these are his witnesses to the people** (13:31).

Paul, who connected ancient history with the contemporary one in terms of promise (Acts 13:22–23), bound the past and the present with witnesses and promise, respectively: **We also proclaim to you the good news that the promise given to our fathers has been realized** (13:32). They were not eyewitnesses but could proclaim that God's promise had been fulfilled on the basis of the OT. Three passages, Ps 2:7, Isa 55:3, and Ps 16:10, are quoted and then interpreted (Acts 13:33–37). We will look at each one in the order Paul laid out in his speech.

First, Ps 2:7 is quoted: **Just as also it is written in the second Psalm, "You are my Son, today I have begotten you"** (cf. Heb 1:5; 5:5), **God has fulfilled this promise to us their children by raising Jesus** (Acts 13:33). Seeing that the word "begotten" can put emphasis on "fathership," this verse can be understood as "You are my son, and I am your father." If "today" is added, the second sentence could be interpreted as "even today I am your father."[83] The initial quotation can be understood as "the enthronement of the king or with the renewal of God's promise to the monarch,"[84] nullifying the kings and the rulers opposing the Messiah (Ps 2:3). Jesus' mission life, which started with the Father's approval of Jesus' sonship in his baptism (Luke 3:22, alluding to Ps 2:7 and Isa 42:1), did not end with his death but was resumed by his resurrection. It can be said that the Father's approval was reaffirmed by Jesus' resurrection, so Ps 2:7 could have been quoted in connection with his resurrection: Paul seems to use this verse not only as the Father's continuing approval of his sonship but also as a proclamation of his victory over leading opponents (cf. Acts 4:25–26), namely of a glorious victory fulfilling God's promise of

83. Marshall 2007: 585 suggests the translation: "[I declare to you] today [that] I begat you." However, the position of "today" in the sentence may not allow this kind of translation.

84. Schnabel 2012: 581 following Marshall 2007: 585.

salvation through the Davidic kingship. The proclamation of this victory is similar to the use of Ps 2:7 in Hebrews where the verse is employed to proclaim the Son's superiority over the angels (Heb 1:5) and Christ's glory (5:5).

Next, Ps 2:7 is applied and interpreted; Paul declared God raising Jesus from the dead and interpreted the event with the word *diaphthora* (destruction, ruin) (Acts 13:34a). According to the usage of *diaphthora* especially in Ps 30:9 [29:10, LXX], Job 33:28, etc., the term could refer to a place similar to a pit, a grave, or the underworld. Being raised from the dead can indicate that he will not return to corruption anymore; thus, Paul could clarify that Jesus "received incorruptible, everlasting life—the prerequisite for his being the Savior of the present generation of Israelites, God-fearers, and Gentiles for all time."[85]

Third, Isa 55:3 is quoted in Acts 13:34b: **Thus he has spoken that "I will give you the holy and sure mercies/blessings/piety of David."** This citation is called "the *crux interpretum* of Paul's speech":[86] Anderson classifies the interpretations of the quoted phrase into three approaches: (1) having "in common an emphasis upon the relationship between Isa 55:3 in Acts 13:34 and Ps 15:10 LXX in Acts 13:35"; (2) emphasizing "the relationship between 13:34 and 13:26, 38–39"; (3) interpreting "the phrase as a reference to God's covenant promises to David." He himself sees the last one reasonable and concludes like this:

> The "holy things of David" pertain to that larger complex of salvation blessings (i.e., life in the kingdom of God) which includes God's "raising up" a promised heir to David and the establishment of an eternal kingship and dominion and inheritance for the people of God, as was promised to Israel's ancestral leaders.[87]

His analysis is quite brilliant, but one point would make his conclusion more established; the genitive of "the holy and sure mercies of David" should be seen as subjective rather than objective, as it is more feasible grammatically in the Greek text and the MT.[88] Olley argues that the subject of *chesed* ("mercy, loyalty") in Isa 55:3 LXX is "man," viz. David; if so, David's mercies may refer to "the establishing of Jerusalem and

---

85. Schnabel 2012: 582.

86. Anderson 2006: 249.

87. Anderson 2006: 249–54.

88. In Isa 55:3, τὰ ὅσια Δαυὶδ is equivalent to חסדי דוד.

the setting up of the temple."[89] David is described as a messianic figure in Isa 9:6; 16:5; 22:22; and 37:35, and while talking about "the servants of the Lord" (Isa 54:17), the Lord's covenant of eternity (*berith olam*)[90] itself is defined as David's *chesed* in Isa 55:3: "I will make with you an everlasting covenant, David's *chesed*, which is trustful."

What kind of logic is flowing inside Paul's speech? After announcing that God's promise found in ancient Israelite history had been confirmed within the Davidic messiah, Paul quoted an eventual promise for the people of God. So the following logic seems hidden beneath Paul's speech: "God's promise was given to David and the Davidic messiah (Acts 13:22; cf. Ps 89:20; 1 Sam 13:14; Isa 11:1, 10; 44:28) and, on the basis of the promise, God swore that the holy and sure mercies of David [the Davidic messiah] would be given to His people (Acts 13:34b; cf. Isa 55:3), so the resurrection of the Davidic messiah should be seen as both the result of the promise and the prerequisite of its fulfillment."

Unraveling Paul's previous message enriches our understanding on Paul's interpretation of the Scriptures and his fourth quotation, and thus helps us to connect Isa 55:3 and Ps 16:10 [15:10, LXX]: **Therefore the Scripture says**[91] **also in another psalm, "You will not allow Your Holy One**[92] **to see corruption"** (Acts 13:35). The Davidic messiah's eternal mercies and blessings can be fulfilled only when he lives forever, so David is praising God that He would not put His Holy One into the pit to see corruption (Ps 16:10). In this psalm "Your Holy One" could not refer to David himself because **David in his own generation served the purpose of God and then fell asleep and then was laid together with his fathers and finally saw corruption** (Acts 13:36; cf. 2:29). Unlike David, **the one God raised up did not see corruption** (13:37; cf. 2:31). David did not sing for himself, but for the Davidic messiah (Ps 16:10). Praise the Lord! God who had made the promise in advance fulfilled His promise perfectly.

89. Olley 1979: 144–45. In regard to David's *chesed*, I would like to count the event of David sparing Saul's life (e.g., 1 Sam 26), too.

90. In the OT, "the covenant of eternity" occurs in many places (e.g., Gen 9:16; 17:7, 13, 19; Exod 31:16; Lev 24:8; 2 Sam 23:5; Isa 24:5; 55:3; 61:8; Jer 32:40; 50:5; Ezek 16:60; 37:26; Ps 105:10; 1 Chr 16:17).

91. Bruce 1990: 310 says, "The subject [of λέγει] is ἡ γραφή understood, not ὁ θεός, since it is to God that the words are addressed." The alteration of the subject from "God" to "the Scripture" may explain the difference between *eirēken* (13:34) and *legei* (13:35).

92. In Ps 16:10 [15:10, LXX] τὸν ὅσιόν σου is equivalent to חסידך. See also 2:27.

Now Paul's words of wisdom come to an end: A promise and a warning to the audience (Acts 13:38–41). Paul, who proclaimed the good news by expounding on the redemptive history of Israel and the evidence found in the OT, carried on with what was promised to the audience: **Therefore, let it be known to you, brothers, that through this man [Jesus] forgiveness of sins is proclaimed to you, and that from everything from which you could not be freed by the law of Moses, by this man everyone who believes is set free** (13:38–39). What would be examples of "everything from which you could not be freed by the law of Moses"? Marshall suggests sins "committed deliberately."[93] However, sins more specific can be discretely extracted from the expression, "that person shall be cut off from" God's people Israel:

> the sin of not being circumcised (Gen 17:14);
>
> the sin of eating what is leavened during the Passover season (Exod 12:15);
>
> the sin of eating "the flesh of the sacrifice of the Lord's peace offering while being unclean" (Lev 7:20–21);
>
> the sin of eating any blood (Lev 7:27);
>
> the sin of the eating any peace offerings left over until the third day (Lev 19:5–7);
>
> the sin of anyone not traveling failing to keep the Passover (Num 9:13);
>
> the sin of defiling the tabernacle of the Lord after touching a dead person (Num 19:13).

In particular, idolatry should be included in this type of sin, since it is written that "whoever sacrifices to gods, other than the Lord alone, shall become *herem* [be separated to destruction]" (Exod 22:20 [22:19, MT]).[94]

The good news of the risen Messiah was wisely explained; then came a desperate plea or a stern warning: **Therefore, beware lest what has been said in the Prophets should come true [to you], "Look, scoffers,[95] be astounded and be hidden away;[96] for I am doing a work in your**

93. Marshall 2007: 587.

94. See Park 2007A: 8, 174.

95. "Scoffers" in the LXX is the equivalent for "at the nations" in the MT.

96. Marshall 2007: 587 sees "vanishing away" as "a paraphrase of the repetitious

days, a work[97] that you will not believe, even if one tells it in detail
to you" (Acts 13:40–41). Just as Habakkuk prophesied the "consequence
of disbelieving God's work through the Chaldeans (Hab 1:5–11, LXX),"
so Paul did warn "of disbelieving God at work through Jesus."[98] From a
similar perspective Paul quotes Hab 2:4b in Rom 1:17b: "Hab. 2:4 is God's
response to the prophet's complaint about God's inaction and injustice. It
instructs the person who is already righteous. . . . In Paul, the quotation
functions to characterize how it is that one can attain right standing with
God and so live eternally."[99]

   Then, Luke reports the responses to Paul's speech, generally positive but to some more pleasing: **As they departed, the people in the
synagogue urged Paul and Barnabas to tell them these words the next
Sabbath. Along the way, after the meeting of the synagogue broke up,
many Jews and many devout converts to Judaism followed Paul[100] and
Barnabas** (Acts 13:42–43a). There was no violent resistance, but a calm
yet deep reluctance to make a decision. Nevertheless, some followed and
talked with the evangelists; Paul and Barnabas **urged them to remain
continually in the grace of God** (13:43b) surely because He is the God
of grace and of fulfilling His will.

Second Stage (13:44–52)

The ministry in Pisidian Antioch seemed to be okay and somewhat
satisfactory. However, the situation changed on the following week: **On
the following Sabbath almost the whole city assembled together to
hear the word of the Lord. But when the Jews saw the crowds, they
were filled with jealousy and began to oppose what Paul was saying,
reviling him** (Acts 13:44–45). The attitude of the Jews became vicious
because almost all of the citizens in the city had been gathered; as Kilgallen insists, it was not because Paul's message guaranteed the gentiles the
justification without being "a physical descendant of Abraham."[101] The

---

'be amazed [in MT],' possibly in the sense of hiding away in utter fear."

97. Wall 2000: 250–1 says that "the repetition of 'work' in the citation emphasizes
its thematic importance for Acts."

98. Cheng 2011: 104.

99. Moo 1996: 77.

100. Paul's name comes in front of Barnabas's for the first time in Acts (so also
13:46, 50; 14:20; 15:2, 22, 35, 36; cf. 14:12, 14; 15:12, 25).

101. Kilgallen 2003: 15.

text clearly declares that the Jews were consumed by jealousy. The jealousy of the Jews was irresistible and would grow stronger and stronger (cf. Acts 14:19), so Paul and Barnabas boldly made it clear that it was the time to evangelize the gentiles rather than the Jews: **It was necessary that the Word of God be spoken first to you [the Jews]. Since you thrust it aside and judge yourselves unworthy of eternal life, behold, we are turning to the Gentiles** (13:46). "Turning to the gentiles" is authorized by the Lord's command: **For so the Lord has commanded us,**[102] **I have made you a light for the Gentiles, that you may exist for the salvation to the ends of the earth"** (13:47). The quoted Isa 49:6 is originally the "part of a statement from Yahweh to his servant Israel, or, more precisely, to whoever has the task of restoring Israel."[103] The evangelists neither escaped as cowards nor kept their further intention hidden, rather they clearly showed their direction they will take along with an understandable reason based on the Scripture.

We do not know what the Jews thought of and felt about them "turning to the gentiles." They could have masked their anger because they did not have enough power to kill Paul. In Jerusalem, the issue of turning to the gentiles made the Jews raise their voices and say, **Away with such a fellow [Paul] from the earth! For it is not proper for him to live** (Acts 22:22b). On the contrary, the gentiles revealed their feeling: **When the Gentiles heard this, they began rejoicing and glorifying the Word of the Lord** (13:48a). This is the only verse where rejoicing and glorifying occur together in the NT (no verse in the LXX). The gentiles' open and honest minds resulted in rejoicing in the good news and glorifying the God of Israel. This must have brought joy to heaven (Luke 15:7, 10). **As many as were appointed to eternal life believed** (Acts 13:48b) is its evidence; further, **the Word of the Lord was spreading throughout the whole region** (13:49). What was happening was enough to create joy in heaven.

Finally, the Jews also revealed their minds: **the Jews incited the devout women of high standing and the leading men of the city, stirred up persecution against Paul and Barnabas, and drove them out of their district** (Acts 13:50). The Jews could not take action to deal with the evangelists' proclamation, so they encouraged some leading people of high authority to rebel against Paul and Barnabas who did not have any

---

102. This *hēin* refers only to Paul and Barnabas, not to the audience (cf. 13:26, 33).
103. Marshall 2007: 588.

social power there. Cowardice does not act but only stimulates others to act.

Even though the evangelists were driven out of their ministry, the ministry did not shrink: **But they shook off the dust from their feet against them and went to Iconium** (145 km on foot from Pisidian Antioch) (Acts 13:51). Shaking dust from their feet is "a gesture which Jesus had commended to his disciples when they left an inhospitable place"[104] (Matt 10:14; Mark 6:11). As a result of their bold speech and honorable departure, **the disciples were filled with joy and with the Holy Spirit** (Acts 13:52).

104. Bruce 1988: 268.

ACTS 14

Mission to Iconium and Lystra, and Completion of the First Mission Trip

Paul and Barnabas departed Pisidian Antioch and went to Iconium (145 km on foot from Pisidian Antioch), then to Lystra (30 km southwest of Iconium), and finally to Derbe (60 km east of Lystra).[1] The location of Iconium, "one of the oldest continually occupied cities in the world," was "linked at various times with both Phrygia and Lycaonia."[2] "It passed into the Roman sphere of influence in 65 BC, and became part of the empire in 25 BC, when the former kingdom of Galatia was incorporated as the province of Galatia."[3] But Iconium "was not a Roman colony: it was a democratic Greek city where the populace held the power."[4]

Lystra and Derbe were categorized as the Lycaonian cities. "The name Lycaones is probably related to Lukka, an Anatolian[5] people and territory mentioned in Hittite texts."[6] Along with Pisidian Antioch, Lystra "was made a Roman colony by Augustus in 25 BC": these "two colonies, which were about 100 miles apart, were connected by a military road which did not pass through Iconium."[7] Coming from Iconium, it is perfectly possible that Paul did not take this road to Lystra. Anyhow, four times Paul visited Lystra (Acts 14:6, 21; 16:1; 18:23), which was also

1. Distances following NET notes. According to Schnabel 2012: 591, 605, distances are 150, 34, and 150 kilometers.

2. *ABD* 3:357: "Founded as a Phrygian settlement and linked with Phrygia both geographically and culturally, the native people would have considered themselves Phrygians." Bruce 1988: 272 argues well that "Iconium was as Phrygian a city in the middle of the first century AD as it had been 450 years earlier."

3. Bruce 1988: 268.

4. Morton 1937 [1936]: 214.

5. Anatolia can be defined as "the Asian portion of the modern republic of Turkey" (*ABD* 1:228).

6. *ABD* 4:419.

7. Bruce 1988: 272. Some (e.g., Witherington 1998: 421) think Lystra became a Roman colony in 26 BC.

Timothy's hometown (16:1), and during his first visit, he was severely persecuted (14:19; cf. 2 Tim 3:11). Paul's final destination, Derbe, "was the last city on distinctively Rom[an] territory, on the road leading from Southern Galatia to the E. [East]; it was here that commerce entering the province had to pay the customs dues."[8]

All of the three cities, Iconium, Lystra, and Derbe, were located at a central plateau in Anatolia, over one thousand meters above sea level north of the Taurus Mountains,[9] and were categorized as southern Galatia.[10] After finishing the ministries in these areas, Paul and Barnabas did not return to Syrian Antioch via Tarsus, Paul's hometown,[11] although that way would have been an easier route and so was taken in the second and the third missionary trips (Acts 15:41—16:1; 18:23); rather they traversed Lystra, Iconium, Pisidian Antioch, and finally Perga in Pamphylia, the place where the gospel had not been proclaimed at the first visit (13:13–14). In the former three regions, they strengthened the disciples (13:21–23), and lastly, in Perga they proclaimed the Word (14:25). Afterward, Paul and Barnabas finished their first mission trip with "an almost directly easterly journey of about 300 miles [480 km]" via Attalia (20 km on foot from Perga) (14:26–27),[12] and the chapter ends when they set their feet on the land of Antioch in Syria.

Mission to Iconium (14:1–7)

Objections raised by the Jews in Pisidian Antioch were strong but unable to prevent Paul and Barnabas from evangelizing in the synagogue of Iconium: **In Iconium in the same manner**[13] **they entered into the**

---

8. *ISBE* 2:830.

9. On the way from Lystra to Derbe in 1936, Morton 1937 [1936]: 236 "thought what a strange experience it was to leave the luxuriant, semi-tropical coast of Asia Minor and to climb to this savage land where bare mountains stand sentinel over a barren plain lifted four thousand feet above sea level."

10. See Hansen 1994: 378, who includes Pisidian Antioch, Iconium, Lystra, and Derbe as a part of the province of Galatia.

11. About 145 kilometers east of Derbe, Tarsus was located; and about 220 kilometers southeast of Tarsus was Antioch, Syria.

12. Campbell 2000: 601.

13. Bruce 1990: 317 understands κατὰ τὸ αὐτό as "'after the same manner' as in Pisidian Antioch"; so also Culy and Parsons 2003: 271 say that this phrase "probably indicates that the apostles used the same approach that they had used when they arrived in Salamis (13:5) and Pisidian Antioch (13:14; cf. Barrett, 667) rather than that

Jewish synagogue and spoke in such a way that a great number of both Jews and Greeks believed (Acts 14:1). However, the attitude of the Jews changed mostly on account of jealousy (cf. 13:45):[14] **But the unbelieving Jews stimulated the Gentiles' natures to do evil against the brothers** (14:2). These "brothers," instead of indicating Paul and Barnabas, who were later called "the apostles" in 14:4, seems to refer to the believers in Iconium.[15] This situation was different from that in Pisidian Antioch, and the main reason can be found in "that Iconium was not a Roman colony" but "a democratic Greek city where the populace held the power," as Morton finds: "The most effective way to expel the apostles was obviously to create a public argument, to rouse the whole city against them, and then sit back and allow democracy to do its worst."[16]

Codex Bezae has a different reading of Acts 14:2. It reads, "Now the heads of the synagogue and the leaders [of the synagogue] launched a persecution against the righteous, but the lord quickly brought a cessation."[17] The scribe of Codex Bezae might have wanted to explain that "the Jewish leaders incited persecution against" not only the believers but also "the Righteous"[18] and to expound that the evangelists remained for a long time with the help of the Lord: these variants can be considered as "comments calculated to remedy the difficulty of the B-text."[19]

The Jews in Iconium treated the evangelism of Paul and Barnabas in a way fit with the Greek culture. As a result, the believers in the city were targeted by the Jews, probably accusing them of being revolutionaries within society. Knowing this, Paul and Barnabas felt a great need to strengthen the disciples (Acts 14:22), thus, **remained for a long time** (14:3a).[20] **They spoke boldly depending on the Lord, who bore witness**

---

the apostles entered the synagogue 'together.'" ESV translates it as "together," and NET as "the same thing."

14. So Bock 2007: 462 also understands this jealousy as "a struggle for power and control of the people."

15. With Witherington 1998: 419. Peterson 2009: 404 thinks that "the brothers must have included the new believers as well as the evangelists."

16. Morton 1937 [1936]: 214.

17. The text of Codex Bezae is quoted from Pervo 2009: 345.

18. Rius-Camps and Read-Heimerdinger 2007: 131.

19. Lake and Cadbury 1933: 161 ("the B-text" refers to Codex Vaticanus); so also Metzger 1994: 371.

20. Marshall 1980B: 247 thinks that Luke intended "to emphasize that it was precisely because of the rise of opposition that the missionaries felt they must stay as long as possible to consolidate the infant Christian community, and departed only when they were absolutely forced to do so."

to the word of his grace, granting signs and wonders to be done by their hands (14:3b). This was the fulfillment of the prayer in 4:29b–30. According to the same phrase "the Word of His grace" in 20:32, this "Lord" in 14:3 could refer to God the Father.[21] Even yet, the context may support the view that this "Lord" actually refers to Jesus: first, this interpretation could be inferred through Dunn's study of the word *kurios* in Acts as he himself insists;[22] second, "because there is the expression, 'the word (λόγος) of God,' and because Paul addresses the 'Lord' of 'the words of the Lord' in 20:35 as Jesus,"[23] as Park says, *kurios* in this chapter and even in the previous chapter, in "the Word of the Lord" (13:48–49), may also be referring to Jesus. So we can understand 14:3b in this manner: Paul and Barnabas depended on Jesus so spoke boldly; in response to their trust, Jesus granted signs and wonders to reveal that their gospel was trustworthy.

The Jews attacked the evangelists tactically, but Paul and Barnabas resisted their attack with "the Word of grace" and with their enthusiasm to support the new believers. And most of all, Jesus the Lord supported them. Eventually, **the multitude of the city were divided; some sided with the Jews and some with the apostles** (Acts 14:4). The disciples in Iconium were unshaken in spite of the refusal of the other citizens; so the Jews failed to expel Paul and Barnabas from their territory. Consequently, the Jews revealed their real intention: **Time came when both the Gentiles and the Jews, with their rulers, showed their zeal to mistreat and stone[24] them [Paul and Barnabas]** (14:5). So the evangelists, due to circumstances beyond their control, **fled to the cities of Lycaonia, viz. Lystra, Derbe, and the surrounding region, and even there they continued to preach the gospel** (14:6–7). They escaped for the time being (cf. 14:21) and went to different nations from the Phrygians and made a mission journey for that area.

21. E.g., Schnabel 2012: 603–4.

22. Dunn 1998: 247.

23. Park 2002: 42–43.

24. This word (*lithoboleō*) occurs here and in Matt 21:35; 23:37; Luke 13:34; Acts 7:58, 59; and Heb 12:20.

Mission to Lystra (14:8–20)[25]

As regards the mission to the Lycaonian cities, Luke reports a story that happened in Lystra,[26] a Roman colony among them,[27] probably to exemplify evangelism for the Lycaonian cities. So a person is introduced just as particular persons, namely Aeneas, Tabitha, and Cornelius, were mentioned for Peter's mission journey (Acts 9:32—11:2a): **In Lystra there was a man sitting who could not use his feet, lame from his mother's womb, who had never walked** (14:8). There was no synagogue, so Paul might have given a speech "in some public place."[28]

At that time, **this man listened to Paul speaking; and Paul, looking intently at him and seeing that he had faith to be saved/healed,**[29] **said in a loud voice, "Stand upright on your feet"** (Acts 14:9–10a). Peterson insists that this man's faith "was not yet a seeking for salvation in the sense of forgiveness, eternal life, and entrance into the kingdom of God (cf. 13:48; 14:22)."[30] However, it is not for us to limit his faith to only his physical healing: rather, we should say that his faith was strong, even to the extent of being healed from his permanent physical handicap. This man was different from the lame man who asked alms of Peter and John at the Beautiful Gate (3:2): the believing man of Lystra heard of Paul, believed in the gospel, and might have reached to a conclusion such as, "This God can heal me." Whatsoever, it was the beginning of his faith, so it would not be proper at this point to judge the characteristics of his faith too much; that he had faith to be saved should be our primary concern.

Two things or four happened in detail as a result of Paul's commandment: the man **sprang up and began walking** (Acts 14:10b), and

---

25. Paul's speech in Lystra (14:14–17) is a part of Park 2016: 49–100.

26. The site of Lystra was found in 1885 by Professor J. R. Sitlington Sterrett (Morton 1937 [1936]: 230; so also see Bruce 1990: 320), but not yet excavated: it lies under an "unexcavated mound near the Turkish village of Hatun Saray" (Accordance Bible 11: PhotoGuide 4).

27. Morton 1937 [1936]: 234 reports that in 1936 "the only object of interest on this desolate site is the altar," that is "a massive, carved stone about three and a half feet high and twelve inches thick, much damaged and cracked, but still bearing in clear-cut Latin characters," which can be translated, "Gemina Lustra, the Fortunate, being a Julian colony, dedicated Augustus Cæsar as a god: [the altar] being decreed by the Urban Council."

28. Peterson 2009: 407.

29. Peterson 2009 prefers "healed" to "saved."

30. Peterson 2009: 407.

the crowds were surprised at not only the miracle of healing but also, according to Strelan, Paul's stare, loud voice, and order.[31] **When the crowds saw what Paul had done, they shouted in the Lycaonian language, "The gods have come down to us in the form of human beings."[32] Thus they called Barnabas Zeus and Paul Hermes** (14:11). As a background of their alarm, a legend spoken by Ovid (Publius Ovidius Naso), the Latin poet, has been generally suggested.[33] The related parts, *Metamorphoses* 8.611–724,[34] can be thematically summarized: "PEIRITHOUS DISPUTES DIVINE POWER TO IMPOSE TRANSFORMATION. Lelex [an old man] refutes him with tale of BAUCIS AND PHILEMON, who welcome gods unaware and are saved from separation in death by *transformation into trees*."[35] In the story, it is said that Jupiter (Zeus to the Greeks) and Atlas's grandson (Mercury to the Romans; Hermes to the Greeks) visited a Phrygian village, but only one old couple welcomed respectfully and fed them extremely well, later survived the waters of a flood, then became priests, and were lastly transformed into trees together at the same moment.[36]

The audience in Lystra, who might have connected the healing of the lame with the myth, identified Paul and Barnabas with the divine figures in the legend. **Thus they called Barnabas "Zeus" and Paul "Hermes," because he was leading the speech** (Acts 14:12).[37] They could not have been free from the thought that a harsh punishment would be imposed on them unless they served these "gods" immediately. **So the priest of the temple of Zeus located before the city,[38] along with the crowds, wanted**

---

31. Strelan 2000: 488–503 insists that the crowds in Lystra recognized Paul's stare, loud voice, and command as divine elements.

32. In regard to "in the form of human beings," see BDAG 707.

33. See Witherington 1998: 421–22 and Peterson 2009: 408.

34. *Metamorphoses* (μεταμόρφωσις) means "transformation" (LSJ 1114).

35. Fantham 2004: 162 (capitals and italics original).

36. This story seems to combine the stories of Gen 18–19: Abraham and Sarah welcomed and fed the Lord and his angels; Lot survived when Sodom was destroyed; Lot's wife was transformed into a pillar of salt. In regard to the connection between Lot's story and Ovid's, see Martin 1995: 153.

37. In regard to this kind of identification, Ramsay 1975 [1897]: 84 says, "The Western mind regards the leader as the active and energetic partner; but the Oriental mind considers the leader to be the person who sits still and does nothing, while his subordinates speak and work for him."

38. For translation, see BDAG 426.

to offer sacrifices [to them], by bringing bulls and garlands[39] **to the city gates** (14:13).

This made the evangelists genuinely perplexed. **When the apostles Barnabas and Paul heard about it, they tore their clothes and rushed out into the crowd, shouting and saying** (14:14–15a). If Paul and Barnabas would have liked to pretend to be Zeus and Hermes in the legend, they could have received their worship and revealed that they were "gods" by performing other miracles to punish or bless the worshipers. If so, such a process would have been disastrous not only for the evangelists but also for the audience. Thankfully, however, they stopped the crowd from sacrificing bulls and from garlanding them with a wreath.

And they expressed why they had gotten these kinds of reactions to such an overwhelmingly respectful welcome (Acts 14:14–17). This short speech can be outlined as follows:

> Who we are (14:15b)
> What we do (14:15c)
> Who God is (14:15d–16)
> What God does (14:17)

They start off by identifying themselves as "human beings": **Men, why are you doing these things? We too are human beings, with the same nature like you** (Acts 14:15b). This identification is the same as Peter's before Cornelius in 10:26, but contrasts with that of Zeus and Hermes in the legend. The feared characters in the legend said, "We are gods" (*Metam.* 8.689).

Second, they introduced what they were doing: **We are proclaiming the good news to you, in order for you to turn from these worthless things to the living God** (Acts 14:15c). "Worthless things" can refer to "idols."[40] According to Bauernfeind, in the LXX "the gods of the ἔθνη are primarily μάταια, i.e., the very gods who in the Greek world are supposed in some way to be the guarantors of that which escapes the μάταιον."[41] So Paul's anti-idols polemic was very strong and strategic in that they

---

39 "Animals were often adorned with garlands (wreaths) as they were led to the place of sacrifice" (Peterson 2009: 408). At a wedding ceremony Morton 1937 [1936]: 239 met a ram whose horns was set round by "a wreath of hill flowers" and heard, "They are going to sacrifice the animal to bring good luck to the bride and the bridegroom."

40. *TDNT* 4:522; Bruce 1990: 323; Cheng 2011: 106n68.

41. *TDNT* 4:521–22.

identified the so-called "the guarantors who help people to escape use-lessness" as useless gods. Consequently, Paul compares these worthless gods with the God alive and working, "an expression used in the Old Testament to describe the one true God who created heaven and earth, who has revealed himself to Israel, and who intervened in Israel's history."[42] Hence, the evangelists revealed the reality of both the idols and the living God.

Third, they explained who this one and only living God is: **He made the heaven, the earth, the sea, and everything that is in them,**[43] **but in past generations He allowed all the nations to go their own ways** (Acts 14:15d–16). He is the Creator with all power and authority, but is generous enough to keep up with all the nations to follow their own lifestyle. Again, in contrast, the divine figures in the legend were not so generous as to punish anyone who stood against them nor provided a place for rest (*Metam.* 8.628–29, 690–700).

Fourth, they revealed what God does: **Yet He really did not leave Himself without witness, for He did good, gave you rains from heaven and fruitful seasons, and filled your hearts with nourishment/food and merriment/joy** (Acts 14:17). Both "rains and fruitful seasons" and "food and joy" are in a sequential order for demonstrating two separate concepts; thus, far from being hendiadys. Rather, they are blessings. All four of them can be formed into a set. Rains result in fruitful seasons, fruitful seasons provide food, and food make people satisfied. In the first phrase, it is stressed that God gives people fruitful seasons as well as rainfalls; in the next phrase, it is manifested that God provides us with not only food for our body but also satisfaction to our hearts. Eventually, all this giving and providing explains God's goodness.

In truth, God had tried to make all the nations return to Him, even by providing all kinds of blessings. Nevertheless, the people had not yearned to follow His way. So up to the point when God finished His perfect way of salvation through His Son Jesus Christ, He permitted all the nations to go on their own ways. However, as Peter realized through God's attitude toward Cornelius, He is always and ever ready to accept

---

42. Schnabel 2012: 610. He provides as a reference, "Cf. Hos 1:10 (MT/LXX 2:1); 4:14; Isa 37:4; Dan 5:23; see also Deut 5:26; Josh 3:10; 1 Sam 17:36; 2 Kgs 19:4, 16; Ps 84:2 (LXX 83:3), where the description of God as 'living' is contrasted with dead idols" (610n24).

43. This sentence is alluding to Exod 20:11 and Ps 146:6 (UBS4).

anyone **who fears Him and does what is right** (Acts 10:35). Like the lame man in Lystra, one can get His salvation if one is a believer of God.

Their speech prevented the crowd in Lystra from sacrificing bulls to Paul and Barnabas (Acts 14:18). However, unfortunately and ironically, they joined the Jews of Pisidian Antioch and Iconium in persecuting the evangelists: **But Jews came from Antioch and Iconium, and after winning the crowds over, they stoned Paul and dragged him out of the city, supposing him to have been dead** (14:19). Paul mentions this event afterward in 2 Cor 11:25b ("Once I was stoned") and in 2 Tim 3:11 ("my persecutions and sufferings that happened to me in Antioch, in Iconium, and in Lystra, all kinds of persecutions that I endured and from all of which the Lord rescued me"). Bruce connects this event with a noun phrase, "the marks of Jesus," in Gal 6:17.[44]

But why did these multitudes stone Paul and not Barnabas? The first assumption attributes it to the absence of Barnabas. Bock explains that "Barnabas is absent because he is not the speaker before the crowd and may not be present on this occasion."[45] However, the text clearly puts both of them on stage: Paul and Barnabas tore "their" clothes and "they" shouted and spoke to the crowd (Acts 14:14–15). Barnabas must have been present beside Paul. Then why? The second assumption is based on a foolproof but untouched presumption. Being regarded as Hermes, Paul could have been stoned solely because he was considered as the lower deity than Zeus. They might have wanted to avoid stoning Barnabas, for the time being, as he was supposed as Zeus, "the greatest of the Olympian gods."[46]

A storm of protest was stirred and erupted, but the ministry steadily marched on: **But when the disciples surrounded him, he rose up and entered into the city [Lystra], and on the next day he went on with Barnabas to Derbe** (Acts 14:20). Peterson suggests that these disciples might have been "converts who cared for him in their homes" in Lystra or "members of his team, perhaps joined by converts from other places who had followed him."[47] Some of them might have been people encountered in Lystra (cf. 14:21–22), even the man healed from lameness; others could have been those who had followed the Jews from Pisidian Antioch

44. Bruce 1990: 325.

45. Bock 2007: 479.

46. *ED* 1419.

47. Peterson 2009: 412.

and Iconium to help the evangelists. After rising up and entering into Lystra, Paul did not hesitate but continued to move on to Derbe. Here, Luke describes who seized the initiative by employing Paul as the subject: **Paul went on with Barnabas to Derbe**.

Completion of the First Mission Trip (14:21–28)

In Derbe,[48] Paul and Barnabas **had proclaimed the gospel and made many disciples, and returned to Lystra, to Iconium, and to Antioch** (Acts 14:21). Lystra exemplified the mission to the cities of Lycaonia, so the mission to Derbe should have been simplified:[49] in the text persecution was not mentioned but could have occurred. The important fact was that many had become disciples in Derbe. On the basis of using a rare verb meaning "making disciples,"[50] Detwiler reads a Lucan summary, which reflects the fulfillment of the Great Commission (Matt 28:19) in the evangelists' ministry.[51]

Further, a more important fact lies in the attitude of the evangelists. They returned to the disciples who had recently converted to Christianity. Morton, who traveled these places in 1936, expresses well what their returning could mean: "Instead of pressing on to the south-east, along the trade road that would have taken them through the Cilician Gates into Tarsus, the apostles turned back from Derbe and with great courage went again through the territory where they had been stoned and persecuted."[52] The characteristics of Paul's attitude at this period are enumerated in 2 Tim 3:10: "manner of life, purpose, faith, longsuffering, charity, patience."

They returned to the previous mission or battle fields **to strengthen the souls of the disciples and to exhort them to remain fixed to the faith, saying "through many tribulations we must enter the kingdom**

48. In 1936, there was in Derbe "nothing left but a huge mound called Gudelisin, strewn with fragments of broken pottery" (Morton 1937 [1936]: 238), but still not yet excavated.

49. Detwiler 1995: 34 summarizes well the related points concerning Derbe in Acts: "Little else is known about the Christians in Derbe, except that Paul eventually returned to strengthen the church there (Acts 15:36, 41; 16:1, 5, and perhaps again in 18:23), and that Gaius, a member of that congregation, later accompanied Paul on part of his third missionary journey (20:4)."

50. *Matēteuō* occurs only in Matt 13:52; 27:57; 28:19, and here, in the NT.

51. Detwiler 1995: 34–35.

52. Morton 1937 [1936]: 238.

of God" (Acts 14:22). Both strengthening and exhorting can be called "shepherding" or "nurturing" and be seen as a part of "making disciples."[53] It is interesting that high expectations[54] for tribulations were included in exhortation. Tribulations have been an essential element of God's salvation: deserts to the Israelites who moved out of Egypt; exile to the Israelites who lived in the promised land; exiled life in the world like deserts to Jesus and his disciples. By the way, this exhortation to the faith became the foundation of Paul's later reproach ("Did you receive the Spirit by works of the law or by hearing with faith? Are you that foolish? Having begun by the Spirit, are you now being completed by the flesh? Did you suffer so many things in vain?" [Gal 3:2–4a]) and his confirmation ("in Christ Jesus . . . only faith working through love" [5:6]).

As the two shepherds returned for their lambs, not only teachings but also systems were provided: **They appointed elders for them in every church, prayed with fasting, and committed them [the disciples] to the Lord in whom they**[55] **had believed** (Acts 14:23). Appointing elders directly appertains to providing "ongoing nurture through qualified leaders," a possible prerequisite for "making disciples."[56] Nevertheless, Luke puts emphasis on the point that the disciples were "committed" to the Lord by the apostles, that is to say, "entrusting the disciples to the care or protection of divine protection."[57] "Returned" and "committed" are the two main verbs of 14:21–23. So these verses give further insights, such as, "they returned and committed their time and effort to nurture disciples, but they trusted only in the Lord."

Trusting in the Lord made it possible. This was their motive as **they passed through Pisidia and came into Pamphylia,** and as **having spoken the Word in Perga they went down to Attalia** (Acts 14:24–25). Via Lystra, Iconium, and Pisidian Antioch, Paul and Barnabas took the journey from Pisidian Antioch to Perga, the place where they arrived right after John Mark left them, walking along the "500km 25-day way-marked

53. See Detwiler 1995: 36–37.

54. As Detwiler 1995: 37 explains, the saying that "through many tribulations we must enter the kingdom of God" does not mean "that suffering is the means to obtaining salvation" but "that suffering is to be expected by those traveling along the narrow way of faith in Christ."

55. Schnabel 2012: 614 identifies this third plural pronoun with "the Jewish and Gentile Christians in Lystra, Iconium, and Pisidian Antioch."

56. Detwiler 1995: 37–38.

57. BDAG 772.

footpath."[58] During their first visit they had no strength to proclaim the gospel, but this time they played their role for all the nations (cf. 13:47). Subsequently, they went to Attalia, which had a bigger harbor: "The missionaries walked down to Attaleia, perhaps on the newly constructed Tiberian road extension, to try to pick up a vessel travelling along the coast to the east from that much busier harbour."[59]

From Attalia **they sailed back to Syrian Antioch, where they had been handed over to the grace of God for the work they had completed** (Acts 14:26). It should have been a buoyant return voyage, but with regretful minds they might have remembered John Mark, who had missed the latter and probably more important part of the first mission journey. They arrived in Syrian Antioch, certainly through Seleucia (cf. 13:4); they **gathered the church together, and they reported all the things God had done with them, and that He had opened a door of faith for the Gentiles** (14:27). They did not focus on what they had completed but on what God had done; in other words, "He had opened a door of faith for the Gentiles." This "door of faith" is articulated not only as "giving them the possibility of believing"[60] or giving "the opportunity to believe,"[61] but also maybe more properly as "a passage for entering"[62] into faith. Here the "faith" would be "the faith that is born through him [Jesus]" in 3:16. At last the gentiles entered into the faith because God had the door of faith open wide enough for anyone to go through. Hallelujah!

Since Paul and Barnabas finished the ministry committed to them, **they spent no little time with the disciples** probably around 48–49 CE (Acts 14:28). "No little time" is the litotes, "the negation of something in order to affirm the opposite; or understatement in order to give emphasis":[63] that is to say, enough time has passed. Since the event of Gal 2:11–21 might have occurred during this period,[64] these years do not seem to have passed quietly.

58. Clow 2013: 4.

59. Campbell 2000: 601.

60. *TDNT* 3:174.

61. Schnabel 2012: 616, possibly based on "'an open door' is used of the opportunity of doing something . . . of getting faith" (Thayer 293) or on "God gave the gentiles an opportunity to become believers" (BDAG 84).

62. BDAG 462.

63. *PDSNTG* 81. Examples of litotes can be found frequently in Luke's writings; see Culy and Parsons 2003: 6.

64. Park 2010A: 274–75 argues that the Jerusalem Council occurred "probably a bit after the time of Galatians 2:11–21."

ACTS 15

The Jerusalem Council and the Departure for the Second Mission Journey[1]

This chapter deals with the renowned Jerusalem Council. Some background information concerning this council can be found in Galatians as we follow the trail of Bauckham's "five conferences."[2] His "five conferences" on how to deal with the gentile Christians in the early church are sequenced to Acts 11:1–18 (first, 34–35 CE), Gal 1:18–19 (second, 35 CE), 2:1–10 (third, 46 CE), Acts 15:1–2a with Gal 2:1–21 (fourth, 48 CE), and Acts 15:1–29 (fifth, 49 CE).[3]

The conferences give us a faint sketch of who took the lead. For example, in Gal 2:11–21, listed as the fourth conference, "certain persons from James" had several messages from James such as, "Break the habit of 'eating Gentile food at Gentile tables'!"[4] At that time Peter had table fellowship with gentile Christians, but for the fear of the circumcision faction, he drew back from the fellowship (2:12). Then the other Jews including Barnabas complied with Peter's "hypocrisy" (2:13). When the table fellowship between the Jewish and the gentile Christians was about to be broken up, Paul scolded Peter for not following both the gospel and Peter's established practice (2:14).[5] On account of Paul's argument, Barnabas should have taken his previous position again. Taking the later Scriptures into account, Peter seems to agree with Paul, as well, and admitting his fallacy, determines not to fall into this "hypocrisy" again. With the help of this backdrop, we can understand why this serious discussion ensued in the Syrian Antioch church. Just like those "certain persons" in

1. In regard to the Jerusalem Council section, main ideas and a lot of expressions are quoted from the author's article Park 2010A: 271–91, without quotation marks, but revised, augmented, and much of it fitted into this book.

2. Bauckham 2005: 137–38.

3. Bauckham 2005: 137–38, and as for the years, see Bruce 1990: 92.

4. Manson 1962: 181; similarly Bruce 1982: 130.

5. This blame continues up to Gal 2:21 according to Bauckham 1996: 125–26.

2:12, "some men" in Acts 15:1 could have been associated with the Lord's brother James. Likewise, the scenes of the conferences seem to imply that James and Paul were the representatives of each group, not only in Syrian Antioch (Gal 2:11–21) but also at the Jerusalem Council.

Preparation for the Jerusalem Council (15:1–5)

When Paul and Barnabas stayed in Syrian Antioch after completing the first mission journey, something important happened to the brethren in Cyprus, southern Galatia, and Pamphylia, as well as in Syrian Antioch: **Some men came down from Judea and began to teach the brothers, "Unless you are circumcised according to the custom of Moses, you are unable to be saved"** (Acts 15:1). This group mentioned the prerequisite for the "salvation" of thegGentile Christians. As a result of this teaching, **no small disagreement and debate[6] was raised by Paul and Barnabas toward them** (15:2a).

Due to "no small disagreement and debate," it was hard for the Antioch church to go further on debating since these Jews raised a fundamental matter, "salvation." The church sent Paul, Barnabas, and some of the church leaders to the "apostles and elders" in Jerusalem in order to deal with this disagreement (Acts 15:2b). On the way, because of their report on the conversion of the gentiles, they got a warm welcome from the believers in Phoenicia[7] and Samaria (15:3), where there was neither disagreement nor debate. However, by the time they arrived in Jerusalem, the circumstances were quite different.[8]

After exchanging greetings, Paul and Barnabas were pulled into debates once more when **they reported all that God had done with them** (Acts 15:4). In the following verse, the demand of "some believers[9] who belonged to the sect of the Pharisees" is briefly introduced: **It is necessary to circumcise them and to order them to observe the law of Moses** (15:5). The Pharisaic believers insisted that the gentile Christians should come within the boundaries which had existed between the Jews and the

6. The expression, "no small disagreement and debate," is again "litotes, by which an affirmative is expressed by the negative of the contrary" (Peterson 2009: 421n15).

7. "Phoenicia was an area along the Mediterranean coast north of Palestine in ancient Syria" (NET notes).

8. Cf. Malcolm 2002: 249.

9. *Pepisteukotes* is viewed "as an attributive modifier of a substantival τινες" (Culy and Parsons 2003: 287). So *pepisteukotes* can mean "even though they believe."

gentiles for a long time, and that they should keep the law of Moses, including the food laws, exactly as the Jewish Christians do.

If we do not mix Acts 15:1 and 15:5, some men who came down from Judea in 15:1, later on unveiled as **certain persons who have gone out from us, though with no instructions from us** [apostles and elders] (15:24), stressed circumcision and the law of Moses in respect to salvation. However, the Pharisaic believers in Jerusalem in 15:5 just emphasized circumcision and the law of Moses, without any relation to salvation. Between the two, 15:1 and 15:5, there was a report from Paul and Barnabas on **all that God had done with them** (15:4). The believers who were already a part of the Pharisees (15:5) seem to have responded to this report, still standing on the side of those **who came down from Judea** (15:1) but omitting reference to the matter of salvation, by reason of what God has done through Paul and Barnabas. The council reaches the issue, as Bauckham says, "evidently not whether Gentiles could join the messianically renewed Israel, but whether they could do so without becoming Jews."[10]

The Jerusalem Council (15:6-23a)

In Acts 10:1—11:18 Luke reports on the first (according to Bauckham) conference, including the backstory to why it was convened—that is, the story of Cornelius's conversion. Then, the birth of the Syrian Antioch church is described. So Luke's audience, including Theophilus, might have expected that a further arrangement would be made by the Jerusalem church because a different kind of group involvement in the faith (that is, the gentiles) had necessitated an action from the mother church. This kind of action was taken from her starting point: the disciples, who were waiting for the fulfillment of the promise made by God the Father, elected Matthias to take the place of Judas Iscariot (1:13–26); after substantial growth of the congregation of the Jerusalem church, the church appointed the seven [deacons] (6:1–6); when people in Samaria received the word of God, the mother church sent Peter and John there (8:14); even after Paul's conversion, a meeting of the apostles was held to receive the eager persecutor of the church as one of them (9:27). After all these incidents, as mentioned above, the first conference was held (11:1–18) after Cornelius's conversion. So it would have been very likely that the

10. Bauckham 1996: 168.

leaders of the mother church met in Jerusalem after many gentiles became believers.

In this Jerusalem Council, however, a very delicate matter was
broached. It was not a matter of electing a replacement for an apostle,
or of appointing a (kind of) deacon, or of examining an apostle who was
blamed for having unlawful relationships with gentiles, instead a very old
and essential subject on how the gentiles can be united with the Jewish
community. Consequently, various groups took part in the council. The
leadership was enlarged from the apostles (cf. Acts 1:26; 2:42; 4:33; 6:6;
8:14; 9:27; 11:1) to "the apostles and the elders" (15:4, 6, 22, 23). Of two
main disputing parties, one side was represented by "some who came
down from Judea" (15:1) and "some believers who belonged to the sect
of the Pharisees" (15:5), and the other by Paul and Barnabas and possibly the Syrian Antioch church leaders since they were sent together.
The main speakers of the council were some disciples who had followed
Jesus in his ministry on earth, namely Peter and probably Barnabas,[11] and
some who became disciples after Jesus' resurrection, namely Paul and
(very likely) James (cf. Luke 8:19–21; Acts 1:14; 1 Cor 15:7). One opinion
is briefly introduced in Acts 15:1, 5, as mentioned previously, that the
gentile Christians should keep the Mosaic law. Another opinion is that
the gentile Christians do not need to keep the law of Moses both to be
saved and to be united with the Jewish Christians.

The following structure of Acts 15:4–29 helps us zoom in each shot
in the flow of the conversation which surely proves the participants'
attitudes.

a. The church and the apostles and the elders
welcome Paul and Barnabas
and some representatives of Antioch (15:4a)

b. Paul and Barnabas's testimony (15:4b)   c. Some Pharisaic believers'
insistence (15:5)

d. Meeting and debating of the council (15:6–7a)

e. Peter's speech (15:7b–11)

f. Silence of the whole assembly (15:12a)

g. Barnabas and Paul's testimony (15:12b)

h. Silence of Barnabas and Paul (15:13a)

---

11. Some manuscripts and ancient translations (D 6s pc it vgmss) have "Barnabas"
instead of "Barsabbas" in 1:23, which means that Barnabas had been with Jesus from
John's baptism to Jesus' ascension.

i. James's suggestion (15:13b–21)

j. The council's agreement (15:22–29)

Preparations for the council started with the Jerusalem church welcoming the Antioch church members (a; 15:4a). Then Paul and Barnabas talked about what God had done without making any complaints regarding the debate that recently arose (b; 15:4b). Some Pharisaic believers, of the other group, mentioned circumcision and the law of Moses, but remained silent about "custom" and "salvation" in 15:1 (c; 15:5). The council gathered to consider this matter and spent a long time discussing, without going away in anger or pushing people into discarding their opinions or making political moves to defeat their opponents: **Both the apostles and the elders met together to deliberate concerning this matter, and there had been much debate** (d; Acts 15:6–7a). It is important to pay attention to "much debate" (*pollēs zēteseōs*): even though its contents are not reported, readers should suspect the discussion was not short. As Peterson says, "It seems likely that the whole body of believers in Jerusalem was involved at some level in the debate and its outcome (cf. vv. 12, 22)."[12]

After an ongoing discussion, Peter, who had been the representative of the apostles and likely the president of this council, spoke (e; Acts 15:7b–11). He at first dealt with what God had done.[13] He gave two pieces of evidence. One is that God chose Peter, his own very self, and the other is that He gave His Spirit to the gentiles: **God made a choice among you that the Gentiles hear through my mouth the Word of the gospel and believe,**[14] **and God, who knows the heart, has testified to them by giving them the Holy Spirit just as He did to us** (Acts 15:7b–8). It was not Peter, but God who decided to make the gentiles hear the Word

12. Peterson 2009: 424.

13. Cf. Bauckham 1996: 154.

14. Bruce 1988: 289n36 sees *en humin ekseleksato* as "a Semitic idiom for 'chose you.'" His reference is 1 Sam 16:9–10; 1 Kgs 8:16, 44; 1 Chr 28:4–5; Neh 9:7 (Bruce 1990: 336). So Culy and Parsons 2003: 288 even put "me" explicitly. However, in the NT this verb normally has an accusative as its object (Mark 13:20; Luke 6:13; 10:42; 14:7; John 6:70; 13:18; 15:16 [2x], 19; Acts 1:2, 24; 6:5; 13:17; 15:22, 25; 1 Cor 1:27 [2x], 28; Eph 1:4; Jas 2:5). So it is hard to assume that Luke uses a dative as the object of the verb only in this verse. Therefore, Peterson's translation seems more reasonable: "God made a choice among you that the Gentiles might hear from my lips the message of the gospel and believe" (Peterson 2009: 424). BDAG 305 sees this verb/idiom as the construction with the infinitive following without an object, and translates the first part of the verse as "in your presence God chose that [they] were to hear through my mouth."

and believe while they were not circumcised, thus not keeping the law of Moses thoroughly. Moreover, God poured out the Holy Spirit to those who were not even proselytes. These hands-on experiences Peter shared meant to him that **He made no distinction between them [the Gentiles] and us [the Jews], cleansing their hearts by faith** (15:9). Further, to Peter, these works of God connoted that if the Jewish Christians, including himself, had forced them to be circumcised and to keep the custom of Moses, they would be **putting God to the test by placing on the neck of the disciples, possibly, the yoke that neither their [our] ancestors nor they themselves [we] had been able to bear** (15:10). Finally, based on what God had done, Peter concluded that **on the contrary, we believe that we are saved through the grace of the Lord Jesus, in the same way as they are** (15:11). He pointed out that there is "no distinction" between the two groups (15:9). His evidence came from Cornelius's case, which had already been finalized in Jerusalem (11:1–18).[15] Rather than *ethos* or *pathos*, the usage of *logos* stands out in Peter's speech.

The whole assembly stepped back from the debate to think and listen (f; Acts 15:12a). Peter's argument silenced the whole assembly effectively. Then the silence broke out with Barnabas and Paul's testimonies; Peter's evidence was supported by the multiplied evidences of **all the signs and wonders that God has done among the Gentiles** through the missionaries for the gentiles (g; 15:12b). Barnabas, probably more than Paul, if presenting his name prior to Paul's holds some kind of significance, spoke of all these miracles that God had done, solely His work. Then they lapsed into silence (h; 15:13a).

After Paul and Barnabas finished speaking (Acts 15:13a), the last speech was given by James, who was not an apostle but an elder and/ or a chief pastor in the Jerusalem church (i; 15:13b–21). The position of James is still in debate; yet, being the last speaker does not seem sufficient to prove that James was the leader of the Jerusalem Council. The group members were composed of "apostles and elders"; however, James the Lord's brother did not belong to the apostles; nor was he yet an elder. Rather, he could be titled as "a leading representative of the so-called *Hebraioi*."[16] According to Farmer, this James was an important figure from the second (Gal 1:18–19) to the fifth (the Jerusalem Council) meeting on

15. So also Bauckham 2005: 117.

16. Ådna 2000: 126.

the condition that the "James" in 2:9 and 12 is identified as "James the Lord's brother" (1:19).[17]

In the fourth conference, as we have seen, James had to do with both parties, the Jews from Judea (Acts 15:1) and with the Pharisaic believers (15:5). So it should have been escapable for James not to speak in the last or fifth conference because he certainly was the representative of the view that the gentiles should keep the custom of Moses to join the new Messianic community. James's final proposal was made in response to Peter's remark on God's recent acts for the salvation of the gentiles, and based on the Scripture, especially the prophets: "Simeon has explained how God took the initiative[18] to concern himself about winning a people from among the nations,"[19] and the words of the prophets harmonize with this, as it is written, **"After this I will return, and I will rebuild the fallen tent of David; I will repair its ruins and lift it up again, so that the rest of humanity may seek the Lord,**[20] **namely all the Gentiles on whom my name has been called on them,"**[21] **says the Lord, who makes these things known from long ago** (15:14–18).

Marshall connects **winning a people from among the nations** (Acts 15:14) with Deut 14:2, and says, "Whereas Deuteronomy refers to God selecting Israel to be his special people *separate from* the nations, James here appears to mean that God is now taking a group of people *out of the Gentile nations* to be a people for himself."[22] On this premise, James identified "God's recent acts for the salvation of the Gentiles" with something like His selecting Israel in the past.[23]

---

17. Farmer 1999: 133. So also Dunn 1993: 108.

18. *Prōton* can have the meaning of "taking the initiative" (Cheng 2011: 164, 164n42).

19. BDAG 378.

20. In regard to "so that the rest of humanity may seek the Lord," which differs from the LXX as well as the MT in Amos 9:12a, Peterson 2009: 432n50 writes, "This version is regarded as authoritative 'midrash' because it interprets the original in the light of its fulfillment in Christ and reflects also the perspective of other eschatological prophecies (v. 15)."

21. In regard to *eph . . . ep autous* Bruce 1990: 341, says, "LXX follows the Heb. idiom, which repeats the personal or demonstrative pron. after the relative *'ăšer* (cf. Mod. Gk. construction with ποῦ." Similarly Culy and Parsons 2003: 293.

22. Marshall 2007: 589 (italics original).

23. And some passages in the OT allude to this point; Hos 3:5; Jer 12:15–16; Amos 9:11–12; and Isa 45:21 are suggested as the Scriptures related to Acts 15:16–17. See Ådna 2000: 128–39, 161; so also Proctor 1996: 474. Cf. Marshall 2007: 589–93.

Consequently, James did not demand the gentile Christians' circumcision but only four items, some essential requisites for the gentile residents among the Israelites: **Therefore, I conclude that we should not cause further trouble for those among the Gentiles who turn to God, but should write to them to abstain from the things polluted**[24] **by idols, and from sexual immorality, and from what has been strangled, and from blood** (Acts 15:19-20). The reason for imposing these four prohibitions was because **from ancient generations Moses has had in every city those who proclaim him; he is read aloud in the synagogue every Sabbath** (15:21).

Ultimately, the apostles and the elders, together with the whole church, decided to send two leading brothers to Antioch with a letter containing the famous fourfold prohibitions (j; Acts 15:22-29). **It seemed best to the apostles and the elders to send men chosen from among them, Judas and called Barsabbas and Silas, leaders among the brothers, to Antioch with Paul and Barnabas, after writing a letter through their hands**[25] (15:22-23a). Two witnesses and a legal letter were prepared.

The Letter of the Council (15:23b–29)

The letter sent to Antioch consists of five parts: Salutation (Acts 15:23b), Background (15:24-26), Witnesses (15:27), Decision (15:28-29a), and Final Greetings (15:29b). To begin with, the salutation follows a general form: the sender (**the apostles and the elderly brothers**),[26] the recipient (**to the brothers of Gentile origin in Antioch and Syria and Cilicia**), and the greetings (**peace be with you**) (15:23b). Then, the backgrounds includes what they had heard (**we have heard that certain persons, who have gone out from us, disturbed you and unsettled your minds by saying words which we had not commanded expressly,** 15:24) and what process had been followed (**it seemed best to us to choose men**

24. Instone-Brewer (Instone-Brewer 2009: 304) suggests the possibility that τῶν εἰδώλων καὶ τῆς πορνείας καὶ τοῦ πνικτοῦ καὶ τοῦ αἵματος modifies τῶν ἀλισγημάτων. If he is right, James's list can be seen quite more ritual-centered.

25. "In this expression (Lit. 'writing through their hand'), the direct object and an intervening event is left implicit: 'writing *a letter to be delivered* by their hand'" (Culy and Parsons 2003: 297) (italics theirs).

26. Or "the Apostles and the elders, brothers" (see Bruce 1990: 345).

unanimously²⁷ and send them to you, along with our beloved Barnabas and Paul,²⁸ the men who have risked their lives for the sake of
the name of our Lord Jesus Christ, 15:25–26). Two were counted as
witnesses (we have therefore sent Judas and Silas, namely those²⁹ who
will tell you the same things by words, 15:27). The decision was made
(it has seemed best to the Holy Spirit and to us³⁰ to impose on you no
further burden than these essentials: that you abstain from what has
been sacrificed to idols and from blood and from what is strangled
and from fornication; if you keep yourselves from these, you will do
well,15:28–29a). And the final greetings were Farewell (15:29b).

The final decision of the council was that the gentile Christians
should abstain from the four prohibitions, but this list is quite different
from what was first urged by James in Acts 15:20:³¹

> 15:20 τῶν ἀλισγημάτων τῶν εἰδώλων καὶ τῆς πορνείας καὶ τοῦ
> πνικτοῦ καὶ τοῦ αἵματος (James's list)

> 15:29 εἰδωλοθύτων καὶ αἵματος καὶ πνικτῶν καὶ πορνείας (the
> council's letter).

27. "It may be possible to take the entire phrase, γενομένοις ὁμοθυμαδὸν
ἐκλεξαμένοις, as an attributive periphrastic expression ('It seemed good to us, who
had unanimously chosen men . . .'), though a temporal expression makes for a better
English translation" (Culy and Parsons 2003: 299).

28. It is interesting that in the council's letter Barnabas precedes Paul (so also 14:12,
14; 15:12; cf. 13:43, 46, 50; 14:20; 15:2, 22, 35, 36 where Paul precedes Barnabas).

29. "This epexegetical expression [καὶ αὐτούς] draws attention to the activity,
state, or role of the referent(s) (cf. v. 32; Mark 1:19; Luke 1:36)" (Culy and Parsons
2003: 299). So, *kai autous* may mean "namely those."

30. The Holy Spirit can be mentioned on the basis of the Cornelius event (10:19–
20, 44–47; 11:12, 15–16) and the first mission journey (13:2, 52). "We" include "the
apostles and the elders and the Jerusalem church" (15:6, 22). So "to the Holy Spirit and
to us" indicates both divine and human evidence. McIntosh 2002: 131–47 suggests
Peter's remark (15:8–9), Barnabas's and Paul's testimony (15:4b, 12), and James's citation (15:16–18) as evidences to state that "it seemed good to the Holy Spirit."

31. In some manuscripts we can find an effort to harmonize these lists, including
the list in 21:25. For example, some minuscules (945, 1739, 1891) change the order of
"blood" in 15:20 (from the fourth to the second) and the numbers of "things strangled"
in 15:29 (from plural to singular), to make the second, the third, and the fourth items
the same in the three lists (see Swanson 1998: 263). Changing the numbers of "things
strangled" can be found in many manuscripts, namely P74 Ac ℵc E H L P Ψ 049 056 1
33 88 etc. (Swanson 1998: 268). However, most scholars prefer the variants adopted in
NA27 and UBS4 as original (see Metzger 1994: 382; Savelle 2004: 450–51).

Through analysis, we can acknowledge few, yet significant, distinctions between the two. To begin with, we see "blood" as the last item on James's list, but as the second in the council's letter. Only James's list included a very ritual term ἀλισγημάτων ("pollutions").[32] In the council's letter the word "idols" (εἰδώλων) changed to a terminology more corresponding to worshiping, "idol sacrifices" (εἰδωλοθύτων). "Strangled" in 15:20 is changed from singular to plural (a more inclusive term) in 15:29. In addition, each item of the four in the former has a Greek article, but none of the four has the article in the latter. This omission of the articles may indicate that the gentile Christians could not understand the ritual aspect of the four prohibitions. However, since the debate had occurred for a long period, at least five times according to Bauckham, the gentile Christians could have been used to and understood some parts of the ritual aspects in the four. Seeing that the church omitted the Greek articles from the four, this strongly suggests a change of aspect from ritual to something broader, such as worship and/or covenant.

Before expanding on this claim, I would like to point out that the characteristics of the four prohibitions offered to the gentile Christians in Acts 15:29 have been debated. Some Western texts, first of all, may show that ritual and moral perspectives had been important even in the past. Some witnesses (D l [VIII] etc.) omit "what is strangled," and more (D 323 614 945 1739 1891 a few manuscripts of the Majority text l [VIII] p [VIII] w [XIV/XV], etc.) add a negative form of the Golden Rule.[33] Savelle evaluates Western texts as "reinvented along ethical lines."[34] Barrett writes, "Just as the circumstances that evoked it had both ritual and ethical elements, so the Old Uncial Decree had both ritual and ethical elements. . . . The Western editor(s) came down strongly on the ethical side."[35] So, considering the text critical issues, Metzger asks if "the three or four prohibitions [are] entirely ceremonial, or entirely ethical, or a combination of both kinds."[36]

In addition to this textual criticism, some aspects of Second Temple Judaism make Bauckham raise the same question. On the basis of Klawans's article on the Second Temple Jewish understanding of the gentiles

32. Savelle 2004: 452 connects this term with "eating food."
33. Cf. Metzger 1994: 380.
34. Savelle 2004: 450–51.
35. Barrett 1998: 736.
36. Metzger 1994: 379.

published in 1995,[37] Bauckham claims, "It is not matters of ritual purity that concern the group opposed to Peter, Barnabas, and Paul, but the moral conversion of Gentiles."[38] This claim as well as the textual variants and the dissimilarity between the lists of James and the council provoked a thought that the two lists might, despite their similarity in content, have been made from different or contrasting perspectives. Therefore, Bauckham's argument has to be examined much more closely, mostly because he had not referred to Klawans's thesis published in 2000.[39]

According to Klawans's thesis, ritual and moral impurity can be distinguished as follows:

	Ritual Impurity	**Moral Impurity**
Source	Bodily flows, corpses, etc.	Sins: idolatry, incest, murder
Effect	Temporary, contagious impurity	Defilement of sinners, land, and sanctuary
Resolution	Bathing, waiting	Atonement or punishment, and ultimately, exile[40]

Klawans clarifies his aim in using these terms:

> By using these terms I am not intending to state that ritual and morality are opposing or mutually exclusive concerns. I am simply trying to drive home the point that there are two kinds of impurity in ancient Israel, one of which is more associated with sin than the other.[41]

However, his treatment of these themes in the NT did not deal with Acts 15.[42] Further, even though he uses Leviticus in defining both "ritual impurity" and "moral impurity" in his thesis, very little mention is made on chs. 17 and 18 of Leviticus, the chapters Bauckham suggests as underlying reasons for these four prohibitions.[43] What is more, Klawans admits that the dietary law has both "ritual" and "moral" aspects.[44] Along these

37. Klawans 1995: 285–312.

38. Bauckham 2005: 118.

39. Bauckham 2005: 91.

40. Klawans 2000: 27.

41. Klawans 2000: 22.

42. See Klawans 1995: 136–57.

43. Klawans 2000: 22–31.

44. Klawans 2000: 31–32.

lines, the conclusion that the four prohibitions are simply linked to moral iniquity seems superficial.

In regard to the Jewish understanding of the gentiles, Bauckham depends on Klawans's article, which has some evidence for the notion that some Jews thought of the gentiles as ritually impure. The evidence comes from Josephus's works (*Ant.* 12.145; 14.285; *War* 1.229; 2.150) and from some rabbinic sources (*T. Zabim* 2:1).[45] Ritual impurity can become morally impure by doing something, and moral impurity can be purified ritually, as well as through punishment.[46] On the basis of Acts 14:1 and 17:1–4, Klawans insists that "Acts as a whole sees no inherent barriers to Jewish-Gentile interaction, even in synagogues."[47] However, we need to remember that 17:1–4 occurred after the Jerusalem Council and even 14:1, after the third conference in 46 CE (Gal 2:1–10). Bauckham's stance on the Jewish understanding of the gentiles as morally impure is also not thoroughly complete.

Moreover, Bauckham's claim seems to result from his presupposition that James's list is the same as the council's,[48] and that the four items are only related to eating food. He pays attention to "the profane food of profane people."[49] However, these lists are different literally and in perspective; simply speaking, the council's list focuses more on worship and/ or covenant than on ritual. I present below five considerations in support of this claim.

First, the council (Acts 15:29) seems to have changed some ritual aspects embedded in James's remark (15:20) into some worship aspects that cover the rituals, from "things polluted by idols" to sacrificing or worshiping other gods. To Proctor, all four prohibitions are connected with "a matter of idolatry," and so, "worship must be given to Israel's God alone. This is the point to be secured; the rest will, it seems, look after itself."[50] He says, "Nor will abstinence from black pudding be much help in healing these deep divisions; the main things that Jews have found

45. Klawans 1995: 286, 298–300.

46. Klawans 1995: 289.

47. Klawans 1995: 301–2.

48. Barrett 1998: 736, says, "It is not surprising that those who accepted the authority of this mixed Decree emphasized sometimes one [ritual] sometimes the other [ethical] aspect of it." This mixture of emphasis here and there may result, in one sense, from the fact that all three lists were dealt collectively.

49. Bauckham 2005: 103.

50. Proctor 1996: 478.

offensive in Christianity are not dietary."[51] Further, Park connects the first item ("idol sacrifices") with a covenantal law, saying that "the first component of the four restrictions, the things sacrificed to idols (εἰδωλόθυτος in Acts 15.29; 21.25; cf. εἴδωλον in Acts 15.20), is related absolutely to mandatory חרם because idolatry is the sin that should result in mandatory חרם."[52] Therefore, the first item employed by the council has to do with worship.

Second, the intention of changing the order of the "blood" could be a hint to its readers to relate the text with the covenant. Proctor suggests this blood should be "a metonymy for violence, wounding or murder, the outcome of human conflict."[53] However, according to Savelle,

> understanding αἷμα in the sense of murder seems unlikely for at least two reasons. First, when αἷμα is used with the sense of murder, the context usually makes it clear that it is to be taken that way. . . . Second, would something as obvious as prohibiting murder be included in what is clearly a highly selective list? This seems unlikely.[54]

Interestingly, four of the nineteen occurrences of the word "blood" in Luke-Acts directly refer to Jesus' blood (Luke 22:20, 44; Acts 5:28; 20:28); six times indirectly to his blood;[55] six times refer to people's blood;[56] and the other three are related to the list (15:20, 29; 21:25). And the blood of Jesus is the very core of the new covenant upon which the new community, the church, is built. The people in this community in any sense drink Jesus' blood at Holy Communion (Luke 22:20; Acts 2:46) and through it they worship (Heb 9:14; 10:19). Paul stresses that the blood of Christ brought the gentile Christians near to Israel, the covenants, and God (Eph 2:12–13); thus, devouring other drops of blood can be interpreted in relation to breaking the new covenant. By and large Jesus' blood is significant as the new covenantal sign since it is compared with circumcision, the sign of the old covenant that was still strongly

51. Proctor 1996: 479.

52. Park 2007A: 174.

53. Proctor 1996: 472.

54. Savelle 2004: 455.

55. Luke 11:50 (of the prophets), 51a (Abel's), 52b (Zechariah's); Acts 2:19–20 (quotation from Joel 2:28–32 [3:1–5, MT, LXX]); 22:20 (Stephen's).

56. Luke 8:43–44 (a woman who had been suffering from a hemorrhage); 13:1 (some Galileans); Acts 1:19 (Judas); 18:6 (Corinthian Jews); 20:26 (Ephesian church members).

held by some Jews in the council. Hence, the council may have moved the "blood" from last to second place so as to lay a greater emphasis on the mark of the new covenant; in addition, the council might prohibit the gentile Christians from consuming "blood" except for Jesus' blood, just as it prohibited them from worshiping other gods except God the Father.

Third, strangling a live being may not merely refer to foods. "Things that were strangled" are considered as "the eating of animals that had not had their blood drained properly (Lev 17:13–14; Deut 12:16, 23),"[57] or outputs of cooking,[58] or choked "sacrifices in pagan temples (a practice which may have occurred but was probably very rare) and smothering infants—a practice which most non-Jews regarded as a normal form of birth control."[59] If we follow Instone-Brewer's highly specialized study, these "smothered" or "strangled" things also do not simply mean foods, but a cruel practice in pagan worship or family life.

Fourth, fornication is a strong term linked to idolatry. Savelle holds that "in the Septuagint πορνεία is used about fifty times, usually as a metaphor for idolatry or unfaithfulness to God" and that "the issue is further complicated by the fact that a number of pagan religions included immoral sexual activities as part of their worship."[60] Moreover, fornication can be identified with idol worship in Exod 34:15–16.[61]

Fifth, backgrounds to the four prohibitions encourage us to see covenant and worship as the characteristics of the four components in the Jerusalem decree. If the "Noachide commandments" proposed by Bockmuehl[62] are the grounds to the decree,[63] the four items may demonstrate a covenantal perspective. Taylor says, "The reference implied in these seven precepts is not the particular Covenant with Abraham or its renewal at Sinai, or even Creation (which would be implied in a precept to observe the Sabbath), but Noah, that is to say, a very general covenant between God and humanity as a whole." Alternatively, many scholars think of Leviticus 17–18 as the background of the decree.[64] Bauckham summarizes the connection between the four restrictions and Leviticus

---

57. Savelle 2004: 456.

58. Proctor 1996: 473.

59. Instone-Brewer 2009: 321.

60. Savelle 2004: 454; so also Park 2007A: 9, 174.

61. Park 2007A: 174.

62. Bockmuehl 2000.

63. *Pace* Taylor 2001: 374–77; *contra* Proctor 1996: 476 Barrett 1998: 733–35.

64. E.g., Jervell 1972: 133–52; Proctor 1996: 474–75.

17–18 as follows: "(a) 'things sacrificed to idols' are prohibited in Lev 17:8–9; (b) 'blood' is prohibited in Lev 17:10, 12; (c) 'things strangled' are prohibited in Lev 17:13; (d) 'sexual immorality' refers to Lev 18:26 and covers all the prohibited forms of sexual practice in Lev 18:6–23."[65] Leviticus 17–18 is part of a bigger structure, that is, Leviticus 17–21, and its center is Leviticus 19.[66] This chapter seems to be used elsewhere in the NT[67] and includes both ritual and moral aspects, such as worship and/or covenant. Leviticus 17–21 is given to "all the congregation of the children of Israel."[68] In addition, Leviticus's main context is worship, so all the cases, including suggested occasions (for example, eating blood, idolatry, Sabbath, fornication), are mentioned in respect of worship based on God's covenant. Each case regulates the time when the Israelites will lose the right as worshipers temporarily, or in another way of putting it, permanently. So the suggested backgrounds to the four items help us to consider the characteristics of each component as worship and/or covenant.[69]

Consequently, we can conclude that the four items in Acts 15:29 were issued precisely from the perspective of worship and covenant rather than that of ritual. The four in James's list, as we have seen, do have a more ritual perspective. Taking Gal 2:11–21 into account, it is possible that James wanted to make the gentile Christians keep some ritual regulations of the Old Testament. However, the council, in accepting the four items suggested by James, seems to have based their stance on covenant, acknowledging the *unity* of both Jewish and gentile Christians. In sum, the council made an agreement that was located between the two positions, very similar to James's suggestion, but adjusting its basic stance to a more covenantal and worshiping perspective.

65. Bauckham 2005: 119.

66. Kim 2011: 34–37; so also Kim 2007: 119.

67. Johnson 1982: 391–401.

68. Kim 2007: 122.

69. My suggestion on the concept of *Herem* as a background to both Luke 16:16–17 and the four prohibitions in Acts 15:29 (Park 2007A: 174) also supports this proposal.

Fusing the Horizons: Concession for Encouragement and Unity[70]

This history of the Jerusalem Council traces a long way back. Through a flow of conversation in Acts 15:6–29, we can notice that there were two groups involved, that the council was divided into two main groups. While the three lists of the four prohibitions all differ significantly, James's list shows to be most associated with the rituals, and the council's to worship and covenant. The fixation of these four prohibitions of the council does not seem to demonstrate any general principle like "the so-called Negative Golden Rule."[71] While scholars like Savelle suggest that Luke intended to present "the unification of the two groups" in Acts,[72] an intriguing remark by Perkins[73] helps us sense that more than mere unification is what Luke is aiming to illustrate through this passage.

In my opinion, "the common sense shared within the council member" is being described here carefully. We will look at what "common sense" they shared and how they look similar, yet contrast to the ones considered ethical. They listened to others carefully and placed trust in each other's speech; they did not doubt their testimonies. Although the members had not experienced Peter's or Paul's and Barnabas's life,[74] they trusted each other. In addition, they were all God-centered (cf. Acts 15:3–4, 7–9, 12, 14, 17).[75] Peter especially is seen as a person who gives authority to God rather than to human beings, in comparing 10:1–16 with 11:1–17. In 11:5 and 9, he used "from heaven" twice, which does not appear in 10:1–17. His conclusive remark was "Who am I that I could hinder God?" (11:17). Moreover, all the council members respected the Scripture and used the same hermeneutics to interpret the Bible. What is more, the council mem-

70. This theme is based on Park 2010A: 286–91.

71. This rule is expressed in some Western manuscripts (D 323 945) meaning that "they should not do to others what they do not like to have done to themselves" (Proctor 1996: 471–72).

72. Savelle 2004: 467.

73. Perkins 1988: 238: "Luke suggests that true peace and unity among peoples is not created by the order of the Roman empire but by a common hope for salvation which is open to all people."

74. The Strongs (Strong and Strong 2007: 138) think, "The council was able to arrive at a harmonious conclusion because it focused on common experiences." However, most of the members had not shared experiences with Peter, Paul, and Barnabas.

75. Strong and Strong 2007: 137.

bers had the attitude of concession to form a better solution even though each part had its own reason for its point of view, based on God's Word and their experiences.

The Jerusalem Council had the characteristic that they shared attitudes such as concession, as well as trusting each other, respecting God and His Word, responding in a sympathetic manner for "encouraging and uniting the members to form a better solution." Nevertheless, these were not attitudes "essential to achieving more global understandings" as the Strongs suggest.[76] The Jerusalem Council did not strive for the globalization of the church but pursued the will of God by taking their stance only on what God had said in the Bible and had done in their lives.

Concessions are achieved in other passages in Acts as well; the attitude of concession was key to solve conflicts even before the council. To begin with, in Acts 6:1–6 the apostles adopted this attitude to find a solution to the problem which arose between two groups within one church. In 9:10–19a, this kind of attitude prevailed in Ananias in the Damascus church when he went to Paul. Further, this attitude helps to explain the continued context since Acts 15 concludes with the division between Barnabas and Paul (15:36–39) and goes on to the second journey that covers going astray (16:6–8) and hesitating to talk about Jesus (18:5; cf. 1 Thess 3:1–8). The division between Barnabas and Paul could be considered as a conflict between "encouragement" and "conviction." Barnabas, literally meaning "son of encouragement" (Acts 4:36), lived a life of encouragement, shown by supporting the church financially (4:37), his defense of Paul (9:27), and his ministry for the gentiles (11:22–26). Paul was a man of strong conviction.[77] He was able to approve even of Stephen's death (8:1). He did not stop breathing **threats and murder against the disciples of the Lord** (9:1). After his conversion, he continued to show this kind of behavior throughout his mission (9:20; 14:20–21). Both encouragement and conviction are good virtues; however, without the attitude of concession both could end fruitless.

Later in the story we see a change in the man of conviction, especially in Acts 21:26. This man, who could not accept John Mark due to his record of deserting colleagues, now accepted even those who were "zealous for the law" (21:20) in order to fulfill the mission of offering the gentiles to

76. Strong and Strong 2007: 134.

77. In the NRSV, the word "conviction" appears only in Rom 14:22; 1 Thess 1:5; Heb 11:1.

God (24:17; Rom 15:16). For Luke, would this change have been positive or negative? When we read the rest of Acts, especially the last verse (Acts 28:31), Luke seems to regard Paul's change as positive. In Eph 2:14, on the basis of offering the gentiles, Paul seems to proclaim boldly that the dividing wall between the Jews and the gentiles has been broken down.

When we apply "the attitude of concession for encouragement and unity" in Acts 15 to our situation, we need to remember that there were no divisions within each group in the Jerusalem Council in terms of hermeneutics and the authority of Scripture. So "the recent dispute over homosexuality within the worldwide Anglican Communion"[78] would *not* be a case to which the attitude can be directly applied because it is said that "from a hermeneutical perspective, the conservative wing of the church follows a hermeneutic based on the finality of Scripture, whereas the liberal wing begins with the ideals of love, acceptance, and compassion and reaches different conclusions."[79]

In conclusion, I suggest that taking an "attitude of concession for encouragement and unity to form a better solution," rather than fighting for one's own opinion, is much more likely to lead to a consensus if the members of a group have the same confession of faith in God the Father and Jesus Christ our Lord. With this attitude, potential splits that can appear so easily in Christian organizations could be transformed into occasions of unity, encouragement, and rejoicing.

The Results of the Council and the Departures for the Second Mission Journey (15:30–41)

The witnesses and the members of the Syrian Antioch church, including Paul and Barnabas, carried out their mission: **So they were sent off and went down to Antioch, and after gathering the congregation together, they delivered the letter** (Acts 15:30). Responses to the letter were quite positive: **after reading it, they rejoiced at the exhortation** (Acts 15:31). The letter, especially the four forbidden items, comforted the gentile believers since it was a concession made by the Jewish Christians. The

78. Strong and Strong 2007: 133.
79. Strong and Strong 2007: 133–34.

Jerusalem Council succeeded in achieving a unity, and resulted in encouragement and rejoicing.

Further, two of the witnesses also completed their mission: **Judas and Silas, who were themselves prophets, encouraged and strengthened the brethren with a lot of words** (15:32). The role Judas and Silas occupied was the same as that of the council's letter, namely encouraging the church members, but they did more, that is, establishing a community of gentile brethren.[80] After finishing the official errand, they returned to Jerusalem: **after staying there for some time, on the one hand, they were sent off in peace by the brothers to those who had sent them** (15:33).

As regards Silas, some manuscripts have one more verse (Acts 15:34). For example, Codex Bezae has the reading of "Silas, however, decided they [Judas and Silas] would remain; but Judas went, alone."[81] This insertion was "no doubt made by copyists to account for the presence of Silas at Antioch in ver. 40."[82] Ordinarily, it was proper for the servants of the Lord not to stay at the mission field in unnecessary occasions; and it was crucial for these two witnesses to return to Jerusalem in order to submit a report on the situation. In these lines, there was no reason for Silas to stay in Antioch anymore. If he had to stay, he could have come back after his trip to Jerusalem.

Judas and Silas departed for Jerusalem, then Paul and Barnabas were able to stay in peace. **On the other hand, Paul and Barnabas remained in Antioch, teaching and proclaiming the Word of the Lord, along with many others** (Acts 15:35).[83] Rather than making himself comfortable, Paul was more consumed with taking an active interest in the welfare of the gentile believers: **after some days**[84] **Paul said to Barnabas, "Let us indeed return and visit**[85] **the brothers in every city where**

80. *Epistērizō* appears just in Acts 14:22, 15:32, 41, and 18:23 in the NT. All the occurrences refer to establishing the church.

81. Rius-Camps and Read-Heimerdinger 2007: 225.

82. Metzger 1994: 388.

83. NET translates *kai heterōn pollōn* as "(along with many others)," considering this as "a parenthetical note by the author" (NET notes). In comparison with 14:28, Luke introduces other leaders who seem to have taken the place of Barnabas and Paul while they were on their mission.

84. In regard to *meta de tinas hēmeras*, Peterson 2009: 447 says, "Time references such as *some time later (meta de tinas hēmeras)* are regularly used in the second half of Acts to begin a new section (cf. 18:1; 21:15; 24:1, 24; 25:1; 28:11, 17)." Italics his.

85. *Episkeptomai* indicates "care" that is both divine (Luke 1:68, 78; 7:16; Acts

we proclaimed the Word of the Lord, and see how they are"[86] (15:36). However, there was a disagreement between them about John Mark: **Barnabas wanted to bring John called Mark, too, but Paul insisted that they should not take along**[87] **this one**[88] **who had left them in Pamphylia and had not accompanied them in the work** (15:37–38). John Mark had gone to Jerusalem on the way to Perga, probably at Magydus (13:13). Nonetheless, he could possibly have come back to Syrian Antioch after the council, along with Barnabas, with a greater resolution to resume his missionary work.

About taking this John Mark for further work, Barnabas and Paul failed to reach a compromise: **There arose a sharp disagreement,**[89] **so that they separated from each other, and eventually Barnabas took Mark with him and sailed away to Cyprus; so Paul chose Silas and departed, having been handed over to the grace of the Lord by the brothers** (Acts 15:39–40). It is ironic that these missionaries, who had taken the same stance at the council, split up, even right after the gracious decision of the church. Anyway, two teams were newly formed for the second missionary journey. One team went to Cyprus, and the other **went through Syria and Cilicia** toward southern Galatia, **strengthening the churches** (15:41). Even the unfortunate conflicts produced positive results: John Mark had an opportunity to recover from a bad reputation; Silas had a chance to go on a missionary journey. According to 15:41, many churches had been already established in Syria and Cilicia, which actually can be fully expected on the basis of the existence of the Syrian Antioch church, and of Paul's staying in Tarsus by and large for ten years (ca. 35–44 CE).[90] In the meantime, while strengthening the churches by delivering the council letter to its recipients, Paul should have arrived in Tarsus (220 km on foot from Syrian Antioch), his hometown.

15:14; Heb 2:6) and humane (Matt 25:36, 43; Acts 6:3; 7:23; 15:36; Jas 1:27).

86. In regard to *pōs echousin*, Culy and Parsons 2003: 303 says, "This independent interrogative clause supplies the reason for the visit," and translates it as "(to see) how they are." Similarly, Peterson 2009: 447 translates it as "see how they are doing."

87. BDAG 94.

88. "This one" came from the last word of this sentence, *touton*, considered as "resumptive" (Culy and Parsons 2003: 304). "Resumptive" means "recapitulating or tending to take up again after a break or interruption." DeMoss 2001: 109.

89. *Paroksusmos*, from which "paroxysm" came, appears only here and Heb 10:24 in the NT, but in Heb 10:24 this word has a positive meaning like "spur, encouragement."

90. Cf. Bruce 1990: 92.

ACTS 16

Beginning of the Second Missionary Journey

While Paul took the second mission trip along with Silas, he passed through the first mission field and went over to Macedonia and Achaia with the unexpected guidance of the Lord. Macedonia had been an important area in the time of the Roman civil war (Thessalonica to Pompey [49–48 BCE]; Philippi to Brutus, Cassius, and Antony [42 BCE]) and had been a senatorial province as well as Achaia from 27 BCE to 15 CE, and from 44 CE to the time Paul arrived (49 CE).[1]

On this trip he encountered Timothy, Luke, and Lydia. All of these people became his lifetime coworkers. Timothy is called Paul's fellow-worker (Rom 16:21), his true child (1 Tim 1:2), and his beloved child (2 Tim 1:2), and moreover his name occurs as a sender of the Pauline epistles (1 Thess 1:1; 2 Thess 1:1; 2 Cor 1:1; Col 1:1; Phlm 1:1; Phil 1:1). Luke, the author of this Acts of the Apostles, accompanied Paul from Troas to Philippi[2] (Acts 16:10–17), from Philippi to Jerusalem (20:5—21:17), and finally from Caesarea to Rome (27:1—28:16); these are called "we-passages."[3] Lydia must have been an important benefactor among

---

1. Gill 1994: 403–4. From 15 to 44 CE, "both Macedonia and Achaia became imperial provinces and were linked to the province of Moesia" (Gill 1994: 436).

2. See comments on 16:24–28.

3. We consider the use of the first plural pronoun as the author's presence. There are four opinions about this matter, as Hemer and Gempf 1989: 316 classifies: "(a) The 'we-passages' should be explained as the writer's device for indicating an ultimate eyewitness source. (b) The device is to be understood as a secondary or redactional signal to draw special attention to the passage, as vivid, or important, or 'typical.' (c) This device is a literary convention applied specially to a sea-voyage narrative genre, without any suggestion of the writer's personal participation in the voyage. (d) The 'we-passages' are used in order to (falsely) claim personal participation." For instance, Porter 1994: 573 belongs to the (b) group, by seeing "that the author of Acts has utilized a continuous, independent source probably discovered in the course of his investigation." Cf. "The Author of the Gospel of Luke" section in the introduction of this book.

the Philippian church members who had supported Paul since the beginning of his gospel ministry (Phil 4:15).

Taking Care of the First Mission Field (16:1–5)

After finishing the ministry for the churches in Syria and Cilicia, Paul **came down to Derbe and to Lystra** (Acts 16:1a). By land, the distance from Tarsus, Paul's hometown, to Derbe was about 145 kilometers on foot via the Cilician gate, and from Derbe to Lystra was 60 kilometers. At the end of the journey of about 425 kilometers from Syrian Antioch to Lystra, Paul found an absolute gem who was qualified enough to replace John Mark just as Silas replaced Barnabas: **And look! There is a disciple named Timothy, the son of a Jewish woman who was a believer[4] and a Greek father; he was well spoken of by the brothers in Lystra and Iconium** (16:1b–2). Luke pays close attention to this young disciple as he focuses on this new team for evangelism. He compares Timothy with John Mark in terms of reputation; not only his hometown people (cf. 2 Tim 3:11) but also the neighbors far away in Iconium (30 km on foot from Lystra) held him in high repute.

Paul, who spurned John Mark because he left the team, chose Timothy as the new member: **Paul wanted this [Timothy] to go out with him, and taking him he circumcised him because of the Jews who were in those places, for they all knew that his father was[5] Greek** (Acts 16:3). As Hemer says, "the circumcision of Timothy, at first sight startling after the controversy preceding, is consistent with Paul's remarkable flexibility in conciliation where the truth of the Gospel was not at stake."[6] Timothy was not merely a gentile, so it was necessary for him to be circumcised despite the decision previously announced at the Jerusalem Council.

---

4. Her name is Eunice (2 Tim 1:5).

5. In regard to *upērchen*, Peterson 2009: 450 says, "The imperfect tense of the verb *hypērchen* probably implies that his father was now dead." He (Peterson 2009: 450n6) adds: "The present tense would have been used if his father was still alive." However, the usage of this verb is not in line with his assertion. See Luke 8:41 (Jairus seems to be a ruler of the synagogue at that time.); Acts 4:34 (those who were owners of land or houses); 5:4; 8:6; 10:12; 16:3; 28:7. Just in these seven cases this verb has the indicative imperfect form. As an indicative present form, this verb appears in Acts 3:6; 21:20; 27:34; and Phil 3:20. The aorist form of this verb does not appear in the NT, but in the OT just in Ps 69:20 [68:21, LXX] and Prob 17:16.

6. Hemer and Gempf 1989: 185–86. He thinks about 1 Cor 9:19–22: "To the Jews I became like a Jew to gain the Jews."

With this new member, Paul and Silas visited the Galatian churches in Lystra, Iconium, and Pisidian Antoich: **As they went through the cities, they passed on the decrees that had been decided on by the apostles and elders in Jerusalem for them [the Gentile believers] to observe** (Acts 16:4). The Christians of these cities were not the direct recipients of the letter of the Jerusalem Council, but the missionaries passed on the decrees to the brothers in southern Galatia because the letter had to do with the brothers; it would have also made them rejoice (cf. 15:31).

Then, a summary verse on the churches is given: **So the churches were being strengthened in the faith and were increasing in number every day** (Acts 16:5). The churches in Syria and Cilicia might have been included in "the churches" as well as those in the southern Galatia. "The faith" contains the belief that anyone who believes in Jesus as the Lord Christ will be saved even if the person has not been converted to Judaism.

Recognizing the Lord's Commission (16:6–10)

Up to this time, everything seemed to go smoothly. Afterward, on account of divine blockage, the mission of Paul, Silas, and Timothy was forced to a halt: **They went through the region of Phrygia and Galatia, having been prevented by the Holy Spirit from speaking the Word in the province of Asia** (Acts 16:6). Hansen accepts Hemer's argument that "the region of Phrygia and Galatia" indicates "a Phrygian-Galatic region in the southern part of the Roman province of Galatia," namely "an area that was ethnically Phrygian and politically Galatic."[7] Further, in concordance with Mitchell, who concludes that "Paul did not visit N. Galatia,"[8] Hansen says, "A detour of 1083 kilometres [the trip from Pisidian Antioch to Ancyra was 312 kilometres; the trip from Ancyra to Troas was 771 kilometres] is indeed 'hardly conceivable'!"[9] However, even if we are to follow this southern Galatian hypothesis, we do not need to suppose that "the region of Phrygia and Galatia" in this verse does not embrace northern Galatia, because the mission team did not evangelize northern Galatia yet. Nor do we need to suppose that the team had visited Ancyra, the capital of Galatia, located at the northern part of Galatia, since the text focuses on regions and directions rather than on exact locations where

7. Hansen 1994: 378; see Hemer and Gempf 1989: 280–89.

8. Mitchell 1993: 3.

9. Hansen 1994: 379. "A detour of 1083 kilometres" is based on Jewett's calculation (Jewett 1979: 60).

evangelizing was done. Phrygia and Galatia were neighboring regions, so "the region of Phrygia and Galatia" can refer to some places belonging to these two neighboring regions. Furthermore, Phrygia was a part of Asia at that time,[10] and Luke connects Phrygia and Galatia with Asia.[11] Hence, it can be concluded that after completing the mission of establishing the churches, the team tried to evangelize the places nearby; however, their path was blocked. Thus they changed direction to the west and went into Asia but were prevented likewise.

The three missionaries went to the northwest and arrived in Mysia, the extreme northwest province of Asia. They then tried to turn to the east in order to get into Bithynia, because otherwise they would have arrived on the shoreline: **When they came to Mysia, they attempted to go into Bithynia,[12] but the Spirit of Jesus did not allow them** (Acts 16:7). Here, we should first note that Peterson rightly sees that the expression "the Spirit of Jesus" rather than "the Holy Spirit" is employed in this verse to recall "an important theological perspective about the Spirit's relation to the ascended and enthroned Messiah."[13] So, with the guidance of the Spirit of Jesus, they could not change to the opposite direction, viz., the east. They kept going to the west and met the Aegean sea[14] in Troas:[15] "so they passed through Mysia and went down to Troas" (16:8). Now if they

10. For instance, see Trebilco 1994: 292: "In the time of Paul the province of Asia incorporated the areas of Mysia, the Troad, Aeolis, Ionia, the coastal islands, Lydia, Caria, Phrygia and Cibyra."

11. Luke seems to use the term "Asia" primarily "in the sense of the Roman province" except 2:9–11, where "used in the narrower sense of the Greek cities of the Aegean coast with the territory adjacent to them, a much smaller area than the province" (Trebilco 1994: 301–2).

12. Cf. 1 Pet 1:1.

13. Peterson 2009: 455 thinks "the Spirit of Jesus" suggests "that the exalted Christ continued to direct the progress of the gospel through the Spirit which he 'received from the Father' and 'poured out' on his disciples at Pentecost (2:33; cf. Rom. 8:9–10 ['the Spirit of Christ']; Phil. 1:19 ['the Spirit of Jesus Christ'])." Similarly, Johnson 1992: 285 says, "We have seen before that Jesus continues to take an active role in the story (7:56; 9:5)."

14. Aegean Sea is "an arm of the Mediterranean Sea extending northward between Greece and Asia Minor" (Accordance Bible 11: PhotoGuide 4).

15. Troas: "A principal seaport on the Aegean Sea located in northwest Asia Minor ca. 20 km. (12 mi.) SSW of ancient Troy (Ilium). The city was founded as Antigonia ca. 310 by Antigonus, the successor of Alexander the Great. After defeating Antigonus, Lysimachus renamed it Alexandria Troas after Alexander the Great (301). One of the more important cities of the Roman Empire, Troas came into Roman possession in 133 and became a Roman colony under Augustus" (*ED*, 1337).

wanted to keep going toward the west as they were led, the sea must be crossed.

Subsequently, **a vision was seen by Paul during the whole night**[16] (Acts 16:9a). "A vision" (*horama*) is often followed by abrupt changes of circumstance in Acts; for example, Moses (7:31), Ananaias in Damascus (9:10, 12), Cornelius (10:3), Peter (10:17, 19; 11:5; [12:9]), and Paul (16:9, 10; 18:9). Paul's first vision was: **A Macedonian man**[17] **was standing and urging him, "Come over to Macedonia and help us!"** (16:9b). Paul, a person lacking flexibility (cf. 15:38), should have been troubled during the whole night by an unfamiliar person who sought for him in a vision where the scenery was unknown to him.

Nevertheless, the team was quick in deciding the strategy for further movement: **Since he had seen the vision, immediately we sought to go on into Macedonia, concluding that God had called us to proclaim the good news to them** (Acts 16:10). The "we-passage" begins. The first plural pronouns indicate that Luke the evangelist had joined them on their wanderings. We cannot pinpoint the exact time or location Luke joined them, but can conjecture that he became a companion on the way to Troas from Syrian Antioch in 15:41—16:8. Divine blockage and human wanderings were not fruitless. Now there were four in the team: Paul, Silas, Timothy, and Luke. The number was doubled; it was enough to deal with the further dynamic ministry in Greece.

Mission in Philippi (16:11–40)

The four moved quickly over to Philippi across "the Thracian sea (the northern part of the Aegean sea)"[18] and started their first mission in Europe for a few at first, but then for more and multiple people later. The rest of the chapter is on their mission in Philippi. The name "Philippi" came from Philip II of Macedon who refounded the city in 356 BCE; its forum (the area used for public business) "was relatively small measuring some 100 m. × 50 m."; its official language seems to have been Latin.[19] Its importance in terms of NT backgrounds is summarized well by Bruce:

16. On account of the article, "whole" is added: in Acts, *dia nuktos* appears in 5:19; 17:10; and 23:31, but *dia tēs nuktos* only here (cf. Luke 5:5: *di holēe nuktos*).

17. The man may have introduced himself as a Macedonian, wearing particular clothing and speaking in a particular dialect.

18. Peterson 2009: 456.

19. Gill 1994: 411–13.

Near Philippi was fought the battle in 42 BC which resulted in the victory of Mark Antony and Octavian (the future Emperor Augustus) over Brutus and Cassius, assassins of Julius Caesar. After the battle, the victors settled a number of their veterans at Philippi and made the city a Roman colony; Octavian settled further colonists there after his victory over Antony and Cleopatra at Actium in 31 BC.[20]

Paul, who had been to Pisidian Antioch, the "little Rome," should have met a number of descendants of Roman veterans who were so proud of their own Roman citizenship.

First Stage (16:11–15)

The first stage of the mission in Philippi ran smoothly, and so did their journey: **After putting out to sea from Troas we went straight to Samothrace, the next day to Neapolis, and thence to Philippi, which is a leading city**[21] **of that district of Macedonia,**[22] **a Roman colony** (16:11–12a). The population of Troas (also called the "Alexandria Troas") is estimated "from 30,000 to 100,000"; this "city grew quickly due to the construction of an artificial harbour which enabled it to become the main seaport of North-Western Asia Minor and a city of great commercial importance."[23] They went directly to Samothrace (160 km by ship from Troas), an island in the northern part of the Aegean sea; the next day, they arrived at Neapolis (100 km by ship from Samothrace), a seaport on the southern coast of Macedonia; and then went to Philippi (16 km on foot from Neapolis). They did not hesitate to go there.

In spite of their immediacy and arrival in double quick time, they thought their time wasted: **in this city we spent**[24] **for some days** (Acts 16:12b). However, they did not continue to have a rest; instead **on the**

20. Bruce 1988: 309.

21. NET following NA25 and 26 prefers *prōtē* to *prōtēs*, translating "a leading city of that district of Macedonia." So also TNIV; Metzger 1994: 395; Marshall 1980B: 266; Bock 2007: 533, 546; Peterson 2009: 459; especially Ascough 1998: 93–103. *Contra* NA27 and 28; UBS4; L&N §1.85; Bruce 1988: 308–10; Bruce 1990: 357.

22. Macedonia was divided into four districts in 167 BCE by Aemilius Paullus: "the capitals of the four different areas were designated: Amphipolis to the first, Thessalonike to the second, Pella to the third, and Pelagonia to the fourth" (Gill 1994: 401).

23. Trebilco 1994: 358–59.

24. The basic meaning of this verb is "to rub hard" (LSJ 416).

Sabbath day we went outside the city gate to the side of the river,[25] **where we thought there would be a place of prayer, and sitting down we began to speak to the women who had assembled** (16:13).

Lydia, **a dealer in purple cloth from the city of Thyatira,**[26] **a God-fearing woman**, was there. She listened carefully and **the Lord opened her heart to pay attention to what Paul was saying** (16:14). She and her family became the firstfruits of Macedonia: **she and her household were baptized** (16:15a). Furthermore, as a devoted worker of God, she urged the mission team, saying, **if you think of me as a believer in the Lord, come and stay in my house**. And she eventually prevailed upon the team to abide in her house (16:15b). She should have been a great comfort to the team. What had happened in Phillipi should have confirmed that the vision had come from the Lord and that the mission team was on the right track. However, it was not long before they met another cycle of crisis and opportunity to evangelize.

Second Stage (16:16–40)

When they went to the same place of prayer, a slave girl with a spirit of a python[27] happened to be following behind the team. The girl brought her owners a lot of business[28] by fortune-telling (Acts 16:16). Her authority came from fortune-telling, so she tried to exert it even about this mission team: **she followed behind Paul and us and she kept shouting, "These men are servants of the Most High God, who are proclaiming to you the way of salvation"** (16:17). The contents were not wrong, but when she continued to do this for many days, Paul became greatly annoyed (16:18a). Why was Paul greatly annoyed? It was probably because she did not deserve to talk about **the way of salvation** (16:17), for she did not believe in Jesus. Paul accepted statements on the grounds of faith.

25. This river "bore the names Gangas or Gangites" and is "the modern Anghista" (*ISBE* 4:2369).

26. Thyatira is a city in the Lycus river valley in western Asia Minor, located between Pergamum and Sardis by which Paul should pass (16:6). In regard to the church at Thyatira, see Rev 1:11 and 2:18–29.

27. *Puthōn*: "According to Strabo 9, 3, 12 the serpent or dragon that guarded the Delphic oracle; it lived at the foot of Mt. Parnassus, and was slain by Apollo. Later the word came to designate a spirit of divination, then also of ventriloquists, who were believed to have such a spirit dwelling in their belly" (BDAG 897).

28. The basic meaning of *ergasia* is "work, business" (LSJ 682), and it has not the meaning of "benefit or gain," which has been generally used for translation.

However, the evil spirit might have used this opportunity to earn money without faith, which the next verse (16:19) reveals. As a result, **turning to the spirit Paul said, "I command you in the name of Jesus Christ to come out of her," and it came out of her at that very time** (16:18b).

Jesus also did not allow the evil spirits to talk about himself (Mark 1:25; Luke 4:35). However, the responses to expelling spirits were different: people were amazed at Jesus (Mark 1:27; Luke 4:36), but Paul was attacked in an instant: **But when her owners saw their hope of business was gone, they seized Paul and Silas and dragged them into the marketplace before the rulers** (Acts 16:19). The owners of the slave girl brought Paul and Silas, not Timothy and Luke, to "the top civic officers in the colony"[29] and accused the two of "disturbing the city" and "advocating customs unsuitable for Romans" (16:20–21).[30] They were not concerned about the girl's soul, neither her freedom nor her happiness; but their thoughts were fixed on using the girl and, in the end, getting money in their hands.

De Vos suggests a possibility of a clear connection between exorcism and these charges on the basis of "deviance theory."[31]

In light of the prominence of such labels of deviance in the ancient world, the lack of a clear distinction between religion and magic, and the fact that only some people were prosecuted for magic under certain circumstances, it should be apparent that an *accusation of practicing magic* involved a process of deviance-labeling. It required someone to perceive that the action involved magic and was harmful, to denounce the perpetrator as a magician, and to gain the support of those in authority via a legal trial (a status degradation ritual). . . . In this particular case, therefore, it does not matter whether Paul and Silas had used magic or not. To be labeled as magicians, and treated as such by the legal system only required that someone denounce them as potential deviants; the

29. Hellerman 2003: 422 translates the *duumviri iure dicundo* (the equivalent Latin title of στρατηγόι) as "the top civic officers in the colony." So also see Hemer and Gempf 1989: 115n34.

30. The expression of "a leading city" in 16:12 indicates the "civic pride" of the Philippians (see Ascough 1998: 100).

31. For "deviance theory," see Malina and Neyrey 1991: 97–122. De Vos 1999: 58 briefly introduces "deviance" as "a social construct," "behaviour that is perceived to be a violation of norms or values," and "what makes something (or someone) deviant."

community would then perceive that it was so, and those in authority would label and treat them as such.[32]

Paul and Silas were harmless "magicians" that cast out a harmful spirit, but losing a means to hear the message from the python-spirit seemed to have made the crowd regard the exorcism as deviant enough to join in the attack on them (Acts 16:22a). Eventually, but "without due process,"[33] the top civic officers decided to punish them: **the officers tore their garments off and ordered lictors**[34] **to beat them with rods; then after having inflicted many blows upon them by lictors,**[35] **officers threw them into prison, ordering the jailer to keep them firmly** (16:22b–23; cf. 2 Cor 11:25a).

During the time when they were treated violently, Paul and Silas did not claim that they each had Roman citizenship just as Paul did in advance while in Jerusalem (Acts 22:25). Was there not enough time to utter this significant news that could ease their pain? Were they beaten and confined in such a short time? Maybe they had a few glimpses of something that would happen after that accusation. Or maybe they were anxious about Timothy and Luke, their team members who were not Roman citizens. For whatever reason, the two bruised men did not stand up for their rights even during their imprisonment; they only did so afterward (16:37).

In regards to the reason for delaying their claim of Roman citizenship, Bruce explains, "In the general excitement it might have been useless to do so, or if he did so his appeal was ignored"; as for the Jerusalem case, he states that "the flogging on that occasion was to be inflicted not with rods but with the murderous scourge."[36] On the other hand, Peterson argues quite reasonably that "Paul had an attitude of detachment to

32. De Vos 1999: 59 (italics original).

33. BDAG, 35 defines *akatakritos* as "not undergoing a proper legal process, uncondemned, without due process."

34. ῥάβδουχος (ῥαβδοῦχος in 16:35, 38) refers to "one who carries a rod or staff of office" (LSJ 1563). The top civic officers of Philippi "had two lictors in attendance on them" (BDAG 902). Hellerman 2003: 422 explains the Greek term as corresponding "to the Latin *lictores*, a title for persons who proceeded before the chief magistrates bearing the *fasces*, which symbolized magisterial authority." Further, Bruce 1988: 315 says, "It was with the lictors' rods that the two missionaries were beaten on this occasion."

35. Bruce 1990: 362 also states, "This beating with rods was carried out by the lictors."

36. Bruce 1990: 366.

his Roman citizenship . . . and believed he should take advantage of this only insofar as it furthered the cause of Christ."[37] We do not know exactly why they permitted themselves to be persecuted. By the way, this was not the first time Paul was persecuted. He had already been stoned in Lystra two years ago (Acts 14:19). At that time he was the only one stoned. But for the present, Paul was beaten at the same time as Silas.

At any rate, because of their silence about their citizenship, the evangelists met a jailer who would have been hard to encounter so naturally unless in this way. The jailer was remarkably faithful to the top officers and obeyed their order: **having received such an order, he not only put them into the inner prison but also fastened their feet between heavy blocks of wood**[38] (16:24). He did his very best to guard Paul and Silas securely; in a sense, the controls exercised were too strict. Bruises were not looked after, nor were they comforted, and pain had to be endured in a cold and damp cage. Nevertheless, **about midnight Paul and Silas were praying and singing hymns to God** (16:25a). Projected is a startling image of faithfulness that is derived from deep within. What a marvelous response! They changed violence into appreciation, reasons for agony into reasons for praise, and human faithfulness into divine faithfulness.

Their praise caught all the prisoners' attention (Acts 16:25b) and, without doubt, definitely the jailer's attention, as well. The audience might have listened in awed silence, surprised by the newcomers' mental power and the heavenly peace that had already prevailed over the dark concert hall through their unbelievable duet. The peace could have induced a deep sleep to the jailer (cf. 16:27a) since it would be unusual for this type of "a still well-disciplined retired soldier"[39] to fall into a sound sleep while doing surveillance. The peace caused by their hymns could be the reason for the prisoners not to run away (cf. 16:27b) even though it might have been expected.[40]

---

37. Peterson 2009: 473–74.

38. GNB has "between heavy blocks of wood." For a picture and an explanation of wood stocks, see Pritz 2009: 221–22.

39. According to Ramsay 1975 [1897]: 222, the jailer was "the orderly well-disciplined character." In addition, he was more possibly "a retired soldier" (Bruce 1988: 315) than "a public slave" (De Vos 1995: 293), considering that Philippi was full of Roman veterans.

40. So also Bruce 1988: 317, who says that "the awed impression which the two missionaries' behavior produced on the other prisoners" may "dissuade those others from making their escape."

As Paul and Silas sang, **suddenly there was a great earthquake, so that the foundations of the prison were shaken; and immediately all the doors were opened and everyone's bonds were unfastened** (Acts 16:26). It was not an earthquake to destroy but to rescue Paul and Silas and everybody else in the prison. The earthquake freed the people and awakened the jailer. The personal position of the jailer, however, drove him to despair: **seeing that the prison doors were open, he drew his sword and was about to kill himself,**[41] **supposing that the prisoners had escaped** (Acts 16:27). The jailer was unable to see the situation clearly because he had been asleep, but Paul was able to recognize the situation because his eyes had already adjusted to the dark. Ramsay describes this situation well:

> The inner prison was a small cell, which had no window and no opening, except into the outer and larger prison, and that the outer prison, also, had one larger door in the opposite wall; then, if there were any faint starlight in the sky, still more if the moon were up, a person in the outer doorway would be distinguishable to one whose eyes were accustomed to the darkness, but the jailer would see only black darkness in the prison.[42]

The jailer did not know what the earthquake meant, but Paul did. He took notice of the Lord's work through this sudden violent movement and the ensuing release.

Paul realized what the jailer was about to do. **So Paul cried with a loud voice, "Do not harm yourself, for we are all here"** (Acts 16:28) lest losing a soul should happen at the moment of salvation. Just as God dealt with them all at once, Paul groups himself with the prisoners. All the remnant, "we," were all there. The pain of the stocks was gone, and fellowship began to sprout. The jailer was probably even more stunned by Paul's voice than the earthquake. Wanting to confirm what he heard, the sound of hope, thus, **searching for [and bringing] lights, he rushed in** (16:29a). He should have passed the outer cells to enter into the inner cell and felt the change of mood. Entering the outer cells, he would have found contrasting looks. He might have found the other prisoners perplexed due to the evangelists' behavior at first, but later because of the

41. Ramsay 1975 [1897]: 222 says that "he preferred death by his own hand, to exposure, disgrace, and a dishonourable death"; so also Pervo 2009: 409.

42. Ramsay 1975 [1897]: 221–22.

beneficial earthquake that opened the doors to freedom. At the inner cell
he should have found two faces lighted with joy and love, unsuitable to
that ghastly place. Instantaneously, **with trembling, he fell down at the
feet of Paul and Silas** (16:29b).

The jailer should have already been informed of what Paul and Silas did, why they had been beaten and confined: they practiced "magic"
strong enough to expel even a python spirit. And now they seemed to
summon up an earthquake to open the prison doors and to loose the
prisoners' bonds. So **bringing them outside, he said, "Lords, what must
I do to be saved?"** (16:30). It is an unthinkable and bizarre but predictable question; unthinkable because he was a jailer and they were the
jailed, bizarre because a loyal jailer accepted these prisoners as "Lords,"
yet predictable because of the Almighty God and the unique phenom-
ena He brings in times preposterous and perfect. So it turns out that the
jailer thought of these powerful "magicians" as "lords" who can give him
salvation. **They, however, immediately address Jesus as "Lord," saying
"Believe on the Lord Jesus"** (16:30a). Paul and Silas "deny their own
Lordship."[43] Further, a promise was added to the imperative: **then you
will be saved, and [probably][44] your household** (16:30b).[45] Bruce understands this "'house' or household included not only the immediate
family in our sense, but all who were under the authority of the master of
the house—slaves, attendants, and other dependents" (also 11:14; 18:8).[46]

The jailer responded positively in faith, so Paul and Silas **spoke the
Word of the Lord to him, along with all those who were in his house**
(Acts 16:32). After hearing the Word, the jailer **took them at that hour
of the night and washed their wounds** (16:33); now he was able to take
care of their pains. Then baptism followed: **he and all who belonged to
him were baptized right away** (16:33b). Next, prepared was a ceremonial feast: **Eventually he took them into his household and set food
before them, and he was overjoyed that he had come to believe in God,
together with his entire household** (16:34).

Here we may not need to pay too much attention to the transitions
between "household" (*oikos*, Acts 16:31 and 34) and "house" (*oikia*,

43. Park 2002: 55. Further, he compares the disciples' committed lordship with
Jesus' own Lordship (Park 2002: 55–56).

44. The subjunctive basically has the meaning of "probability."

45. The subject of *sōthēsē* should be the second singular, so "your household"
seems to have been added denoting possibility.

46. Bruce 1990: 269.

16:32)—as de Vos did. He thinks of "these two terms" as referring "to two separate institutions," especially, of *oikia* as referring to "enlarged family including other public slaves."[47] However, as even de Vos himself admits,[48] *oikos* primarily represents all the members of a family, and *oikia* the building for a family. So it would be suitable to organize Lucan usage of family-related words in 16:31–34 before we go on. First, the promise Paul made to the jailer was related to the jailer's family members (16:31, *oikos*); then, all the family members in his house (16:32, *oikia*) were gathered; at last, he brought them into "the place for all the family members" (16:34a, *oikos*) and all of them (16:34b, *panoikei*) rejoiced.

Things were brightening up. Paul and Silas were put into their cell again. Without being fastened in the stocks, they were guarded by the same jailer who now approached the evangelists with a different perspective of life and his two prisoners. The earthquake seems to have affected the top civic officers as well. They decided on their release: **the top civic officers sent lictors, saying, "Release those men"** (Acts 16:35). The top civic officers could have possibly, as added in Codex Bezae, come "together, united in purpose, in the market place, and remembering the earthquake that had happened, they were afraid,"[49] and ended up changing their plans. Otherwise, this flick of their minds could have been simply because they thought the orders they had given were complete: they "had simply exercised their police right of *coercitio*—summary correction or chastisement" "by having Paul and Silas locked up overnight after their beating."[50] After hearing from the lictors, who were officers who bore an ax and fasces or rods, **the jailer reported these words to Paul: "The top officers have sent orders to release you, so come out now and go in peace"** (16:36). The conspicuous expression "in peace" seems to mirror the jailor's state of mind.

But Paul and Silas make an abrupt switch: **Paul said to them, "Having had us beaten in public without due process—even though we are Roman citizens—they threw us in prison, and now they want to send us away secretly? Absolutely not! Rather, they themselves must come and escort us out!"** (Acts 16:37). Paul did not totally set aside the matter

---

47. De Vos 1995: 293–96.
48. Cf. De Vos 1995: 295.
49. Rius-Camps and Read-Heimerdinger 2007: 264.
50. Bruce 1988: 319.

of Roman citizenship; at the very moment he considered proper, he made claims about their Roman citizenship.

Immediately, the lictors **reported these words to the top civic officers**, and hearing these words, the officers were frightened since they now knew that **they [were] Roman citizens** (Acts 16:38). So the officers could not refrain from coming, comforting them, and escorting them out as requested. Further, presumably much more politely than before, **they asked them to leave the city** (16:39), certainly **hoping to avoid a trial where their mistake would come to light**.[51] This event "may have helped to protect his [Paul's] converts from persecution."[52]

Before leaving Philippi as asked, Paul and Silas stopped by Lydia's house, and **after exhorting the brothers** [surely including Timothy and Luke], **they departed** (Acts 16:40). We may agree with Bruce, in concluding that "Luke may have stayed behind in Philippi, where he reappears in 20:5,"[53] howbeit not with his insistence: "From Philippi Paul and Silas, with Timothy, took the Egnatian Way westward through Amphipolis on the Strymon"[54] to Thessalonica. Examining both the reason why Paul and Silas should have departed away from Thessalonica[55] and the fact that Timothy had been sent there (1 Thess 3:2), it seems that Paul and Silas were not in the company of Timothy thoroughly on the journey from Philippi to Thessalonica; hence, Luke seems to have been residing together with Timothy in Philippi during Paul and Silas's absence.

51. Witherington 1998: 499.

52. Bruce 1990: 367.

53. Bruce 1990: 367.

54. Bruce 1988: 322.

55. See "Mission in Thessalonica (17:1–9)."

ACTS 17

Mission in Thessalonica, Berea, and Athens

Paul and Silas left Philippi bruised, but with a comforted mind on the basis of the conversion of Lydia's family and also of the jailer's. Paul and Silas walked through the Roman military road *Via Egnatia*, stopping by Amphipolis (50 km on foot from Philippi) and Apollonia (40 km on foot from Amphipolis) and finally reached Thessalonica (55 km on foot from Apollonia),[1] which became the capital of Macedonia in the reign of Claudius in 44 CE (Dio Cassius, *History* 60.24.1). There they found a Jewish synagogue so they could do as Paul's custom. Then, as usual, some Jews stood against Paul but with a new matter, Caesar's decree; Jason and the new believers should pay for their belief.

During the mission work in Berea (Beroea) the Jews showed different attitudes toward the gospel. They thought carefully and acted thoughtfully. Verifying Paul's speech strengthened their belief. When the riot stirred up by the Jews from Thessalonica began, some sincere friends accompanied Paul to Athens, located 357 kilometers from Berea on foot or 460 kilometers via ship. In addition, those whole-hearted guides delivered a message from Paul to Silas in Berea, and to Timothy, who was probably in Thessalonica.

While in Athens, Paul can be pictured as a soldier solely carrying the duties of a whole army. He was neither frozen nor silent; rather, he walked around here and there and conversed with all kinds of people. As a result, he had the privilege of standing on the Areopagus in front of the multitude. He revealed the unknown God, "we," and what kind of relationship should be established between the two, the creator God

---

1. According to Rainey and Notley 2006: 374, the distance between Philippi and Amphipolis is approximately 40 miles (67 km), and that between Amphipolis and Apollonia 24 miles (40 km), and that between Apollonia and Thessalonica 36 miles (60 km). NET notes 2005: 2160 provides each distance as 33 miles (53 km), 27 miles (43 km), and 33 miles (53 km). Peterson 2009: 477 introduces Amphipolis as "the capital of the first district of Macedonia in which Philippi was situated, about 30 miles (48 km) west-southwest."

and the created beings. His speech, almost a revelation, educated and persuaded the audience, and warned the listeners. Paul guided more people into God's kingdom. They had been neglected, but now the neglected were found.

Mission in Thessalonica (17:1–9)

Paul's company passed through Amphipolis and Apollonia on route to Thessalonica. Thessalonica, the capital of the province of Macedonia, was a suitable place to spread the gospel. "It was important, not only as a harbor with a large import and export trade, but also as the principal station on the great Via Egnatia, the highway from the Adriatic to the Hellespont."[2] In addition, a synagogue of the Jews was there; accordingly, Paul had no reason not to follow his custom—that is, to evangelize the Jews first, then the God-fearers, and finally the gentiles (Acts 17:2).

At the first stage (Acts 17:1–4) Paul entered into the synagogue for the Jews[3] and the God-fearers. He was a complete stranger, and yet was bold, with his courage much strengthened by the ministry in Philippi. In his letter, he declared, "But though we had already suffered and been shamefully treated at Philippi, as you know, we had boldness in our God to declare to you the gospel of God in the midst of much conflict" (1 Thess 2:2 ESV). Without pause and in earnest he conversed with the Thessalonians, both Jews and God-fearers, throughout the first three weeks at the Sabbath meetings (Acts 17:2).

A glimpse of Paul's teaching in Thessalonica is shown through a summary Luke provides. The writer sums it up as the Christ's suffering and resurrection: **The Christ should be suffered and be resurrected among the dead** (Acts 17:3a). As to the related Scripture passages, Wright says, "We can only guess at the passages he employed, but our guesses can be pretty accurate in view of his use of scripture in his letters on this topic: Isaiah 53, of course, but also Genesis 22 (Abraham's sacrifice of Isaac, referred to in Rom 8:32), Psalm 22 (read as a prayer of the Messiah), perhaps Zechariah's dark oracles of suffering and vindication."[4] However, we cannot let these following passages slip through our fingers:

2. *ISBE* 5:2970.

3. According to Ellington 2003: 414, the "synagogue of the Jews" is better translation than "Jewish synagogue" or "Jewish meeting place" on account of pronoun reference.

4. Wright 2008: 76.

Deut 21:23 quoted in Gal 3:13, and further Josh 8:29; 10:26–30, 38–39, referring to the hanged Canaanite kings as mandatory *herem*.[5] Even though the concept of "the suffering Messiah" is rarely found in Second Temple Jewish literature, the suffering Messiah was at the center of Paul's teachings in general.

Luke's sketch then moves on to the Messiahship of Jesus: **This is the Christ [the] Jesus whom I declare to you** (Acts 17:3b). Paul's argument flows from the old covenant to the new covenant, from the prophesied Messiah to Jesus the Messiah. Theoretically, if anyone has the right notion of the Messiah prophesied in the OT, the person can follow up to Jesus' suffering and resurrection, the Messiahship of Jesus, unraveling the puzzle of the "prophesied Christ." Paul started with the OT that the Jews and the God-fearers had already known well. "Christ, suffering, and resurrection" were not unfamiliar to them. They only needed someone to merge these concepts into one, namely "the suffered *and* resurrected Christ," and subsequently to connect the merged idea with "Jesus" the Savior.

In the meantime, **some of them [the Jews] were persuaded and joined with Paul and Silas, and finally a large number of God-fearing Greeks and furthermore not a few wives of the chief men** (Acts 17:4).[6] The copulative coordinating conjunction *te* (so, finally, as a result) shows the process of the gospel spreading and conviction in sequential order: starting from some of the Jews and the God-fearers, next the common Greeks, and finally, the Greek leaders' wives. The latter two groups may not have been in the synagogue on the first Sabbath day among the three. The God-fearing Greek might invite them into the synagogue on the second Sabbath meeting, and then on the third Sabbath not a few Greek leaders' wives could be involved with learning the new merged teaching, "the suffered and resurrected Christ Jesus."

This persuasion was prompted by Paul's **explaining and proving** (Acts 17:3), which was evaluated "not simply with words but also with power, with the Holy Spirit and deep conviction" (1 Thess 1:5 TNIV). In comparison with Paul himself, Luke does not use expressions such as "power," "Holy Spirit." Again, in comparison with Paul, Luke focuses not only on the Jews but also on the gentiles, especially the prominent Greek wives, possibly on the procedure during the three Sabbaths. Paul

5. Park 2007A: 149–51.

6. Bruce 1990: 369 suggests *gunaikōn tōn prōtōn ouk oligai* in 17:4 be translated into "many of the chief women" or "many of the wives of the chief men."

proclaimed the gospel on the Sabbath meetings, and the audience spread it between the meetings. Likewise, the Christian community can spread the gospel in between its weekly meetings.

At the second stage (Acts 17:5–9), all of the main verbs and participles have "the Jews," not "some Jews," as the subject. "The Jews" were jealous. They made a mob by employing some wicked riffraff and setting the city of Thessalonica in an uproar. Jason's house became a target, because they thought Jason had welcomed Paul and Silas. The Jews sought to bring them out from Jason's house. In this uneasy situation, fortunately, Paul and Silas were not to be found; they might have been informed by the leaders' wives. Since the Jews could not find Paul and Silas in Jason's house, they dragged Jason and some brothers before the city administrators, shouting, **"Those who turned the whole inhabited region[7] upside down, these men also came here. By the way Jason welcomed them. And they all behaved against the decrees of Caesar, saying that there is quite a different king, Jesus."** (17:6b–7). This shouting had an effect on the mob and the city administrators who were disturbed.

Had Paul and Silas been in Jason's house? If they were in his house, it would have been for fellowship and/or worship. Jason was a Greek version of a Jewish name,[8] so he could have been a Jew. He and his family possibly became believers at the first meeting with Paul and Silas; and like Lydia and the jailer in Philippi, he might have invited Paul and Silas to stay with him for a few weeks. Naturally, a house church would have been founded at his house. This is supported by the fact that some brothers had been in his house when the Jews visited suddenly. Further, he must be wealthy enough to pay a sufficient amount, possibly 1,000 bronze sesterces, roughly 250 denarii,[9] for the **security** to be released (17:9). So in spite of the short three-week ministry, Paul was able to describe it as: "Just as a nursing mother cares for her children, so we [Paul and Silas]

7. According to LSJ 1205, *oikoumenē* means "inhabited region" or "the Roman world."

8. According to BDAG 465, "It was a favorite practice among Jews to substitute the purely Gk. name Ἰάσων for the Hebrew-Gk. Ἰησοῦς." In the NT, this name occurs in Rom 16:21, and in the Apocrypha, 1 Macc 8:17; 12:16; 14:22; 2 Macc 1:7; 2:23; 4:7, 13, 19, 22, 23, 24, 26; 5:5, 6.

9. Hardin 2006: 46, on the basis of "a recently discovered municipal constitution in Spain, the *Lex Irnitana*, which dates to the Flavian period (69–96 CE)," argues, "The free city of Thessalonica may have reflected a similar penalty [1,000 sesterces] in their civic constitution." In NT times, "the bronze sesterce" were "equal in value to one fourth of a denarius" (*ED* 370).

cared for you. . . . Surely you remember . . . we worked night and day . . . you know that we dealt with each of you as a father deals with his own children, encouraging, comforting and urging you to live lives worthy of God" (1 Thess 2:7b, 9a, 11–12 TNIV).

Jason and the believers were released by the disturbed city magistrates after paying the security. Scholars are left to wonder what "the decrees of Caesar" that were referred to are, and how they were violated. In this regard Hardin suggests that these decrees should be related with "Roman restrictions on Graeco-Roman voluntary associations," rather than "*maiestas* (treason)" or "ruler changes or the oath of loyalty."[10] He rejects them being related to *maiestas*[11] not only because it "was exclusively reserved for those of elite status, such as those among the senatorial class in Rome," but also because that kind of low-level leader, city magistrates, could not release "the absent party without their having made an appearance" after receiving only the security, since *maiestas* was a matter that should be dealt with by the proconsul of Macedonia.[12] Hardin also discards "any prediction on the next ruler or oath of loyalty" opinion[13] mainly because "the imperial legislation of Augustus and Tiberius" should be "restricted to Italy."[14]

In this way, Paul and Silas's fatherly ministry in Thessalonica was accompanied by financial matters. The mob and the Jews were assuaged after making Jason and some believers suffer a financial loss. Even so, the believers in Thessalonica "turned to God from those idols to serve the living and authentic God, and to wait for His Son from heaven" (1 Thess 1:9b–10a). They were not disappointed with losing the money. This suffering was just the beginning (2 Thess 1:5–7a).

Mission in Berea (17:10–14)

At night the brothers in Thessalonica brought Paul and Silas to Berea (Beroea), a "town of southwestern Macedonia, in the district of Emathia . . . at the foot of Mt. Bermius"[15] "about 45 mi (75 km) west of

10. Hardin 2006: 29–49.

11. "Maiestas is an abbreviation for maiestas populi romani minuta ('diminishing the majesty of the Roman people')" (Hardin 2006: 30n4).

12. Hardin 2006: 32.

13. Judge 1971: 1–7.

14. Hardin 2006: 33–35.

15. *ISBE* 1:440.

Thessalonica"[16] along the Egnatian Way. After about a two-day journey from Thessalonica to Berea, Paul and Silas entered into the Jewish synagogue again, a place where suffering was generally expected.

The first stage proceeded smoothly (Acts 17:10–12). The Jews in the Berea synagogue were **more open-minded than those of Thessalonica**[17] (17:11). The term "open-minded" (*eugenēs*) has the meaning of "well-born, noble-minded, generous, noble (of outward form)."[18] That is to say, they were neither too strict to reject the new idea without considering the reality, nor bound to their views too much to neglect any new belief. They received the Word everyday enthusiastically, weighing up the gospel carefully with the Scriptures, checking if what they were being told was in accordance with the Scriptures. Their experience or philosophy based on traditions were not the criteria; instead, the Scriptures (OT) were their benchmark for distinguishing the right from wrong contexts. Through this examination, surely with the help of the Holy Spirit, the biblical evidence of "the suffering Messiah" must have been found. Hence, many Jews believed in the gospel. Moreover, not a few Greek men and women of high standing also believed.

This peaceful evangelism did not go a long way. At the second stage (Acts 17:13–14), the Thessalonican Jews, stricter and inflexible in their doctrines, heard that Paul was now preaching in Berea. They came to stir up the crowds in Berea against Paul (17:13). So the brothers, both the Jews and the gentiles in Berea, solved this by sending Paul out of their city, while Silas and Timothy remained (17:14).

Here we may need to ask when and from where Timothy came to Berea. Timothy must have arrived in Philippi earlier (Acts 16:3, 6) but seems to have stayed there even after Paul and Silas's departure for Berea (17:10). In regard of the presence or the absence of Timothy, Peterson explains that "since Luke tends not to mention secondary figures unless they are central to a particular narrative, it is a [*sic*] reasonable to presume that Timothy accompanied Paul and Silas from Lystra to Berea."[19] At Berea "Paul and Silas were rejoined by Timothy,"[20] and when objection against Paul's companion was raised, Paul was sent away to the coast

16. NET notes 2005: 2161.

17. Bruce 1988: 326.

18. LSJ 708.

19. Peterson 2009: 485.

20. Bruce 1988: 327.

(about 45 km) while Silas and Timothy certainly stayed behind to take care of the church in Berea.[21] Meanwhile, Luke might have been lodging in Philippi.

Mission in Athens (17:15–34)

Those who accompanied Paul escorted him to the sea and as far as to Athens, on land about 357 kilometers (222 miles),[22] or by sea about 460 kilometers.[23] It would had been a long journey that lasted more than ten days. After arriving in Athens, the so-called "City of Idol Worship,"[24] Paul intended to reorganize his ministry. He sent a letter through the Berean brothers to Silas and Timothy, imploring them to come over from Berea to Athens as quick as they could. In Macedonia, the two companions of Paul were still working hard and evangelized diligently in three cities (Philippi, Thessalonica, and Berea).

According to 1 Thess 3:1–2, Timothy had been in Athens before his arrival in Acts 18:5. From this, we can conjecture that when Paul, Silas, and Timothy gathered in Athens due to Paul's call, Paul was informed by his fellow workers about the church in Berea; right away, a meeting was summoned over the guidance of the Macedonian church. Consequently, Timothy was sent to Thessalonica (1 Thess 3:2) and Silas to somewhere in Macedonia (Acts 18:5), possibly to Berea or Philippi. Their next meeting would be held in Corinth (18:5), but until then Paul stayed in Athens.

Athēnai, the Greek word indicating "the city of Athens" and "generally" referring to "the whole country,"[25] started toward "military and economic gravity" after the revolt of Ionia against Persia had failed in 498–493 BCE.[26] Right after the first Persian war (492–479 BCE), "that city-state [Athens] eventually became the head of the Delian league."[27]

---

21. With Peterson 2009: 485: "presumably to nurture and encourage their new converts."

22. Following Peterson 2009: 485. NET notes 2005: 2162 have an estimate of "about 340 mi (550 km)" for the distance of traveling overland.

23. Bruce 1988: 328 presumes that "some of his Beroean friends took him to the coast—to Methone or Dium—and put him on board a ship bound for Piraeus (the port of Athens)." See also *ISBE* 1:319.

24. Broneer 1958: 2.

25. LSJ 32.

26. Rainey and Notley 2006: 287.

27. Rainey and Notley 2006: 288. The Delian League, "an anti-Persian alliance,"

About fifty years later, however, the Peloponnesian War (431–404 BCE) resulted in a drastic decline in her political force. Nonetheless, Alexander the Great (356–323 BCE) made her the center of culture, and even in NT times she still had a cultural influence.[28] The Athenians must have been very proud of the Athenian reputation for academic excellence.

Moreover, Athens, "named for the Greek goddess Athena, whose world-renowned temple, the Parthenon, stood on top of the Acropolis in the heart of town,"[29] was the heart of religion as well as that of ancient Greek philosophy. The Parthenon temple at the Acropolis was built and decorated in 447–432 BCE, and then "was dedicated to the Greek goddess Athena Parthenos (Athena the Warrior Maiden)."[30]

During his stay in this influential city, Paul met with people in the synagogue and in the Agora, and got a chance to speak before the council at the Areopagus, the highest judgment seat in the city. The Agora was "the central square of a Greek city, . . . surrounded by public buildings, temples, shops and so forth."[31] And as for the Areopagus ("hill of Ares [Ares, the Gk. god of war = Rom. Mars, hence the older 'Mars' Hill']"),[32] it was located at a place where the Acropolis can be easily seen, or "other locations, such as the Stoa Basileios."[33] The council of Areopagus probably had gathered to hear from Paul because it "would have been the body responsible for initiating action for the assimilation of the new god,"[34] though its main function was to judge criminals.[35]

---

was formed in 478–477 BC, and it was "called the Delian League since it was headquartered on the island of Delos" (*ED* 530; cf. Thucydides 1.4.96–97).

28. With Bruce 1988: 329: "Although Athens had long since lost the political eminence which was hers in an earlier day, she continued to represent the highest level of culture attained in classical antiquity."

29. *DNTB* 139.

30. PhotoMuseum.

31. *PDBS* 7.

32. BDAG 129.

33. Croy 1997: 24–25 suggests that "the Royal Stoa seems to be a more likely setting for the speech than Mars Hill." See also Bruce 1990: 379, who on the basis of "in the middle of the Areopagus" in 17:22 says, "The construction with *en mesō* indicates the court, not the hill."

34. Winter 1996: 78.

35. Geagan 1967: 48 states, "In the democratic constitution of Athens the Areopagus had ceased to occupy the foremost place, but under the Roman Empire there is ample testimony that it had regained a position of predominance. . . . The Areopagus never did lose its judicial significance."

First Stage (17:15–18)

Paul, when first brought into Athens, felt that Silas and Timothy should join him. **While waiting for them** (17:16a), he found the city full of idols and idolatry. This irritated his spirit very deeply and left him troubled. In spite of what he had seen, Paul seems to have been calm and careful in delivering the Areopagus speech. Besides following his custom of entering the synagogue on the Sabbath days for the Jews and the God-fearers (non-Jewish worshipers),[36] he made his way to the Agora each day as well, following the habit known as "the method of Socrates,"[37] in order to encounter sellers, buyers, or even wandering philosophers.

At the Agora, the marketplace, Paul was confronted[38] by some of the Epicurean and Stoic philosophers. Epicureanism began from Epicurus (341–270 BCE), who "established the school named after him in what became known as 'the Garden,' a plot of ground northwest of the city."[39] This school considered *ataraksia* ("utter freedom from disturbing thoughts and influences") as an essential value;[40] its view of the afterlife is revealed in Epicurus's letter to Menoeceus: "Death, therefore, the most awful of evils, is nothing to us, seeing that, when we are, death is not come, and, when death is come, we are not."[41] This school rejected the notion of the resurrection of the body. As for Stoicism, it was founded by "Zeno of Citium in Cyprus (ca. 340–265 BC),"[42] "who had come to Athens in 313."[43] This school's view of the afterlife is a bit complicated, but can be summarized as "a soul would exist quite a while after the death of the composed body, but all the souls cannot exist as their own individual forms after *ekpurōsis* (a cosmic conflagration)."[44] Hence, even to

36. Culy and Parsons 2003: 333 think "the 'worshippers' were non-Jews."

37. Bruce 1990: 376 indicates that "Paul's entering into conversation with persons who happened to be around in the *agora* . . . is reminiscent of the method of Socrates."

38. In *suneballon*, Culy and Parsons 2003: 334 read a "confrontational sense ('to debate')" rather than "a neutral ('to meet with')" one.

39. Croy 1997: 23.

40. Croy 1997: 29.

41. Diogenes Laertius, 10.125. See also Croy 1997: 29–32, who insists that Epicureanism can never be compatible with the resurrection of the body after death.

42. Bruce 1990: 377.

43. Croy 1997: 23.

44. Croy 1997: 32–36, who scrutinizes the Stoics' views on the afterlife, especially of Zeno (the founder), of Panaetius (a middle Stoic), and of Seneca and Epictetus and Marcus Aurelius (the later Stoics). As regard to *ekpurōsis*, he explains, "A common

the Stoic philosophers, just as the Epicureans, the idea of "resurrection" would have been odd. Therefore, just as the Pharisees argued with Jesus the Christ, so did the philosophers with the evangelist, merely for the difference in doctrines and teachings, and fundamentally due to the fear that they would lose followers.

Luke introduces two kinds of attitudes these pursuers of "wisdom" had toward Paul. On the one hand, some despised[45] him for being a babbler, "an idle and worthless character who collects the 'scraps' of others' ideas and disseminates them."[46] They dismissed any possibilities of hearing, anything of value, or they believed resurrection was beyond the bounds of possibility. Their response was an "unmistakably negative."[47]

On the other hand, some were interested in Paul's teaching and identified Paul as the proclaimer of "foreign divinities or inferior divine beings"[48] because he mentioned "Jesus" and "*anastasis* (resurrection)." In regard to "Jesus," Chase suggests, "The name Ἰησοῦς, otherwise unintelligible, would be naturally connected by the Athenians with ἴασις (Ionic ἴησις) and Ἰασώ (Ιησώ), the goddess of healing and health,"[49] and Chase's suggestion has been broadly adopted.[50] "Anastasis" also can be "construed as the name of a deity."[51] In regards to *ton Iēsun kai tēn anastasin*, Fizmyer guesses that "such a person [a pagan Athenian] would have understood the fem. Greek noun *anastasis* as the name of a consort for the foreign deity, Jesus, 'Jesus and Anastasis,'" and states that "John Chrysostom understood it (*Hom. in Acta* 38.1; PG 60.267), and many after him."[52] Indeed, these public responses portray their "perplexity" and "curiosity" on foreign deities.[53] The curious were driven to bring Paul to the Areopagus

---

Stoic doctrine was that periodically a cosmic conflagration . . . would occur, in which all things, including the souls of individual persons, would be dissolved into the elements from which they came" (Croy 1997: 33).

45. They called Paul "this babbler." Here "this" is thought of as "contemptuous" (BDF §290.6.1; cf. 6:13, 14; 19:26; Croy 1997: 23n5; Culy and Parsons 2003: 334).

46. Croy 1997: 23. Bruce 1990: 377 defines "seed-picker" as "one who picked up scraps of learning wherever he could."

47. Croy 1997: 23.

48. LSJ 365.

49. Chase 1902: 205–6n3.

50. See Bruce 1990: 331n35; Croy 1997: 23.

51. Croy 1997: 23.

52. Fitzmyer 1998: 607; so also Wright 2008: 84.

53. Croy 1997: 24.

council in order to learn about these unknown gods. As Winter argues, "Acts 17:18–20 is to be connected with the role of the Areopagus in examining the claim for introducing new deities into Athens."[54]

Second Stage (17:19–34)

Without question, the Athenians tried to satisfy their philosophers' instincts by staging Paul at the Areopagus council, "the predominant corporation of Roman Athens."[55] The council members were called "Areopagites," such as Dionysius (Acts 17:34), and the council was composed of probably "between 91 and 104 Areopagites."[56]

Even though "it has not been unusual for commentators to view Paul's ministry in Athens as a failure,"[57] Paul's speech in the Areopagus has been evaluated as a good model for preaching the gospel. Charles points out that Paul was born in Tarsus, "the native city of several famous Stoic philosophers—among them, Zeno, Antipater, Athenadorus, and Nestor" and "one of three 'university' cities of renown" (Athens, Alexandria, and Tarsus), and that Paul's speech shows "a model for cultural apologetics" literarily and rhetorically.[58] Especially, Dahle argues, Paul's speech has historical authenticity and can be "an apologetic model then and now."[59]

54. Winter 1996: 88.

55. Geagan 1967: 41.

56. Geagan 1967: 57 estimates this amount as the size of the Areopagus: "for three tribes there are between twenty-two and twenty-four names of Areopagites preserved, an average of seven or eight each. A projection of this for thirteen tribes makes a total of between 91 and 104 Areopatites."

57. Charles 1995: 47–48 quotes W. M. Ramsay, C. Munsinger, A. Daniel-Rops, etc.

58. Charles 1995: 49, 50, 52–60.

59. Dahle 2002: 313–316 in the summary of his thesis indicates four items to see Paul's speech in Athens as an apologetic model: "convictions about who God is and how he has revealed himself"; "the apologist's contextual understanding, his application of appropriate justification procedures and his 'positive deconstruction' of alternative worldviews"; "from . . . natural theology through the plausibility and implications of God's ultimate authority . . . to the significance and evidence of the Resurrection"; and "Paul's threefold aim ('to interest,' 'to persuade,' and 'to confront')."

Questions and Responses (17:19–31)

In the council the Athenians claimed, **"We possess the right to judge what this new teaching is being spoken of by you. You are bringing strange [foreign] things to our ears: we therefore wish to judge what it is being claimed [or decreed] these things are"** (17:19–20).[60] They wanted to know who "Jesus and Anastasis" were, "like Venus and Adonis or Zeus and Dione,"[61] so as to judge if they were gods proper to serve.

Luke introduces the Athenians' and also the visitors' habit, that is, to spend time on saying something or listening to something new.[62] These queries are melded in their habit: **Can we know?** (Acts 17:19) and **We want to know** (17:20). According to their knowledge, Paul's teaching was new and exotic, in a sense, unheard-of, so they wanted to evaluate this new teaching on Jesus and *Anastasis*.

Paul was left to clarify that *Anastasis* does not refer to a goddess but to "resurrection" itself. How was he able to do it for those who did not pay attention even to the afterlife, not to mention "resurrection"? Paul stood in the middle of the Areopagus and affirmed that the Creator, the real deity, calls all the nations to repent because God has provided a clear evidence, specifically, by Jesus' resurrection. Paul's answer to the Athenians' habitual questions is well-organized by Cheng.

> 17:22–24a Identification of an Athenian unknown god with the one true God
>
> Point out an Athenian unknown deity (vv. 22–23)
>
> Bring out the God of creation (v. 24a)
>
> 17:24b–29 Elucidation of the nature of God the Creator
>
> Supreme over the creation (v. 24b)
>
> —*Lord of heaven and earth*
>
> Self-sufficient from the creation (v. 25)
>
> —*Giver of life and all things*
>
> Sovereign over humankind (vv. 26–27)
>
> —*Ruler of humankind*
>
> Self-existent from humankind (vv. 28–29)

60. Winter 1996: 90 posits the term "judge" to indicate the Athenians' intention after scrutinizing the characteristics of the council.

61. Gray 2005: 113.

62. Here the comparative *kainoteron* is employed, but this can "have the force of the simple positive" (Zerwick 1963 [2001]: 150).

—*Begetter of humankind*

17:30–31 Explication of the plan of God in Jesus

Past: God disregarded human ignorance (v. 30a)

Present: God commands all to repent (vv. 30b–31)

—*Reason for humankind's repentance (v. 31a)*

—*Proof for God's judgment (v. 31b)*[63]

First, Paul calls the gatherers **men of Athenians**, who were "thoroughly Greek, allowing the audience immediately to feel at home,"[64] and characterizes them as **more religious or superstitious**[65] **in all respects**, generally accepted as "Luke's artful use of ambiguous religious language that can be read in either way, for either rhetorical or ironical purposes."[66] This term, *deisidaimōn*, can be compared with *daimonion* (divinities or inferior divine beings) in Acts 17:18. Paul seems to dismiss the Athenians' claim that Paul is a proclaimer of the foreign inferior or the evil spirits, by saying, "If I have to do with some spiritual beings, you would do more than I."

Then, Paul mentions the altar engraved "**To an unknown god**" (Acts 17:23) as an evidence of their religious curiosity. As Bruce states, "When a derelict altar was repaired and the original dedication could not be recovered, ἀγνώστῳ θεῷ would have been a suitable inscription for it."[67] Even if there could have been many altars of this sort,[68] Paul simplified it by employing the singular form. Further, the "god" is neutralized by the neutral relative pronoun (*ho*) and the demonstrative pronoun (*touto*), which may refer to one of "the objects of worship" (*ta sebasmata*). Bruce believes, "Paul starts with his hearers' belief in an impersonal divine essence, pantheistically conceived."[69] Paul grabbed hold of their lack of knowledge of "a god" to introduce the one and only true God.

---

63. Cheng 2011: 108 (italics hers).

64. Charles 1995: 54.

65. *Deisidaimonesterous* is "the comparative adjective" (Oxley 2004: 336), and *deisidaimōn* has the meaning "in good sense, religious" and "in bad sense, superstitious" (LSJ 375).

66. Gray 2005: 110.

67. Bruce 1990: 381; *contra* van der Horst 1992: 32–37, who connects this altar with an altar erected by Godfearers for the God of the Jews.

68. See Bruce 1990: 380–81; Cheng 2011: 108n73.

69. Bruce 1990: 381.

Next Paul tells the Athenians that **the God who made the whole universe**[70] **and everything in it**, identifying "the God" with **Lord of heaven and earth**, and he proclaims that **the God does not dwell in hand-made temples** (Acts 17:24). The term "hand-made" (*cheiropoiētos*) can be "used metaphorically for idols" in light of the OT.[71] Pao reads "the anti-idol program in Isaiah 40–55" in several expressions used in this speech: "the description of God as one 'who made the world and everything in it, he who is Lord of heaven and earth'" (v. 24) alluding to Isa 42:5; "shrines made by human hands" (v. 24) echoing Isa 46:6; "we ought not to think that the deity is like gold, or silver, or stone, an image formed by the art and imagination of mortals" (v. 29) alluding to Deut 29:16–17 (29:15–16, MT) and Isa 40:18–20; and to "search for God" who "is not far from each one of us" (v. 27) recalling Isa 55:6.[72] Paul's polemic against idols is very well combined with pro-God dialogue by using the simplest form of chiasm.

> God made the world and this God is the Lord (v. 24a–b).
>
> So He is not an idol which lives in hand-made shrines (v. 24c).
>
> He neither needs nor expects any help from human beings (v. 25a).
>
> Rather He distributes life and breath and everything to everyone (v. 25b).

In v. 25, Bruce reads "approximations to the Epicurean doctrine that God needs nothing from human beings and to the Stoic belief that he is the source of all life (see on 17:28)."[73] So Paul seems to relieve the Athenians' unfriendly feeling caused by the anti-idol theology.

After comparing the true God with idols and providing relief for the audience, Paul explains the relationship between God and human beings by employing a chiasm order in vv. 26–31.

> God made every nation of mankind from one man . . . (vv. 26–27).
>
> We live and move in Him . . . (v. 28).
>
> We need to change the concept of divinity . . . (v. 29).
>
> God commands all mankind to repent on the basis of **one man** . . . (vv. 30–31).

70. Mundhenk 2002: 442 suggests that the *kosmos* in Acts 17:24 means "the whole universe."

71. Litwak 2004: 206.

72. Pao 2000: 194–96.

73. Bruce 1990: 382.

First, the fact that God's creation of every nation of humankind was made only by one is declared (v. 26a), which is connected with the appointed one in v. 31. Schnabel describes vividly the listeners' understanding of Paul's declaration of the creator God as follows.

> There is no parallel for *the notion of a common ancestor of the entire human race* in Greek or Roman mythology. If we assume that the educated listeners in the Areopagus Council, who were certainly aware of the presence of a Jewish community in Athens, had some knowledge of Jewish cosmology, they would have realized at this point of Paul's speech that the God whom Paul proclaims in Athens is indeed not a foreign deity but *the God of the Jews*, whose holy Scriptures claim that the human race began with the creation of Adam, the first human race inhabits, as one, the earth.[74]

Paul's proclamation of the unique originality of humankind is followed by the multiplication of humankind and its purpose. **God made all the nations from one man, so as to live on all the face of the earth** (v. 26b). This statement reminds us about God's first commandment, "Be fruitful and multiply and fill the earth" (Gen 1:28). This was also given to Noah and his sons (9:2). However, it had not been obeyed since people did not want to be "scattered all over the face of the earth" (11:4). Consequently, God had "to make them scatter all over the face of the earth" (11:9b).[75]

Paul continues with God's determination of **times and places** (Acts 17:26c), that is, "periods of history" and "the political boundaries between the places where people live—whether cities, regions, provinces, or continents."[76] The thought behind this statement reflects Daniel's vision (Daniel 2 and 7) and the song of Moses (Deut 32:8: "For the most high divided the nations as he separated the sons of Adam; he established regions for the nations").[77] The fact that God rules humankind can be recognized when an empire arises and perishes. The Greeks should be

74. Schnabel 2012: 734 (italics mine).

75. Litwak 2004: 207 says that Acts 17:26b "is similar to Gen 11,9b," but the situation is different. The former echoes God's original purpose of making nations, but the latter indicates God's interruption for completing His creation purpose.

76. Schnabel 2012: 735; cf. Pervo 2009: 436; *contra* Bruce 1990: 383 who suggests seeing this *kairous* as "the seasons of the year" rather than "divinely ordained periods." The "times" in this verse should be different from "seasons" in 14:17.

77. Litwak 2004: 207 says that "the thought of Acts 17,26 is expressed in Deut 32,8."

unable to deny it because they, too, had set up an empire and experienced its collapse.

Here, Paul pays attention to God's purpose in determining times and places, that is, to make all the nations **seek God** (Acts 17:27a). Seeking God is an essential theme in the OT.[78] Jesus also taught the disciples to "seek first the kingdom of God and His righteousness" (Matt 6:33a). Paul connects human limits on times and places with their necessity of seeking God, and makes a weak promise that **they would probably indeed touch and find him** (Acts 17:27b).[79] This is comparable to Jesus' remark "seek and you will find . . . and the one who seeks finds" (Matt 7:7–8). The difference between Paul's promise and Jesus' remark can be explained in terms of the audience: the Athenians did not even have the notion of the true God, but the disciples "came near to" Jesus (5:1). In spite of the remoteness of the Athenians from God, Paul was able to give the Athenians a positive notion that **the God is not far from each of us** (Acts 17:27c).

Second, Paul changes the subject from a third singular, referring to God, to a first plural, including the Athenians and Paul himself. **For in Him we live and move around and exist, just as some of your own poets have already said, because we belong to His offspring, too** (Acts 17:28). According to Bruce, the former phrase ("For in Him we live . . . exist") might have been quoted from a poem written by "Epimenides the Cretan (*c.* 600 BC)," namely, "For in thee we live and move and have our being," and the latter phrase ("we belong to His offspring too") is "part of the fifth line of the *Phainomena* of Paul's fellow-Cilician Aratus (born 310 BC)."[80] Borrowing its exact words and its word order could have had steered the audience to open their ears to this foreigner's monologue.

Third, Paul resumes the anti-idol polemic along with using the same first plural subject. **Therefore, being God's offspring, we should not consider the deity such as gold or silver or stone, also such as products of human skill and imagination** (Acts 17:29). Similar expressions can be found in Ps 115:4 [113:12, LXX]; Isa 40:18–19; and 46:5–6.[81] However,

78. Litwak 2004: 208 finds this theme in Deut 4:29; 1 Chr 22:19a; 28:9b; Ps 9:25; 13:2; Isa 55:6; 58:2; Hos 3:5; Amos 5:6, etc.

79. According to Culy and Parsons 2003: 339, "The use of εἰ with two optative verbs forms a (double) fourth class condition (always incomplete in the NT), which is normally used to express something that has only a remote possibility of happening in the future."

80. Bruce 1988: 338–39. So also Schnabel 2012: 736–37, etc.

81. Litwak 2004: 209.

these expressions are declared posterior to calling the idol worshipers "God's offspring," extending the boundaries to the Athenians unlike the Psalter or Isaiah. He positively "reinterpreted" Greek poets in terms of OT theology, as Bruce indicates, "Before a pagan audience he naturally does not make his points by formally quoting from the OT, as he did in the synagogue at Pisidian Antioch, but if instead he introduces quotations from Greek poets, he does not adopt those poets' perspective; rather, he reinterprets their words in a biblical sense."[82] Paul's reinterpretation of secular literature was biblical, not vice versa.

Fourth, on the basis of the one Creator theology and the unique originality of humankind, Paul claims that all the Athenians are required to repent. **The God, who has overlooked such times of ignorance, now**[83] **orders people to repent everywhere without exception** (Acts 17:30). This order has been founded on Jesus' resurrection, and the urgency of broadcasting this good news was stressed greatly by God's D-Day, when "He is going to judge the whole inhabited earth in righteousness,[84] by the man whom He appointed" (17:31a).

At his last remark Paul mentions "faith" (*pistis*) or "proof." Although most commentators interpret this *pistis* as "proof" ("a token offered as a guarantee of someth. [something] promised"),[85] Paul could still have declared that God **offered faith to everyone** (Acts 17:31b). In this verse "righteousness" and "the resurrected Jesus" are key concepts along with "faith/proof." In Pauline letters (e.g., Rom 3, 9–10) and in Paul's speeches recorded in Acts (only 13:39 and here), these three concepts are combined together in many verses.[86] Therefore, just as Paul declared at the synagogue in Pisidian Antioch that "by this one, everyone who believes is

82. Bruce 1990: 382.

83. In regard of "now," Culy and Parsons 2003: 341 say, "The use of the neuter accusative plural article (as a nominalizer; see 1:3) with the adverb νῦν may make the shift in time more emphatic (cf. 4:29 ὅτι καὶ τὰ νῦν)."

84. Litwak 2004: 209–10 reads a "scriptural tradition" on God's judging the world in righteousness in Ps 9:8 [9:9, MT, LXX]; 96:13b [95:13b, LXX]; and 98:9 [97:9, LXX].

85. BDAG 818; e.g., Bruce 1990: 386; Culy and Parsons 2003: 342; Schnabel 2012: 741 etc. *Ant.* 2.218 and 15.260 are suggested as examples, but *pistis* in the former may have the meaning of "faith or faithfulness." And *pistis* in the latter has a modifier but the one in Acts 17:31 does not.

86. In the NT, these three concepts, namely, "faith," "righteousness," and "Jesus," occur together in the following verses: Acts 13:39; 17:31; Rom 1:17; 3:22, 25, 26, 28, 30 (4:3, 5, 9, 11, 13); 5:1; 9:30; 10:4, 6, 10; Gal 2:16 (3:6, 8, 11), 24; 5:5; Phil 3:9; 1 Tim 3:16 (Jam 2:23, 24); 2 Pet 1:1.

justified," so he seems to unwrap before the Athenians that **God offered the faith to everyone after resurrecting him [Jesus] from the dead** (17:31b). Paul, born a Jew, did not separate the Athenians from the Jews; rather he merged them into one: "us" and "everyone."

The Responses (17:32–34)

Luke introduces two main responses to Paul's speech from the Athenians. One is clearly included as derision, but the other can be interpreted as curiosity or as a polite rejection. "We will hear from you about this once more" may infer their indifference, saying something such as, "Let's hear from him again another day even though it would not be important." As Croy suggests, it is quite feasible that "Luke intended the contrasting responses of derision and curiosity to refer to the Epicureans and Stoics respectively."[87] As the Epicureans mocked Paul, the Stoics showed interest in this strange account; however, "as far as we know, no Stoic ever entertained the notion of the resurrection of the body."[88] Hence, it is more likely that after Paul implored repentance to God, the Stoics were firmly and tactfully rejecting what they heard in a more civilized manner. As a matter of fact, the text does not mention any further meeting with philosophers. Rather, the next step Paul took was to leave this crowd: in this way Paul departed from their midst (Acts 17:33).

Nevertheless, there were firstfruits of faith. **By the way, there were some men/husbands who joined Paul. They believed. Among them even Dionysius the Areopagite was included. In addition, a woman/wife named Damaris joined and believed. Furthermore, there were others along with them [Dionysius and Damaris]** (Acts 17:34). Dionysius was one of the 91 to 104 Areopagites or Areopagus council members.[89] It is said that "Greek archaeologists have uncovered the ruins of a church of Dionysios, the Areopagites."[90] In the meantime, Damaris—who is mentioned next—may not have been Dionysius's wife, but an important figure both socially and "in the church of Athens (or in the churches of Achaia)."[91] John Chrysostom presupposed that Damaris was Dionysius's

---

87. Croy 1997: 38.
88. Croy 1997: 37.
89. Geagan 1967: 57.
90. Broneer 1958: 82.
91. Schnabel 2012: 743.

wife in his work "On the Priesthood" (*De sacerdotio*) 4.7: "How was it that that Areopagite, an inhabitant of Athens, that most devoted of all cities to the gods, followed the apostle, he and his wife?"[92] However, this presupposition is evaluated as "no evidence."[93] On whatever the occasion, Paul's speech did bear fruits; he convinced the Athenians to change their minds and receive the faith.

---

92. *NPNF*1 9:67.

93. Schnabel 2012: 743n99. Further, Damaris is very less likely to have been "invented by Luke" as insisted by Gill 1999: 489–90.

ACTS 18

Mission in Corinth and the Dawn of the Church in Ephesus

After fruitful evangelism, Paul departed from Athens and went to Corinth.[1] In 27 BCE this city "became the seat of administration of the Roman province of Achaia."[2] Strabo points out that "Corinth is called 'wealthy' because of its commerce, since it is situated on the Isthmus and is master of two harbours, of which the one [Cenchreae] leads straight to Asia, and the other [Lechaeum] to Italy; and it makes easy the exchange of merchandise from both countries that are so far distant from each other."[3] Strabo had first passed through Corinth in 44 BCE, then visited the city fifteen years later (29 BCE), and accomplished his *Geography* [*Geographica*] before 2 BCE at the least. When Paul visited Corinth, it was like a commercial center in Achaia. Even Murphy-O'Connor draws a parallel between Corinth and "San Francisco in the days of the gold rush."[4]

To trace back Paul's arrival and departure time in Corinth, it is necessary to examine these three key points: the year of Claudius's edict (Acts 18:2), the period of Gallio's term of office, and the time sequence in 18:1–18. First, 41 and 49 CE are proposed as the year Claudius's edict was issued. In regard to this edict, Luke informs us that Emperor Claudius,

1. According to Pausanias, who "visited Corinth not long after AD 165," "that Corinthus was a son of Zeus I have never known anybody say seriously except the majority of the Corinthians" (Murphy-O'Connor 2002: 5–6; see Pausanias, *Description of Greece* 2.1.1).

2. Bruce 1988: 345–46.

3. Strabo, *Geogr.* 8.6.20; see Murphy-O'Connor 2002: 52–53. So also Broneer 1951: 78, 80: "It [Corinth] dominated the neck of land that joined the southern part of the Greek peninsula with the mainland, and since the trade of the Roman Empire was carried overland from sea to sea, Corinth controlled the traffic between the east and the west. Through its two harbors, Cenchreae on the east side of the Isthmus and Lechaeum on the west, flowed the commerce of the world."

4. Murphy-O'Connor 1984: 147.

who reigned from 41 to 54 CE, had ordered all the Jews to leave Rome (18:2). This edict of Claudius had been dated to 49 CE on the basis of the testimony of Orosius,[5] but Murphy-O'Connor suggests 41 CE instead; having judged that Orosius's testimony is unreliable, he reinterprets Suetonius, *Claud.* 25.4, Dio Cassius, *History* 60.6.6, Philo, *Embassy to Gaius* 156–157, and so on.[6] For example, he translates Suetonius's text slightly differently than the Loeb Classical Library version: "Since the Jews constantly made disturbances at the instigation of Chrestus, he expelled them from Rome" was rephrased to "He expelled from Rome the Jews constantly making disturbances at the instigation of Chrestus." Since Murphy-O'Connor's version emphasizes that not all the Jews but only the Jews making disturbances were expelled, it makes it possible for him to say that "as the result of a disturbance concerning Christ in a Roman synagogue, Claudius expelled the missionaries who were not Roman citizens."[7] That is to say, the possession of Roman citizenship was placed as the standard for compartmentalizing the displaced. However, according to Luke's testimony, Claudius forced "all" the Jews, not just some Jews, to leave Rome (18:2); thus, Luke attests that the nationality known as the "Jews" was the benchmark for drawing the line between the expelled and the permitted.[8] Henceforth, we can plainly say, as in the traditional view, that Claudius's edict was ordered in 49 CE.

Subsequently, the date of Gallio's term of office can be simply fixed between 51–52 CE,[9] probably from "1 July 51 to 30 June 52."[10] Winter's detailed description of Gallio can be summarized as follows: Gallio was born as the first son of the ambitious and famous Stoic philosopher Annaeus Lucius Seneca (c. 50 BCE–40 CE), but was named Lucius Junius Gallio Annaeus after being adopted by a leading senator, L. Junius Gallio; Gallio became a senator in 37 CE and then the proconsul of Achaea;

5. See Bruce 1990: 347n9; Fitzmyer 1998: 619–20; Bock 2007: 577–78; etc.

6. Murphy-O'Connor 2002: 152–58. Pervo 2009: 446 also prefers this earlier date.

7. Murphy-O'Connor 2002: 152, 156.

8. Regarding a further objection to Murphy-O'Connor's view, see Fitzmyer 1998: 620.

9. See Fitzmyer 1998: 622–23; Peterson 2009: 516, 516n43; etc.

10. Murphy-O'Connor 2002: 165. His argument is based on the date of the Delphi inscription identified as Emperor Claudius's letter to the Delphians. Murphy-O'Connor 2002: 164 concludes that "the letter of Claudius was probably written in the late spring or very early summer of AD 52." So also Winter 2006: 296. Pervo 2009: 447 dates this letter from Claudius more precisely "between January 25 and August 1, 52."

he was called Claudius's "friend" and became Rome's consul; he suffered from hypochondriasis right after his proconsulship of Achaea; and he hated flattery.[11]

Finally, as for the time sequence mentioned in 18:1–18, several expressions of time that Luke employs to describe Paul's ministry in Corinth should be examined: **every Sabbath** (Acts 18:4), **one and a half years** (18:11), and **sufficient days** (18:18). While some see the sum of this period as "one and a half years,"[12] some scholars suggest that adding each period could be the total length of his stay in Corinth;[13] thus, Paul would have stayed in Corinth more than one and a half years. Slingerland thinks of the variant in Codex Bezae Cantabrigiensis, that is "in Corinth," as one and a half years or "eighteen months may be the total length of Paul's sojourn in Corinth."[14] However, the experts at the Codex say, "The 18 months seem to be viewed as additional to any time Paul had spent so far in Corinth, going up to, and beyond, his appearance before Gallio (18.12, cf. 18.18)."[15] Furthermore, this seems more credible on account of Luke's usage of conjunctions.[16]

Seeing that Paul's stay in Corinth was longer than one and a half years and that Claudius's edict was issued in 49 CE and Gallio's term of office in 51–52 CE, this leads to a conclusion that Paul arrived in Corinth probably between 49 and 50 CE.[17] There Paul met Aquila and Priscilla who were expelled from Rome, and after a while he, possibly together with this couple, founded a church very influential in Greece. Applying Luke's illustrations of time, Paul's stay in Corinth could be calculated at one and a half years at the very least, for instance, from the spring of 49 CE to the autumn of 51 CE, or from the autumn of 50 CE to the spring of 52 CE: there would be no problem to put these dates together, viz., from the spring of 49 CE to the spring of 52 CE.

11. See Winter 2006: 293–301.

12. See Witherington 1998: 551n332.

13. E.g., Peterson 2009: 514–15.

14. Slingerland 1991: 442.

15. Rius-Camps and Read-Heimerdinger 2007: 379.

16. See Slingerland 1991: 442.

17. Murphy-O'Connor 1984: 148, who have studied a study on Corinth thoroughly, prefers the autumn of 50 CE as the time of Paul's arrival in Corinth, but later Murphy-O'Connor 2002: 159 places Paul's arrival "in late AD 49 or more probably early AD 50."

Thereafter, he stopped by Ephesus and moved on to Jerusalem and Syrian Antioch. Murphy-O'Connor introduces Ephesus compactly:

> It [Ephesus] was the western terminus of the road from India and the capital of perhaps the richest province in the Roman empire. It enshrined the Temple of Artemis, one of the seven wonders of the world. The city was also Paul's base for just over two years, and because of the letters he wrote from Ephesus it is the best documented period of his career. Toward the end of the first century CE the city became the home of the evangelist [John the Apostle] who produced the final version of the Fourth Gospel. Ephesus, in consequence, has a claim on the attention of anyone interested in the origins of Christianity or in the life of one of the most extraordinary cities of antiquity.[18]

This city was also known as the birthplace of Artemis and Apollo.[19] The first temple of Artemis in Ephesus "measured 142 × 73 meters" and was known as "the largest building of its time in Rome, Greece, or Asia."[20] If Paul arrived in Ephesus in the autumn of 51 CE—or even if he arrived there in the spring of 52 CE—he could have not stayed much longer there "because the end of the sailing season was approaching."[21]

Mission in Corinth (18:1–17)

After finishing the ministry in Athens, Paul departed and arrived in Corinth, "located 55 mi (88 km) west of Athens."[22] By ship he would have boarded on "a boat going from Piraeus via Salamis to Schoenus or Cenchreae," otherwise "he would have crossed the *diolkos*[23] at Schoenus."[24] In

18. Murphy-O'Connor 2008: xiii.

19. See Strabo, Geogr. 14.1.20 and Murphy-O'Connor 2008: 15–17.

20. Murphy-O'Connor 2008: 22, 116–18. This measure is based on the report of Pliny the Elder, "Gaius Plinius Secundus" who "was born about 23 CE and died heroically on August 24, 79, when an expedition to study the eruption of Mount Vesuvius turned into a rescue mission and his ships were trapped on a lee shore" (Murphy-O'Connor 2008: 104).

21. Murphy-O'Connor 2008: 187.

22. NET notes.

23. *ABD* I, 1136: "Periander (ca. 625–585 BC) built a paved road (the *diolkos*) across the isthmus, which permitted light ships to be hauled from one sea to the other on a platform running in grooves cut in the pavement. Excavations have revealed a dock and 460 m of the road on the W side of the isthmus."

24. Murphy-O'Connor 1984: 148–49.

those days the city walls of Corinth were ruined; the length of the walls "is closer to 10 kilometers"; and the walls used to enclose "an area of about 4 square kilometers."[25] It might have been the first sight Paul encountered in Corinth; a city surrounded by the walls tumbled down but flourishing as a commercial center; a city having no more the necessity to be defended with physical walls visual to the eye but with spiritual walls against sins.

First Stage (18:1–11)

In Corinth, Paul met a Jewish couple, Aquila and Priscilla. Aquila had been born in Pontus, one of the places highly religious Jews had lived (cf. 2:9); but there is no particular information on his wife Priscilla. This couple had recently come from Rome, Italy. They could be introduced not only as evangelists but also as merchants regularly on the move. After having been acquaintances with Paul for nearly two years (49–51 or 50–52 CE), they moved to Ephesus between the years 51–54 or 52–54 CE (18:18–26 and 1 Cor 16:19); and before Paul wrote the Epistle to the Romans while spending the winter in Corinth (56–57 CE), they journeyed back to Rome (Rom 16:3) probably because they were able to move to Rome due to the death of Claudius in 54 CE; and around 64/65 CE they were in Ephesus again (2 Tim 4:19). In this sense, during the occasion of their acquaintance with Paul, the evangelistic partners came to Corinth as merchants since the city was easily reachable from Rome via Lechaeum the trade port.

Paul joined up with Aquila and Priscilla, who might have already been Christians,[26] and they lodged and worked together since Paul shared the same trade, that is, **leather-work** (Acts 18:3).[27] Paul did work on weekdays, probably being employed by the couple rather than having his own business; however, on the Sabbaths, he argued in the synagogue and tried to persuade both the Jews and the Greeks. The subject matter Paul argued is not revealed, but the next verse does allow us to guess that Paul talked merely about "the Messiah." Paul paid attention to talking about

25. Murphy-O'Connor 1984: 149.

26. Witherington 1998: 545 regards this couple as having been Christian converts before meeting Paul, because their conversions are not mentioned in Acts.

27. Bruce 1990: 392 says, "While the etymological sense of σκηνοποιός is 'tent-maker,' it was used in the wider sense of 'leather-work' (cf. Eng. 'saddler,' which has a wider sense than 'maker of saddles')."

the Messiah every Sabbath (18:4) but not to the core of the gospel, Jesus Christ (proclaiming that the Messiah is Jesus), maybe feeling anxious about the Thessalonian church. Since he had left Thessalonica after only a three-week ministry, he might have been worried about the stability and growth of this very young church (cf. 1 Thess 3:1–10). Nevertheless, when Paul heard from Silas and Timothy what God had done during his absence in Thessalonica, he resumed his core ministry of evangelizing, proclaiming Jesus as the Messiah first to "the Jews" as was his custom: **When both Silas and Timothy came down from Macedonia, Paul was occupied**[28] **with the Word and so declared to the Jews that "the Messiah is Jesus"** (Acts 18:5).[29]

Then, the situation changed. The Jews who had been in silence opposed and held Paul in contempt for his proclamation of Jesus as the prophesied Messiah (Acts 18:6a). When the gospel is proclaimed, objection is raised. Persecution began and Paul, possibly taking the dust off from his clothes, shook off the clothing just as Jesus taught his followers (Matt 10:14; Mark 6:11) and as he had done at the synagogue in Pisidian Antioch (Acts 13:51). He said, **Your blood (be) on your own heads! I am free (of debt or blame). From now on I will go to the Gentiles** (18:6b–c).

Paul's action is parallel to Neh 5:13,[30] and his saying alludes to Ezek 33:4.[31] Nehemiah commanded the Israelites, who had been restored from exile, to show deep sincerity toward any poor neighbors and proclaimed that anyone who lacks this sincerity shall be "shaken off" from God and be emptied (Neh 5:13). This emptiness means receiving none of God's inheritance. Moreover, "shaking off" also refers to a disconnection—disengagement from God. When we explicate what Paul meant by "shaking off his clothing" in terms of 5:13, his pronouncement becomes more

28. Culy and Parsons 2003: 345 think, "The verb should probably be viewed as middle rather than passive." However, this verb can have the passive form in Acts where the Word has the subjective power (see 6:7; 12:24; 19:20).

29. In terms of articularity and word order, "the Messiah" should be the subject. So also Bruce 1990: 393 who takes account of articularity; Wallace 1996: 197n78 and Culy and Parsons 2003: 345 who focus on word order; on commentaries see Marshall 1980B: 311, Conzelmann 1987 [1972]: 150, Witherington 1998: 549, Bock 2007: 576, Wright 2008: 94, Pervo 2009: 443, etc.

30. Schnabel 2012: 759n20.

31. NA28; Bruce 1988: 349n25. Schnabel 2012: 759n21 connects this formula with "Lev 20:9; Deut 21:5; 2 Sam 1:16; 3:28–29; 14:9; 1 Kgs 2:31–33, 44–45; *As. Mos.* 9:7; *T. Levi* 16:3; *m. Sanh.* 4.5; cf. Ezek 33:1–9; Matt 27:25; Acts 5:28; 20:26."

straightforward: "You are not related to this gospel, to the Messiah, thus even to God's salvation and inheritance." Further, Ezek 33:4, the passage related to the sentinel and the sword, clarifies his criticism to a greater extent. While Ezekiel was appointed as the sentinel by God Himself and for the house of Israel (33:7), Paul is being identified as that sentinel. He stood watch and sounded a warning signal with the gospel since it is not only the only way for the people to avoid falling into God's judgment, but also the only way for Paul not to bear any responsibility for their fatal consequences.

Paul announced that the Messiah, the savior prophesied in the OT, had come, and that the Messiah was Jesus (Acts 18:5b). He completed his task; he is free from any obligation to tell them about Jesus or more on God's salvation history and will not be accountable for their resulting judgment. After stating his prophetic formula of ministry, Paul declares that now he will go to the gentiles (18:6c; Greeks in 18:4).

Paul did not go far; he entered the house next door to the synagogue (Acts 18:7). An easy accessibility from the synagogue was not the reason Paul moved into this new place; rather, the house's owner, Titius Justus, seems to have had an effect on this matter. Titius Justus was a God-fearer and the order of his name is seen as "a Roman *nomen* and *cognomen*."[32] However faint, this offers a possibility that he could had been a Roman citizen. If his *praenomen* is Gaius,[33] he could be recognized as the "Gaius" in 1 Cor 1:14 and Rom 16:23. Occupied with the Word (Acts 18:5a), Paul changed his mind, and ultimately his behavior and resolution as well; accordingly, it can be said that it was not Paul who grabbed hold of Titius Justus, a significant convert, but the Word.

Paul withdrew from the synagogue because of the Jews' resistance to the gospel. Still, Crispus the ruler of the synagogue and his family became believers of the Lord (Acts 18:8a). Crispus seems to have been succeeded by Sosthenes who appears in 18:17 as he was considered unsuitable to

32. Bruce 1988: 503. Roman names are composed of *praenomen* (personal name), *nomen* (clan name), *cognomen* (house or family name), and *agnomen* (additional name). For example, the first Roman emperor was named Gaius Julius Caesar Octavianus.

33. This idea was first suggested by Ramsay 1910: 205, 205n2, who thinks of Titius Justus as "a Roman citizen" and suggests that "his name was in full probably Gaius Titus Justus, the Gaius of Rom. XVI. 23," and was articulated by Goodspeed 1950: 382–83, and then was followed by Bruce 1988: 503, etc., but was doubted by Witherington 1998: 550, etc. So Gaius can be Titius Justus's *praenomen*, but that idea "must remain hypothetical," as Schnabel 2012: 759 says.

take charge of the office on account of his belief in Jesus. Besides him and this new family, many Corinthians and were baptized (18:8b). The latter could have had occurred after Paul went to the gentiles (like he said he would). It is possible that while Paul was in Titius Justus's house, crowds gathered inside and many went through the door as converts after listening to Paul's message. Faith came by hearing.

Luke seems to emphasize that all these events from Acts 18:5 to 18:8 occurred within one day by writing an episode of that very night in the next two verses. That night,[34] when Paul changed his message while the Word grabbed hold of him, the Lord said to Paul through sheer ecstasy or in a vision, **Do not fear! Rather speak[35] and do not be silent, for the reason that I am with you and that no one will lay a hand[36] on you to harm you,[37] and for the reason that a lot of people in this city belong to me** (18:9–10). It seems reasonable to infer from this remark that Paul had not revealed Jesus as the Messiah until this day of **every Sabbath** (18:4); his silence should have prevented the Lord as the Word from calling many Corinthians into the kingdom of God. To prevent further silence, the promise of Immanuel is reaffirmed. "I am with you even in Corinth the wealthy, commercial city," Jesus confirmed, and then promised both protection from harm and a successful result in his ministry.

34. To be translated not into "one night" but "that night," see BDAG 682; NET.

35. If *lalei* is translated as "go on speaking," as the ESV does, it may mean "as you speak today, keep on speaking."

36. Robertson 2010 [1934]: 477 teaches that "χεῖρας must be supplied."

37. Culy and Parsons 2003: 348 see this articular "infinitive may either indicate purpose or be epexegetical."

Fusing the Horizons: Inclusiveness and Absoluteness in Christianity[38]

Neither opposition nor revilement occurred in the synagogue in Corinth before Paul **declared that "the Messiah is Jesus"** (Acts 18:5). Here we can read both the inclusiveness and absoluteness in Christianity. A proclamation was issued to the Corinthians; this is related to its inclusiveness. Related to its absoluteness is the message that is the one and only reason trouble is stirred: Messiahship belongs to Jesus alone.

Christianity's inclusiveness remarkably stands out in Acts 1:8: **But you will receive power when the Holy Spirit comes upon you, and you will be my witnesses not only in Jerusalem but also in all Judea and Samaria and to the end of the earth**. Jerusalem where Jesus was crucified is included; no revenge but blessings were promised. Galilee, especially Nazareth, was despised at Jesus' time (John 1:46; 7:52; Acts 2:7); however, Jesus the Nazarene did not exclude Judea from the proclamation of the gospel. It is surprising that Samaria was included not only because "Jews did not have dealings with Samaritans" (John 4:9b) but also because even the disciples of Jesus did not like them, and said in hatred, "Lord, do you want us to call fire to come down from heaven and consume them?" (Luke 9:54). Above all, "the end of the earth," referring to the gentiles, reveals Christianity's inclusiveness. There is no exception. Anyone can be included. Even Saul, who **was trying to destroy the church** (Acts 8:3), was not excluded. Even idol worshipers were invited to believe in the gospel (14:15–16; 17:29–30). This attitude is compared to that in Wis 14:8, where both idols and idol worshipers are accursed; in Acts, they are not accursed but invited and welcomed. The invitation was sent out even to the Roman officers (Felix and Festus) and the Herodian family members (Drusilla, Agrippa II, and Bernice; Acts 24–26).

This inclusiveness of Christianity is based on its absolute criterion, that is, Jesus and his gospel. Peter confirmed that **there is salvation in no one else, for there is no other name under heaven that was given among people, by which we must be saved** (Acts 4:12). This Jesus is the person who was crucified on the cross at "the site of skulls" (*Golgotha*) in Jerusalem during the Passover so as to die the death of representative substitution for our

38. Park 2013A: 65–76. Inclusiveness may be defined as welcoming and accepting everyone equally and warmly, and absoluteness as an independent and unchangeable condition.

salvation. Peter loudly trumpeted solely this Jesus (2:36; 3:6, 16; 4:30; 10:39–43; 15:11). Paul also broadcast Jesus, only him, at any time to everyone, even to the Jews who tried to silence him by death (22:8, 16, 17–21), and finally to **all who came to him** in Rome (28:30). Jesus is the perfecter as well as the founder of faith (Heb 12:2): he not only started and established the law of faith but also will complete the law of faith until the end of days.

Christianity's inclusiveness and absoluteness can be defined as fol- lows: anyone, even Jews or Samaritans or gentiles or persecutors or idol worshipers, can be saved at any plac, and at any time up to the judgment day *if* they believe in the Lord Jesus' Messiahship. As a matter of fact, its absoluteness makes its inclusiveness feasible. No creature can embrace other creatures. Only the creator, the incarnated Son of God, "who is in the bosom of the Father" (John 1:18), can embrace all creatures. He can take in any believer as a member of God's family, as His child. However, while Christians became one single family owing to Jesus' calling (Matt 23:9; Acts 2:32, 44–46; Gal 3:28; 4:6; Eph 2:14–19), it is this calling that divides people residing in one house (Luke 12:52–53//Matt 10:34–36).

Both Christianity's inclusiveness and absoluteness work together at any time. Even Barnabas, **son of encouragement** (Acts 4:36), turned from the Jews, who contradicted the gospel, to the gentiles (13:45–46). Paul, who had an ardent passion for the salvation of the Jews (Rom 9:3), shook off his clothing toward the Corinthian Jews who opposed the gospel and said, "**Your blood (be) on your own heads! I am free (of debt or blame). From now on I will go to the Gentiles**" (Acts 18:6b–c). A metaphor for Christianity's inclusive- ness can be "politeness," and for its absoluteness, "strictness"; however, indeed, both exist together. Its inclusiveness is based on its absoluteness, and the latter highlights Jesus' inclusiveness.

Nowadays, some blame Christianity for its exclusiveness; but it seems that they misunderstood its absoluteness, formed a false impression of its inclusiveness, and made Christianity open the door of salvation to anyone, even to unbelievers or to those who have different beliefs or so-called reli- gions. They seem to misunderstand Christianity's inclusiveness and ignore its absoluteness and the fact that both are features of Christianity.

Second Stage (18:11–17)

This in-depth ministry caused a different kind of opposition against Paul. It was the time when Gallio was the proconsul of Achaia (Acts 18:12a), as we have seen, probably from July 1, 51 to June 30, 52. The Jews who previously allowed Paul to proclaim the gospel to the gentiles attacked Paul with one accord and brought him before the tribunal of the proconsul (18:12b). They were not satisfied with putting unofficial blame on him; for them, a more effective and holistic treatment might have been necessary in order to cool down the Christian movement in Corinth.

Before the proconsul, the Jews claimed that Paul persuaded people to worship God in ways contrary to their law (Acts 18:13). The Jews always felt the gospel was against the law. Even Paul himself had thought of the Christian doctrine as contrary to the law before his conversion (6:13; 9:1–2). Even among early Christians, how to deal with the law was a burning issue (cf. 15:6–29). Consequently, the Jews' negative responses to Paul's message in Corinth were not atypical.

Gallio's reaction toward the Jews is an important point to take notice of. The Jews first had a say in the tribunal; **This man is persuading people to worship God in a way contrary to the law** (Acts 18:13). Now it was Paul's turn to respond, so he opened his mouth to begin (18:14a). Paul must have had an answer to the Jews in Corinth, as was spoken to the Jews in Jerusalem in 22:1–21. However, Gallio blocked Paul's defense and said, **"If there were[39] some crime or wicked wrongdoing, O Jews,[40] I would accept a complaint to judgment.[41] But if there are matters concerning words** (logou)**, names/people,[42] and your own law,[43] see to it**

---

39. *Ei men ēn* is seen as "unreal" (Zerwick 1963 [2001]: 108) or "second class" condition (Wallace 1996: 696).

40. Winter 2006: 301 understands "O Jews" as a polite address.

41. *Kata logon an aneschomēn* can be translated into "to accept a complaint in court, to admit a complaint to judgment" or "to be reasonably patient with" (LN §56.10). Bruce 1990: 396 says, "In a judicial context (as here) it has the technical sense of taking up a case, accepting a complaint."

42. Culy and Parsons 2003: 350 regards *onamatōn* "perhaps as a metonym (see 1:9 on τῶν ὀφθαλμῶν αὐτῶν) for 'people' (it is clearly used this way in Acts 1:15 and Rev 3:4)."

43. Culy and Parsons 2003: 351 understand *tou kath humas* as "'Your own law' (cf. 17:28 on καθ* ὑμᾶς) as opposed as Roman law."

yourselves. I do not want to be a judge[44] of these things." (18:14b–15). Then Gallio forced the Jews to leave the tribunal (18:16).

Even though Witherington writes, "In Gallio's eyes, Paul was a Jew and the dispute was a Jewish one, not an intramural debate between two religions,"[45] Gallio seems to display a very strong willingness to avoid being involved with religious matters between Judaism and Christianity. First of all, it is true that Paul was a Jew, but he declared **"I will go to the Gentiles"** (Acts 18:6b).[46] Paul's announcement would have clarified that the dispute did not occur in the Jewish community. In addition, as Winter argues, "Gallio was 'meticulous' as a lawyer."[47] He should have known Claudius's edict (18:2)[48] so may have wanted to follow the Emperor's way, viz., expelling them.[49] But anyhow, Gallio's reason is clear: "I will not receive matters of 'words, names/people, and your own law' as legal cases." Gallio, who knew very well that Jewish law was at the core of this, mentioned "words" first, originally *logou*, of which Winter accepts as its meaning "a declaration of legal immunity" in the *Revised Supplement to Liddell and Scott* (1996).[50] However, this word cannot only be defined as "common talk, report, tradition" or "rumour"[51] but also "divine utterance, oracle"[52] according to the context. In 18:5, it is expressed that Paul was occupied with the Word, the divine agent. Consequently, Paul's ministry should be related to the Word; and further, Gallio could have employed the same word to summarize Paul's ministry. Therefore, we can

44. Why does *kritēs* have nominative, not accusative, as a complement of *einai*? Culy and Parsons 2003: 351 explain, "When (at least some) verbs of wishing are modified by an infinitival construction with εἰμί and an unexpressed subject of the infinitive, the predicate of εἰμί occurs in the nominative rather than accusative case (see also Mark 10:44; Matt 19:21; 20:27//Mark 9:35; for examples with an expressed subject of the infinitive, see Rom 16:19; 1 Cor 7:7, 32)."

45. Witherington 1998: 555. Similarly, Bruce 1988: 353, etc.

46. So also Winter 2006: 306.

47. Winter 2006: 307.

48. See also Winter 2006: 303.

49. In considering Seneca the younger's description of his elder brother, that is, "He would not unmask you, but he would reject you," Winter 2006: 302 says that Luke's report reflects "that he [Gallio] handled the Jews during the actual proceedings by unmasking the plaintiffs but in this case rejecting them as the law required in any criminal action if there was no case to answer."

50. Winter 2006: 305, 305n51. See Glare 1996: 198.

51. LSJ 1058.

52. LSJ 1059.

infer from Gallio's refusal that "the Jews had no legal case to bring against the Christians under Roman law,"[53] which was the matter between the two religions, Judaism and Christianity.

Gallio's refusal to judge prompted all the Jews to seize Sosthenes, the ruler of the synagogue (Acts 18:17a). As mentioned above, Sosthenes seems to be "the successor or former colleague of Crispus"[54] and can be identified with the Sosthenes in 1 Cor 1:1. In regard to those who beat Sosthenes, there are textual variants: "According to the Alexandrian text, the people who were responsible for beating Sosthenes are not defined . . . Codex Bezae [or the Western text in a broad sense], on the other hand, is clear that the people who took Sosthenes were Greeks."[55] The Western texts has the reading of "all the Greeks," which might be a text emendation caused by the incomprehensibility of why the Jews would beat their own ruler, and thus in order to respond to the query, writing that the Greeks, not the Jews, beat the ruler of the synagogue. Then, why would "all," who can be identified in the previous verse as "the expelled Jews,"[56] beat their leader? Schnabel rightly proposes that the "disappointed members took out their frustration against Sosthenes for the way he had handled the legal case."[57] Well, at least in their view.

Seizing and beating, grabbing and smacking, this terrible commotion was not enough to grab Gallio's attention (Acts 18:17b). Gallio might not have thought of their violent behaviors as **crime or wicked wrongdoing** (18:14) but as a simple response of an argument. Sosthenes became the political scapegoat. As for Paul, the Lord's promise given to Paul, **no one will lay a hand on you to harm you** (18:10), was fulfilled; no one laid a hand on Paul to harm him. Furthermore, Sosthenes who was persecuted instead of Paul became an important leader, significant enough to be written as a sender in an epistle (1 Cor 1:1). This is the way the Lord handles his church; the Lord keeps his promise in many ways

53. Winter 2006: 303. To get this statement, he presupposes that the plural demonstrative pronoun in 18:17 refers to "words, names/people, and the law, your own." However, without this presupposition, we can still state that Gallio compared Judaism with Christianity.

54. Bruce 1990: 397. So also Rius-Camps and Read-Heimerdinger 2007: 381; Schnabel 2012: 765, etc. *Contra* Myrou 1999: 207–12, who identifies Sosthenes with Crispus in Acts 18:8 and 1 Cor 1:1.

55. Rius-Camps and Read-Heimerdinger 2007: 381.

56. See also Rius-Camps and Read-Heimerdinger 2007: 381.

57. Schnabel 2012: 765.

and to people like Simon of Cyrene, the father of Alexander, and Rufus (Mark 15:21) takes care of anyone who was persecuted for the gospel even not by his or her own will.

The Dawn of the Church in Ephesus (18:18–28)

Paul stayed in Corinth for a sufficient number of days, probably "for six months or more,"[58] even after the Jews' legal action against Paul had been rejected (Acts 18:18a): in the meantime, he should have done something **to strengthen the souls of the disciples and to exhort them to remain fixed to the faith** (14:22) as he had done at the end of his first mission trip. Then **he said goodbye to the brothers and set sail for Syria, and with him Priscilla and Aquila** (18:18b).

Why did Silas, Timothy, and Luke not join him to Syria? As we have said, Luke seems to have stayed in Philippi until Paul visited there after the ministry in Ephesus (cf. Acts 16:40). Silas and Timothy came back from Macedonia (18:5) and then probably stayed with Paul in Corinth; they appear as the senders of the Second Epistle to the Thessalonians (2 Thess 1:1). On this account, we can conjecture that when Paul departed from Corinth, Silas and Timothy remained in Corinth while Luke was in Philippi. Instead of them, Priscilla and Aquila accompanied Paul partly up to Ephesus. It was about the autumn of 51 CE or the spring of 52 CE.

Paul stopped by Cenchreae (9 km on foot from Corinth), a seaport of Corinth that "leads straight to Asia,"[59] and before departure **he had cut his hair, for he was under a vow** (Acts 18:18c). Some queries about this vow have been raised; namely, whether or not this vow started or finished at Cenchreae, the underlying cause for the vow, the characteristics of the vow, the feasibility of cutting hair outside Jerusalem. In regard to the first query, Johnson suggests this vow started at Cenchreae and finished "at least two years" later—but if Paul cut his hair about the autumn of 51 CE or the spring of 52, the event in 21:24 occurred around five years later—in Jerusalem (21:24).[60] However, as Marshall says, "There is no evidence that this [cutting of hair] could be done at the beginning of a vow."[61] Moreover, if Paul's vow had begun in Cenchreae, he should not

---

58. Bruce 1990: 397.
59. Strabo, *Geogr.* 8.6.20.
60. Johnson 1992: 330.
61. Marshall 1980B: 318.

have touched the corpse of Eutychus (20:10) and should not have taken part in the Eucharist (20:11). It is better to think of this cutting as an action for ending a vow, rather than the one for beginning a vow; it is also better to uncover the reason behind this vow from the events in the past rather than in the future: as Peterson suggests, the reason the vow could be attributed to "the Lord's promise of protection from danger and Paul's determination to stay in the city and keep preaching (vv. 9–11)."[62] Bruce says more confidently: "Paul's cutting his hair at Cenchreae was probably an expression of thanksgiving to God for his protection, which had enabled him to complete his ministry at Corinth, in fulfilment of the promise of v. 10."[63]

In connection with the possibility of cutting hair outside Jerusalem, Marshall insists that "the shaving of the hair was permissible elsewhere (M.Nazir 3:6; 5:4)."[64] However, references do not refer to his statement. Hence, it would be better to consider as Bruce thinks: "Paul's present vow was rather a private religious exercise, not conforming to the require-ments of a Nazirite vow, which in any case could not be observed outside the land of Israel, because of the constant exposure to defilement in a Gentile environment (m*Nazir* 7.3; cf. 3.6)."[65] Understanding Paul's vow as a "private religious exercise" seems adequate since the other two vows in Acts are related to personal purposes: one appears in Acts 21:23 (**four men who had a vow on themselves**); the other occurs in 23:12, 14, 21 (those who separated themselves to kill Paul).

Hence we can come to a conclusion: If Paul's haircut in Acts 18:18 was done to be released from a vow to the Lord, that *personal* vow could have started in Corinth, possibly due to his repentance over concealing the Messiahship of Jesus from them, his decision about concentrating only on the gospel of Christ, and *his thanksgiving to Jesus on his promise for protection*.

At last Paul and the couple came to Ephesus (380 km via ship from Cenchreae); **and he [Paul] left them [the couple] there** [possibly at their house; cf. 1 Cor 16:19],[66] **and he himself went into the synagogue and**

62. Peterson 2009: 519.

63. Bruce 1990: 398.

64. Marshall 1980B: 318.

65. Bruce 1990: 398.

66. Alternatively *autou* may refer to Ephesus herself: "Paul may have parted com-pany with Priscilla and Aquilla when they landed in Ephesus and then headed for the synagogue, or αὐτοῦ may refer to Ephesus in a sort of parenthetical proleptic clause"

conversed with the Jews (Acts 18:19). Maybe Paul wanted to protect the couple from the expected harmful effects of the Jews not only because his full-scale ministry in Ephesus was not planned at the time of this visit but also because the couple themselves were not primitively missionaries but primarily merchants.

The Jews in Ephesus responded positively at the first stage: **they asked Paul to stay for a longer period** (Acts 18:20a). Luke does not mention what Paul said, but taking the ministry in Corinth in consideration we may expect that Paul did not delay talking about the Messiahship of Jesus. In spite of this positive response, Paul declined: **But on taking leave of them he said, "I will return to you when or if[67] God wills," and he set sail from Ephesus** (18:20b–21). Lake and Cadbury insist, in relation to "if God wills," that "strange as it may seem this is a heathen rather than a Jewish formula" and that "there is no evidence for its use by Jews in Biblical or Talmudic times."[68] However, this expression is important both in the Lord's prayer in Matt 6:10b and in his Gethsemane prayer in 26:39 (par. Mark 14:36; Luke 22:42). Moreover, this expression appears in 2 Macc 12:16 and *Ant.* 2.333, 348. What's more, in Luke-Acts this expression appears strategically as to formulate another concept of this prayer: to begin with, "God's will be done" cannot be found in the Lord's prayer in Matthew but can be in Luke 11:2–4; second, it is stated in Jesus' prayer at "the place," "Father, if thou be willing, remove this cup from me: nevertheless not my will, but thine, be done" (22:40a, 42, KJV); lastly, this expression is employed in Acts particularly related to Paul, in this passage and Acts 21:24 (Paul's companions and the Christians in Caesarea prayed, **The Lord's will be done**). Thus, Luke's strategic usage of "the Lord's will be done" could connote the following: if the Lord's will be done, someone can die; Jesus died after praying this prayer; Paul was about to die after this prayer had been prayed.

Paul did set sail from Ephesus. This was his second journey. And almost three years could have passed after he had departed from Syrian Antioch in 49 CE for this secondary journey. Paul might have strongly felt it necessary to report to the Syrian Antioch church on what had

---

(Culy and Parsons 2003: 353).

67. *Tou theou thelontos* is seen as conditional (Wallace 1996: 633) or temporal (Culy and Parsons 2003: 354). In general, this present participle is translated into the "if" clause: however, the "when" clause seems to better express this participle because Paul seems to be concerned about the time, not about whether or not.

68. Lake and Cadbury 1933: 231.

happened during that journey, and even to the Jerusalem church, especially for Silas.[69] So **having come down to Caesarea** [990 km via ship from Ephesus], **he went up and greeted the [Jerusalem] church** [100 km on foot from Caesarea] **and then went down to Antioch** [490 km on foot from Jerusalem] (Acts 18:22). Paul took this journey alone. Lake and Cadbury think Paul went down to Caesarea[70] because "the winds prevalent in the summer rendered a journey to Caesarea easier than one to Antioch."[71] However, if Paul's voyage to Caesarea was caused by the winds, he would not have visited Jerusalem since he could have gone straight to Antioch from Caesarea directly: then over 200 kilometers would have been reduced from his 1,580 kilometer trip.

Paul arrived at the church that sent Silas and him off, but could not have spent a long time there (Acts 18:23a) because his mission partner Silas was in Corinth and the others, Timothy and Luke, were still in mission, in Corinth and in Philippi; so **he left and went through the region of Galatia and Phrygia, strengthening all the disciples** (18:23b). He passed through the region of his first trip; this is a similar situation to the one mentioned from 15:41 to 16:6. But some differences can be observed: first, Paul was unaccompanied; second, he was going straight to Ephesus so he did not stop by the Syrian and Cilician churches (cf. 15:41); for the same reason, he passed through southern Galatia (Derbe, Lystra, Iconium, and Antioch) and Phrygia, where in the meantime some churches should have been established. His ministry in these regions might have been done around the summer of 52 CE.

At this point Luke inserts an episode on the firstfruits in Ephesus (Acts 18:24–28):[72] **a Jew named Apollos, a native of Alexandria, arrived in Ephesus; he was a learned man [or an eloquent speaker], well-versed in the Scriptures; this man had been instructed in the Way of the Lord and boiling in spirit/Spirit he spoke and taught accurately**

69. Ramsay 1975 [1897]: 264 conjectures that Paul could not have delayed in Ephesus because of the Passover, March 22, 53 CE, that drew near.

70. See comments on 10:1–23a.

71. Lake and Cadbury 1933: 231.

72. Culy and Parsons 2003: 354 divide the text between 18:23 and 18:24, following Levinsohn 2000: 178–79, who thinks "that Apollos' earlier ministry in Ephesus (18:24ff.) provides the general background to the new episode" starting 19:1. So also Conzelmann, Marshall, Bruce, Bock, Pervo. Those who divide the text between 18:22 and 18:23 are Peterson and Fitzmyer. As for Williams and Wright, they see 18:18–28 as a unit.

the things concerning Jesus; [nevertheless] he knew only the baptism of John (18:24–25).

He is somewhat mysterious. First, the fact that he was an Alexandrian Jew does not reveal many things except that he could have been disciplined to think like a philosopher such as Philo.[73] Second, "learned" or "eloquent" may imply the formal education he received that included enhancing his rhetorical ability,[74] or just that he was "a man of culture."[75] Third, "well-versed in the OT" may mean "that he understands how the Scriptures make promises about the Christ (vv. 25, 28)"[76] or that he was "powerful in explaining them in sermons and effective in using biblical texts in debates."[77] Finally, the most mysterious one is how he merely knew the baptism of John even though he had previously been **instructed in the Way of the Lord and,** boiling in spirit/Spirit (*zeōn twpneumati*), **taught the things concerning Jesus accurately** (Acts 18:25). "The Way" of the Lord can function "as a symbol evoking the transformed foundation story of Israel found in Isaiah 40–55 in the construction of the identity of the community";[78] hence, he can be a Christian. Then how about "boiling in spirit/Spirit"? Most scholars connect this phrase with the Holy Spirit.[79] However, this stance is not in complete conformity with Apollos's knowledge merely on the baptism of John, and further with the characteristics of the disciples in Ephesus in 19:1–7. Even Bruce, who translated the phrase as "aglow with the Spirit," doubts: "It may seem strange, no doubt, that someone who was indwelt and empowered by the Spirit should nevertheless know nothing of Christian baptism."[80]

Apollos **began to speak boldly in the synagogue; but when Priscilla and Aquila heard him, they took him aside and expounded on the Way of God to him more accurately** (Acts 18:26). "Speaking boldly" is a piece of circumstantial evidence of one's fullness of the Holy Spirit in

73. However, we cannot go too much further only with this evidence (see Trebilco 2004: 115n56).

74. Schnabel 2012: 784 suggests: "He was both eloquent and cultured (the two meanings of the Greek term that suggest rhetorical training, which was an integral part of Greek and Roman education"); so also see Trebilco 2004: 115.

75. See Bruce 1990: 401.

76. Bock 2007: 591.

77. Schnabel 2012: 784.

78. Pao 2000: 68, 68n110.

79. E.g., Bruce 1990: 402; Witherington 1998: 565; Schnabel 2012: 785; etc.

80. Bruce 1988: 358–60.

Acts.[81] However, in this case it is a bit awkward to say so; he had boldness in speech but lacked something about the Way of God. Before Paul came back, Apollos **wished to cross over to Achaia**: and **the brothers encouraged [Apollos] and wrote**[82] **to the disciples to welcome him** (18:27a). Aquila and some of the people who came from Corinth at the time being may certainly be included in "the brothers"; this group of people could also be composed of those who had learned from Priscilla and Aquila, just as Apollos had.

Luke adds another episode on Apollos that would happen after Paul's arrival in Ephesus: **When he [Apollos] arrived, he by grace[83] greatly helped those who had believed; for he refuted the Jews vigorously in public, demonstrating from the Scriptures that the Messiah is Jesus** (Acts 18:27b–28). The content that **the Messiah is Jesus** was also previously important to Paul (18:5). The Corinthian churches had such a helpful minister. Bruce summarizes well the position of Apollos in Corinth:

> Some of the Corinthian Christians declared themselves his special followers (1 Cor 1:12; 3:4f.). Paul acknowledges that Apollos continued at Corinth the work which he himself had begun (1 Cor 3:6) and seems to appreciate him as a colleague with whom he stands on terms of mutual confidence (1 Cor 4:9). Paul met him some two years later in Ephesus and urged him (unsuccessfully) to pay a further visit to Corinth (1 Cor 16:12).[84]

---

81. See 9:27, 28; 13:46; 14:3; 19:8; 26:26; cf. 2:29; 4:13, 29, 31; 28:31.

82. Zerwick 1963 [2001]: 262, in regard to προτρεψάμενοι οἱ ἀδελφοὶ ἔγραψαν, says: "The sense may be that the brothers exhorted Apollo (first) and (afterwards) wrote, though the more obvious sense is that they wrote exhorting the disciples to receive him (two verbs referring to the same action)." So, it can be translated as "the brothers wrote exhorting the disciples to receive him."

83. In regard to διὰ τῆς χάριτος, Bruce 1990: 404 says that connecting it with συνεβάλετο, rather than with πεπιστευκόσιν, "makes better sense."

84. Bruce 1990: 404.

ACTS 19
Ministry in Ephesus

After finishing the ministry of strengthening the disciples in the region of Galatia and Phrygia (Acts 18:23b), Paul went directly to Ephesus, probably around the autumn of 52 CE. Trebilco estimates the population of Ephesus in the Roman period "at between 200,000–250,000" and wants to call this city "the third largest city in the Empire after Rome and Alexandria."[1] Murphy-O'Connor conjectures that Paul chose Ephesus as the core course of the third mission not only because it was "roughly equidistant from his churches in Achaia, Macedonia, and Galatia," but also because "as a capital city at the head of an excellent road system and with an important port it offered him superb communications."[2] Nevertheless, we should keep in mind that he had already said to the Ephesian Jews, **I will return to you when (or if) God wills** (18:21a). The guidance of God would surely have been involved in his coming back to Ephesus, just as it had been in the starting point of the secondary journey (16:6–10).

After revisiting the essential position of Asia Minor, Paul had stayed there three years, probably from the autumn of 52 CE to the summer of 55 CE (Acts 20:31). Those three years were "the longest stable period of ministry without trial or expulsion"[3] in Acts. During this term the first Corinthian correspondence was written probably in the spring of 55 CE; then "Paul's sorrowful visit to Corinth (2 Cor 2:1; 13:2)" (summer of 55 CE), "Titus' reconciling mission in Corinth (2 Cor. 2:13; 7:5–16)" (summer or autumn of 55 CE), "Paul in Troas (2 Cor. 2:12)" (autumn of 55

---

1. Trebilco 1994: 307. It is more feasible that Syrian Antioch had the position of the third largest city of the Roman world: "Ancient sources range from 600,000 (Pliny *HN* 6.122 for Seleucia Ctesiphon's population) to 200,000 (Chrysostom *Pan. Ign.* 4)" (*ABD* 265).

2. Murphy-O'Connor 2008: 187.

3. Witherington 1998: 572.

CE), and "Paul in Macedonia and Illyricum"[4] (Acts 20:1–2; Rom 15:19) (winter of 55–Autumn of 56 CE) followed.[5]

While Paul stayed in Ephesus, Marcus Junius Silanus, the proconsul, was murdered in 54 CE by Publius Celer and Helius. They were sent by Agrippina (Claudius's niece, his fourth wife, and Nero's mother), who was worried that Silanus, "the son of a great-grandchild of Augustus," would avenge his brother's death (Tacitus, *Ann*. 13.1) and that Silanus would "be preferred to Nero" by the people (Dio Cassius, *History* 61.6.5). When Paul started his mission in Ephesus, Claudius (41–54 CE) was the emperor, but on the occasion of finishing it, Nero (54–68 CE) took the position; this is important because Asia had been a senatorial province after 27 BCE to the time of Paul but had been influenced by the emperors since Augustus.[6]

First Stage (19:1–7)[7]

First of all, Luke points out that while Apollos was in Corinth, Paul re-visited Ephesus, and that Paul found some disciples there. In the process he mentions the fact that Paul passed through the inland of the upper regions (Acts 19:1). In other words, Paul "did not take the main road through the Lycus and Maeander valleys but a higher road farther north, which left the main road at Apamea (modern Dinar) and approached Ephesus from the north side of Mt. Messogis (modern Aydin Dağlari)."[8] Paul's taking a detour may indicate that he wanted to arrive in Ephesus via a way not blocked by any ministry in some intervening cities. If he had wanted to evangelize other cities, he would have taken the main road; however, he chose a road that was a bit farther and more silent. It seems that Paul went directly to Ephesus, possibly in order to focus just on the mission in Ephesus.

4. Illyricum signifies "a vast area lying between the Danube on the N. [North] and Macedonia and Thrace on the S. [South], extending from the Adriatic and the Alps to the Black Sea, and inhabited by a number of warlike and semi-civilized tribes known to the Greeks under the general title of Illyrians" (*ISBE* 3:1449).

5. Bruce 1990: 93. For a slightly different chronology, see Schnabel 2012: 792–93.

6. Trebilco 1994: 298n20 says that "Asia however, seems to have regarded Augustus rather than the Senate as its ruler and subsequent emperors were certainly also involved in the affairs of the province."

7. As regards the spiritual status of the Ephesians in this passage, see Cho 2005: 154–59.

8. Bruce 1990: 405.

Having intended to go straight to Ephesus, Paul met some disciples arriving there. The disciples must have resembled Apollos. Paul asked them whether or not they received the Holy Spirit when they believed (Acts 19:2a). Schnabel interprets this query well: "Since Paul believed and taught that being a Christian and receiving God's Spirit is one and the same reality, his opening question expresses suspicion, designed to reveal whether they are Christians or not."[9] They answered: "Rather, we have not even heard whether there is a Holy Spirit" (19:2b).[10] The OT has "some idea of the Spirit of God, sometimes called his 'Holy Spirit.'"[11] In addition, John the Baptist declared clearly that one more powerful than he "will baptize you [people] with the Holy Spirit and fire" (Luke 3:16). So they may have had a notion of the Holy Spirit and may have waited for its baptism, but they may not have known yet that this baptism had already begun; in other words, "They were ignorant of Pentecost."[12]

Thus Paul asked a question of confirmation: **Into what then were you baptized?** (Acts 19:3a). In the letter to the Corinthians, written in Ephesus, Paul says to the Corinthian Christians that "in one Spirit we were all baptized into one body" (1 Cor 12:13a). It was important to him "into what someone was baptized." According to the previous verse, the "one body" referred to "Christ": so Paul seems to have wanted to know if they were baptized into the Christ.

"To baptize" basically means "to dip or plunge";[13] hence, the Christ must be bigger than all the Christians in order for them to be dipped into him. In John's Gospel this is expressed as "I am in my Father and you are in me" (John 14:20a). This is possible only when Jesus is bigger than all the disciples put together. Jesus' greatness guarantees the oneness of the church. Further, this baptism is parallel to the fullness of the Holy Spirit: so in 1 Cor 12:13b, "whether Jews or Greeks or slaves or free, we were all made to drink of the one Spirit" is added; John 14:20b has "and I am in

9. Schnabel 2012: 788,n28 provides verses Rom 8:9, 1 Cor 12:3, Gal 3:2–3, 1 Thess 1:5–6, Tit 3:5, Acts 11:17, and 1 Pet 1:2 as evidences.

10. Wallace 1996: 312 suggests three options as a translation of οὐδ' εἰ πνεῦμα ἅγιον ἔστιν ἠκούσαμεν: "(1) 'We have not heard whether there is a Holy Spirit'; (2) 'we have not heard whether the Holy Spirit was [given]' (cf. John 7:39); or (3) 'we have not heard whether a spirit can be holy.'" We prefer the second translation.

11. Bruce 1990: 363n9, who as references provides Num 11:16–17, 24–29, Joel 2:28–32, and Isa 63:10–11.

12. Stott 1990: 304.

13. LSJ 305.

you"; likewise, this episode in Acts 19:1–7 contains baptism (19:5) and fullness (19:6) of the Holy Spirit.

In the process of the disciples' baptism and drinking of the Holy Spirit, Paul first recognized that they had been baptized into[14] John's baptism, not into Jesus' (19:3b); then Paul reminded them of the characteristics of John's baptism, that is, "the baptism of repentance," and of John's teaching on "the one who was to come after him," which would include the baptism of the Holy Spirit and fire (Luke 3:16); finally, Paul linked "the one who was to come" with Jesus (19:4). Eventually, the disciples whom Paul met should have concluded that they should now be baptized with the Holy Spirit via Jesus. Thus the narrator naturally continues that **when they heard this, they were baptized in the name of the Lord Jesus** (19:5). This result reminds us of the Pentecost: **when Paul laid hands on them, the Holy Spirit came upon them, and they began to speak in tongues and to prophesy** (19:6). Owing to this verse, Peterson thinks Luke "affirms the fulfillment of Joel 2:28–29 for this particular group of people,"[15] so called "a mini-Pentecost."[16]

Luke finishes the episode with a remark on the number of the disciples: **there were twelve men in all** (Acts 19:7). Some read a symbolic meaning in "twelve,"[17] but others do not.[18] Symbolism should not be completely excluded from this number, first because this "considerable number of family members"[19] probably became "the nucleus of the Ephesian church" and also because "Ephesus was to be a new center for the Gentile mission—the next in importance after Antioch on the Orontes."[20] Paul took in a good number of John the Baptist's disciples, just as Jesus did at

---

14. εἰς of εἰς τὸ Ἰωάννου βάπτισμα may not be used for "instrumental" (*contra* Zerwick 1963 [2001]: 33) but for "usual" usage, that is, "with verbs of motion when the motion and the accusative case combined with εἰς ('in') to give the resultant meaning of 'into,' 'unto,' 'among,' 'to,' 'towards' or 'on,' 'upon,' according to the context" (Robertson 2010 [1934]: 593).

15. Peterson 2009: 532.

16. Stott 1990: 305; so also Bruce 1988: 364, who describes it as "in pentecostal fashion."

17. E.g., Johnson 1992: 338 strongly insists: "he clearly intends this one [number] to symbolically represent a realization of 'Israel' (compare Acts 1:15—2:13)."

18. E.g., Bock 2007: 600, who also says insistently: "There is no symbolism in the number, especially given the estimation."

19. Peterson 2009: 533.

20. Bruce 1988: 365.

first (John 1:35–42); interestingly Paul's three-year ministry in Ephesus can be parallel to Jesus' three-year public ministry.

Second Stage (19:8–20)

The twelve converts could have been Jews or at least proselytes in that they had been baptized into John's baptism. So they could have been members of the synagogue and the ones who paved the way for Paul's ministry there: **So entering the synagogue, he [Paul] spoke out fearlessly for three months, conversing with and convincing people about the Kingdom of God** (Acts 19:8). Beforehand he just conversed with the Jews (18:19); but at this time he both conversed with and convinced the Jews of the kingdom of God. Domestic tranquility lasted three months, which was quite a long time in comparison with the ministry in Thessalonica that lasted for three-weeks (17:2), as well as with the case in Corinth where the opposition arose on that very day when Paul proclaimed the gospel (18:6).

Three months later, however, strong opposition to Paul's teaching arose from the Jews against Paul: **some became hardened and refused to believe, reviling the Way before the congregation** (Acts 19:9a). Relatively speaking, the Jews in Ephesus do not seem to have opposed the gospel as vigorously as those in Pisidian Antioch or Thessalonica. Nevertheless, on account of the opposition of the Jews in the synagogue, Paul found a new place for ministry: **leaving them, he [Paul] separated the disciples and conversed with them everyday in the lecture hall of Tyrannus** (19:9b). "Tyrannus" could be a personal name[21] since this name "is inscribed on a column in the Prytaneum as one of a list of Curetes."[22] Just as Titius Justus's house performed the function of a mission center in Corinth, so also did Tyrannus's lecture hall serve the same function. Tyrannus, in this sense, could have been a believer; otherwise, Paul could have rented it. The "separated" (*aforizō*) disciples may include the twelve converts.

This lecture-hall ministry lasted for two years and achieved marvelous results: **all who settled in the province of Asia, both Jews and Greeks, heard the Word of the Lord** (Acts 19:10). As Bruce says, "all seven of the churches of Asia addressed in the Apocalypse" (Rev 2–3) and

---

21. Bruce 1990: 408 associates Tyrannus with a personal name.
22. Hemer and Gempf 1989: 120–21n53.

"the churches of the Lycus valley, at Colossae, Hierapolis, and Laodicea" (Col 1:2; 2:1; 4:13) could have been founded at this period.[23]

After sketching out Paul's ministry in Ephesus, Luke then provides several other clips, particularly on the power ministry of Paul in Ephesus (Acts 19:11–12), the Jewish exorcists (19:13–16), and the vindication of the gospel (19:17–19); then, the third major summary verse follows (19:20).

The power ministry of Paul in Ephesus was based on God's deeds: **God was performing miracles, which cannot be met easily** [(or could be also translated as) performing extraordinary miracles], **by Paul's hands, so that even when handkerchiefs or aprons that had touched his skin were brought to the sick, their diseases left them and the evil spirits went out [from them]** (Acts 19:11–12). "Handkerchiefs and aprons" would have been "used in his tent-making or leather-working—the sweat-rags for tying around his head and the aprons for tying around his waist"[24] or could have been a "part of the uniform of an orator."[25] The latter seems to be more suitable for the context because it is said that Paul conversed with the disciples everyday (19:9). The reading of Codex Bezae for this verse also seems to support this latter notion. This Codex provides information about the teaching time as "from the fifth hour to the tenth," which "corresponds to 11am to 4pm, the hottest hours of the day, perhaps a time when the hall was not required by other teachers";[26] through this addition it is stressed that Paul would have been sweating due to the heat of the lecture building.

Anyhow, this phenomenon may indicate that "Paul's bodily fluid is stronger than that of the demons":[27] Bruce connects this description with "the healing of those who touched the fringe of Jesus' cloak (Mark 5:27–34; 6:56)" and with "the healing effect of Peter's shadow in Acts 5:15."[28] God's power was so powerful as to have influence even on Paul's sweat, which echoes the bones of Elisha in 2 Kgs 13:21: a corpse of a man was thrown into the grave of Elisha, and as soon as it touched the bones of Elisha, he revived and stood on his feet.

23. Bruce 1990: 409.
24. Bruce 1988: 367.
25. Strelan 2003: 155.
26. Rius-Camps and Read-Heimerdinger 2009: 37, 40.
27. Strelan 2003: 156.
28. Bruce 1988: 367.

Paul's power ministry was mimicked: **some Jewish exorcists who traveled about attempted to address the name of the Lord Jesus over those who were possessed by evil spirits, saying, "I make you swear by Jesus whom Paul preaches"** (Acts 19:13). Their habit reveals the general usefulness of addressing Jesus' name for exorcizing evil spirits. However, a transition occurred owing to an event that happened to Sceva's seven sons.[29] Even though Sceva is called "a Jewish high priest," it could be "his self-designation, set out on a placard."[30] So 19:14 can be translated as **seven sons of a man named Sceva, so called "a Jewish high priest," were doing this.**[31] One day **the evil spirit replied to them, "Jesus I know and I am acquainted with Paul, but who are you?" Then the man, in whom the evil spirit was, jumping and beating them all**[32] **into submission, prevailed against them so that they fled from that house**[33] **naked and wounded** (19:15–16).

It can never be over-emphasized that the evil spirit's utterances should not be trusted: if the spirit really knew Jesus and was acquainted with Paul, why did it not repent of being evil to be "good"? So when translating *ginōskō* ("know") and *epistamai* ("recognize"), verbs such as "be influenced or be controlled" need to be substituted for "know or be acquainted" because in reality the evil spirit was influenced or controlled by Jesus or Paul. In addition, this event shows that Paul's power ministry did not take effect simply through copying and pasting.

The event of Sceva's sons **became known to all who lived in Ephesus, both Jews and Greeks; fear came over them all, and the name of the Lord Jesus was extolled** (Acts 19:17). Fear brings a community much

29. Because of this event, it is possible that "the use by Jews of Jesus' name in healing was sternly denounced by some rabbis" (Bruce 1988: 368n32).

30. Bruce 1988: 368. So he suggests that "Luke might have placed the words between quotation marks."

31. The names of Jewish high priests from 4 BCE to 58 CE are as follows: Eleazar (c. 4–3 BCE), Jesus (c. 3 BCE–6 CE), Joazar (6 CE), Annas (Luke 3:2; John 18:13–24; Acts 4:6; 6–15 CE), Ishmael (15–16 CE), Eleazar (16–17 CE), Simon (17–18 CE), Joseph Caiaphas, son-in-law of Annas (Matt 26:3, 57; Luke 3:2; John 11:49; 18:13–14, 24, 28; Acts 4:6; 18–36 CE), Jonathan (36–37 CE), Theophilus (37–41 CE), Simon Kantheras (41–42 CE), Matthias (42–43 CE), Elioenai (43–44 CE), Joseph (44–47 CE), Ananias (Acts 23:2; 24:1; 47–58 CE) (Bruce 1990: 94–95).

32. *Amfoterōn* refers to "all seven of the sons of Scephas, the Jewish exorcists mentioned in verse 14": this happens as a result of "the obsolescence in Hellenistic Greek of the category of duality" (Zerwick 1963 [2001]: 153).

33. Culy and Parsons 2003: 367 view *ek tou oikou ekeinou* "as a shorter equivalent of 'the house where they had been.'"

progress with the gospel.[34] Schnabel reads "further conversions among the Jews and Greeks in the city" in this verse and v. 20.[35] Furthermore, this event resulted in repentance of "partially socialized Christians who did not immediately give up all their old religious practices when they converted."[36] **Many of those who had already believed[37] came, confessing and making their deeds known; large numbers of those who had practiced magic collected their scrolls and burned them up in the presence of everyone** (19:18–19a). Marshall describes this situation well:

> Christians are not fully converted or perfected in an instant, and pagan ways of thinking can persist alongside genuine Christian experience. . . . The demonstration of the futility of pagan attempts to master evil spirits led many of Paul's Ephesian converts to realize that the pagan magic to which they were still attached was both useless and sinful.[38]

The scrolls in flames can be seen as "the books in which the spells were written down and thus kept ready for use."[39] Ephesus seems to have had a special relation to magical practices, which "is reflected in the term Ἐφέσια γράμματα" found in "scrolls containing magical spells, like the famous magical papyri in the London, Paris, and Leiden collections."[40] These believers could have earned money by selling the scrolls but burned them. Before having turned into ashes, their value was calculated as "fifty thousand silver drachmas [or denarii]," "a single worker's wages for 137 years without a day off,"[41] "in excess of 8,300 weeks of labor (the weeks are calculated at six working days because of the Jewish cultural context)," worth fifty thousand sheep, since "one drachma could buy one sheep."[42]

---

34. See comments on 2:43 and 5:11.

35. Schnabel 2012: 798.

36. Witherington 1998: 582.

37. The perfect tense of *tōn pepisteukotōn* helps us to see these people as those who had already believed, not as new converts (see Marshall 1980B: 330; Witherington 1998: 582; contra Schnabel 2012: 798). So it is hard to see these believers as newly converted magicians (contra Bruce 1988: 369).

38. Marshall 1980B: 330.

39. Barrett 1998: 913.

40. Bruce 1990: 412.

41. Bock 2007: 605.

42. NET notes 2005: 2170.

After the illustrations of the power ministry of Paul in Ephesus (Acts 19:11–12), the Jewish exorcists (19:13–16), and the vindication of the gospel (19:17–19), the third major summary verse follows: **In this way the Word of the Lord continued to grow in power and to prevail** (19:20).[43] Together with 6:7a and 12:24, this is a very important summary verse; the strength of the Word increases in proportion to the purity of the repentance of believers as well as to God's power.

Third Stage (19:21–40)

The third missionary trip went well. Paul was still in Ephesus. In the meantime, some events took place: (1) Epaphras established churches in Colossae, Hierapolis, Laodicea (Col 1:7; 4:12); (2) Apollos came from Corinth to Ephesus (1 Cor 16:12) and Paul wrote the "Previous Letter" to the church in Corinth (5:9); (3) Chloe's people came from Corinth to Ephesus (1:11), but Timothy went from Ephesus to Corinth possibly with Paul's instruction (4:17); (4) Stephanas, Fortunatus, and Achaicus came from Corinth to Ephesus with a letter (16:17; 7:1).[44]

Then, Paul had a future plan in the Spirit **to go to Jerusalem, passing through Macedonia and Achaia; he said, "After I have been there, I must also see Rome"** (Acts 19:21). Some think that the phrase "in the Spirit" (*en tō pneumati*) refers to Paul's spirit or mind,[45] but many scholars consider it representing the Holy Spirit.[46] The latter view seems a better one to take: first, the divine must (*dei*) is engaged in the sentence; second, the further context supports the guidance of the Holy Spirit (see 20:22–23). The purpose of Paul's visiting Macedonia and Achaia was to collect "some contribution for the poor among the saints in Jerusalem" (Rom 15:26; cf. 1 Cor 16:1–3; 2 Cor 8–9; Acts 21:26; 24:17). Paul wanted to visit Jerusalem with "some generosity": probably in order to "remember the poor" (Gal 2:10); certainly in order for the Jewish churches to produce thanksgiving to God through the gentile churches (2 Cor 9:11); and possibly in order for the gentile churches to be joined and built together with the Jewish churches (Eph 2:21–22).

43. NASB translates this verse alternatively: "according to the power of the Lord the word was growing." Wright 2008: 116 translates it similarly: "the word of God grew and was strong in accordance with the power of the Lord."

44. Schnabel 2012: 793.

45. See Barrett 1998: 919; Fitzmyer 1998: 652.

46. See Marshall 1980B: 331; Bruce 1990: 413; Rapske 1994: 404; Walton 2000: 88.

Being scheduled to travel to Macedonia, Achaia, Jerusalem, and Rome, Paul appears to have written 1 Corinthians, where his future plans are told: "I will come to you after I have gone through Macedonia—for I will be going through Macedonia—and perhaps I will stay with you, or even spend the winter. . . . I will stay in Ephesus until Pentecost, because a door of great opportunity stands wide open for me, but there are many opponents" (1 Cor 16:5-6a, 8-9); the time of writing could be the spring of 55 CE[47] or 54 CE.[48] Paul seems to have sent Timothy and Erastus[49] to Macedonia right before or after writing 1 Corinthians: **he [Paul] himself stayed on for a while in the province of Asia** (Acts 19:22). The duties of Timothy and Erastus "would have included the task of preparing the congregations in Macedonia for Paul's farewell visit."[50] Then "Paul's sorrowful visit to Corinth (2 Cor. 2:1; 13:2)" (summer of 55 CE) and "Titus' reconciling mission in Corinth (2 Cor. 2:13; 7:5-16)" (summer or autumn of 55 CE)[51] might have occurred right before the riot in Ephesus (Acts 19:23-40).

According to 1 and 2 Corinthians, in Ephesus Paul "toiled harder than all of" the apostles (1 Cor 15:10) and was "burdened excessively, beyond strength, so as to despair even of living" (2 Cor 1:8b). In addition, he would have continually paid attention to the churches in Macedonia and Achaia and, despite not being mentioned, even to the churches in Galatia, Phrygia, and Cilicia; Paul jotted down that "there is the daily pressure on me of my anxious concern for all the churches" (11:28). The riot in Ephesus occurred at this period (autumn in 55 CE), probably in between two epistles to the Corinthian churches: **At that time no little[52] disturbance took place concerning the Way** (Acts 19:23). So the records in these two letters reveal what kinds of difficulties Paul had in Ephesus.

---

47. Bruce 1990: 93.

48. Schnabel 2012: 793.

49. Erastus could be the same person in 2 Tim 4:20, but probably not the one in Rom 16:23 because, as Marshall 1980B: 332 puts down, "it is doubtful whether a person who held an official post of this kind would have been free to move about on missionary work." See also Witherington 1998: 589-90.

50. Schnabel 2012: 801.

51. Bruce 1990: 93. For a slightly different chronology, see Schnabel 2012: 792-93.

52. Litotes.

There was a silversmith at the core of the riot: his name was Demetrius[53] **who, by making silver shrines of Artemis, brought no little**[54]
business to the craftsmen (Acts 19:24). As we have seen, Artemis was
worshiped in Ephesus in a special way and the temple of Artemis greatly
contributed toward the city economy. This man's business also had to do
with her temple. Hence, we can read money and business matters as the
reasons for the riot. Even though religious items were wrapped around
this financial matter, the essence of the problem for them was "Paul would
make us poor." The fear of these self-proclaimed Artemis lovers contrasts
to their fear in 19:17; financial matters seem to be stronger than religious
ones. In contrast, the followers of Jesus' repentance should have reached
the point where losing money was not important to them (19:18–19).

According to Rowe, Demetrius read "the prospective disintegra-
tion of religiously dependent economics" in Paul's theology: "That those
whose livelihood depends upon the Ephesian goddess should vigorously
defend her greatness is only natural."[55] In this sense, Demetrius can be
comparable to the religious leaders of Jerusalem in Jesus' time. For example, after Jesus demonstrated the characteristics that the Jerusalem
temple had (Luke 19:45–46), "the chief priests and the experts in the
law and the prominent leaders among the people sought to destroy him"
(19:47b). Temple traffickers were very actively involved in both of the
temples, holy and secular.

Demetrius, seen as "the head of the local guild of silversmiths,"
gathered fellow craftsmen along with workmen in similar trades (Acts
19:25a), "for example workers in lead, marble, and semiprecious stones."[56]
His speech consists of three primary arguments: (1) our wealth is based
on the temple of Artemis; (2) Paul's instructions on gods—namely that
things made by hands are not gods—put our wealth and its basis in
danger; (3) Artemis is the great goddess **whom all the province of Asia
and the world worship** (19:25b–27).

In order to understand his speech, we need to know about the fairy
tale behind Artemis. Ancient myths inform us of Artemis as follows:

---

53. Demetrius means "of or belonging to Demeter" (LSJ 385). Demeter was
thought of as a goddess, "the Grain Mother," by the Greeks.

54. Litetos.

55. Rowe 2012: 261.

56. Witherington 1998: 591.

Artemis was the virgin daughter of Leto and Zeus, the older twin of Apollo, and the goddess of the hunt. Although Zeus married Hera, he had had a sexual liaison with Leto, during which she conceived Zeus's twins—Artemis and Apollo. When the time came for Leto to give birth, she learned the full power of Hera's jealousy. Banned from Olympus, Leto discovered that no one would welcome her for fear of angering Hera. But eventually Leto took refuge in Ortygia, a site believed to he [sic] near Ephesus. There she gave birth to her first twin, a daughter. According to legend, at birth gods and goddesses had fully developed mental capacities, so this daughter, Artemis, was completely aware of her mother's travail during the delivery that followed. The difficult birth of Apollo took nine days, during which Artemis watched her mother writhe. As a result, Artemis had no desire to give birth herself, so she asked her father to make her immune to Aphrodite's arrows, a request that Zeus granted. Thus, Artemis, having special sympathy for women in travail from her first days, come to be associated with virginity and, especially in Ephesus, with midwifery.[57]

Artemis was perceived as a goddess of many things. On the basis of this myth and of some literary and epigraphic evidences, Glahn insists that "rather than viewing Artemis Ephesus as a fertility goddess or even as sexually active, people at the time of the earliest Christians appear to have seen in her the ability to deliver a woman through life's most dangerous passage, childbirth."[58] In addition, Artemis is known as "a 'forest goddess'; 'queen of all wild beasts'; a quiver-and-bow-carrying 'archer goddess'; and one 'not fated to be caught.'"[59] Artemis was also "worshipped because of her lordship over supernatural powers," acclaimed as Lady, Savior, a heavenly goddess, and the Queen of the Cosmos, and described as greatest, great, holiest, and most manifest.[60] This goddess was worshiped at least thirty-three places in the Roman world.[61] Apropos to this identity of Artemis, Hooker interprets "if according to a human [way of life] I fought with wild beasts at Ephesus, what did it benefit me"

---

57. Glahn 2015: 318–19.
58. Glahn 2015: 334.
59. Glahn 2015: 319.
60. Trebilco 2004: 22.
61. Trebilco 1994: 332.

(1 Cor 15:32a) as referring to Paul's proclaiming the gospel against the worship of Ephesian Artemis:

> It is highly probable that considerably earlier in his two-year stay in Ephesus Paul would have been seen as a threat to the worship of Artemis, and would have been involved in danger-ous confrontations with those who were devoted to her and whose livelihood he was thought to be undermining. . . . In proclaiming Jesus, rather than Artemis, he was, as *we* would say, putting his head into the lion's mouth. The riot described by Luke may have taken place *after* Paul wrote 1 Corinthians, but it could well have been the culmination of a series of incidents.[62]

Hooker's connection between "wild beasts" in 15:32a with Artemis is plausible; in other words, the "wild beasts" Paul fought with seems to connote Artemis.

Furthermore, the temple of Artemis had a huge amount of influence over "the economic structures of Ephesus and of the province of Asia": "large deposits of money were stored in the Temple"; "Artemis also had her own financial estate, which was one of the largest in Asia"; so the temple of Artemis can be seen as "the biggest bank in Asia."[63] As Rowe more broadly describes, "It functioned not only as a 'house of worship,' but also as the arbiter for regional disputes, a bank, a holding facility for important civic archives, and an asylum for debtors, runaway slaves, and other persons in dire trouble."[64]

Artemis was the most important figure to the Ephesians not only religiously but also socially and economically; and consequently, Demetrius's warning about the dangers of Paul's theology was convincing enough to infuriate those craftsmen and workmen, especially whose livelihood depended upon the temple, and triggered them to shout, **Great is Artemis of the Ephesians!** (Acts 19:28). This slogan had made them wealthy so it should have been continually proclaimed and trusted. Why? The answer is clear: "for their private affluence." They seem to have gone around the whole city so as to agitate all the citizens: **the city was filled with the uproar, and they [the citizens] rushed to the theater**

---

62. Hooker 2013: 45–46 (italics original).
63. In detail, see Trebilco 2004: 25–26.
64. Rowe 2012: 261.

with one accord, dragging with them Gaius[65] **and Aristarchus,**[66] **the Macedonians who were Paul's traveling companions** (19:29). Demetrius tried to use mob violence to attack Paul's view of God; so did the religious leaders in Jerusalem (Luke 23:18, 21, 23). The silversmith took Paul's two companions, maybe because "there was no time for a systematic search for Paul."[67] Or he might have feared Paul's spiritual abilities (Acts 19:11–12); he dragged away less "effective" men, just as the crowds in Lystra had only stoned Paul, regarded as Hermes, a lower deity, but not Barnabas, who, even for a temporary moment, was believed to be Zeus (14:19).

The citizens gathered within "the great theater in Ephesus[68] which was carved out of the side of Mount Pion, was 495 feet [150.88 meters] in diameter, and could hold close to twenty-five thousand people."[69] When Gaius and Aristarchus were in danger of coming to actual bodily harm, Paul heard of it and **was willing to appear before the citizen-body**[70] (Acts 19:30a). Paul was used to suffering (cf. 2 Cor 11:23–27); as a person of sufferings he knew how difficult suffering is; that would be the reason that he threw himself in again; he would not have wanted his companions to be substituted for himself. In spite of Paul's willingness, disciples and friends stopped Paul from entering into the theater: **the disciples did not permit** Paul to enter the public assembly, **and Asiarches**[71] **who were his friends sent [a special messenger] to him, urging him not to venture into the theater** (Acts 19:30b–31). The disciples and Paul's high-ranking friends seem to have prepared a solution to deal with this riot, one brought by the city secretary (19:35–40).

In the meantime, the theater was in a state of turmoil: **So then some were shouting one thing, some another; for the assembly was in confusion, and most of them did not know why they had assembled together**

---

65. This Gaius may refer to the Gaius in 1 Cor 1:14 and Rom 16:23, but not to Gaius from Derbe in 20:4 (see Witherington 1998: 594).

66. This Aristarchus occurs in 20:4 and 27:2 again and "may be the same as the Aristarchus mentioned in Col 4:10 and Philem. 24" (Witherington 1998: 594).

67. Witherington 1998: 594.

68. "The first theater in Ephesus was built sometime in the first decades after Asia became a Roman province in 133 B.C.E., but need expansion in the first half of the first century CE" (Murphy-O'Connor 2008: 93).

69. Witherington 1998: 594.

70. Marshall 1980B: 337.

71. The Asiarches were members of "a wealthy and influential group in the city at all periods" (Murphy-O'Connor 2008: 93).

(Acts 19:32). Demetrius, his fellow craftsmen, and related workmen could have gone on stage, probably with Gaius and Aristarchus. Tens of thousands of citizens might have packed into the stadium to deal with the matter abruptly raised; however, little did they know that they had been called to defend the welfare of these craftsmen.

At that time, the Jews pushed Alexander to the stage and he wanted to defend something (Acts 19:33), probably the fact that the Jews were different from the Christians even though "Jews were known to be opposed to idolatry and were unpopular in the Roman Empire."[72] But the Jews' attempt at defending themselves was unsuccessful, possibly because of the "general anti-Jewish agitation":[73] **recognizing that he [Alexander] was a Jew, they all shouted with one voice for about two hours, "Great is Artemis of the Ephesians!"** (19:34). This was the power of the mob. Also, this shouting reflected their close connection with Artemis. The Jews would not have shouted the same thing just as the mob: "At this point, Jews and Christians found themselves facing the same irrational and angry opposition."[74]

Unresolved tension mounted up in the city. And the city secretary or the town clerk, "the chief executive officer of the *dēmos*"[75] as "one of the highest local officials in Ephesus,"[76] appeared to preside over this uproarious matter (Acts 19:35a).[77] His speech could be explained in four parts, but all aim for dispersing the mob at the theater. First of all, he tried to break up the mob by indicating that their insistence is too general to be dealt with in the citizen-body: **Men of Ephesus, what person is there who does not know that the city of Ephesians is the temple keeper of the great Artemis and of what fell from Zeus?**[78] So because these

72. Peterson 2009: 549.

73. Bruce 1988: 377.

74. Peterson 2009: 549.

75. Bruce 1990: 420.

76. Trebilco 1994: 351.

77. "The 'assembly of the people' (*ekklēsia tou dēmou*) did in fact meet in the theater, and was headed by a *grammateus tou dēmou*" (Murphy-O'Connor 2008: 93).

78. τοῦ διοπετοῦς is often translated as "that fell from heaven or the sky," and this interpretation makes Rowe 2012: 262 conclude that "the official's point is thus clear: Paul's central criticism—'gods made by hands are not gods'—does not apply to Artemis, because, in actuality, the cultic object was not made by hands." However, this word basically has a root referring to Zeus so it means "that fell from Zeus" (LSJ 433) and no other. In addition, Demetrius and his fellows surely made silver shrines of Artemis *by hands* and they also admitted it (19:26b–27a). So the secretary's first point

things are indisputable, you must keep quiet and not do anything reckless (19:35b–36).

Then he dealt with Gaius and Aristarchus, insisting that they were innocent: **you have brought these men here who are neither temple robbers nor blasphemers of our goddess** (Acts 19:37). Just as Rowe points out, this could not have meant that "business is booming as usual."[79] If the business had really been booming as usual, why did Demetrius make his fellows enraged by mentioning the danger of an industrial decline? Together with the decline of the magical book business (19:19), the silver shrine business would also have been declining in Asia as well as in Ephesus.

The secretary's third point is that a legal action should follow legal requirements (Acts 19:38–39). He seems to be saying: Who is the accuser? If Demetrius and his fellows are the accuser,[80] come to the courts,[81] not to the theater. Then the proconsuls will deal with the charge. If the whole citizenry are the accuser, follow the correct procedure. Then that will be settled in a legal meeting of the citizens[82] here for sure.[83] The plural, "proconsuls," can be understood as "simply generic"[84] or "three deputies (*legati pro prætore*)"[85] of the proconsul (Marcus Junius Silanus) murdered in 54 CE: the latter seems to be more plausible.[86]

This third point would have affected the citizens emotionally. It may have made the audience frightened: the term "proconsuls" sounds scary enough to remind them about the death of the previous proconsul.

---

is not that "Artemis is not made by hands," but that "you need to be quiet."

79. Rowe 2012: 262.

80. Or they "have a complaint against someone" (BDAG 600).

81. *Agoraioi* basically refers to "the things pertaining to the market" (Culy and Parsons 2003: 380).

82. Chrysostom says that "there were three assemblies according to law in each month" (*Hom. Act.* 42; *NPNF*1 11:259); so also Bruce 1990: 421.

83. "The theatre in Ephesus was the regular meeting place of the assembly" (Trebilco 1994: 349).

84. Duncan 1929: 106.

85. Ramsay 1900: 335.

86. Duncan 1929: 106 suggests "that the two agents of the murder [Publius Celer and Helius] exercised proconsular authority until the arrival of the new governor." However, Ramsay 1900: 335 disagrees with him since the murderers "are not said to have taken over the authority of Julianus" and "they could not possibly have done so as 'proconsuls,' for Celer was only a knight and Helius a freedman." So also Bruce 1988: 379n82; Trebilco 2004: 163.

Moreover, it could remind them of an event that happened around ten year ago: "the Temple of Artemis was censured by the Romans during the reign of Claudius" and an edict concerning the Temple of Artemis was ordered around 44 CE; so we can perceive "the interest of the proconsul, and probably of the Emperor himself, in the welfare of the cult and temple of Artemis, and the proconsul's willingness to intervene to set matters right."[87]

Finally, with the secretary's last point, his goal is attained: **we are in danger of being charged with** rioting **for what has happened today,**[88] **since there is no cause we can give to account for this commotion** (19:40). This rioting (*stasis* in Greek) "means 'riot-interpreted-by-the-Romans-as-sedition'; i.e., a breach of the civic order required to sustain the *pax Romana*."[89] The city secretary was responsible not only for "keeping the records of the city" but also "drafting important documents which were submitted to the assembly and he often moved decrees or took the lead in the assembly, either alone or in conjunction with the board of magistrates."[90] This being the case, the mob had no reason to be gathered at the front of this official notice; they would not have wanted to lose "the peace of Asia that began with the reign of Augustus."[91] Consequently, the secretary succeeded in dispersing the mob.

---

87. Trebilco 1994: 344.

88. *Peri tēs sēmeron* can be translated as "for what has happened today" because "the article functions as a nominalizer . . . changing the adverb into a noun" (Culy and Parsons 2003: 370, 381).

89. Rowe 2012: 262.

90. Trebilco 1994: 351.

91. Trebilco 1994: 299: this peace of Asia "had lasted throughout the first century AD, and indeed continued throughout the second century."

ACTS 20
Recruiting Ministry in Greece and Asia

Paul's gospel of Jesus reached all the people in Asia Minor (Acts 19:10). Thereafter, Paul first planned to visit Macedonia, then Corinth and to remain there for quite a while, including the winter (1 Cor 16:5–6). However, his first plan seems to have changed; Paul undertook a second and sorrowful visit to Corinth before revisiting Macedonia (2 Cor 2:1; 13:2). After this second visit to Corinth, in Ephesus Paul devised a new plan, that is, to go back to Corinth first and then into Macedonia, next from Macedonia to Corinth again and then travel to Judea (and Jerusalem) (1:15–16). However, Paul did not succeed in sticking to this second scenario either; instead, Paul sent Titus to Corinth along with the "severe letter" (2:4, 13) to bring about a reconciliation between himself (Paul) and the Corinthian Christians (2:13; 7:5–16). After a time of hardship had passed in Ephesus, Paul went to Corinth after visiting Macedonia (Acts 20:1–3a); he ultimately carried out his premier plan.

According to Bruce, Paul arrived in Troas (2 Cor 2:12) in the autumn of 55 CE and, after going through Macedonia and Illyricum (Acts 20:1–2; Rom 15:19; from the winter of 55 CE to the autumn of 56 CE) and writing the Second Letter to the Corinthians,[1] he reached Achaia and wrote the Letter to the Romans (16:23) while spending the winter in Corinth (56–57 CE; Acts 20:2–3; Rom 15:25–28).[2]

Chapter 20 can be divided into four episodes: (1) Paul revisited Macedonia and Achaia (including Corinth), the places of his second missionary journey (Acts 20:1–2); (2) Paul had to return to Macedonia from Achaia on account of the Jews' plot to hurt him (20:3b); (3) Paul preached the Word and had fellowship with the Christians in Troas where he had not finished entirely in spite of a good opportunity (20:5–12; cf. 2 Cor

---

1. Schnelle 2005: 236 thinks that "2 Corinthians was probably written in the late autumn (cf. 8:10) of the year 55 CE in Macedonia (cf. 7:5; 8:1–5; 9:3–4)" (his references refer to 2 Corinthians).

2. Bruce 1990: 93. For a slightly different chronology, see Schnabel 2012: 792–93.

2:12–13); (4) Paul gave a farewell speech to the elders of the Ephesian church in Miletus first of all in order to encourage and strengthen them by reminding them about his past ministry among them, also to warn them by giving some information in advance about what was to come, and finally to entrust them to God and His gracious Word (Acts 20:17–38).

The four episodes add up to a one-and-a-half-year journey, and go under the title of "the recruiting ministry in Greece and Asia" for several reasons. First, via this journey Paul revisited Macedonia and Achaia and indirectly Ephesus. Second, the purpose of this journey was not only to strengthen the churches of the region but also to collect relief supplies for the Judean Christians (Acts 24:17; 1 Cor 16:1–4; 2 Cor 8–9; Rom 15:25–28). Paul had a notion that the gentiles "are indebted to them [the Jerusalem saints]; for if the Gentiles have shared in their [the Jerusalem saints'] spiritual things, they [the Gentiles] are obligated also to serve them [the Jerusalem saints] in material things" (15:27). Paying off their spiritual debts with material funds would free the gentiles to come together with the Jews.

Revisiting Macedonia and Achaia (20:1–4)

The commotion in Ephesus died down (Acts 20:1a): there is no record of any further accusations raised by Demetrius's party or by the Jews, so it is not plausible to think that Paul went through a special affliction such as illness, "fighting with beasts" in Ephesus,[3] or legal accusations by Demeterios or even by the Jews right after the rioting.[4] "The affliction that happened to us [them] in the province of Asia" in 2 Cor 1:8 could be describing a general situation in Ephesus or the rioting itself, not indicating a particular situation right after the rioting. Paul actually would have felt "the sentence of death" already at hand, since most of the citizens ran riot, and thus could not but confess God's salvation from "so great a risk of death" (1:9–10).

After the severe affliction elapsed, **Paul sent for the disciples, encouraged them, and said farewell** (Acts 20:1b). He always put himself in the shoes of the persecutors. He did so in Lystra (14:19), in Philippi (16:19), in Corinth (18:12), and intentionally in Ephesus, too (19:30). At

---

3. See comments on Demetrius's speech in 19:25b–27: Hooker 2013: 45–46 sees fighting with wild beasts in Ephesus in 1 Cor 15:32a as referring to Paul's proclaiming the gospel against the worship of Ephesian Artemis.

4. In detail, see Kruse 1987: 68–70.

the time of a shift in the situation of persecution, as usual, Paul comforted the disciples (20:1b; cf. 14:20, 22; 16:40; 18:18).

Saying farewell to the Ephesian Christians, **Paul left to go to Macedonia** (Acts 20:1c). He then arrived in Troas and waited for Titus, hoping to get positive responses from Corinthian Christians; however, not finding Titus there, he had no relief in his spirit (2 Cor 2:12–13). Still Paul went on and arrived in Macedonia. He could not rest though, neither physically nor mentally, owing to all kinds of troubles, "struggles from the outside, fears on the inside" (7:5).

Even so, Paul was encouraged in Macedonia. He finally met Titus; he was encouraged "not only by his arrival but also by the encouragement" that the Corinthian Christians provided (2 Cor 7:6–7). Paul should also have met Timothy in this region, who had been sent there beforehand (Acts 19:22; cf. the senders in 2 Cor 1:1 and the first plural pronouns in 7:5–7). Lots of encouragement from fellow workers and churches might have helped him go through regions in Macedonia, probably including Illyricum (Acts 20:2a), as Hemer says:

> If "those parts" may reasonably be taken in a broad sense, of territories adjoining and beyond Macedonia proper, we have a placing for a mission including Illyricum, which newly completed the geographical range at the date of Romans. Then we may assign this work in Macedonia and Illyricum to the year 56 before wintering in Corinth.[5]

In Macedonia (and Illyricum) Paul encouraged the believers with many words (20:2b); then he came to Greece (20:2c), which, as "the more popular term, is used as a synonym for 'Achaia,' the name of the Roman province found in 18:12; 19:21."[6] He stayed there for three months. At this time he wrote the Epistle to the Romans, to be precise, probably when he spent the winter (56–57 CE) in Corinth. In Romans, we can read his future plans: he was going to Jerusalem to serve the poor saints in the city with funds collected in Macedonia and Achaia (Rom 15:25–26); and after that ministry he longed to go to Rome and then Spain later on (15:28).

After wintering in Achaia or Greece in 56–57 CE, Paul intended to sail for Syria from the region but discovered that the Jews made a plot against him. As a result, a decision was made to return via a different

---

5. Hemer and Gempf 1989: 260; so also see Schnabel 2004: 1250, who specifies that Paul's missionary work in Illyricum took place "in the summer of AD 56."

6. Bruce 1990: 423.

route, Macedonia (Acts 20:3b).[7] Here "Syria" can be seen being "used in its wider sense to include Judaea, Syria Palaestina":[8] to begin with, even at the end of the second journey, Paul stopped by Jerusalem while on the way to Syrian Antioch (18:22); second, he planned to go to Macedonia and Achaia, and next, to Jerusalem and Rome (19:21; Rom 15:25–26); third, he carried with him the considerable funds collected from Macedonia and Achaia, so he took a shortcut to Jerusalem; fourth, the Antioch church had already helped the saints of Jerusalem (Acts 11:29–30) so her members could have been exempted from contributing to the present relief supplies.

The Jewish plot can be connected with the previous accusation (Acts 18:12–17). Ramsay imagines the illustration of their ambitious scheme reasonably: "Paul's intention must have been to take a pilgrim ship carrying Achaian and Asian Jews to the Passover.... With a shipload of hostile Jews, it would be easy to find opportunity to murder Paul."[9] The Jews were unable to harm Paul in public, so Paul only needed to avoid taking the "pilgrim ship." Along these lines we do not need to presume that Paul went "overland through Macedonia," as Witherington thinks.[10] Schnabel also says: "Paul and several companions traveled overland from Corinth to Philippi, a journey of about 450 miles (730 km.), which took about five weeks."[11] However, this journey would have been difficult to arrange from the beginning. Accordingly Paul would have taken a ship to Philippi after March 21[12] and there would have been enough time for Paul to celebrate the Passover "on Thursday, April 7 in Philippi and depart right after the days of the Unleavened Bread, 'on the morning of Friday, April 15.'"[13]

Hence, it is more apt to conjecture that Paul took a ship sailing to Neapolis in Cenchreae (cf. Acts 18:18) at the end of March 57 CE in order

7. By the way, Codex Bezae has a different reading, "since a plot had been made against him by the Jews, he wanted to sail to Syria. The Spirit, however, told him to return through Macedonia" (Rius-Camps and Read-Heimerdinger 2009: 82); this reading attaches too much weight to the guidance of the Holy Spirit.

8. Bruce 1990: 423. Contra Witherington 1998: 602: "Perhaps Paul was planning to go there [Syria] first on the way to Jerusalem, and then on to Rome."

9. Ramsay 1975 [1897]: 287. Paul's danger of being killed in a ship can also be read in 27:42.

10. Witherington 1998: 603.

11. Schnabel 2012: 834.

12. According to Ramsay 1975 [1897]: 264, "navigation began as a rule" seventeen days before the Passover.

13. For the dates, see Ramsay 1975 [1897]: 289.

to go to Philippi (cf. 16:11–12). First of all, like mentioned above, it is least likely that Paul took a course overland. Moreover, it is supported by several facts: (1) the representatives of Berea and Thessalonica had already arrived in Achaia (20:4); (2) Philippi is mentioned as a place Paul stopped (20:6); (3) other companions sailed directly to Troas (20:5).

Paul's traveling companions came from his previous mission fields: **Sopater son of Pyrrhus from Berea, Aristarchus** [Col 4:10; Phm 24] **and Secundus from Thessalonica, Gaius from Derbe, Timothy** [from Lystra (Acts 16:1)], **Tychicus** [Eph 6:21; Col 4:7; Tit 3:12; 2 Tim 4:12] **and Trophimus** [Acts 21:29; 2 Tim 4:20] **from the province of Asia** (Acts 20:4). Certainly "these persons were converts in these places and thus represented the churches Paul founded in these places."[14] Previous to their meeting in Troas for the time being, they would have gathered probably in Corinth in the winter of 56–57 CE so as to accompany Paul to Jerusalem.

On account of the Jews' plot, however, Paul sent them to Troas in advance (Acts 20:5) possibly to move the funds more safely, to prepare his ministry in Troas, and to rent a ship for safety (cf. 20:13—21:1). Meanwhile, Paul went to Philippi (20:6a). The reason is unclear. Probably it was to celebrate the feast of Unleavened Bread with Passover;[15] but why not in Troas? Maybe it was to bring Luke,[16] but if Luke's companionship had been originally planned, he must have joined Paul in Corinth. The literal expression of 20:5 infers that Luke accompanied Paul from Achaia; only the variant of Codex Bezae, "these men had gone on ahead and were waiting for *him* in Troas,"[17] rejects this idea. So probably it was in order to nullify the Jews' plot that Paul and Luke together took a ship to Neapolis in Cenchreae while the other five companions took another ship sailing to Troas. This guess is helpful in explaining why Paul and Luke departed Philippi right after the days of Unleavened Bread (20:6a): at that time no Jewish pilgrims would have been left in Macedonia.

It took five days for Paul and Luke to travel from Philippi to Troas (Acts 20:6b), from Philippi to Neapolis (16 km on foot), and from Neapolis via Samothrace to Troas (260 km by ship). Because it had taken

14. Witherington 1998: 603.

15. Witherington 1998: 603–4.

16. Bruce 1990: 424 says: "Luke appears to have been left behind at Philippi after Paul's first visit to that city. If so, he and Paul met again there, for Paul, instead of joining the others who sailed to Troas, now went north to Philippi to catch a ship at Neapolis."

17. Rius-Camps and Read-Heimerdinger 2009: 82 (italics mine).

two days for Paul, Silas, Timothy, and Luke to travel from Troas to Philippi over seven or eight years before (around 49 CE),[18] this time it took two and half times longer than before.[19] Schnabel sees "five days" as "a plausible time since the ship would be sailing against the wind in the springtime."[20] Hence, Luke seems to be paying attention to the delays caused first by the Jews' plot and then by the winds. Very important ministries are sometimes confronted by unexpected difficulties. Nevertheless, the real reasons for the delays could be linked with Paul's reluctance to get into Jerusalem at full tilt (see further comments).

From Troas to Miletus (20:6c–16)

Paul and Luke met the other companions in Troas, where they all stayed for seven days (Acts 20:6c): "the first of which was April 19 [Tuesday], and the last, Monday, April 25."[21] On the first day of the week,[22] Sunday, April 24, the church of Troas gathered to break bread along with Paul's companions (20:7a). "The breaking of bread is the term used especially in Acts for the celebration of the Lord's Supper (2:42; cf. 1 Cor. 10:16)."[23] The exact time of gathering would be Sunday evening: "since elsewhere Luke reckons the hours of the day from dawn (3:1), he appears to follow the Roman method of time-reckoning and the Jewish calendar (cf. Luke 24:1)."[24] The context of Acts 20:7b–8 supports this idea, too: **since Paul intended to leave the next day, he talked with them and further prolonged the Word until midnight; now there were many lamps in the upstairs where we gathered.**

The contemporary Christians seem to have already gathered on the first day of the week (see 1 Cor 16:2; also cf. Mark 16:2; Luke 24:1; John 20:1) to worship and have the Eucharist (see 1 Cor 11:20–21). So this gathering in Troas could be seen as a regular meeting for worship and the Lord's feast "rather than an ad hoc gathering because of Paul's presence

18. See comments on 16:11–12.

19. Bruce 1990: 425 says: "The voyage took over twice as long as the voyage in the reverse direction had taken some years earlier; probably the wind was favorable on that occasion but contrary this time."

20. Schnabel 2012: 834.

21. Ramsay 1975 [1897]: 289.

22. Literally "the first day between Sabbaths" or "the first day after the Sabbath."

23. Marshall 1980B: 344.

24. Marshall 1980B: 344. See also Bruce 1988: 384; Witherington 1998: 606; Peterson 2009: 557.

in the city."[25] This weekly meeting lasted until midnight, so **a young man named Eutychus** [meaning "fortunate"], **who was sitting in the window, was sinking into a deep sleep because Paul spoke for a long time, and then, caught hold of by sound sleep, he fell down from the third story and was picked up dead** (Acts 20:9). It should have been a tragedy, giving a great shock, as well as deep sadness. Crying, screams of pain, and all kinds of cries could have been heard (cf. 20:10b). In addition, some suspicious eyes could have been seen piercing Paul. The blame could have fallen on Paul.

This tribulation could have been much harder for Paul and his companions to handle than they had had to for the Jews' plot and the adverse wind. However, we cannot read any surprise or complaint or fear in Paul: **he went down and threw himself on him [Eutychus] and put his arms around him, and said, "Do not be distressed, for he is still alive," and then he went upstairs and, after breaking bread and eating, talked a long time until dawn, and then he left** (Acts 20:10–11).

Did Paul not have any emotion? He surely was a man of devotion, but he too had feelings in that he served the Lord with tears (Acts 20:19) and that others' weeping broke his heart (21:13). Had he expected it beforehand? Certainly not. If so, he should have warned the young man not to sit in the window. Then, what made him so peaceful and quiet at this tragic moment? The following Miletus speech gives a hint: he was bound by the Holy Spirit (20:22); he did not consider even his life worth anything to himself (20:24); he put his trust only in God and His gracious Word (20:32).

Eutychus's[26] resuscitation greatly comforted the saints (Acts 20:12) and surely Paul as well. Paul had already known that imprisonment and persecutions were waiting for him (20:23b); so Eutychus's death and resuscitation might have not only made Paul prepare himself even to martyrdom in the process of fulfilling the ministry but also strengthened him in the hope of resurrection. The impact of this experience could be mirrored through how Paul walked from Troas to Assos in solitude (40 km on foot; 71 km by ship): **Going on ahead to the ship, we put out to**

---

25. Schnabel 2012: 834–35.

26. Interestingly, Luke calls Eutychus *pais* (child, boy, servant), which apart from Eutychus in Acts refers only to Jesus (3:13, 26; 4:27, 30) and David (4:25). Codex Bezae has a different reading, *ton neaniskon* (the young lad), rather than *ton paida* (see Rius-Camps and Read-Heimerdinger 2009: 95, 98). The reading of Codex Bezae seems to avoid designating Eutychus with the same title used for Jesus and David.

sea for Assos, intending to take Paul aboard there; for he had arranged it this way, intending to go there on foot (20:13).

This ship that Paul's companions had taken from Troas to Patara (Acts 20:13—21:1) must have been rented;[27] otherwise, it should not have missed Ephesus, the most important port in Asia and Cnidus (cf. 27:7); in addition, several private plans, namely waiting for Paul in Assos (20:13–14), skipping Ephesus (20:16) and waiting for Ephesian elders in Miletus (20:17–18), could not have been devised and made. The rented ship should have guaranteed swiftness and their safety. The route shows this: among the ports they stopped at, Mitylene (20:14), Chios (Samos), Miletus (20:15), Cos, Rhodes, and Patara (21:1), only two of the ports were not islands: one was Miletus, where Paul met Ephesian elders, and the other was Patara, where they changed their means of transportation. In other words, the ship anchored herself only to islands with the exception of when it was required.

Paul was reunited with his eight companions including Luke in Assos, "an ancient city of Mysia in the Rom[an] province of Asia," which had a beautiful, high, and so steep rock "that Stratoricus wrote of it: 'If you wish to hasten your death, try and climb Assos.'"[28] On the terraces of this rock Paul might have prayed and looked back on his three missionary journeys: in spite of many opponents, the Lord had made him produce fruits of faith; he was about to suffer from serious persecution; like Jesus praying on the Mount of Olives, Paul would have prayed, "Let the Lord's will be done."

They passed through Mitylene (about 70 km by ship from Assos), "the most important city of the Asiatic Aeolians and of the island of Lesbos"[29] (Acts 20:14). Then on the following day they went to Chios (about 160 km by ship from Mitylene), the principle city of the island Chios (20:15a): this city was "situated between the islands of Lesbos and Samos" and "had the advantage of a good harbor which could contain 80 ships (Strabo 14.1.35; Herodotus 6.8; Thucydides 8.15)."[30] On the next day they approached Samos (approximately 130 km by ship from Chios) (20:15b), "a mountainous island" that "lies at the mouth of the bay of

27. The article (*to ploion*) that is employed without a precedent also supports the idea of a lent ship. In Acts, *to ploion* occurs seven times (20:13, 38; 21:3, 6; 27:17, 38, 39). Among these occurrences, only the one in 20:13 has no precedent.

28. *ISBE* 1:289.

29. *ISBE* 3:2068. Mitylene is now part of Greece.

30. *ABD*, 910.

Ephesus,"[31] and finally they arrived in Miletus (approximately 130 km by ship from Samos) (20:15c), "famous early Ionian Gr[eek] city on the coast of Caria, near the mouth of the Meander River."[32]

Here Luke informs us of why Paul did not stop by Ephesus: **Paul had decided to sail past Ephesus so as not to spend time in the province of Asia; for he was hurrying to arrive in Jerusalem, if possible, by the day of Pentecost** [May 29, 57 CE] (Acts 20:16). This decision could have been made when he walked in solitude to Assos from Troas; earlier, safety seems to have been more significant than swiftness, but now the opposite. He had actually wanted to avoid meeting the Jewish pilgrims, but he decided to meet them in Jerusalem by arriving there before their departure. The events on Euthychus might have affected his change of decision.

Miletus Speech (20:17–38)[33]

In Miletus, Paul called for the Ephesian elders (Acts 20:17). Superficially speaking, this could have made his journey to Jerusalem longer, because the messengers must have walked 100 kilometers to get to Ephesus[34] and the elders should have come to Paul. Walking 200 kilometers for a round trip might have made Paul stay in Miletus for at least five days; since Paul departed for Troas on April 25 and it took at least five days to reach Miletus, there would have been less than a month time gap till May 29, 57 CE when he arrived in Miletus. If Paul had visited Ephesus by ship, he could have given his speech within two days in Ephesus. So calling for the Ephesian elders in Miletus could be thought of as an unconventional arrangement in shortening the travel time to Jerusalem. However, the rioting in Ephesus that recently occurred might have made Paul think that calling the elders to come could be more effective than visiting Ephesus again; in Miletus, there would be more chance for him to escape the risk

31. *ABD* 948 and *ISBER* 4:308.

32. *ISBE* 3:2051.

33. Paul's speech to the Ephesian elders (20:18–35) is published as a part of Park 2016: 49–100.

34. Schnabel 2012: 838n27 describes very well the route from Ephesus to Miletus: "Actual travelers on foot had to cross over the spur between the Thorax Mountains and the Mycale Mountains, travel southwest upon reaching Magnesia on the Maeander River, reaching the coast via Priene, then turn east along the northern shore of the Gulf of Latmos, turning west at Heracleia, continuing along the southern shore of the Gulf of Latmos, reaching Miletus after about 62 miles (100 km.)."

of uprising or legal proceedings. Moreover, Ephesus was too big a city to visit carrying the enormous funds. So we can conjecture that Paul arrived in Miletus on April 30, 57 CE and left there on May 5, 57 CE.

Walton cleverly compares "Luke's Last Supper discourse" with this Miletus speech. As Jesus sent for Peter and John before his Last Supper discourse (Luke 22:8), so did Paul for the messengers before his Miletus speech (Acts 20:17).[35] Further, thematically both are connected: "suffering to come" (Luke 22:15, [28, 31–32, 37]; Acts 20:22–24); "efficacy of the death of Jesus" (Luke 22:19–20; Acts 20:28); "leadership" (Luke 22:24–30; Acts 20:28); and "money and work" (Luke 22:35–36; Acts 20:33–35).[36] Paul's Miletus speech lays out his teaching syllabus for the Christian leaders. Its contents can be structured as follows:

> Paul's ministry principles (20:18–21)
> Paul's present ministry (20:22–24)
> Paul's previous ministry in Ephesus (20:25–27)
> Ephesian elders' task for the present and the future (20:28–31)
> Shared ministry principles (20:32–35).[37]

First, Paul summarized his ministry principles that the elders had already experienced (Acts 20:18–21): (1) he served the Lord with all humility and tears, in spite of continuous tests from many adversaries (20:19; cf. 1 Cor 16:9); (2) he boldly[38] proclaimed all of the useful teachings in public and in private (Acts 20:20); (3) he **testified both to the Jews and to the Greeks about conversion to God by faith in Jesus the Lord**[39] (20:21). He had the identity of a servant of the Lord. Even at times

---

35. Walton 2000: 100–101.

36. Walton 2000: 100–117.

37. The Miletus speech is sectioned in various ways (see Walton 2000: 66–75): Walton 2000: 75–84 outlines it: introductory retrospect (20:18–21), the future of Paul in Jerusalem (20:22–24), prospect and retrospect (20:25–27), a charge to the elders (20:28–31), and conclusion (20:32–35); Cheng 2011: 119–20, who scrutinizes all Paul's speeches in Acts, summarizes it as "Paul states his past ministry" (20:18–21), "Paul testifies to the divine will for his future" (20:22–24), "Paul expresses his present concern for the Ephesian Church" (20:25–31), and "Paul gives his final word to the elders" (20:32–35).

38. Bruce 1990: 431 says that οὐδὲν ὑπεστειλάμην . . . τοῦ μὴ ἀναγγεῖλαι "is equivalent to ἐπαρρησιασάμην."

39. "In Acts 20,21 the object of the apostle's preaching is well said to be 'conversion to God and faith in Christ,' but under the one article, so that one may almost understand 'conversion to God by faith in Christ'" (Zerwick 1963 [2001]: 184).

in despair, sadness, and trouble, he did not forget what and to whom he should proclaim. From the beginning and to the end, his unique focus had been fixed only on God and the Lord Jesus. He was both a humble soldier as well as a brave servant. By his standards, there are no extraordinary miracles that God performed by Paul's own hands, probably because these belong to God; they were not his.

Second, Paul revealed his present circumstances (Acts 20:22–24): (1) bound in the Holy Spirit,[40] he was going to Jerusalem where imprisonment and persecution awaited (20:22–23); (2) he had great resolution in facing any difficulties so as to fulfill what the Lord Jesus assigned him (20:24). The direct speech of the Holy Spirit seems to be negative, but his famous response eats up any possible sign of the pessimism in the contents: **I do not account my life of any value . . . to testify to the gracious gospel of God.** Ironically, the gracious gospel has been proclaimed while the evangelists have risked their lives.

Third, Paul's present situation reverberates his previous ministry in Ephesus (Acts 20:25–27): (1) he proclaimed the kingdom of God, going among them (20:25); (2) he was innocent of the Ephesians' blood, because he had not once held back from declaring the purpose of God to them thoroughly (20:26–27). Here we can learn that Paul originally did not intend to come back to Ephesus;[41] however, subsequent to unexpected events, namely two years of confinement in Caesarea and two years of detention in Rome, Paul was able to revisit Ephesus with Timothy (1 Tim 1:3). The expression of Paul's innocence of their blood alludes to Ezek 3:16–21 and 33:1–6[42] and indicates that Paul "has fulfilled the responsibility that the prophet Ezekiel had been given as 'a watchman for the people of Israel,' whom God had commissioned to warn the wicked of their wicked ways in order to save their lives."[43]

Fourth, in retrospect to his past ministry and the present, Paul charged the Ephesian elders with some tasks for the present and the future (Acts 20:28–31): (1) they became overseers **to shepherd the**

40. Cf. 19:21; 21:4, 11. *tō pneumati* in 20:22 can be seen as the Holy Spirit (so also Marshall 1980B: 350; Bruce 1990: 432; Rapske 1994: 404; Walton 2000: 88; Gaventa 2004: 45).

41. Bruce 1990: 433 says: "If he survived his visit to Jerusalem, his intention was not to return to the Aegean world but to evangelize the western Mediterranean (cf. 19:21; Rom. 1:15; 15:23f., 28f.)."

42. Cf. Marshall 2007: 596.

43. Schnabel 2012: 844.

church of God that He obtained with the blood of His own one,[44] so they should watch out for themselves and for all the flock (20:28); (2) the church was about to be faced outwardly with fierce wolves, "heretical teachers,"[45] surrounding the church, and inwardly with some elders who would speak perverted teachings in the church to draw the disciples toward themselves (20:29–30); (3) they must **be alert, remembering that day and night for three years Paul did not cease admonishing**[46] **each of them with tears** (20:31). The elders were like shepherds for the sheep; thus, they should be alert and watch out in order not only to take care of the sheep assigned but also to prevent any wolves from devouring the sheep. Their responsibility for the church had to do with the Trinity, God her owner, His own Son as the subject of the Word, and the Holy Spirit her guide.[47] "Whatever the implications of these complexities may be for the church's trinitarian theology, the implications for this portrait of the intramural life of the church seem clear: the church is God's own," as Gaventa says.[48]

Now then from God's ownership of the church, the last and main[49] point of the syllabus is extracted, that is, "shared ministry principles" (Acts 20:32–35): (1) God and His gracious Word[50] could build up the church and give the saints one inheritance among all those who are sanctified (20:32);[51] (2) Ministers should not desire any possessions, even silver or

44. *Dia tou haimatos tou idiou* can be translated as "with the blood of his own one" (Bruce 1990: 434) because of the article (cf. Heb 9:12; 13:12). Cf. Gaventa 2004: 48n38. For a robust study on textual and exegetical discussions of this phrase, see Walton 2000: 94–98.

45. Bruce 1990: 435.

46. The middle form of παύω with participle is used to mean "to cease doing" something (BDAG, 790).

47. See Cheng 2011: 122.

48. Gaventa 2004: 49.

49. With *ta nun* (also see 4:29; 5:38; 17:30; 27:22), "the speaker is about to make his or her main point" (Culy and Parsons 2003: 78).

50. The subject is grammatically "the Word," "but the real enabler is God, who uses his words as the means of building up the church and securing its members' eternal inheritance" (Bruce 1990: 436).

51. "The idea of an inheritance among the sanctified (cf. 1 Cor 1:2) is repeated in 26:18; cf. Eph 1:14; Col 1:12; 3:24; also Heb 1:14; 6:12" in the NT (Bruce 1990: 436). In the OT, this idea appears in Gen 15:7; Exod 15:17; Josh 11:23; Deut 33:3–4; and Ps 15:5 (see Marshall 2007: 597).

gold or clothing, of the saints[52] but work for himself and his companions and even for the weak[53] (20:33–35). God nurtures His church, so "the future health of the church rests with God rather than with the faithfulness to a model established by Paul."[54]

Paul and the elders became one-minded on the ministry principles: Paul **knelt down and prayed along with them and they wept loudly and fell on Paul's neck and kissed him** (Acts 20:36b–37). Paul's saying that **they were not going to see his face again** (20:38a) made this teaching a farewell speech, his last words; so the elders **accompanied him to the [rented] ship** (20:38b). Paul had eight companions. He should not have been lonelier than Jesus.

Fusing the Horizons: "All Things to All Men" Speech[55]

Paul's speeches form the predominant part in his three missionary journeys, namely the speech in Pisidian Antioch (Acts 13:16–41), the speech in Lystra (14:15–17), the speech in Athens (17:22–31), and the speech to the Ephesian elders (20:18b–35). In 1 Cor 9:19–22, Paul declares that he became "all things to all men": to the Jews like a Jew; to those free from the law like one free from the law; to the weak like a weak one. How did he articulate this principle in his speech? By simple yet thorough exegesis of Paul's four speeches in Acts, we can learn how he spoke to versatile audiences.

First of all, in the synagogue of a Romanized city, Pisidian Antioch, Paul proclaimed the gospel to the Jews and the God-fearers by focusing on (1) what God had promised through the ancient history of Israel, (2) how God has fulfilled the promise in Jesus and his resurrection, (3) how salvation by the Davidic kingship could be realized through the permanent blessings Jesus provided, (4) a gracious way that is open to people along with a serious warning concerning rejection. In the process of expounding each statement, Paul largely relied on the OT: Ps 89:20; 1 Sam 13:14; Isa

---

52. Paul's "negative confession" is parallel to 1 Sam 12:1–5 (Bruce 1990: 436; Walton 2000: 89; Marshall 2007: 597).

53. Paul's "pattern of self-support" can be found in his Epistles too (1 Cor 4:12; 2 Cor 7:2; 1 Thess 2:9) (Gaventa 2004: 46).

54. Gaventa 2004: 44.

55. This was published as a part of Park 2016: 49–100.

11:1, 10; 44:28; Ps 2:7; Isa 55:3; Ps 16:10; Hab 1:5. In addition, the contemporary history of Palestine in that period was shared with the audience: John the Baptist, Jesus' death on the cross and resurrection.

Second, in the speech to the idol-worshipers in Lystra, a Lycaonian city, we can find neither Israel's ancient history nor God's promise and fulfillment. Rather, Paul proclaimed some statements that were tailored to the background of the situation, particularly considering the legend about Zeus and Hermes: (1) the evangelists are human beings; (2) idols must be compared with the living God; (3) unlike Zeus and Hermes, the living God is generous; (4) the living God provides human beings with satisfaction as well as food. The OT and the contemporary history in Palestine were not employed; the Lycaonian legend and the audience's mindset form the backdrop to his statements.

In the following Areopagus speech to the Areopagites in Athens, Paul must have clarified that God made Jesus' resurrection the crucial evidence for His final salvation because the council was gathered to judge Paul's religion and the members of the council did not pay attention to the afterlife or even resurrection. In the heart of religion and Greek philosophy, Paul first of all admitted their religious nature and recalled the altar engraved with "To an unknown god" as a piece of evidence for the one and only one true God. He proclaimed "the God" as the creator while relieving the Epicureans and the Stoics by mentioning an Epicurean doctrine that "God needs nothing from human beings" and a Stoic belief that "He is the source of all life." Further, Paul declared that the God of creation determined human history and political boundaries: this notion goes to the human necessity of seeking God. Paul's final statement demanded their repentance to receive righteousness based on the resurrected Jesus. To be precise, in this third speech Paul considered and reinterpreted the altar engraved with "To an unknown god," the beliefs of the Athenian philosophers, and a few poems (of Epimenides the Cretan and Aratus) they were familiar with. He did not quote the OT but echoed or alluded to it: Deut 29:16–17; 32:8; Dan 2, 7; Ps 115:4; Isa 40:18–20; 42:5; 46:5–6; 55:6. In addition, he explored some of the OT themes: "the one Creator theology," "the unique originality of humankind," "seeking God," and "repentance to God."

Fourth, Paul gave a farewell speech to the elders of the Ephesian church in Miletus in order to primarily encourage and strengthen them by reminding them about his past ministry that had been done among them, also to warn them by giving some information about the future in advance, and finally to entrust them to God and His gracious Word. Meanwhile, he used mainly what they had experienced together. None of the cultural background was employed. The OT was not quoted but only some verses (namely, 1 Sam 12:1–5; Ezek 3:16–21; and 33:1–6) reverberated; some NT verses (Luke 6:38; 11:9; and John 13:34) were alluded to. His focus was given only to God and His gracious Word, and to the guidance of the Holy Spirit. Ministers should not value themselves, not even their lives, in order to fulfill the ministry given by their Lord Jesus.

Through the analysis above we can find out that Paul was very sensitive to the listeners: to their knowledge, background, and needs. To the Jews and the God-fearers he quoted from the OT and recalled what had happened in Palestine; for the Lycaonian idol-worshipers he remembered their legends and agricultural life; in order to answer the Greek philosophers he made use of their conceptions and his abundant knowledge of literature; and for the Ephesian elders, what they themselves had seen and heard from Paul was essentially employed.

In spite of various materials for speeches, Paul aimed at having each audience know God and fit for His will. First, to the Jews and the God-fearers in Pisidian Antioch, Paul made known how God's promise had been fulfilled and then urged them to believe and follow the gospel. Second, to the idol-worshipers in Lystra, Paul made known who the living God is and what He has done, and urged them to stop worshiping idols. As for the Areopagites and the Greek philosophers, Paul taught them about their lack of knowledge on the one true God and then prompted them to accept Jesus' resurrection as the basis of righteousness. Lastly, to the Ephesian elders, Paul made known what had happened and would have happened in the church of Ephesus and pleaded with them to trust God and His gracious Word and to follow the principles of the ministry.

Paul expressed different ideas in his speeches given to different audiences in different places. Nevertheless, he remained consistent with his attitude and speech principles: (1) he carefully considered the audiences' background; (2) he used and reinterpreted the audiences' knowledge and notion in terms of the biblical thoughts; (3) he was always theocentric; (4) he urged people to change their life and thoughts so as to fit into God's will at their spiritual level. These speech principles can be of practical use to current missionaries and preachers.

ACTS 21
Paul's Arrival in Jerusalem for Relief Ministry

For the journey from Miletus to Patara, Paul's companions continued to use the rented ship (Acts 21:1). Later they took a general ship sailing to Ptolemais via Tyre (21:2–7). Then they stopped by Caesarea, where their resolve to visit Jerusalem was renewed (21:8–16). Afterward, they finally reached Jerusalem (21:17).

In Jerusalem, in spite of the disciples' anxiety over Paul's security, everything seemed to go well at first: they were warmly welcomed by James and the elders (Acts 21:18–19); and Paul accepted the Jerusalem leaders' request for demonstrating that he had respect for the law of Moses. However, before satisfying the requirements of their request, Paul was attacked by a mob agitated by pilgrims from Asia, especially from Ephesus. At the moment of being nearly killed by the angry mob, Paul was saved by the chiliarch (the tribune of the cohort) and got an opportunity to speak directly to the mob.

All the events of this chapter happened in the spring of 57 CE. Paul would have left Miletus on May 5 and might have arrived in Jerusalem at least nine days before the Pentecost (May 29; cf. 21:18, 26, 27), thus possibly on May 20. Within these fifteen days, Paul traveled from Miletus to Jerusalem and stayed shortly both in Tyre and in Caesarea.

Miletus to Jerusalem (21:1–17)

After having a meeting with the Ephesian elders, Paul's companions left Miletus and, via two islands, Cos[1] (around 73 nautical km from Miletus) and Rhodes[2] (around 120 nautical km from Cos), went to Patara (about

---

1. Cos "was famous in antiquity for excellent wine, amphorae, wheat, ointments, silk and other clothing" and "was the birthplace of Hippocrates ([460–375 BCE] the father of medicine)" (*ISBE* 2:723).

2. Rhodes was related to Herod the Great in two ways: first, he escaped to this island in the autumn of 40 CE when he fled to Rome (*Ant.* 14.377; cf. *War* 1.280); second, after Marc Antony and Cleopatra were defeated by Octavianus in 31 BCE,

110 nautical km from Rhodes), "a prominent seaport city of Lycia"[3] (Acts 21:1). It would have been easy to find there a ship sailing to Syria because "many of the coast trading ships stopped at Patara" on account of its excellent quality as a harbor.[4]

In Patara, they "found a ship crossing over to Phoenicia" (Acts 21:2a). The "crossing over" refers to "a cross-sea voyage instead of a coasting voyage; the journey was thus considerably shortened."[5] This ship sailed directly to Tyre, a famous seaport on the coast of Phoenicia along with Sidon (cf. Isa 23), in order to unload its cargo there, so it passed the island of Cyprus on her left-hand side (Acts 21:2b–3): any map of the Mediterranean Sea shows that a straight line can be drawn from Patara to Tyre (620 km from Patara).

In Tyre, they should have stayed for seven days searching for the disciples and staying put with them (Acts 21:4a) since it took time for the ship to discharge its cargo. The disciples in Tyre told Paul **through the Spirit not to go on to Jerusalem** (21:4b). "Through the Spirit"[6] indicates that "not to go on to Jerusalem" was not a direct speech of the Holy Spirit; but the Tyrian believers' interpretation of a revelation from the Spirit,[7] probably on account of their poor education on predestination;[8] or a personal counsel based on their misunderstanding of a divine communication, as Rapske denotes,

> The expression "not to go up to Jerusalem" represents not the divine portent itself but the personal counsel given to Paul by the Tyrian Christians. They have 1) *misunderstood* the communication as either a) warning Paul against going to

---

Herod went to Rhodes to surrender to the winner (*Ant.* 15.187; cf. *War* 1.387).

3. *ABD* 177: Patara "served as the port for the city of Xanthus. . . . The importance of Patara is indicated by its inclusion in the Lycian League of which it was the 6th largest member."

4. *ISBE* 4:2262.

5. Bruce 1988: 398.

6. Among the primary texts for NT studies, *dia tou pneumatos* does not appear in Second Temple Jewish literature, but in the LXX (Isa 30:1) and in the NT (Acts 11:28; 1 Cor 2:10; 12:8; Eph 3:16).

7. Schnabel 2012: 854n117 thinks that "one believer received a revelation from the Spirit, which the Tyrian believers interpreted to mean that Paul should not go to Jerusalem."

8. Marshall 1980B: 358 suggests: "The disciples at Tyre may not have been well informed on the finer points of predestination, and could have thought it possible to say to Paul, 'If this is what is going to happen to you, don't go.'"

Jerusalem or b) of providing a divine insight so that he might
prudently avoid trouble.[9]

In comparison with Agabus's prophecy in 21:11, the counsel of the
Tyrian Christians did not have an influence on Paul's companions; possibly because Jerusalem was still far away and the prophetic authority of
the Tyrian disciples were weaker than that of Agabus (cf. 11:28). After
the cargos were discharged from the ship, the Tyrian disciples and their
families accompanied Paul's companions to the beach; then they knelt
and prayed together and went their own ways (21:5–6).

Paul and his companions continued the voyage to Phoenicia from
Tyre to Ptolemais (48 km from Tyre) (Acts 21:7a), the southern tip of
Phoenicia, so "perhaps the last port at which their ship was due to put
in."[10] Ptolemais was called Accho [or Acco or Akko] in OT times, and
Ptolemais's name change was "in the late 3rd or early 2nd century BC by
Ptolemy I or II of Egypt"; this seaport is located "on the N point of the
Bay of Acre (named from Accho), about 13 km N of Carmel headland
which faces it across the bay"; at this time this city was a Roman colony,
"the emperor Claudius having settled a group of veterans there."[11] Paul's
companions stayed there for just one day, so no teachings but only greetings were given to the believers of the city (21:7b).

The next day Paul and company arrived in Caesarea (48 or 60 km
from Ptolemais)[12] (Acts 21:8a) probably on foot, since there is no mention of any ship: in addition, there was a well-trodden path between
Ptolemais and Caesarea following the seashore.[13] Here we may ask, as
Marshall did, "why Paul had waited [in Tyre] a full week for a ship that

9. Rapske 1994: 408 (italics original). He adds a sentence, "On the other hand, they
may have 2) *understood* the communication properly and counselled disobedience"
on the basis of Marshall's commentary; however, Marshall 1980B: 358 points out their
poor education on predestination.

10. Bruce 1988: 399.

11. *NBD3* 988–89. After the Roman period, the original name was restored.

12. Many commentators (e.g., Peterson 2009: 579) think the distance from Ptolemais to Caesarea as 48 km (30 miles) following Hemer and Gempf 1989: 125; according to Witherington 1998: 632, it is 32 miles (51.2 km); but Pervo 2009: 536n27 sees it
as "about sixty kilometers" and NET notes suggest 65 km.

13. Even though Bruce 1988: 399 (so also Hemer and Gempf 1989: 126; Peterson
2009: 579) says that "it is not clear whether they took another ship to Caesarea or
went there by road," some commentators simply assume that they went to Caesarea
by sailing (Witherington 1998: 632; Bock 2007: 637; Schnabel 2012: 856) or on road
(Pervo 2009: 535–36).

merely went one day's journey when he could have traveled the same distance more quickly by land."[14] They probably had paid the ship fare in full for Ptolemais, or the companions could have needed a rest due to the nonstop sea voyage, or maybe Paul felt a need to talk, or to be precise, to search and stay put with the Tyrian Christians like in Troas (cf. 20:6).

In Caesarea, Paul and his companions stayed in **the house of Philip the evangelist, who was one of the seven** (Acts 21:8b). Paul's staying in Philip's house may have formed a very meaningful friendship between the two: first, since, when Stephen was martyred, Philip was one of the seven deacons and Paul kept the executioners' garments; second, about twenty-two years ago the two belonged to the same group as the seven deacons; subsequently, by passing through many tribulations, Paul had enough discipline to understand Stephen's mind in his martyrdom; fourth, both became evangelists for the Roman people living in Romanized cities; lastly, this would have been to further their acquaintance because they had met each other beforehand (cf. 9:30; 18:22).

Here Luke adds further information on Philip (cf. Acts 6:5; 8:5–40): **he had four unmarried daughters who prophesied** (21:9). Then, are there any intentions included in this explanation? Possibly not: neither that "women needed to be unmarried to prophesy, nor that they needed to be virgins."[15] Besides being with four virgin prophetesses, it would have been a great blessing to be a father to four daughters.[16] With the given information on Philip's family, the readers would be prepared to read about a new prophet in the following verse.

While they remained in Caesarea for several days,[17] **a prophet named Agabus came down from Judea** (Acts 21:10). He was one of the prophets who came down from Jerusalem to Antioch (11:27). When Paul had been in Achaia, Macedonia, and Asia, Agabus seems to have been in Judea; and after Paul arrived in Caesarea, Agabus came down to the city "which was, in Jewish geographical perspective, part of Samaria."[18]

---

14. Marshall 1980B: 358.

15. Witherington 1998: 633.

16. I also have four daughters.

17. *Hemeras pleious* literally means "for a (large) number of days, for many days" (BDAG 848). However, they had no time to remain there many days, so this expression should be understood relatively in comparison with a one-day stay in Ptolemais in 21:7.

18. Schnabel 2012: 857. "Caesarea was officially the provincial capital, though geographically in the section called Samaria, rather than in Judaea in the narrower sense"

The Holy Spirit had guided Paul from the beginning of his missionary journeys (13:2–3), so the advent of Agabus is not a coincidence; also, the readers are reminded of the previous account of Agabus's prophecy of a severe famine in 11:28 followed by James's death, Peter's imprisonment and escape, and Herod Agrippa I's death in 12:1–23 despite the fact that these three incidents should have occurred about 43 to March 44 CE[19] while Agabus's prophecy was delivered between 44 and 45 CE.

Agabus's statement was dynamically provided with an action: **taking Paul's belt and tying his own feet and hands, he said, "The Holy Spirit says this: 'The man whose belt this is, in this way the Jews in Jerusalem will tie up, and will hand him over to the Gentiles'"** (Acts 21:11). His prophecy would have had an enormous impact on the listeners. To begin with, his spiritual authority had already been verified (cf. 11:27–28) and since a dozen of years had passed from that time onward, he should have been regarded as a very famous and prominent prophet. Additionally, he should have known about the Jews in Jerusalem. Third, and especially, he appeared on time in Caesarea when Paul arrived, and prophesied about what was to become of Paul.

Consequently, both Paul's companions and **the local people begged him not to go up to Jerusalem** with weeping (Acts 21:12–13a). Their begging and weeping broke Paul's heart, but he revealed his one-track mind by saying, **I am ready not only to be bound up but also to die in Jerusalem for the name of the Lord Jesus** (21:13). Paul had already been bound by the Holy Spirit (20:22), so he should not have been afraid of being bound by anything else, not even ropes; since his sufferings had been so severe (14:19; 2 Cor 4:8–10; 6:4–10; 11:23–28) and he preferred "to be away from the body and at home with the Lord" (5:8), he would not have feared nor longed for being safe.

Then, a prayer follows: **because he could not be persuaded, we became silent, after saying, "The Lord's will be done!"** (Acts 21:14). This prayer is parallel to a part of the Lord's prayer, "Thy will be done in earth, as in heaven" (Matt 6:10b), and to Jesus' prayer in Gethsemane, "Father, if Thou be willing, remove this cup from me: nevertheless, not my will, but Thine, be done" (Luke 22:42; cf. Matt 26:42; Mark 14:36). The Lord's prayer in the Lucan Gospel (Luke 11:2–4) does not include this part; so both Jesus' prayer in 22:42 and Paul's companions' prayer in Acts 21:14

(Hemer and Gempf 1989: 126n72).

   19. Bruce 1990: 92.

can be seen as a piece of the Lucan Lord's prayer puzzle. If all the parts of the Lord's prayer in Luke-Acts were considered, the Lord's will could be easily identified with suffering. It was not any kind of success in life, but just as the Lord wanted Jesus to be hanged up on the cross, His will was for Paul to go up to the dangerous city Jerusalem.

Agabus's prophecy did not influence Paul's resolution but his companions' preparation for the journey to Jerusalem: **after these days we got ready and went up to Jerusalem; by the way, some of the disciples from Caesarea came along with us too, and brought us to the house of Mnason of Cyprus, a disciple from the earliest times, with whom we were to lodge** (Acts 21:15–16). Some disciples in Caesarea devoted more time to Paul's ministry in Jerusalem; they helped Paul and the company to find Mnason's house.

There are two ways of locating "Mnason's house."[20] On the one hand, Mnason's house could have been on the way from Caesarea to Jerusalem, probably in the middle, such as Joppa (cf. Acts 9:36—10:24) or Antipatris (cf. 23:31).[21] We can infer from the close context that Paul and his companions stopped just for one night in Mnason's house: the Caesarean disciples departed together (21:16a); they guided Paul's company to Mnason's house to lodge (21:16b); "we" (Paul's company) arrived in Jerusalem (21:17a). Codex Bezae's longer reading supports this idea.[22] It is possible that the Caesarean disciples guided Paul and his companions to Mnason's house to stay for one night and then returned home while Paul's company went up to Jerusalem. The distance from Caesarea to Jerusalem is about 100 kilometers, so it is hard to get to Jerusalem within one day without riding on horseback (cf. 23:31–33).[23] On the other hand,

20. KJV translates 21:16b as "[certain of the disciples of Caesarea] brought with them one Mnason of Cyprus, an old disciple, with whom we should lodge," which indicates that Mnason lived in Caesarea; however, it translates the dative (*Mnasōni tini Kupriō*) wrongly.

21. With Hemer and Gempf 1989: 126, who says: "The implication, made explicit in D, is perhaps that Mnason's home was not in Jerusalem, but an overnight stopping-place *en route.*"

22. Rius-Camps and Read-Heimerdinger 2009: 175 translate 21:16 of Codex Bezae as follows: "Some from among the disciples from Caesarea came with us. These men took us to the people with whom they wanted us to lodge; when we arrived in a certain village, we found ourselves at the house of Nason, a certain Cypriot and an early disciple."

23. Schnabel 2012: 859 thinks that 100 kilometers "required four days of walking"; however, it would require only two days of walking since it normally takes one hour to walk four to five kilometers.

Mnason's house could have been located in Jerusalem or her suburban districts.[24] In this case, the Caesarean disciples would have accompanied Paul and his companions to Mnason's house located in Jerusalem or her suburb. If so, the first plural pronoun in 21:17 indicates both Paul's company and the Caesarean party.

In summary, Paul and his companions left Caesarea to make a journey to Jerusalem (21:15), and some disciples in Caesarea accompanied them to Mnason's house, located probably on the way to their destination (21:16). About two months prior, around March 21 in 57 CE, Paul and Luke departed Achaia (Acts 20:3); then around April 19, the other seven companions joined them in Troas (20:5); then, possibly in the middle of May before the Pentecost [May 29, 57 CE], some disciples unexpectedly joined the company in Caesarea (21:16). Assistants had been added each month.

After Paul and his companions left Mnason's house, they arrived in Jerusalem and got a warm welcome from the brothers (Acts 21:17), who seem to be somewhat different from most of the contemporary Jerusalemite believers, viz., "all ardent observers of the law" (cf. 21:20). Having been warmly welcomed by these brothers, Paul should certainly have gotten a brave heart.[25]

Fusing the Horizons: The Lord's Prayers in Acts[26]

The Lord's prayer appears not only in Matt 6:10–13 but also in Luke's former book (Luke 11:2–4). Both have some differences; (1) "Our Father in heaven" in Matt 6:10 differs from "Father" in Luke 11:2; (2) Luke does not have "Thy will be done on earth, as in heaven" (Matt 6:10b); (3) "this day" in Matt 6:11 differs from "day by day" in Luke 11:3; (4) the related verbs meaning "give" differ between the aorist imperative (*dos*, Matt 6:11) and the present imperative (*didou*, Luke 11:3); (5) in Matt 6:12 "our debts" are compared with "our debtors," but in Luke 11:4 "our sins" with "every

24. Most commentators support this idea (e.g., Bruce 1990: 443; Schnabel 2012: 859).

25. Bruce 1990: 444 seems to have some confusion over whom these brothers refer to: "These 'brethren' are probably Mnason and his associates. But the clause may anticipate the account of the visitors' reception by James and the elders in vv. 18ff. If so, then James and the elders will be 'the brethren' mentioned here."

26. This theme is based on Park 2012: 137–52.

one that is indebted to us." Most of these can be explained as the Lucan Lord's prayer occurring in the journey narrative (9:51—19:46); this prayer is mirrored in Acts as well.

The Lord's prayer in Luke was written with a journey motif: a traveler arrived but his friend did not have food, though the friend went to his other friend; food will be provided not because of friendship but because of the persistent and shameless demand due to the traveler's urgency (11:5–8). In journeys, one's needs become urgent. Having exigent matters to deal with, supplicants would not have the time to call God "our Father in heaven"—in Greek six words—so may call Him quickly in short "Father." They would have yearned to satisfy their needs, so it would be necessary for them to talk about "day by day" referring to "each day" rather than about "this day" indicating "days in general." And the urgency can be expressed with the present imperative (*didou*) better than the aorist (*dos*). Moreover, urgency would make the supplicants humble, thus they might differ between what they get, "forgiveness from their sins," and what they give, "forgiving debtors." God will forgive them their sins, then they will share this grace with their debtors.

Interpreting the Lord's prayer in Luke as a prayer during a cold journey explains all the differences it has with the prayer in Matthew, except for the second one: Luke does not have "Thy will be done on earth, as in heaven" (Matt 6:10b). Interestingly, Jesus' prayer in Gethsemane at the end of his journey contains this supplication: "Father, if Thou be willing, remove this cup from me: nevertheless, not my will, but Thine, be done" (Luke 22:42; cf. Matt 26:42; Mark 14:36). In the same way, Paul's companions and the Christians in Caesarea prayed, **The Lord's will be done**! (Acts 21:14). Hence, as we have seen, if all the expressions of the Lord's prayer in Luke-Acts were considered, the Lord's will could be easily identified with suffering, not with any kinds of success in life since God the Father wanted Jesus to be hanged up on the cross and the Lord guided Paul to Jerusalem, the city where danger awaits.

The Lord prayed the prayer he taught till the end of his journey, and Paul's companions and the Caesarean Christians prayed the Lord's prayer. Then, how about other prayers recorded by the same writer? We find three prayers in Acts 1:24–25, 4:23–31, and 7:60. The first one is linked to appointing a substitute for Judas the Iscariot. The disciples would have desired Barsabbas, a person well-known in the community, to be elected rather than Matthias, probably less known.[27] However, they wanted God's will to be fulfilled, so they prayed: **You Lord, Heart-knower of everyone! Show us which one of these two you have chosen to take the place in this service and apostleship from which Judas turned aside to go to his own place** (1:24–25). The church sought the Lord's will to decide on a surrogate apostle.

The second prayer was offered when the apostles were threatened and forbidden to preach in the name of Jesus. The disciples in unison literally prayed for themselves to be strong enough to face the persecution fearlessly (Acts 4:29), unlike Nehemiah or the psalmist, who sometimes would ask God to take revenge on their enemies (cf. Neh 4:4; Pss 44:13; 79:12; 123:3–4).[28] The disciples called God **Sovereign Lord, Creator of the heaven, the earth, the sea and everything in them** (Acts 4:24). Sovereign Lord "expresses God's sovereign position."[29]

The third prayer is Stephen's: he prayed, **Lord Jesus, receive my spirit, and kneeling down he cried with a loud voice, Lord, lay not this sin to their charge** (Acts 7:59b–60a). Just as Jesus prayed to the Father and asked for the forgiveness of those who were killing him, so Stephen appealed to Jesus for forgiving those who were killing him.[30] Stephen's prayer can be compared with Zachariah's request in 2 Chr 24:22b: "May YHWH see and avenge!" Zachariah sought for fair judgment, but Stephen for His loving forgiveness: the latter reminds us of a part of the Lord's prayer, viz. "forgive us our sins; for we also forgive every one that is indebted to us."

To sum up, all the four prayers found in Acts can be connected with the Lord's prayer. The first and the last one can be equated with the God's-will-be-done part. The second can be linked with the God's-name-and-kingdom part. The third one, Stephen's prayer, can be identified with the forgiveness part. The disciples did not repeat the Lord's prayer again and again literally, but did pray it during their lives in many figures.

---

27. See comments on 1:23–26.
28. See comments on 4:23–31.
29. Bock 2007: 204.
30. See comments on 7:59–60.

Nine Days in Jerusalem (21:18–40)

Luke goes into detail in reporting Paul's twelve-day sojourn in Jerusalem (Acts 21:18—23:30), and this section includes the first nine days. A day passed after Paul had arrived in Jerusalem safe and sound: **On the following [2nd] day Paul went in with us to James, and all the elders appeared** (21:18). This "us" refers to Paul's eight companions. In this verse, as Bruce says, "Paul is distinguished from 'us' at the end of a 'we' section":[31] Paul is identified with the apostle of the gentiles, and his companions with the representatives of the gentile churches. It would have been a formal meeting with the Jerusalem church leaders and the gentile church delegates, which is verified by the appearance of the elders.

After exchanging greetings among them, a report was submitted to the Jerusalem church leaders: Paul **related one by one the things that God had done among the Gentiles through his ministry** (Acts 21:19). What God has done was always the subject of Paul's report (cf. 14:27; 15:4, 12). The first response to the report was glorifying God; but their heartfelt sincerity of praise passed away so soon, in comparison with their following request. In their praise, Bruce reads two causes, "not only for the conversion of the Gentiles, but also for the practical evidence of their conversion in the contributions to the relief fund being handed over there and then by delegates from Gentile churches."[32]

Their request is introduced in Acts 21:20b–25, composed of two parts, presenting Paul's problem (21:20b–22) and providing a solution of their own (21:23–25). They seem to say: "Well done, you did a good job. Nevertheless, there is a problem with you. Well, you are the problem actually. There are many thousands of Jewish believers here, who are very zealous for the law. They have already heard about you that **you teach all the Jews who are among the Gentiles to rebel against Moses, telling them not to circumcise their children or walk according to the customs**. They will also hear that you have come. What shall we do? We have a solution. Demonstrate that you yourself also live in observance of the law. Fortunately, we have four men who have been under a vow. Purify yourself along with these men, and pay their expenses so that they might have their heads shaved.[33] Then the problem will be solved. The Jewish

---

31. Bruce 1990: 444.

32. Bruce 1990: 445.

33. *Xurēsontai* can be seen as "causative middle," so can be translated as "they might have their head shaved" (Wallace 1996: 424). "The future tense is used with ἵνα

believers will know that there is nothing right in what they have heard of
you, but that you keep the law. Don't worry about the Gentiles. We know
that they need to keep only the four restrictions."

The leaders of the Jerusalem church paid attention to the Jewish
believers, and not to what God had done; to what people said about Paul,
and not to what God had done through Paul. It is hard to read in their
request any defense of Pauline theology or any efforts to listen to Paul's
defense. They just demanded a show in public in order to silence the
church members by paying some expenses. The legitimacy of their request was based on the decision of the Jerusalem council (Acts 15:29).
Their expression, however, shows that they were concentrating on something different from the council's:

> The list in 21:25 seems to be the same as that in 15:29. How-
> ever, all four items in 21:25 have the singular even though
> "idol sacrifices" and "things strangled" in 15:29 have the plu-
> ral. Also, only one article τό is applied to all four or at least to
> the first three, which may be the reason for two items to be-
> come singular. Moreover, in respect of situation and function,
> this list is very different from that of 15:29. In 21:21 it is said
> that Paul teaches the Jews to forsake the law of Moses so as
> not to circumcise their children and not to keep the customs.
> Paul's teaching to the Jews, not to the gentiles, is at issue. The
> fourfold list in 21:25 is mentioned to emphasise the distinc-
> tion between the Jews and the gentiles. However, the list in
> the council letter in 15:29 was given to emphasise the *unity*
> between the Jewish and the gentile Christians.[34]

Luke reports that their solution did not work well; before completing the purification ceremony for the four Jewish believers under a vow,
Paul was attacked by another angry mob and was bound with two chains
(21:30–33).

Even though their request sounded discourteous, Paul accepted it:
**Paul took the men, and the next day he purified himself along with
them and went into the Temple, giving notice of the completion of the
days of purification, when the sacrifice would be offered for each of
them** (Acts 21:26). Luke does not mention Paul's answer to their request,
but merely his action in which his endurance could be read. In regard

---

... to express purpose" (Culy and Parsons 2003: 412).

34. Park 2010A: 280.

to Paul's acceptance, some commentators remind themselves of Paul's famous expression, "All things to all men" in 1 Cor 9:22.[35]

Nonetheless, the "two problems with this explanation" are pointed out by Schnabel: (1) in 1 Cor 9:19–23, Paul "does not exclude anybody from his preaching" and "he does not set limits on his identification with the people whom he seeks to win for faith in Jesus"; (2) "Paul cannot 'live like a Jew' and treat the temple as the central place of God's presence (and continue to bring sin and guilt offerings), or regard the Jewish people as the only place where salvation is possible (and require Gentiles to become Jews if they want forgiveness)."[36]

We need another explanation. According to Witherington, Paul "may have felt it was necessary to maintain the bond of peace between the mother church and his converts."[37] It is possible, but we cannot set aside Paul's transition; in other words, the man of conviction (Acts 15:38–40) could have become tenderer to approve of this kind of request; not because of his wisdom to *comply* "with the elders' plan,"[38] but on the basis of his faith in God and His gracious Word (20:32). Even though the Jerusalem church leaders retreated a bit from the decision of the Jerusalem Council by separating the Jewish Christians from the gentile Christians, Paul seems to have shown the "attitude of concession."[39]

Paul's acceptance to the elders' request, along with Paul's activity itself in Jerusalem, has been viewed in many angles.[40] If we deal with them one by one, to begin with, Paul's purification would not have been a ceremony to complete his previous vow in Cenchreae.[41] In addition, the four men's vow was related to a Nazirite vow, which no one denies. Also, the four men's purification would not have been for ritual defilement: some scholars think that the four men should be cleansed from their ritual defilement during their Nazirite vow.[42] If they had been defiled, they had no need to purify themselves with Paul for the first time; on the contrary, they purified themselves with Paul (Acts 21:26) and then

---

35. E.g., Bruce 1990: 447; Fitzmyer 1998: 697.

36. Schnabel 2012: 878–79; also see Schnabel 2004: 955–56.

37. Witherington 1998: 651.

38. Bruce 1988: 407.

39. In regard to Paul's attitude of concession in 21:26, see Park 2010A: 289–90.

40. For basic information, see Marshall 1980B: 364–65n3 and Bock 2007: 647.

41. See comments on 18:18.

42. E.g., Schnabel 2012: 876.

waited for **seven days**, surely for another purification (21:27). Besides, the elders might not have asked Paul to pay eight doves or eight young pigeons since only "two doves or two young pigeons" were mandatory to be cleansed from uncleanness during a Nazirite vow (Num 6:9–10). Moreover, Paul's purification should not have had to do with his recent return from a "Gentile territory";[43] not only because this purificatory ritual must be performed both on the seventh day *and* on the third day (cf. 19:12) but also because Paul was purified together with these four men. Hence, we may conclude that Paul and the four men started their Nazirite vow at the same time and planned to finish it on the seventh day.[44] This view has been rejected on the basis of the statement that a Nazirite vow "would last for thirty days."[45] However, the text of *m. Naz.* 6:3 admits a Nazirite vow for seven days: "A Nazirite vow for an unspecified period of time is [to apply] for thirty days." The "thirty days" regulation is related to "a Nazirite vow of an unspecified period of time." Therefore, we may conclude that Paul aimed at keeping peace with the elders by accepting their request with the "attitude of concession."

After the purification ceremony "perhaps in the Pool of Siloam at the junction of the Tyropoeon and Kidron Valleys, or in the Pool of Bethesda near the Sheep Gate"[46] or more probably in "the ritual baths near the Temple Mount,"[47] Paul should have prepared another means for purification even though the relief fund had already been delivered to the Jerusalem church leaders. The amount would have been five male lambs a year old without blemish for burnt offerings, five ewe lambs a year old without blemish as sin offerings, five rams without blemish as peace offerings, and five baskets of unleavened bread, cakes of fine flour mixed with oil, wafers made without yeast and smeared with olive oil, and their grain offerings and their drink offerings (Num 6:14–15); thus fifteen animals, a bunch of bread, cakes, and wafers, and a lot of fine flours and tons of wine.

Nevertheless, Paul could not finish his Nazirite vow: **When the seven days were almost completed** [on the tenth day], **the Jews from Asia,**

43. Bruce 1990: 447 supports this view in connection with Num 19:12.

44. E.g., Marshall 1980B: 364–65n3.

45. E.g., Bruce 1988: 406; Witherington 1998: 649.

46. Schnabel 2012: 877–78.

47. Regev 2005: 194–204 argues that "the public ritual baths near the Temple Mount" were used for "an extra-purification of an already ritually pure person, before the entrance to the sacred domains of the Temple."

seeing him in the Temple, stirred up the whole crowd and laid hands on him (Acts 21:27). The pilgrim Jews, probably having known the riot in Ephesus (19:23–41), seem to have resolved to harm Paul in their religious base camp, that is, Jerusalem. They shouted: **Men of Israel, help! This is the man who is teaching everyone everywhere against the people and the law and this place. Furthermore, he even brought Greeks into the Temple and has defiled this holy place.** (21:28). They might have failed to take notice of Paul's purification; otherwise, it would have been strong enough to cool down their anger.

Right at this point, Luke explains what these Jews misunderstood: **For they had previously seen Trophimus the Ephesian with him in the city, and they supposed that Paul had brought him into the Temple** (Acts 21:29). Among the seven delegates (20:4), only Trophimus the Ephesian was recognized, which may indicate that the Jews from Ephesus took the lead in the riot. They saw one Greek, Trophimus, but claimed that Paul brought "Greeks" into the temple. Anger causes one to be delirious. On top of Luke's narrative, if they had followed "the law of purity" written in the inscription on the stone partitions that separated the inner court from the outer court, namely "no foreigner should go within that sanctuary,"[48] not Paul but Trophimus should have been brought out to be judged: two inscriptions found in Herod's Temple area in 1871 and 1935 revealed the exact contents; "No stranger is to enter within the balustrade (τρυφακτος) round the temple and enclosure. Whoever is caught will be responsible to himself for this death, which will ensue."[49] They can be accused of cowardice—the Jews in Ephesus showed the same attitude at the Ephesian riot (19:33).

All the city was stirred up and must have been louder than the Ephesian riot since **the people ran together, seized Paul, and dragged**

---

48. See *J.W.* 5.194 and *Ant.* 15.417. Philo informs us that "death is inexorably pronounced against all those who enter into the inner circuit of the sacred precincts (for they admit all men from every country into the exterior circuit), unless he be one of their own nation by blood" (*Legat.* 212).

49. Clermont-Ganneau 1871: 132 (cf. Ilife 1938: 1–3). The text in Greek is Μηθένα ἀλλογενῆ εἰσπορεύεσθαι ἐντὸς ποῦ περὶ τὸ ἱερὸν τρυφάκτου καὶ περιβόλου. Ὃς δ' ἂν ληφθῇ, ἑαυτῶι αἴτιος ἔσται διὰ τὸ ἐξακολουθεῖν θάνατον (Llewelyn and van Beek 2011: 3). τρυφάκτου had been thought of as "one of the faults of pronunciation in use among the Jews speaking Greek at this period" (Clermont-Ganneau 1871: 133; so also Bruce 1990: 449); however, Llewelyn and van Beek 2011: 1–22 argue well not only that it was not a fault (p. 18) but also that the whole contents of the inscriptions are quite well-organized and expressed by the Greeks for the Hellenistic law to recognize their authorship of kings.

him out of the Temple, and at once the gates were shut (21:30). These gates would be those "leading from the inner courts to the outer court (like the Beautiful Gate of 3:2)," which were to be shut probably in order "to prevent further desecration of the sacred precincts."[50] Schnabel reads in this verse an ironic juxtaposition of the geographical phrases: "'the whole city' moves from their 'secular' activities in the city into the inner courts of the temple (potentially rendering the inner courts impure), while Paul, who is engaged in 'holy' activities in the temple in a state of ritual purity, is moved 'out of the temple.'"[51] Anger defies logic; and it still makes sense.

Once more, an angry mob tried to kill Paul (Acts 21:31a) like the one in Lystra (14:19) and in Ephesus (19:29). According to Rapske and Thompson, Paul would have seen some members of the Jerusalem church in the mad mob. Rapske says:

> Luke's silence concerning the reaction of the Jerusalem church to this disaster, when earlier he consistently indicates to his reader the Jerusalem church's solidarity with its leaders in times of severe opposition (4:23–31; 8:1–3; 12:5, 12–17), also tells in favour of a Jewish Christian rejection of Paul. While Paul's arrest created its own ministry opportunities (23:11), nothing positive can be said of the Jerusalem church here. This very silence suggests that the Jerusalem church, at least in part, was not reconciled to the plan of God.[52]

Moreover, Thompson literally expresses the possibility of the presence of the Jerusalem church members in the enraged mob.[53]

Paul would have shut his eyes to these circumstances for he had already done what he could do. He might have remembered both Stephen's face like the face of an angel (Acts 6:15) and his last prayer, **Lord, do not hold this sin against them** (7:60). At the same time, he may have recollected his earlier plan to see Rome (19:21). "What would the Lord do to lead this situation? If I would be beaten to death, would I be able to rise up as in Lystra? Or is this the time for my earthly home to be destroyed (cf. 2 Cor 5:1)?" At that moment, the Jews started to beat Paul, probably with their fists and feet (cf. Acts 21:32).

---

50. Bruce 1990: 450.
51. Schnabel 2012: 894.
52. Rapske 1998: 245.
53. Thompson 2006: 233.

All Jerusalem is in confusion! (Acts 21:31). In the meantime, the tidings of this riot were brought to the tribune of the cohort.[54] Being worthy of a high-ranking military officer, the tribune **at once took soldiers and centurions and ran down to them** (21:32a) probably via "the steps that led from the Antonia Fortress[55] into the outer court of the temple complex" (cf. 21:35).[56] He and his soldiers were quick enough to get to the outer court before Paul was murdered. The Jews **stopped beating Paul when they saw the tribune and the soldiers** (21:32b). Again, God used law enforcement authorities: Gallio in Athens (18:12–17), the town clerk of Ephesus (19:35–41), and this time the tribune of Jerusalem. He would not have "come to save Paul but to restore order,"[57] but he happened to prevent Paul from being beaten to death.

The Jews, especially those who had beaten Paul, were probably standing in awe. Paul would have suffered from pains, bleeding. The tribune seems to have thought that this guy should be arrested to avoid further disorder. Approaching and arresting Paul, the tribune **ordered him to be bound with two chains and inquired who he was and what he had done** (Acts 21:33). The tribune neither arrested those who had beaten Paul nor asked Paul who he was and what he had done; rather, he only grabbed hold of the victim and asked about the situation to the mob. Through this prejudicial process, apoplectic shouts from the mob were what he could collect (21:34a), such as, "His name is Saul; he defiled the Temple," or, "His name is Paul; he violated the law of purity by bringing Greeks into the inner court." In addition, he might have been overwhelmed with the mob's anger toward Paul because two hundred soldiers were too small a number to impose control of all the Jerusalemites and the pilgrims (cf. 21:35). Hence, **he ordered** his soldiers **to bring him into the barracks** [the Antonia Fortress] (21:34c).[58] As Witherington says, it

---

54. In *J.W.* 5,244, it is said that "there always lay in this tower [the Antonia Fortress] a Roman legion." Here "legion" is a translation of τάγμα: in a sense it is a correct translation (cf. LSJ 1752), but scholars understand this term as referring to a cohort (for instance, see Hemer and Gempf 1989: 126 and Witherington 1998: 656). This cohort seems to be an auxiliary cohort composed of 760 infantry and 240 cavalry (see Hanson and Oakman 1998: 170, 186; Witherington 1998: 656).

55. As Herod the Great's first building in Jerusalem, "Antonia combined a palace and a fortress (controlling the Temple Mount which was just to its S[outh])" (*ABD* 169). Viewed toward the east, it was on the left-hand side of the temple.

56. Schnabel 2012: 895.

57. Schnabel 2012: 895.

58. His "barracks" "must be the Fortress Antonia" (Rapske 1994: 137).

is important that the Romans, not the temple police, arrested Paul: if the latter had arrested him, "he would have been tried and sentenced by the Sanhedrin."[59] Jesus and Stephen were judged by the Sanhedrin; however, a different legal process was applied to Paul merely because the tribune arrested him.

Still, the Jews seem to have wanted to snatch and harm Paul: **when they arrived at the steps** ["the two flights of steps connecting the outer court with the fortress"],[60] **he [Paul] had to be carried by the soldiers because of the violence of the mob; the multitude of people followed, screaming, "Away with him!"** (Acts 21:35–36). Paul was about to be torn apart, though already covered in bruises and bound in chains. Thereby, the barracks could have been thought of as a shelter from the mob. Silent screams of pains and ear-piercing screams should have been strong enough to make Paul lose his senses.

Nevertheless, a miracle happened. At the very moment Paul entered into the barracks (Acts 21:37a), he made the cohort of the soldiers stop and informed the mob about who he was and what the Lord had done (22:37—23:21). First of all, Paul asked the tribune in Greek if he could say something to him [the tribune] (21:37b). Paul's asking in Greek seems to be natural because "Greek was the language used by Roman officials in the cities of the eastern Mediterranean."[61] However, this made the tribune surprised: the tribune asked, **Do you know Greek? You are not [you can be] then**[62] **the Egyptian who recently stirred up and led**[63] **the**

59. Witherington 1998: 657.

60. Bruce 1990: 451–52; see also *J. W.* 5.243.

61. Schnabel 2012: 897.

62. The expression, *ouk ara su ei*, may refer to astonishment or inference (see Schnabel 2012: 896n18); but I prefer the latter for these reasons. First, the tribune "could not learn trustworthy facts because of the uproar" (21:34b). Second, the opinion that Paul's speaking in Greek guided the tribune to think that he was an Egyptian, is completely in accord with the language preference of the Egyptian Jews: "many Egyptians spoke Greek, the language preferred by the Jews living in Egypt" (Schnabel 2012: 897). Third, it is almost impossible to suppose that the tribune did not know the language situation in Egypt. Fourth, the conjunction *de* is employed in 21:39, which means that Paul did not admit of the tribune's supposition. Lastly, the Egyptian agitator's name, "Ben Stada" (Bruce 1990: 452), is too different from "Saul" or "Paul" to cause confusion.

63. *Anastatoō* has an object in the LXX and the NT (see Dan 7:23; Acts 17:6; Gal 5:12). So the four thousand men can be considered as the object of *anastatōsas* as well as *eksagagōn*.

four thousand[64] **men of the** sicarii[65] **out into the wilderness?** (21:37c–38). Witherington describes well this situation:

> The tribune knows very well that Greek was spoken widely in Egypt as a result of the long-standing Hellenistic influence there, and since he assumes Paul is a rebel of some sort, the fluency of Greek suggests to him that Paul is no mere local Jewish troublemaker, whose Greek would not likely be this good.[66]

We can read great happiness in the tribune's remark; this officer of Felix might have thought that "he had a real prize—the Egyptian revolutionary who had recently slipped Felix' grasp after organizing and leading a revolt."[67]

However, Paul's answer should have made him disappointed: **I am a Jew, from Tarsus in Cilicia, a citizen of no obscure city; I beg you, permit me to speak to the people** (Acts 21:39). Schnabel understands Paul's insistence on his Tarsian citizenship "as a rebuttal of someone who resents being mistaken for an Egyptian."[68] Paul's citizenship is "in heaven" (Phil 3:20); he also had a Roman citizenship (cf. Acts 16:37–38; 22:25–29; 23:27); but his Tarsian citizenship seems to have been important enough to get an opportunity to speak to the crowd.[69]

The tribune permitted Paul to speak. The soldiers should have lowered him on the ground; so Paul **stood on the steps and motioned with**

---

64. There is a gap between Josephus and Luke in terms of the number: according to Josephus (*J.W.* 2,261) it is 30,000 in Greek Λ; according to Luke, it is 4,000 in Greek Δ (see Bruce 1980 [1969]: 340n15. Rapske 1994: 136n5). In relation to this gap, Bruce 1980 [1969]: 340 says: "Four thousand is a more reasonable estimate of the Egyptian's army than Josephus's thirty thousand." Josephus might have desired to increase the number of the *sicarii*.

65. "The name is derived from Latin *sīca*, 'a dagger.' The *sicarioi* were implacable in their hatred to Rome and to those Jews who were suspected of leaning toward Rome. They took a leading part in the Jewish rebellion and in the disturbance previous to it, and also in the faction quarrels during the war" (*ISBE* 1:288).

66. Witherington 1998: 661.

67. Rapske 1994: 136.

68. Schnabel 2012: 898.

69. Via Tarsian citizenship, according to Witherington 1998: 663, Paul "is making a claim here to be a person of considerable social status, indeed probably higher status than the tribune himself." For a deeper level discussion, see Rapske 1994: 72–83, who concludes: "Textually and contextually, then, Paul should be understood to declare his full Tarsian citizenship at Acts 21:39."

his hand to the people (Acts 21:40a). A calm and orderly atmosphere: the soldiers did not enter into the barracks carrying Paul on their shoulders; after a strange conversation between the tribune and Paul, Paul stood on the steps, gesturing for the mob to be silent. Thus, silence reigned over the disordered mob, and Paul addressed them in the Hebrew language (21:40b). This Hebrew language may refer from Aramaic or Hebrew;[70] "it is not impossible that he spoke in Hebrew, a language still in use, as the Dead Sea Scrolls have demonstrated," as Schnabel says.[71]

---

70. For references, see Fitzmyer 1998: 701.

71. Schnabel 2012: 898. I hold that Paul spoke in Hebrew rather than Aramaic; first, on account of the effect on the audience—speaking in Hebrew would have influenced the Jews to be silent more than speaking in Aramaic—(22:2); second, Paul's education at the feet of Gamaliel (22:3) could have been proved by using Hebrew, not by employing just "the *lingua franca* of non-Greek speakers in the eastern Roman world and in the Parthian Empire" (Bruce 1990: 453).

ACTS 22
Paul's First Defense and One Day Interval

From this chapter, Paul's trial speeches are continued on from the last chapter. Goulder compares Luke 20–24 with Acts 21–28 as follows:

Luke		Acts	
20–23 Jesus' passion and four trials		21–26	Paul's passion, and four trials[1]
23	Jesus' death	27	Paul's "death"
24	Jesus' resurrection	28	Paul's "resurrection"
	Jesus' ascension		Paul's arrival at Rome[2]

This is a meaningful parallel, but it cannot be denied that Paul's trial did not come to an end in Acts, as written in the last point of his first imprisonment in Rome. Paul describes himself as a runner who forgets the things that were behind and strives to reach out for the things that were ahead (Phil 3:12–14).

In this chapter, Luke provides Paul's speech to the Jews, who had intended to beat him to death, and then describes what happened in the barracks for one day: all these would have happened around the Pentecost, May 29 in 57 CE. In regards to the meaning and significance of Paul's conversion and calling, see the section "A Historical Figure's Conversion/Call" (Acts 9:1–19a). As for now we will focus on the narrative flow and the differences between 9:1–19a and 22:1–21.[3] To analyze the repetitions, some rhetorical terms related to means of persuasion will be used. "The means of persuasion" used by characters can be categorized as artificial or inartificial, and as *ethos*, *pathos*, or *logos*. Aristotle says that "proofs are

---

1. A summary on "Parallels between the Trial of Jesus and the Trials of Paul" can be found in Rius-Camps and Read-Heimerdinger 2009: 359–61.

2. Goulder 1964: 61; so also see Walton 2000: 38.

3. As regards the differences of Paul's two conversion/call stories, the main idea and lots of expressions came from Park 2011: 146–68 without quotation marks.

the only things in it that come within the province of art"⁴ and that "it is obvious, therefore, that a system arranged according to the rules of art is only concerned with proofs."⁵ He says,

> As for proofs, some are inartificial, other artificial. By the former I understand all those which have not been furnished by ourselves but were already in existence, such as witnesses, tortures, contracts, and the like; by the latter, all that can be constructed by system and by our own efforts. Thus we have only to make use of the former, whereas we must invent the latter.
>
> Now the proofs furnished by the speech are of three kinds. The first [*ethos*] depends upon the moral character of the speaker, the second [*pathos*] upon putting the hearer into a certain frame of mind, the third [*logos*] upon the speech itself, in so far as it proves or seems to prove.⁶

We will examine which "means of persuasion" are employed by Paul, artificial or inartificial, and *ethos* or *pathos* or *logos*.

Paul's Defense before the Jews (22:1–21)

Paul's speech was called "defense" by himself, and his language of speech, Hebrew or Aramaic, made the Jews even quieter (Acts 22:1–2). His defense is composed of the following parts:

Who he was (22:3–5)

Who made him find the new way of faith (22:6–16)

What Jesus did (22:6–11)

What Ananias did (22:12–16)

Why he had gone to the gentiles (22:17–21)

[What God had done through him among the gentiles].

If his defense had not been interrupted, he should have talked about what God had done among the gentiles, namely his main repertoire (cf. 14:27; 15:4, 12; 21:19).

Who was Paul? He introduced himself as a Jew who had four features: (1) **born in Tarsus in Cilicia**, (2) **brought up in this city [Jerusalem]**,

---

4. *Rhetoric* I.1.3.

5. *Rhetoric* I.1.11.

6. *Rhetoric* I.2.2–3.

(3) **educated at the feet of Gamaliel according to the strictness of the law of our fathers**, and (4) **being zealous for God as all of you** [the Jews in front of him] **are this day** (Acts 22:3). We will look at each one since this background information on Paul does not appear in 9:1–19a.

Point 1, he was born in Tarsus. On the basis of his Tarsian citizenship (21:39), Ramsay conjectures that his "family had been planted in Tarsus with full right as part of a colony settled there by one of the Seleucid kings [possibly under Antiochus IV (175–164 BCE)] in order to strengthen their hold on the city."[7]

Point 2, he had been brought up in Jerusalem. His bringing up in Jerusalem may explain how he was able to speak in Hebrew or Aramaic. Additionally, he would not have been adjusted fully to any language and culture so his speech could have been evaluated as "contemptible" (2 Cor 10:10), even though, as Schnabel observes, "he was bilingual and bicultural, moving with ease between Jewish culture and Gentile culture."[8]

Point 3, he learned from Gamaliel, the grandson of Hillel (c. 50 BCE–10 CE) who had more easygoing views on the law.[9] Gamaliel is described as **a teacher of the law, respected by all the people** in Acts 5:34, so this name should have given Paul the authority to talk further.[10]

Point 4, he was zealous for God as much as the listeners. This expression may allow the listeners and the readers to connect Paul with the Zealot and can pave the way for "Paul's Zealot associations,"[11] while this zeal for God was criticized in Rom 10:2, for it was "not in accord with knowledge." Nevertheless, these authoritative characters and associations in their minds should have made Paul more trustworthy, so mentioning them can be seen as *ethos*. And *pathos* can be read in his remark on the Zealot. Overall, these personal backgrounds could be grouped as inartificial proofs.

Paul's biographical account continues: I[12] **persecuted this Way even to the point of death, binding up both men and women and putting**

7. Ramsay 1975 [1897]: 32.

8. Schnabel 2012: 900.

9. Ferguson 1993: 461.

10. Rapske 1994: 94 provides three features of Gamaliel: "In the first instance, Gamaliel himself was, like Paul, a Benjaminite. In the second, Gamaliel was arguably the most significant and influential Pharisaic educator in the early first century AD. Third, Gamaliel had breadth of popular impact."

11. Fairchild 1999: 531.

12. *Hos* in 22:4, which modifies *anēr* in 22:3 (Culy and Parsons 2003: 423), seems

them in prison (Acts 22:4). He admitted that he had been the same as the audience even in terms of conduct, particularly of the reaction toward the Christians (the same logic flows in Phil 3:6a, "In my zeal for God I persecuted the church"). There were official witnesses to Paul's persecution of the church, that is, the high priest[13] and the whole council of elders, for they issued official letters to the brothers in Damascus (Acts 22:5b). While Paul's initiative is emphasized in 9:1–2 (**he requested official letters**),[14] in 22:5b the members of the Sanhedrin have the initiative and perform the function of witnesses. But why Damascus? Probably since it was prophesied as the northern extremity of the promised land (Ezek 47:16–18; 48:1), Paul was about to arrest some as prisoners and bring them even from Damascus to Jerusalem because they were to be punished (Acts 22:5c), which reveal that Paul had been extremely zealous for God and had done more than any other Jew to persecute the church. Paul's mentioning of the high priest and the whole council of elders can also be seen as *ethos* from Paul. His persecuting the church may have moved the Jews' mind, so it can be categorized as *pathos*. And these proofs can be seen as inartificial.

Most of the Jews, especially those from Asia, would have been surprised at his past career and would have queried what made this "official agent of the Sanhedrin"[15] change. Paul answered the expected question with what Jesus and Ananias had done (Acts 22:6–16). Both came near to Paul to meet and converse with him: Jesus met him on the way to Damascus; Ananias in Damascus.

Subsequently, Paul expounded on the life-changing event slightly differently from how Luke had laid out in ch. 9. Coming near to Damascus, **a great light from heaven** (22:6) flashed around him: a stronger expression than **a light from heaven** (9:3) is employed. He fell to the ground and heard a voice talking to him (22:7a). In Acts 9, it is recorded that **he [Paul] understood the voice** [the accusative] **speaking to him** (9:4), and then the companions were **hearing the voice** [the genitive] (9:7). The narrator seems to point out that Paul understood the contents

---

to objectify Paul.

13. This high priest should be "Joseph Gaiaphas, son-in-law of Annas (Mt. 26:3, 57; Lk. 3:2; Jn. 11:49; 18:13f., 24, 28; Ac. 4:6)," who had been the high priest in 18–36 CE (Bruce 1990: 95). Schnabel 2012: 902 thinks that "Caiaphas may still have been alive in AD 57."

14. So also Schnabel 2012: 902.

15. Rapske 1994: 100.

spoken by the voice but the companions heard the sound only.[16] In Acts 22, Paul confesses, **I listened to the speaking voice toward me** (22:7). **They did not understand the voice of the one speaking to me** (22:9b), he says. Chapter 22 seems to emphasize first Paul's obedience and then how others did not take notice of the meaning of the voice speaking.

In the previous description of Paul's journey to Damascus, Jesus' sudden appearance, and Paul's response (Acts 9:1b–4a), the narrator focuses on Paul's act of asking, the actual process of the event, and his cognition, according to main verbs in 9:1b–4a.[17] By the way, in 22:5b–7a the main verbs show Paul putting emphasis on his "doings," namely his departure and falling, his own cognition, and the whole process of the incident.[18] Then, the heavenly voice asked Paul why he persecuted him (22:7b). Paul did not answer the question but asked him back who the Lord was (22:8a); he did not answer, but by calling him the Lord showed that he had a very respectful attitude toward the voice. The Lord answered that he was Jesus of Nazareth, whom he persecuted (22:8b). At this point, the heavenly voice was identified with Jesus of Nazareth;[19] however, the audience did not barge in. Before finishing his talk about the communication with Jesus, Paul mentioned the circumstances of the companions: those who were with him indeed saw the light, but did not understand the voice of the one who was speaking to him (22:9). While Luke the narrator says in 9:7b that the companions heard the voice but could not

16. Robertson 2010 [1934]: 506 insists, "The accusative (case of extent) accents the intellectual apprehension of the sound, while the genitive (specifying case) calls attention to the sound of the voice without accenting the sense." Wallace 1996: 133 doubts this stance: however, his "examples of ἀκούω + genitive indicating understanding" seem to be inaccurate. The genitive in 3:23 quoting Deut 18:19 may accent unquestioning obedience to the prophet like Moses, not understanding him. The genitive in 11:7 should not include Peter's understanding. Even after it was repeated three times Peter could not understand what it meant. Furthermore, Wallace's "instances of ἀκούω + accusative where little or no comprehension takes place" (1996: 133) also are unsuitable. The accusative in 5:24 does not indicate that "the commander of the temple guard and the chief priests" do not understand the report. They understood the report but wondered what this could be. So, Robertson's opinion seems to be still effective in identifying the meaning of ἀκούω in relation to the case. So also see Moulton 1998: 66; BDAG, 38.

17. There are four main verbs in 9:1b–4a: *ētēsato* (he asked, 9:2), *egeneto* (it happened, 9:3), *periēstrapsen* ([a light] flashed, 9:3) and *ēkousen* (he heard, 9:4).

18. There are also four main verbs in 22:5b–7a: *epopeuomēn* (I went, 22:5), *egeneto* (it happened, 22:6), *epesa* (I fell, 22:7) and *ēkousa* (I heard, 22:7).

19. *Ho Nazōraios* does not appear in 9:5.

see anyone, paying attention to the hearing ability, in 22:9 Paul emphasized their visual ability. Paul seems to have employed the companions as eyewitnesses.

Then, Paul expressed another query: **what should I do, Lord?** (Acts 22:10a). In Acts 9, the answer to this question was given to Ananias (9:15–16); in Paul's own speech before the Jews, it was given to Paul himself (22:21). This answer made the Jews agitated (22:22). Foreseeing their reactions, Paul seems to have tried to put this answer at the end of his speech. It should have been quite necessary that the voice in heaven sent Paul to the gentiles. The narrator put this pivot within the communication between Jesus and Ananias (9:15); Paul put it within his conversation with Jesus (22:21), which particularly occurred in the Jerusalem temple (22:17).[20] In this sense, the two passages (9:10–16 and 22:17–21) are parallel to each other in relation to the two workers of God: (1) both Ananias and Paul called Jesus "Lord" (9:10; 22:10, 19); (2) Jesus gave a mission to both (Ananias should go to Saul and lay hands on him, 9:11–12; Paul should go out from Jerusalem, 22:18); (3) both Ananias and Paul at first refused to obey Jesus' orders (9:13–14; 22:19–20); (4) Jesus persuaded Ananias and Paul to obey his command (9:15–16; 22:21); (5) ultimately, both obeyed (9:17; if the Jews had not interrupted Paul, the story of his submission to Jesus' demands would have followed).[21] To answer his second question ("What should I do, Lord?" 22:10a), Paul shared a conversation that took place in a trance, which Aristotle might categorize as an artificial means of persuasion. Particular expressions Paul applied to describe his persecution of the church—namely imprisoning and beating the believers, and guarding the cloaks of those who were killing Stephen (22:19–20)—could easily have stirred the audience's mind; therefore, *pathos* is used.

In the middle of Paul's speech, his blindness and Ananias's utterances are explained (Acts 22:11–16). Paul's inability is mainly described in 9:8–9 (**could see nothing . . . without sight . . . neither ate nor drank**), but in 22:11, the reason behind Paul's inability is emphasized (**I could not see because of the brightness of that light**). Ananias is introduced as **a**

20. Paul's prayer in the temple of Jerusalem may have happened "during his first visit to Jerusalem after his conversion" so can be related to 9:26–29 (Bruce 1990: 458; so also Schnabel 2012: 906).

21. See also Park 2002: 90–91, 96–97: according to him, Ananias's change in 9:10–16 can be dealt with Paul's change in 22:17–21 with the same point of view, viz., disciples' change of attitude following their Lord Jesus' commandment.

disciple in 9:10, but Paul introduced him as one **who was a devout man according to the law and well spoken of by all the Jews living there** (22:12); Paul used *ethos*. In 22:13, Paul's obedience is underlined: he regained his sight at that very moment when Ananias commanded him to regain his sight. In 9:17–18, there's no mentioning of Ananias uttering a command to Paul to regain his sight.

Moreover, Ananias's speech in Acts 9:17b is quite different from that in 22:14–16: (1) the former focuses attention on Jesus, but the latter on the God of Israel: the subject of 9:17b is Jesus, but that of 22:14–15 is the God of our fathers (Jesus is called the Righteous One); (2) in the former the spotlight is on Jesus' sending Ananias to Paul, but in the latter God's sending Paul is highlighted; (3) being filled with the Holy Spirit was important in the former, but in the latter, knowing God's will, seeing and listening to the Righteous One,[22] and having oneself baptized and having one's sins washed away[23] were suggested as the essential components.

To sum up, in Paul's speech we can read a lot of *ethos*, some *pathos* (identifying himself as a Zealot; recounting how he persecuted the church), inartificial means of proofs (in relation to his basic information), and an artificial means of persuasion (providing a personal experience to authenticate his mission for the gentiles). Paul seems to have thought that these kinds of means of proofs and persuasion could have worked to persuade the Jews to know God's will, be baptized, and have their sins washed away. However, they did not.

One Day Interval in the Barracks (22:22–30)

Paul's speech was interrupted by the audience since they could not bear the notion that the heavenly voice commanded Paul to go to the gentiles: **they raised their voices and shouted, "Away with this one from the earth; for it is not appropriate for him to live"** (Acts 22:22). According to the Jews, Paul should have been doomed like Stephen: similar verbs of the same root were used to describe Stephen's public assassination and Paul's destruction (22:20, 22);[24] throwing off their cloaks (22:23) is also in line with the cloaks of those who were putting Stephen to death (22:20).

22. "Hearing the voice from his mouth" may allude to Deut 18:15.

23. Wallace 1996: 426 designates both βάπτισαι and ἀπόλουσαι as "permissive middle," saying "if βάπτισαι were a direct middle, the idea would be 'baptize yourself'—a thoroughly unbiblical concept."

24. *Anairountōn* and *aire.*

The tribune should have been astonished by the Jews' uncouth response to Paul's speech partly because he had actually given Paul a chance to speak, believing he would somewhat tranquilize the angry mob, and partly because his trust in Paul and doing him a favor could return to him as the blame for misjudgment and inability. The tribune's hurt feelings are disclosed in his orders to bring Paul back into the barracks to interrogate him by beating him with a scourge (Acts 22:24). This scourge "(Lat.: *flagrum*) was a fearsome inquisitorial instrument."[25] Witherington portrays its danger and usage:

> The instrument would be used on the subject's back and could tear flesh, and so maim a person for life, or even kill him if used repeatedly. According to Roman law (cf. *Digest* 48.18 prol. 1) this procedure was recommended only when all non-coercive means had failed to resolve the matter, or perhaps when the situation was so extreme it was deemed necessary.[26]

It is hard to think that the tribune had used "all noncoercive means."[27] As Bock notes, "If there were a translator, the tribune might be perplexed at the reaction Paul's words provoke."[28] In the tribune's order, Schnabel reads, "his second mistake: having wrongly believed that Paul was an Egyptian, he now believes that he is only a Jew, i.e., a Jew who is no different from most other Jews and who can thus be interrogated under torture."[29]

While Paul was stretched out on the straps to be bound for whipping, Paul claimed to a centurion that it was illegal to whip a Roman citizen without a proper trial (Acts 22:25). In those days, centurions kept a watch on an important prisoner[30] or superintended executions.[31] The

---

25. Rapske 1994: 139.

26. Witherington 1998: 677.

27. *Contra* Witherington 1998: 677, who says, "The tribune may have felt that he had exhausted the earlier methods (see 21:33–34, 39–40)." However, 21:34–35 shows that the tribune did not understand the situation. In addition, 21:39–40 reveals why the tribune allowed Paul to speak; there is no disagreement between Paul and the tribune.

28. Bock 2007: 664.

29. Schnabel 2012: 922.

30. For instance, Josephus talks about the centurion who kept a watch on Agrippa I at Rome (*Ant.* 18.230–233).

31. For instance, Philo mentions a centurion who, together with a captain of a thousand, superintended the execution of Tiberius's son, viz., Gaius's cousin (*Legat.*

centurion understood what his claim meant, immediately went to the tribune and reported it, connoting a complaint to some extent: **What are you about to do? For this man is a Roman citizen** (22:26). Culy and Parsons understand the centurion's question as "a mitigated command (appropriate in addressing a superior): 'Stop what you're about to do!'"[32] Because of the tribune's misjudgment, the centurion would have also been accused of illegal torture.

The tribune should have been extremely perplexed; so he came by himself and asked Paul if he was a Roman citizen. And he got the positive answer: **Yes** (Acts 22:27). The tribune's following remark on his own citizenship obviously uncovers his complete perplexity: **the tribune answered, "I acquired this citizenship with a large amount of money";**[33] **then Paul replied, "I was even born a citizen"** (22:28). As a matter of fact, the tribune did not need to reveal how he had got his citizenship. He seems to have been knocked out by Paul, in terms of the way how, individually or collectively, Roman citizenship was obtained: starting from the most recognized "1) by being citizen-born; 2) by manumission; 3) on completion of military service; 4) by reward; 5) by *en bloc* grant; or 6) for financial considerations."[34]

The game was over: **those who were about to interrogate him withdrew from him, and the tribune was afraid, realizing that Paul had a Roman citizenship and that he had him tied up** (Acts 22:29). Paul would have had a sound sleep, but the tribune might have sat up all night to mull over how to deal with Paul. He would have known the actual circumstances, so the very next day he summoned the chief priests and the whole Sanhedrin (22:30a) to get some sensible advice; "for as a military commander Lysias lacked the official *imperium*, 'authority,' to institute a formal Roman trial."[35] Paul stood before the council (22:30b) even though he should have been tried and sentenced by Roman tribunals. "A Council House for legal proceedings" was located on the southern wall

---

30).

32. Culy and Parsons 2003: 435.

33. On the basis of "the tribune's *nomen*, Claudius (23:26)," Bruce 1990: 461 guesses that "he acquired the citizenship in the principate of Claudius."

34. Rapske 1994: 86.

35. Fitzmyer 1998: 716, as regards the possibility of the tribune's summoning the Sanhedrin, writes, "The summoning of chief priests and the Sanhedrin in an advisory role is not as impossible as has been claimed."

of the Temple Mount, and the Roman soldiers were stationed in the Antonia Fortress at the northeast corner of the Temple Mount; the distance between the council house and the fortress was about one kilometer.[36] The wounded citizen was carried to the council house from the fortress.

36. Currid and Barrett 2010: 216–17.

ACTS 23

From the Sanhedrin to Felix's *Praetorium*

Luke continues to go into detail to report Paul's sojourn in Jerusalem. Chapter 23 includes events that occurred within three days; if Paul arrived in Jerusalem at least nine days before the Pentecost (May 29; cf. Acts 21:18, 26, 27), thus possibly on May 20, these three days would be from May 31 to June 2 in 57 CE. The first day, counting from his arrival in Jerusalem, was the eleventh day; that day Paul stood and was questioned before the Sanhedrin. On the second, so the twelfth day, some Jews plotted against Paul. Their plan was revealed to Paul and the tribune. That night, two centurions escorted Paul to Antipatris (56 km on foot from Jerusalem).[1] On the third in this chapter, or the thirteenth day in Jerusalem, Paul was convoyed to Felix the procurator in Caesarea (55 km on foot from Antipatris). As a result, within two weeks, Paul came back to the place where the prayer that "the Lord's will be done" had taken place (21:14).

Before the Sanhedrin Council (23:1–11)

Paul stood before the Sanhedrin council. It would not have been the first occasion for him to stand before the council, for he had received the letters from the council to the Jews in Damascus (Acts 22:5). On this account the council would have been somewhat familiar to him. **Paul, looking directly at the council, said, "Brothers, I have lived my life as a citizen with a good conscience before God to this day"** (23:1). His statement can be seen as an extension of his interrupted speech on the previous day (22:1–21); he did not need to introduce himself or defend

---

1. The distance between Jerusalem and Antipatris is variously estimated: "An attempt to measure on a map the Roman road distance from Jerusalem to Antipatris (via Lydda) gives c. 35 (English) miles, as compared with 37 (Marshall), 40 (Haenchen), 45 (Hanson)" (Hemer and Gempf 1989: 128n79); 35 miles equal to 56 kilometers.

his beliefs or even his ministry. **Living as a citizen**[2] can be connected with the context of Paul's citizenships, the Tarsian (21:39) and the Roman one (22:25–29): before the council, Paul seems to have pointed out how he performed his heavenly citizenship (cf. Phil 3:20). He carried it out with a good conscience, "i.e., with a self-awareness that resulted from the knowledge that his behavior in thought, word, and deed consistently followed the standard of God's laws."[3]

After hearing Paul's testimony, **the high priest Ananias ordered those standing near him [Paul] to strike him on the mouth** (Acts 23:2). Bruce provides a very good biographical note about this high priest.

> Ananias, son of Nedebaeus [Nebedeus], a notoriously rapacious politician, had been appointed high priest by Herod of Chalcis *c.* AD 47. Like most of the high priests of the period, he was a Sadducee. About 52 he was sent to Rome by Quadratus, legate of Syria, charged with fomenting disorder in Judaea, but was acquitted and was now at the height of his power. Even after his supersession in 57/58 he wielded great authority. He was assassinated at the outbreak of the revolt in AD 66 by followers of the Zealot leader Menahem; his son Eleazar, captain of the temple at that time, took a suitable revenge when Menahem fell into his power.[4]

On the basis of his pro-Roman sentiments, moreover, Witherington evaluates that "as a collaborator with Rome, it is quite believable that he would work closely with Claudius Lysias, and would have been willing to call a council meeting or at least an informal hearing if the tribune required it."[5] This powerful and pro-Roman high priest first brutalized Paul by ordering him to be struck on the mouth, "a gesture which suggests a

---

2. The verb *pepoliteumai* appears here and Phil 1:27 in the NT: it means "'live as a citizen,' i.e., 'conduct oneself in public'" (Bruce 1990: 463).

3. Schnabel 2012: 925. He suggests "the term 'good conscience' (συνείδησις ἀγαθή; also 1 Tim 1:5, 19; 1 Pet 3:16, 21; cf. συνείδησις καλή in Heb 13:18) is synonymous with 'pure conscience' (συσείδησις καθαρά; 1 Tim 3:9; 2 Tim 1:3) and 'clear conscience' (συσείδησις ἀπρόσκοπος; Acts 24:16)" (Schnabel 2012: 925n12).

4. Bruce 1990: 464. For a reference, see *Ant.* 20.103 (appointment), 131 (in bonds to Rome in 52 CE), 205–7 (wickedness under Albinus the procurator in 62 CE), 208–10 (difficulties caused by the sicarii in 63 CE), 213 (conflicts among the high priests in 63 CE); *J.W.* 2.243 (in bonds to Rome in 52 CE), 426 (his house caught on fire in 66 CE), 441–42 (death in 66 CE).

5. Witherington 1998: 688.

strong rejection of what Paul had just claimed."[6] A similar attitude can be found in an officer of another powerful high priest, Annas, who struck Jesus on the face (John 18:22).[7]

As Jesus had been struck on the face at his first trial, so Paul was about to be hit on his mouth. But he escaped from this kind of unlawful and impudent treatment via a swift reply: **God is going to strike you, you whitewashed wall! You sit to judge me according to the law, but even so in violation of the law you order me to be struck?** (Acts 23:3). Paul's reply alludes to Deut 28:22, 28; Ezek 13:8–15 (cf. Matt 23:27); and Lev 19:15:[8] Ananias violated the law that the judges must judge fellow citizens fairly without showing partiality to the poor or honoring the rich (Lev 19:15); further, he hypocritically pretended to be a fair judge by ordering people to strike Paul (Ezek 13:8–15); so God will strike him due to his disobedience and hypocrisy (Deut 28:22, 28).

Paul's sharp riposte seemed to have made those standing near him perplexed, probably because the high priest was blamed for disobedience and hypocrisy before they obeyed his order. **Do you insult God's high priest?** (Acts 23:4), they scolded Paul. In their counter-question, Calvin reads both hypocrisy and pride: "They look narrowly into other men's faults and wink at their own. Again, this pride is coupled with tyranny, so that their subjects, and those who are under them, may do nothing, but as for themselves, they may do whatsoever they will."[9]

Paul immediately and politely replied to their biased and hypocritical response, **I did not know, brothers, that he was the high priest, for it is written, "You must not speak evil about a ruler of your people"** (Acts 23:5). If the first sentence, that "I did not know that he was the high priest," had been a sarcastic remark,[10] Paul would have assigned fault again to the high priest with a form of apology; then a charge of hypocrisy would have been brought on Paul. It is hard to read heavy sarcasm or irony in this verse. Moreover, it may be impossible that Paul was not able

---

6. Witherington 1998: 688.

7. Marshall 1980B: 382 says that the order of the high priest may "remind the reader of how Jesus was treated at his trial (John 18:22f.), although this detail is not recorded in Luke's own account of it."

8. Marshall 2007: 598.

9. Calvin 2009: 316–17.

10. Marshall 1980B: 384 thinks "that Paul was speaking in bitter irony: 'I did not think that a man who could give such an order could be the high priest.'" So also Schnabel 2012: 927.

to see who addressed him.[11] Rather, his expression clearly shows that he really did not know the title of the man speaking to him. There are several conjectured reasons for Paul's unawareness: (1) there had been seven supersessions of the high priest from the time of Paul's conversion;[12] (2) further, he may not have taken notice of the recent replacement for the high priest because he focused only on the ministry that he had received from the Lord Jesus (20:24); (3) the council would have assembled for advisories, not for a trial; so the high priest might not have sat down in accordance with "the manner of the Great Sanhedrin's seating"[13] nor have worn his formal robes.[14] Paul quoted Exod 22:28, "one of a collection of miscellaneous laws,"[15] as the basis for regret at an offensive remark he made about the high priest. On the whole, the Jews charged Paul with transgressing the law (Acts 21:21, 28), the high priest broke the law in public (23:2), and some council members took the high priest's part (23:4); in contrast, Paul apologized even for breaking unintentionally a miscellaneous law (23:5).

This situation may have made Paul have doubts about this council's usefulness to examine his case. Instead of continuing his defense, Paul paid attention to the council composition, "the main of the Sadducean majority [including Ananias the high priest] and the strong Pharisaic minority":[16] **noticing that part of them were Sadducees and the others Pharisees, Paul shouted out in the council, "Brothers, I am a Pharisee, a son of Pharisees. I am on trial concerning the hope and resurrection of the dead!"** (Acts 23:6). Via Ananias's interruption, "keeping the law" became a main issue, and Paul did not miss the opportunity to split the council up into two groups by associating himself with one group. He identified himself with a Pharisee. "Pharisaism" in those days can be understood as "the fundamental and most influential religious move-

11. Two reasons can be related to this case: "that Paul had bad eyesight, and that he did not see that it was the high priest who had given the command to strike him" (Marshall 1980B: 383).

12. See Bruce 1990: 95: when Paul met Jesus, Joseph Caiaphas was the high priest; then Jonathan (36–37 CE), Theophilus (37–41 CE), Simon Kantheras (41–42 CE), Matthias (42–43 CE), Elioenai (43–44 CE), Joseph (44–47 CE), and Ananias (47–58 CE) got the office.

13. For "the manner of the Great Sanhedrin's seating," see Rapske 1994: 105n197.

14. Keener 1993: 391 thinks it a possibility that the high priest did not normally sit in a special place nor wear distinctive robes because the gathering was informal.

15. Marshall 2007: 598.

16. Bruce 1988: 427.

ment within Palestinian Judaism between 150 BC and AD 70," as Deines argues.[17] Hence, he seems to reply in haste: "It is very lamentable for the high priest not to keep the law. Why did it happen? Let's see, um, because he is a Sadducee! Sadducees do not keep the law properly; in addition, they do not have any hope of resurrection. However, I keep the law and have the hope to be resurrected since I am not only a Pharisee but also a descendant of Pharisees. In fact, I am here on trial on account of my hope of resurrection."

Paul did not fail to point out his main arguments, "hope" and "resurrection." "Hope" appears afterward in his defense before Felix (Acts 24:15) and in his final testimony before Agrippa II (26:6, 7). In Acts, half of this word usage (*elpis*) belongs to Paul's trial speeches (23:6; 24:15; 26:6, 7).[18] In addition, "resurrection" also has an important role in his defense (24:15, 21) and final testimony (26:23). In Acts, this word (*anastasis*) appears four times in the part about the early Jerusalem church (1:22; 2:31; 4:2, 33); it occurs in Paul's speech in the Areopagus (17:18, 32); and then only his trial speeches (23:6, 8; 24:15, 21; 26:23). Hence, it would be very attractive to see how Paul used these two elements in his trial speeches.

Paul's quick response made the assembly divided while **there came about an argument between the Pharisees and the Sadducees** (Acts 23:7). Luke provides the reason for division within the council: **for the Sadducees say there is no resurrection, or angel, or spirit, but the Pharisees acknowledge them all**[19] (23:8). Parker interprets this verse logically. First of all, he argues on the basis of Josephus that there were different beliefs concerning "fate" at that time: "the Sadducees deny fate altogether, favoring free will; the Essenes attribute everything to fate, and the Pharisees allow for a mixture of fate and free will (*Ant.* 13.171–173; 18.13; *BJ* 2.162–165)." And supernatural beings such as angels had to do with "fate" and "providence."[20] Second, he suggests three options as to how the difference between angel and spirit can be distinguished: (1) "'spirit' refers to disembodied humans prior to resurrection"; (2) "'angel'

17. Carson, O'Brien, and Seifrid 2001: 503.

18. The other half appears in 2:26; 16:19; 27:20; and 28:20.

19. Zerwick 1963 [2001]: 51 says that *amphoteroi* is allowed "to be used of a plurality with the meaning 'all'" on account of "the obsolescence in Hellenistic Greek of the category of duality": so this word in this verse "refers to three doctrines there listed: the resurrection, angels, the spirit."

20. Parker 2003: 360–62.

and 'spirit' are used to distinguish genera (e.g., Cherubim, Seraphim, and Ophanin) or rank (e.g., archangel and angel) of heavenly beings"; (3) "'spirit' could refer to the Holy Spirit."[21] Among these options, he seems to prefer the first for he also provides some evidence that may show the Jews' conception of spirits of dead people, e.g., "Josephus, the Pharisee, accepts that the witch of Endor brought back the soul (ψυχή) of Samuel from Hades and gave a message to Saul (*Ant.* 6.332)," "when the disciples see Jesus walking on the sea they thought he was a 'ghost' (φάντασμα; Matt 14,26)," and "when they [the disciples] first encountered the resurrected Jesus, they thought they were seeing a 'spirit' (πνεῦμα; Luke 24,37.39)."[22] Third, he argues that "angel or spirit" in 23:8 should not have been regarded "as forms of resurrection."[23] According to him, "resurrection could entail a simple restoration of the body to life (Sib 4.181–182; ApcBar(syr) 50,2; *LAB* 3.10, *animam et carnem*), a transformation of the body (ApcBar[syr] 51,1; 1 Cor 15,51; Phil 3,21), or the soul's migration to a new body (*Ant.* 18.14; *BJ* 3.374; *Ap.* 2.218)."[24]

To sum up, the Sadducees and the Pharisees did not coincide with the same political, financial, and theological backgrounds. The Sadducees had hegemony in politics and were generally wealthy, so their doctrines did not allow any space for supernatural (such as angels) or spiritual (such as disembodied humans) beings to provide human beings with fate or providence; moreover, they did not have a lingering affection for any further life after death probably because they seized enough power during their lifetime. On the contrary, the Pharisees had a small portion of political hegemony for a long period so they could have had a tendency to wait for some interventions of supernatural powers and to attach too much importance to life after death; hence, their doctrines might have permitted plenty of space for interventions of angels or spirits and for life after death. Eventually, some scribes among the Pharisees voiced their objections to the Sadducees' philosophy: **we find nothing evil with this man; what if a spirit or an angel has spoken to him?** (Acts 23:9b).

A clamor of voices (Acts 23:9a) and the heated argument made the tribune anxious. He **feared that Paul would be torn to pieces by them; so he ordered the detachment to go down, take him away out of their**

21. Parker 2003: 362–63.
22. Parker 2003: 362–63n71.
23. Parker 2003: 359.
24. Parker 2003: 358.

midst, and bring him into the barracks (23:10). Although the furor amid the council pertains to Paul, he himself would not have been happy about their commotion; his national leaders continued fighting each other while many gentiles were coming back to God. After coming back to the place where he had spent one day before (cf. 22:30), Paul might have had a sleepless night: **that night**[25] **standing near him [Paul], the Lord said, "Be of good courage, for just as you have testified about me in Jerusalem, so you must also testify in Rome"** (23:11). In Corinth the Lord said, **Do not fear! Rather speak and do not be silent** (18:9), which referred to Paul's fear and silence. In Jerusalem, on the contrary, the Lord encouraged Paul, acknowledged that he had done his job well, and then reassured him that he must go to Rome. There was no rebuke; there were "no more miraculous releases or escapes for Paul,"[26] but only encouragement and reassurance. Boosted up by Jesus' remark, Paul would have confronted the remaining trials with a strong conviction.

Fusing the Horizons: The Vision to Follow

Paul came back to Jerusalem after having three missionary journeys over twelve years from 45 to 57 CE. On one hand, he endured many hardships, even physical ones such as being stoned to death in Lystra (Acts 14:19); on the other hand, he also experienced extraordinary miracles; for example, **when even handkerchiefs or aprons that had touched his skin were brought to the sick, their diseases left them and the evil spirits went out** [of them] (19:11–12). In both circumstances he had toiled hard and did not run away from his responsibilities as the apostle for the gentiles. Even when he was told about the sufferings waiting ahead in Jerusalem (20:23), he completed his duty; and even to the enraged mob, involving abusive Jews (21:30, 32), that was trying to kill him, Paul was not reluctant to proclaim the gospel (22:1–22). Moreover, it must have seemed in vain to spread the Word to the Jews when an enormous group of the gentiles repented and turned to God (26:20). Even in these spirals of depressing situations, Paul stood firm and carried on with his duty.

25. Literally the text has "the following night," which may be reckoned by Jewish time (cf. 3:1; Witherington 1998: 693).

26. Witherington 1998: 693.

This Paul stood before the Sanhedrin council, the meeting of the top leaders of the Jews. What did he see? He saw faces of hatred and judgment, Ananias the whitewashed wall (Acts 23:3), and signs of dissension within the council (23:9–10). What did he hear? He heard an unlawful yell of the high priest (23:2), biased and hypocritical advocacy (23:4), and noises created from conflicts (23:9–10). He saw hopeless situations and heard unlawful and biased babbles among people of his own nation while the gentiles were turning toward God. His heart should have grown weak in those painful circumstances because he earnestly prayed for the salvation of his own people (Rom 9:3). Nevertheless, at that night Jesus appeared, **stood beside Paul, and said, "Be of good courage, for just as you have testified about me in Jerusalem, so you must also testify in Rome"** (Acts 23:11). In Jesus' encouragement, we may discern what Paul would have felt in the council, i.e., a mood of despair or the impression that his efforts were useless. He should have felt discouraged. However, Jesus encouraged him by asserting that what Paul said in the council in Jerusalem was a testimony about Jesus. Indeed! Paul did a good job although no fruit was yet to be seen. Actually his nephew, who apprised Paul and Lysias of the oath of more than forty Jews, should be a sprout of the outcome of his ministry in Jerusalem. Jesus admitted that Paul did not gain "nothing" for his pains. Paul testified about Jesus; being his messenger, this was sufficient. Messengers can deliver messages, but not force people to believe in the good news. The audience was always divided into two groups, believers and unbelievers, just as Simeon's prophecy foretold (Luke 2:34b). Further, Jesus added that Paul would do the same thing in Rome. Paul's ministry for Jesus did not yet come to a close. Paul needed to go to Rome. Due to his further ministry, he should not have felt discouraged.

Both Jesus' acknowledgment of Paul's present ministry in Jerusalem and his guidance of Paul's further ministry in Rome could be the generative power for Paul's testimony in following trials and his journey to Rome. Paul defeated Tertullus the professional orator (Acts 24:1–23). Paul mentioned **righteousness, self-control, and the coming judgment** even to Felix the notorious procurator and Drusilla, his third wife (24:25). Paul defended his innocence influentially and finally appealed to Caesar (25:8, 10–11). He proclaimed the gospel to Felix, Agrippa II, Bernice, the senior military officers and the prominent men of Caesarea, and he blessed them all the more (25:23—26:29). In spite of being in the storm, Paul encouraged all the people in the vessel to have hope and eat food (27:21–26, 33–36).

One statement of the Lord was strong enough for Paul to keep on doing his ministry in an anchored manner. Paul should have zoomed in not on what he saw and heard in the Sanhedrin council, but on what he saw and heard in the attitude and speech of Jesus his Lord. Paul did not "look at what can be seen but at what cannot be seen; for what can be seen is transient, but what cannot be seen is eternal" (2 Cor 4:18). What Paul saw and heard in the council may be categorized as an earthly vision, and what he noticed and learned in the presence of Jesus can be called a heavenly vision. Paul followed the heavenly vision, not the earthly one.

Sometimes what we see and hear on earth could make us disappointed. Conflicts, noises, unlawfulness, hypocrisy, selfishness, and all kinds of nasty things can be seen and heard in our countries, nations, churches, and families, or even within ourselves. Even at that moment, we need to straighten our eyes and ears to our Lord and to his Word, his solution and his perspective. Then we can walk in the very way of Jesus and his disciples, walking without being contaminated with an earthly sense of values. Paul did not bribe Felix to find favor (cf. Acts 24:26, 27; 25:3, 9). He wanted all the passengers, including those who did not listen to his advice (viz., the centurion, the captain, and the ship's owner; 27:11) and those who had bad intentions (viz., the sailors and the soldiers; 27:30, 42), to be saved. We do not always go by the earthly norm. But like Paul, we follow heavenly visions given to us.

Jewish Plot against Paul (23:12–22): Paul's Twelfth Day in Jerusalem

The Jews, by the way, not unrelated to either the Sadducees or the Pharisees, seem to have been annoyed, probably thinking that all the Jews had been made fun of by Paul because the council had been split simply on account of Paul's brief remark on the law: more than forty Jews formed a conspiracy and **separated themselves, saying that they would neither eat nor drink until they had killed Paul** (Acts 23:12–13). This "separation" has to do with the *herem* concept in the OT,[27] particularly with voluntary *herem* initiated by human beings;[28] they should have been put to

---

27. Johnson 1992: 403–4; Barrett 1998: 1072; esp. Park 2007A: 116.

28. On the basis of OT usage, Park 2007A: 7–52 categorizes *herem* into mandatory, voluntary, and pagan *herem*. Park 2007A: 50 defines voluntary *herem* like this: "It is

death (Lev 27:28–29), but death seems to have been amended to "neither eating nor drinking."[29]

The high priests and the elders were informed of these conspirators' oath and plot: We have separated ourselves as (voluntary) *herem* not to partake of anything until we have killed Paul; so now you request the tribune to bring him down to you, as if you were going to investigate the things about him more thoroughly; we are ready to destroy him (cf. Acts 22:20) before he approaches [this place] (23:14–15). The distance between "a Council House for legal proceedings" on the southern wall of the Temple Mount and the Antonia Fortress at its northeast corner was about one kilometer.[30] Accordingly, it would take the detachment of Roman soldiers about twenty minutes to bring Paul down from the fortress to the council hall, "either across the outer court of the temple to one of the gates in the western boundary of the Temple Mount that gave access to the road below, or via the direct access from the Antonia into the city."[31] Those who planned to lie in ambush might have thought that twenty minutes would be enough to grab Paul. Their oath and ambush allude to 2 Chr 20:23 where the concept of *herem* is combined with ambushes; the Lord's agents carried out the ambushes to give victory to Jehoshaphat and the Israelites.[32]

The Jews' ambush[33] was known to the son of Paul's sister, who **came and entered the barracks and reported to Paul** (Acts 23:16).[34] This young man could have had information about the ambush from some acquainted Pharisees. Paul's nephew, probably a teenager[35] or one "between

---

initiated by human beings. It is most holy and never able to be substituted or redeemed or ransomed (Lev 27.28). It can be lawfully given only when the owners make what belongs to them voluntary 'separation' to the Lord. Any thing or living creature can be 'separated' to the Lord (Lev 27.21, 28)."

29. See Park 2007A: 116.

30. Currid and Barrett 2010: 216–17.

31. Schnabel 2012: 933.

32. Park 2007A: 47–48 categorizes this *herem* as mandatory "separation" initiated by God.

33. The Jews "will be posted along the route traveled by the detachment of Roman soldiers taking Paul to the council hall, perhaps hiding in crowds" (Schnabel 2012: 933).

34. On the presence of Paul's nephew in Jerusalem, Witherington 1998: 695 reads the possibility "that not just Paul, but his family, had moved to Jerusalem some time ago."

35. Bruce 1990: 469 guesses his age to be less than twenty in accordance to "the

twenty-two and twenty-eight,"[36] is introduced as Paul's sole helper in those days except for the tribune who helped Paul unintentionally; none of the church members are mentioned as his helper. This youth might have heard Paul's speech in 22:1–21 and gotten a favorable impression of him. Paul, who had been strengthened by the Lord on the previous day (23:11), should have been comforted that night by his young but brave relative. After hearing of the plot, Paul neither despised nor hesitated to call one of the centurions, and strongly recommended taking the youth to the tribune (23:17).

The centurion also did not delay in doing what he should do (Acts 23:18); for the past two days he should have already realized that Paul was involved with a delicate matter. The tribune should also have detected signs that the youth had some news of intrinsic value; **the tribune took him by the hand, withdrew privately, and asked, "What is it that you possess to report to me?"** (23:19). The nephew informed the tribune of the Jews' consensus on his uncle, then warned him not to be persuaded to accept their request, and mentioned the oath and the ambush of the more than forty as his conclusive argument (23:20–21). The young man set out the time as "tomorrow" (23:20), so the tribune must have dealt with the report without hesitation. He sent Paul's nephew away, confirming that he should not tell anyone about this report (23:22).

From Jerusalem to Caesarea (23:23–35): Paul's Thirteenth Day in Jerusalem

Promptly, the tribune summoned two of the centurions and commanded them to prepare almost half of the cohort along with mounts by nine o'clock that night so as to take Paul safely to Felix the procurator[37] (Acts 23:23). The tribune's auxiliary cohort might have been composed of 760 infantry and 240 cavalry,[38] so 470 soldiers (200 soldiers, 70 horsemen, and 200 javelin throwers[39]) count up almost half of the troop, which in-

---

diminutive form νεανίσκος (vv. 18, 22) and the fact that the tribune took him by the hand to a place where they could have privacy."

36. Witherington 1998: 695.

37. "The term procurator, 'agent,' in ordinary Latin refers to a person, usually a free citizen, who managed the estates and business affairs of a wealthy Roman" (*ISBER* 3:978–79).

38. See Hanson and Oakman 1998: 170, 186; Witherington 1998: 656.

39. LSJ 379. *Dexiolabous* literally means "holding with the right hand," so

dicates that the tribune treated Paul very exceptionally. Mounts were also prepared for Paul: "This may mean a horse for Paul and a pack animal for his baggage, or both mounts may be simply for Paul, the one spelling the other in a rapid journey."[40]

The tribune planned to send Paul away to Felix the governor. Unlike Paul, Felix had been a slave before becoming a freedman.[41] His origin remains wrapped in mystery; he might have had two tribal names (*nomen* [*gentilicium*]), Antonius (according to Tacitus) and Claudius (according to Josephus);[42] Luke seems to avoid the issue of Felix's origin by providing only his cognomen since both Lysias's *nomen* (Claudius, Acts 23:26) and Festus's *nomen* (Porcius, 24:27) are informed. Felix was appointed as procurator of Judea, Samaria, Galilee, and Perea by Claudius in 52 CE,[43] which might be "an unusual appointment for a mere freedman rather than someone of equestrian rank."[44] Even though Nero had the power of Caesar in 54 CE, the procuratorship of Felix was preserved. Brenk and de Rossi assess his ability as a procurator as follows:

> As for Felix, the Imperial court seems to have regarded him as effective or competent. He remained in his post as *procurator* quite some time, outlasting his brother Pallas, who had been Claudius' financial secretary (*a rationibus*)[45] before moving into the government of Nero. Moreover, before becoming procurator, Felix may have been active in Judaea in some sort of commanding position (Tacitus, *Annals* 12.54, in contrast to Josephus). Judging by *Acts*, Felix was procurator from AD 52 to around 60, a period of almost eight years. His successors

---

"spearmen, slingers, and javelin throwers" are suggested as its meaning (Bruce 1990: 470).

40. Witherington 1998: 697.

41. See Bruce 1990: 470: "Felix was a brother of Pallas, most influential of the imperial freedmen under Claudius."

42. Bruce 1978: 33–36 argued that Felix's full name was Tiberius [praenomen] Claudius [nomen] Felix [cognomen]; however, it was doubted by Hemer 1987: 45–49; eventually, Brenk and de Rossi 2001: 410–11 think that both Claudius and Antonius are possibly correct as Felix's *nomen*.

43. *Ant.* 20.137, 142; *J.W.* 2.247.

44. Walton 2012: 554; so also see *ISBER* 3:979.

45. *A rationibus*, the chief of accounts for the *fiscus Caesaris*, "became the real minister of finance" during Claudius's time (*DNTB* 959).

did much worse: Porcius Festus 60–62; Lucceius (?) Albinus
62–64; Gessius Florus 64–66 (followed by the Revolt).[46]

The tribune wrote a letter to Felix (Acts 23:25–30). On the basis of
the expression, *tupos*,[47] Schnabel thinks that Luke "is providing a direct
citation of a transcript of the letter, not a rhetorical approximation of
what the Roman commander might have written."[48] In regard to how
Luke obtained this copy, two possibilities can be counted:

> (1) This letter surely would have been read out loud upon
> Paul's arrival at the initial meeting between the prefect and
> Paul, in which case Paul heard what is said and could have
> conveyed its contents to Luke, if Luke himself did not ac-
> company Paul on this journey. . . . (3) Precisely because it was
> an official report, it was the sort of document that would be
> preserved for the trial of Paul as an important reference work
> for Felix (and others?) to use.[49]

This letter can be regarded as a legal document,[50] surely attached
to the legal document for Paul's trial; it should have been read by Felix,
Festus, Agrippa, and finally Nero.

The document starts with the prescript; the sender (Claudius
Lysias), the recipient (His Excellency[51] Procurator Felix), and the salutation (greetings) (Acts 23:26). The four main verbs have the first singular
subject: **I rescued** (23:27), **I brought down** (23:28), **I found** (23:29), and
I sent (23:30). In addition, all of them have the same object, viz., Paul.
Hence, this letter has a very simple format: "I rescued this man, I brought
him down to the Sanhedrin council, I found him innocent, and I sent

---

46. Brenk and de Rossi 2001: 413 (italics original). Felix's predecessors also had
shorter procuratorships: Cuspius Fadus (44–45 CE), Tiberius Julius Alexander (45–48
CE), and Ventidius Cumanus (48–52 CE) (Bruce 1990: 94).

47. This word has the meaning of "engraved mark" (LSJ 1835).

48. Schnabel 2012: 936. So also Witherington 1998: 698–99, who suggests 3 Macc
3:12–29 as further evidence; Winter 1993: 309; *TDNT* 8:248. *Contra* BDAG 1020.

49. Similarly Schnabel 2012: 936–37: "the letter was likely read in court, where
Paul, who was Luke's source, became familiar with the text; or the letter likely became
part of the official documentation of Paul's legal case and would thus have been available to the defendant."

50. This kind of report is called *elogium* ("short saying, inscription") (see Schnabel
2012: 937).

51. This word (*kratistos*) appears only four times in the NT: for Theophilus (Luke
1:3); for Felix (23:26; 24:3); and for Festus (26:25).

him to you."[52] This document should have been more officially composed, something like: "Some things happened to this man; the Jewish council treated him as such; I found him innocent; and he is sent to you." It seems that the tribune's writing was not professional, especially in its format.

However, his skill in covering his own faults seems to be very high. First, by arranging the contents of the document in chronological order, he concealed his carelessness in his command to flog a Roman citizen (without a trial): what is written in Acts 23:27 can be plainly put as, "This man was seized by the Jews; he was about to be destroyed by the Jews; coming up with the detachment, I rescued him; I learned that he was a Roman citizen." The tribune selected "I rescued him" as the main verb and added the fact about his recognition of Paul's Roman citizenship; the emphasis was laid on the tribune's coming to Paul's rescue, so the tribune's wrong treatment of Paul was buried away. Schnabel enumerates what Lysias failed to mention:

> Lysias fails to mention the tumult of Jewish crowds (which may have called his precautions to prevent turbulences in Jerusalem in question), the location of these events in the temple courts (which were right under the nose of his troops stationed in the Antonia Fortress), his suspicion that he was the Jewish-Egyptian insurrectionist, as well as the fact that he chained Paul and called for his interrogation under torture without establishing his identity.[53]

Then, he closes with, "he portrays himself as the protector of a Roman citizen who had been attacked by Jews in Jerusalem."[54]

Second, the tribune reported the council meeting (Acts 23:28) but omitted the severe conflict between the Sadducees and the Pharisees (23:7–10), that occurred because he had brought Paul down to the council. Rather, under the Jewish controversy over the law (cf. 18:15) and his judgment on the case, he hid his incautious ushering of Paul into the Jewish council: **I found he was accused with reference to issues about their law, but having no charge worthy of death or imprisonment** (23:29). This might not indicate Paul's pure innocence; Schnabel says, "There may

---

52. In a sense, it is too simple in comparison with 3 Macc 3:12–29, which has mainly the third plural and the first plural subjects.

53. Schnabel 2012: 937.

54. Schnabel 2012: 938.

be other charges deserving the death sentence that Paul might be guilty of."[55]

Third, the Jewish plot to kill Paul was diminished to a simple plot (Acts 23:30a). As a matter of fact, the oath (23:14, 21b) and ambush (23:15b–16, 21c) that over forty men made can be evaluated as a very serious problem: their oath had to do with "the strictest form of giving to the Lord, demanding complete giving and the giver's perfect faithfulness";[56] to add, lying in ambush is a military action. However, the tribune did not give an account of the severity and stratagem of the Jews' plot.

Lastly, his follow-up measures were described in advance: **I sent him to you at once, also ordering the accusers to state the things against him before you** (Acts 23:30b). Rapske reads a favor to Paul in the tribune's emergency measures:

> As Caesarea was the administrative and judicial centre for Judea, Paul might despair of a speedy hearing. The case load there would be particularly heavy. It might therefore have been considered an additional favour to Paul that Lysias orders the accusers to appear at Caesarea post-haste to present their case before Felix. They are not to await a summons. This would presumably pre-empt the governor's trial calendar.[57]

To sum up, in the tribune's letter, readers may have easily caught Lysias's hiding his faults and exaggerating his own merits, and further have read his sensitivity to self-protection, which contrasts with Paul's attitude to his ministry (cf. 20:24).

The strength of the Roman troop is detected in the unquestioning obedience of the soldiers (cf. Luke 7:8; Acts 10:7–8): the soldiers, in accordance with the assigned order, took Paul and brought him to Antipatris during the night (23:31). They left Jerusalem at nine p.m. and arrived in Antipatris (56 km on foot from Jerusalem) during the night, which means that they should have walked eight hours at a speed of seven kilometers per hour without rest or sleep, an incredible speed.[58] In Antipatris,

---

55. Schnabel 2012: 938n58.

56. Park 2007A: 10.

57. Rapske 1994: 153.

58. Schnabel 2012: 939 thinks about a possibility of "a full day of marching between the night during which they leave Jerusalem and their arrival in Antipatris" and suggests that "the next morning" in 23:32 could refer "to the departure of the infantry escort before the company reaches Antipatris." However, the subject of the main verb in 23:31 makes reference to the whole troop, and that in 23:32 to all of the

there was a fort built by Herod the Great, which was better than Jericho.[59] Thus they could have stopped there for a rest. However, they did not take a rest; the 70 horsemen convoyed Paul to Felix the procurator in Caesarea (55 km on foot from Antipatris) while the others, 200 soldiers and 200 javelin throwers, returned to the barracks in Jerusalem (23:32); for, as Bruce expounds, the country between Antipatris and Caesarea "was open and inhabited mainly by Gentiles" and further "as the conspirators had now been left far behind, the large escort was no longer necessary."[60] The Roman soldiers were strong, swift, and committed to perform the confronted task.

Most likely on June 2 in 57 CE, Paul was presented to the notorious Felix along with the tribune's letter. The procurator read the letter (Acts 23:34a); through the letter he might have discovered that Paul was a Roman citizen hated and accused by the Jews. On account of Paul's citizenship, Felix **asked what province he was from and learned that he was from Cilicia** (23:34b–c). The procurator might have certified that Paul was under his jurisdiction because "Cilicia (at least Eastern Cilicia, including Tarsus) belonged from 25 BC to AD 72 to the united province of Syria-Cilicia."[61] Rapske explains Felix's reasoning:

> The question is jurisdictional and suggests that Felix might have avoided trying the case. An accused could be tried in his own home province, the province in which he had allegedly committed the crime, or in the province where he had been apprehended. The discovery that Paul was from Cilicia foreclosed the option of a transfer as Cilicia was at this time under the authority of the Legate of Syria to whom Felix was responsible. A refusal to try the case in these circumstances would probably have been read as an annoying avoidance tactic by the Legate. A sudden change of trial venue would also strain relations with the members of the Jewish supreme court who were soon to arrive in Caesarea to accuse Paul. Felix was boxed into handling the case.[62]

---

200 soldiers and 200 javelin throwers except for the 70 horsemen. Hence, the context should be interpreted that the troop moved from Jerusalem to Antipatris nearly at their full speed.

59. *J.W.* 1.417.
60. Bruce 1990: 473.
61. Bruce 1990: 473.
62. Rapske 1994: 155.

The tribune could have faced a similar dilemma, but he dispatched Paul to the governor. Now that Lysias is released from his duty and the possibilities of accusation, Felix will take on the burden; however, later on, Felix also had Paul's case tossed back to the tribune (24:22) and finally left it for Festus to solve (24:27).

What Felix could say at that moment was only to promise Paul to hear him speak when the accusers arrived; he ordered Paul to be guarded in Herod's *praetorium* (23:35). Felix's official residence[63] was called by the name of "Herod the builder." According to Josephus, after successfully surviving the great famine in 28–27 BCE and marrying Mariamme, the daughter of Simon the high priest, Herod the Great rebuilt Strato's Tower for twelve years (probably between 22–10 or 21–9 BCE) and changed its name to Caesarea;[64] some splendid palaces were included in his building projects.[65] As regards to Paul's state of confinement, Rapske infers "that Paul was placed under strict restraint, perhaps even in bonds in a cell," by comparing the first state in 23:35b with the latter one in 24:23.[66]

---

63. "The *praetorium* (originally the headquarters of the *praetor* or military commander) was (among other things) the official residence of the Roman governor of an imperial province" (Bruce 1990: 474).

64. See *Ant.* 14.76; 15.293, 299–341; *J.W.* 408–14.

65. *Ant.* 15.331; *J.W.* 408.

66. Rapske 1994: 157: "Paul would be closely watched and virtually immobile. Furthermore, the later command that visitors not be forbidden him (Acts 24:23) suggests that the first phase of his Caesarean imprisonment involved complete isolation from friends and associates and from the help they might provide."

ACTS 24
In Felix's *Praetorium*[1]

In this chapter, Paul's trial before Felix the procurator is fully described. This trial proceeded in Caesarea, probably on June 7 in 57 CE. The representative of the plaintiffs was Tertullus (Acts 24:1). After his claim was proclaimed (24:2b–8), Ananias the high priest and some elders supported him (24:9). Then, Paul defended himself (24:10–21). Subsequent to hearing both sides, Felix postponed his decision on the pretext of hearing the tribune (24:22); however, Lysias does not appear anymore. Rather, Felix's wife emerges in sight with her husband (24:24a). In the end Felix quit his post without dealing with Paul's case, so it was passed on to his successor, Festus (24:27). In the meantime, Paul remained in custody, in some measure free (24:23) even to proclaim the gospel (24:24b–26).

The Plaintiffs' Claim (24:1–9)

Five days passed by **after Paul's arrival**[2] in Caesarea (Acts 24:1a). Some events would have occurred throughout these days. First, Ananias the high priest and the elders would have requested the tribune to bring Paul down to the council house again (23:14–15, 20); by then the tribune would have answered that Paul had already been taken to Felix the procurator in Caesarea (23:24, 30a), and that any charge against Paul should have been brought to the governor (23:30b). Otherwise, the tribune should have informed the council of extraditing Paul to Caesarea before the Sanhedrin council appealed for Paul. Subsequently, Ananias and the elders might have discussed of this unforeseen change with the conspirators (23:12–15, 21). Next, more than forty Jews might have deferred carrying out the oath in that their ambush was available even after two years (25:3). Fourth, Ananias and some of the elders must have taken the trip

---

1. Main ideas and a lot of expressions in Felix's *Praetorium* were published in Park 2017: 70–99.

2. Park 2017: 158.

from Jerusalem to Caesarea "either on foot (four days) or on horses (two days)."[3] Lastly, via a professional advocate[4] they might have indicted Paul for stirring up riots (cf. 24:5); it would have taken at least "one full day in Caesarea to arrange for a meeting with the governor and to lodge the petition to initiate trial proceedings against Paul."[5] Normally five days would not have been long enough to handle all of these affairs; hence, it can be said that Ananias and the elders dealt with the matter very quickly.

At that time Paul **in bonds in a cell** would have prayed and praised as usual (Acts 16:25), and pondered over his next move like this: "The Lord said to me that I must also testify about him in Rome (23:11); what shall I do? (22:10); I must not be defeated at the trial in order to perform the committed task; how should I vindicate myself?" His well-argued testimony in 24:10–21 had to be prepared within these five days.

The plaintiffs, viz., Ananias, elders, and Tertullus, arrived (Acts 24:1b). Ananias and the elders were very strong accusers, as Rapske notes:

> Their birth credentials were superior, and they possessed of-
> fices and honors which put them at the pinnacle of religious
> and political power in Judaism. They would have been heads
> of some of the wealthiest families in Judaea. As high as Paul's
> status was his accusers were superior. In one respect only
> would they be at a disadvantage: Paul was a Roman citizen.[6]

These strong accusers must have employed a very outspoken advocate. Tertullus the legal representative of the plaintiffs, Bruce states, "is a common Roman name,"[7] and Rapske sees the possibility that this rhetor had Roman citizenship.[8] This notion seems to be plausible not only because he had a Roman name and a title indicating "professional legal advocate"[9] but also because the Jews might have already known that Paul's Roman citizenship became the pivot on which the situation changed course. Moreover, Tertullus's Jewishness is insisted on the basis

---

3. Schnabel 2012: 951.

4. If Tertullus had not been under exclusive contract with the Sanhedrin council, he could have been employed in Caesaea because professional attorneys must have remained active around the judicial center for Judea.

5. Schnabel 2012: 951.

6. Rapske 1994: 159.

7. Bruce 1990: 475.

8. Rapske 1994: 159–60.

9. Hogan 2002: 79 understands this usage of *hrētōr* as carrying "the sense of professional legal advocate (cf. Josephus, *Ant.* 17.226 [Ireneus the orator])."

of the first-person plural in 24:3 and 6b.[10] However, this idea is open to question since he could have used the first-person plural in generic terms as a hired legal representative. Even though he said, **we arrested him** (24:6b), this "we" must not have referred to the Jews and Tertullus; even Ananias and the elders should not have seized Paul. Likewise, the first-person plural in 24:3 (**we acknowledge** [your administrative ability]) can also be seen as a generic pronoun referring to the Jews. Above all, **the Jews** in 24:9 excludes Tertullus from "Jewishness." Hence, it is inappropriate to assume that Tertullus had Jewishness. Ananias and the elders represented all of the Jews (**this nation** in 24:2b), and Tertullus made his claim as the official spokesman of the Jews; so it would be proper for him to use the first-person plural not only in 24:3, 6 but also in 24:8, where the first-plural pronoun (*hēmeis*) is also used to emphasize that the accusation was made by all of the Jews.

The accusers **brought formal charges against Paul to the governor** (Acts 24:1c); this was the first action of Roman judicial procedure.[11] As the second action, Paul the accused was summoned (24:2a). Then, as the third action, accusations were made, in this case, by a professional advocate (24:2b–8). Winter argues that Tertullus, as "an able professional rhetor,"[12] followed well the form of official petitions composed of *exordium* (introduction, 24:2b–4), *narratio* (statement of facts, 24:5), *confirmatio* (confirmation, 24:6–8), and *peroratio* (conclusion, 24:8).[13] Meanwhile, Hogan puts stress on Tertullus's omission of *probatio* (proof), in analyzing his charge in terms of Quintilian's five parts of forensic speech, namely "the *exordium* (introduction), *narratio* (statement of facts), *probatio* (proof), *refutatio* (refutation), and *peroratio* (conclusion) (*Inst.* 3.9.1),"[14] and attests that Tertullus undertook "an impossible case"

10. Bruce 1990: 475 mentions 24:6, and Rapske 1994: 160n40 mentions 24:3 along with the Western reading, "according to our law."

11. Witherington 1998: 703 summarizes the order of Roman judicial procedure as follows: "(1) the prosecution comes before the governor and reports its case, (2) the accused is then summoned, (3) the prosecution makes its accusations, (4) the defendant must respond, (5) the judge must decide the issue."

12. Winter 1991: 520–21.

13. Winter 1993: 312, 314, 315–22; Winter 1991: 515–21: he sees 24:2b–3 as the *exordium* in the introduction, but in the body 24:4 is regarded as the conclusion of the *exordium* (see Winter 1991: 518).

14. Hogan 2002: 73, who sees these five parts as "common although not universal among manuals": according to him, "Aristotle omits the *refutatio*, preferring to see it instead as a part of the *probatio* (*Rhet.* 2.26)."

and had no proof to provide.[15] We may assume that Tertullus did not follow the general forensic speech form but instead skillfully employed the form of official petitions because he had no contents to organize the parts of the *probatio* and *refutatio*. Tertullus's mixture of *confirmatio* (confirmation) and *peroratio* (conclusion) in two verses (24:6–8)[16] also can be seen as his own exquisite treatment, and he is not to be blamed for not fully employing the general forensic speech form. In this sense, Brown's evaluation of 24:1–23 as "not a legal text, and therefore not an historical text" should be rejected.[17]

Let's see how the professional pleader claimed the unprovable accusation. In *exordium*, Tertullus made the judge closely connected with the plaintiffs through flattery: **Having experienced[18] much peace through you, and reforms[19] being made in this nation through your providence, everywhere and in every way we acknowledge this, Most excellent Felix, with complete thankfulness; in order not to weary you any further, I beg you to listen to us briefly with your customary indulgence** (Acts 24:2b–4). First of all, Winter notes two facts in connection with having **experienced much peace through you**:

> First, the plaintiffs were duty bound to support Felix [52–59,
> CE], for it was the present high priest, Ananias [47–59 CE], son

15. Hogan 2002: 80–81. Sherwin-White 1978 [1963]: 49 explains the case that the *probatio* is omitted, as an example of the extra ordinem procedure, in which charges are alleged without evidence or witnesses.

16. Codex Bezae has 6b–8a: "[6b we] wanted to judge him according to our own law. 7 However, Lysias the tribune intervened and with a great deal of force removed him out of our hands, 8a ordering his accusers to appear before you" (Rius-Camps and Read-Heimerdinger 2009: 300). It should not be original; first because the charge would make the main point vague (further comments would show that Tertullus accused Paul of being a peace breaker, but the reading of Codex Bezae would make the tribune accused); second because this reading is inconsistent with Tertullus's *exordium* in 24:2b–4 where he flattered the judge; third because this reading formulates another *narratio*.

17. Brown 1996: 329: he says, "We know it is not a legal text because it does not have the language, the structure, or the purpose of legal texts such as those surviving accounts of the proceedings from the courts of the Roman era, the papyri."

18. Winter 1991: 515n41 pays attention to the passive form: "Unlike the three forensic papyri which use the verb in the active form, it is used in the passive by Tertullus to indicate to Felix that the petitioners have enjoyed much peace through his administration."

19. This may refer to "periodic revision of legal ordinances" probably "relating to the procedures of the Sanhedrin or temple administration" (Winter 1991: 517).

of Nedebaeus, the former high priest Jonathan [36–37 CE], and the son of the former occupant of that position in his capacity as captain of the Temple, who, while in Rome, all urged the emperor, Claudius, to appoint Felix to the procuratorship. It was a high unprecedented appointment of a freedman to a post normally given to a member of the equestrian order. The Jews who came down from Jerusalem included the high priest, Ananias, before whom Paul had recently appeared. They were therefore duty bound to endorse the administration of Felix.

Secondly, and more importantly, Felix had very recently restored law and order by quelling the rebellion of an Egyptian prophet as mentioned by Claudius Lysias in Acts and recorded elsewhere.[20]

Talking to Felix about his relationship with Ananias, Tertullus then admired the judge for his foresight: he seems to say, "You know the relationship between you and the high priest as well as the importance of peace in your point of view, so you need to judge this case with providence." After passing a tense remark, the orator comforted the judge by accentuating all-embracing acceptance of the judge and by calling him **Most excellent** (24:3), a title unsuitable for a freedman. In the last part of *exordium*, Tertullus provided both human apologies like "I am wearying you" (24:4a) and "the promise of brevity"[21] (24:4b). Haenchen regards *captatio benevolentiae* (winning of goodwill) in 24:2–4 as "unusually broadly developed,"[22] but, as Winter concludes, Tertullus's "*captatio benevolentiae* was carefully linked to his accusations in the hope of mounting a formidable case against Paul, who was portrayed as an agitator in Jerusalem and an insurrectionist in world-wide Jewry."[23]

Since a powerful and strategic *exordium* was bestowed, Tertullus briefly, but skillfully as before, composed *narratio* (statement of facts, Acts 24:5), *confirmatio* (confirmation, 24:6–8), and *peroratio* (conclusion, 24:8). In *narratio*, Paul was charged with riots: **Being found that this man is a plague, that he stirs up riots among all the Jews throughout the world, and that he is a ringleader of the sect of the Nazarenes** (24:5). Riots (*stasis*) "was the right charge to bring against an opponent

---

20. Winter 1991: 515–16.

21. Winter 1991: 518, 518n57 talks about the usefulness of a lengthy introduction and a brief body in a complicated case.

22. Haenchen 1971 [1965]: 657.

23. Winter 1991: 521.

in criminal proceedings."[24] Through this charge, Tertullus might have reminded Felix about Claudius's edict ordered against the Jews in Rome in 49 CE,[25] as well as the emperor's letter "to the Alexandrians stating that he intended to proceed against Jews from Syria or Egypt who came to Alexandria as 'fermenters of what is a general plague infecting the whole world.'"[26] Furthermore, the rhetor linked Paul with "Jesus of Nazareth, who was crucified by the Roman governor twenty-seven years earlier."[27] At that time even Pilate the prefect was not able to resist Jewish demands for crucifying Jesus (Luke 23:13–25). In this short *narratio*, therefore, Tertullus succeeded in reminding the judge about three elements: the emperor's letter sent to the Alexandrians, his edict given to the Jews in Rome, and the most sensational former trial in Palestine in relation to riots.

The *exordium* and *narratio* of Tertullus seem to have been strong enough to press Felix to declare Paul guilty; to the three elements above the judge might also have recalled Pilate's deposition occurred in 36 or 37 CE. As a result, a very short[28] mixture of *confirmatio* and *peroratio* was added in the end: [first] **he [Paul] even tried to desecrate the Temple;** [second] **him we even arrested;** [third] **from him, by examining, you yourself will be able to perceive all these things of which we are accusing him** (Acts 24:6–8). The "three relative pronouns presenting the proof"[29] are related with the participants in this trial; at first Paul the defendant, then "we" the accusers, and finally "you" the judge. With this very carefully arranged order, Tertullus puts the finishing touches to his claim like this: "Okay, Governor, now it's your turn, so examine him."

Who could have made a better claim on Paul? Felix should have had a stern look while listening to the excellent rhetor. The Jews seem to have been satisfied with Tertullus's claim. It was reinforced by the Jews: they **also joined in the attack, affirming that these things were so** (Acts 24:9).

24. Winter 1991: 518.

25. For this edict, see the introduction of chapter 18 and comments on 18:2.

26. Winter 1991: 518–19.

27. Schnabel 2012: 955.

28. This is very short in comparison with Paul's defense: Tertullus's *confirmatio* and *peroratio* (24:6–8) are equivalent to Paul's *probatio* (24:12–13), *refutatio* (24:14–18a) and *peroratio* (24:18b–21).

29. Winter 1991: 519.

The Defendant's Testimony (24:10–21)

How could Felix deal with these capable and influential plaintiffs? He just followed the Roman judicial procedure, by making the fourth action—that is, the defendant's response: he nodded toward Paul to speak (Acts 24:10a). Paul's defense is analyzed diversely probably "because Paul's speech does not exactly fit the rhetorical pattern."[30] However, Winter evaluates it as following Quintilian five parts: *exordium* (24:10b), *narratio* (24:11), *probatio* (24:12–13), *refutatio* (24:14–18), and *peroratio* (24:19–21).[31]

Paul's *exordium* is very brief in comparison with Tertullus's: **Knowing that for many years you have been a judge over this nation, I cheerfully make my defense** (Acts 24:10b). There was no threat nor flattery like the ones Tertullus carried out to persuade the judge, but a polite acceptance of Felix's status qualified as a judge on account of his lengthy judicial control.

Then, Paul's *narratio* makes it clear that he came to worship and spent only twelve days in Jerusalem: **As you can perceive for yourself, it is not more than twelve days from when I went up to Jerusalem to worship** (Acts 24:11). Paul used the same verb ("perceive") that Tertullus employed in his finale (24:8). Paul seems to say, "Yes, Felix, as Tertullus said, you can calculate and perceive that I had spent only twelve days in Jerusalem." Luke has already provided the reader with how many days passed by in Jerusalem: nine days before Paul's arrest (21:18–40), one day interval in the barracks (22:22–30), one day for the Sanhedrin council (23:1–11), and one day to move from Jerusalem to Caesarea (23:23–35); they all add up to twelve days.

In *probatio*, Paul first declared his lack of involvement in any of the riots and then criticized his accusers for having no proof of things they accused him of doing: **They did not find me arguing[32] with anyone or stirring up a crowd in the Temple[33] or in the synagogues or throughout the city, nor can they present any proof to you concerning the things**

30. See Hogan 2002: 81: in reference, Winter's *refutatio* and *peroratio* was incorrectly divided into "14–18a and 18b–21."

31. Winter 1991: 522–25.

32. "The verb 'arguing' is a standard one Paul uses to describe his preaching and teaching" (Schnabel 2012: 958); he suggests eight occurrences (17:2, 17; 18:4, 19; 19:8, 9; 20:7, 9) as reference (Schnabel 2012: 958n35).

33. Paul's "emphasis on the temple, mentioned first, corresponds to the charge that he was trying to desecrate the temple (v. 6)" (Schnabel 2012: 958).

that they are accusing of (Acts 24:12–13). If Paul had tried to incite a riot, he should have had insistent appeals or stirred up a crowd in a public meeting place; however, he did not demand anything forcibly, nor did he provoke a crowd. Moreover, as Felix could have confirmed in Tertullus's charge, the accusers were not able to prove Paul guilty. Thus Paul's *probatio* nullified the claim of riots that was pointed out in Tertullus's *exordium* and *narratio* (24:2b, 5a).

After invalidating Tertullus's main charge, Paul delivered *refutatio* (Acts 24:14–18). First of all, Paul dealt with his link with Jesus; Tertullus in his *narratio* employed this link to strengthen the claim on Paul's action for riots (24:5b), but Paul used this link to proclaim his faith along with a confession of his belonging to the sect: **But I confess this to you, that, according to the Way (which they call a sect), I worship the God of our ancestors, believing everything that is according to the law and that is written in the prophets** (24:14). Keener evaluates Paul's confession cleverly:

> When Paul admits a deed, he does not admit that it is wrong or ask pardon for it. Instead, he creates a masterful defense: First, this is an issue of internal Jewish law, not a crime under Roman law, and therefore worthy neither of Roman trial nor of Roman execution at Jewish instigation. Further, the Christian faith springs from the Old Testament and is thus an ancient religion, which should be protected as a form of Judaism under Roman toleration.[34]

Thus, Paul's connection with the Nazarene sect should not have been a problem for the Romans.

Together with the sect's basic faith, Paul identified himself with the plaintiffs in terms of the hope of resurrection: **I have a hope in God, which these men themselves accept, too, that there is going to be a resurrection of both the righteous and the unrighteous** (Acts 24:15). Jesus clarifies these two groups as "the ones who have done what is good to the resurrection resulting in life, and the ones who have done what is evil to the resurrection resulting in judgment" (John 5:29; cf. Rev 20:12–13; Dan 12:2).[35] The same notion can be found in Rom 2:6–11; in His judgment God will give eternal life to those who do good, but wrath to those who do evil. Resurrection was the issue that Paul raised in the council (Acts

---

34. Keener 1993: 395.
35. Schnabel 2012: 959n43.

23:6); when Paul mentioned resurrection, the plaintiffs would have been under a lot of strains just like they were a week ago; and if the issue had been addressed among the plaintiffs, they would have broken up again like they did two days ago.

Moreover, Paul touched upon "conscience": **This is the reason I do my best to have a clear conscience toward God and people at any time** (Acts 24:16). He stated this "conscience" in his first remark at the council (23:1).[36] At that time Ananias the high priest ordered people to strike Paul on the mouth (23:2) and then received Paul's sharp and clever riposte (23:3). In retrospect, both conscience and resurrection would have made the plaintiffs nervous.

Furthermore, Paul added the purpose of his appearance in Jerusalem, that is, **to bring alms to my** [his] **people and to present offerings**; as a matter of fact, it took **many years** for Paul to carry it into effect (Acts 24:17), which means that Paul spent a long time bringing alms to his people. Hence, stirring up or rioting people had not been Paul's interest; instead, he was concentrated on helping his nation and offering sacrifices. Unlike the prior spokesman, Paul had evidence to his statement: when he was caught, he was ritually purified in the temple (24:18a). Finally, he repeated that he had nothing to do with any gathering or disturbance (24:18b); that was told in the first part of *probatio* as well (24:12). This final refutation on riots can be juxtaposed with Tertullus's first flattering remark in his *exordium*, **Having experienced much peace through you** (24:5a).

In summary, in his *refutatio* Paul first clarified that his link with Jesus could not be connected with any riots but with the Israelites' tradition of faith (Acts 24:14). Then, Paul dealt with the previous issues, namely resurrection and conscience (24:15–16) that might have provoked the plaintiffs again (cf. 23:7–10). Then he explains his real purpose as his logical conclusion; he came to bring alms to his nation, not to stir up dissent (24:18). At this point, Tertullus and the Jews should have sensed their defeat.

Lastly, in *peroratio* Paul gave his final punches to the plaintiffs. One was related to "the absence of the accusers, the Asian Jews":[37] **But there are some Jews from the province of Asia who should be here before you [Felix] and bring charges, if they have anything against me**

---

36. This noun appears only twice in Acts (23:1; 24:16).

37. Winter 1991: 525.

(Acts 24:19). Since Paul was charged with riots and the crowds had been agitated by some Jews from Asia (21:27–28), only the Asian Jews could have been the witnesses to the whole account. However, not only no evidence but also none of the witnesses were presented. The Sanhedrin council and the plaintiffs were the only group of witnesses present, but they were already disqualified to stand as one: **Or these men themselves should tell what crime they** [Ananias the high priest and the elders, 24:1] **found me guilty of when I stood before the Sanhedrin; otherwise [they should talk] about this one utterance I shouted out while I stood before them, "I am on trial before you** [the members of the Sanhedrin council] **today concerning the resurrection of the dead"** (Acts 24:20–21). The Sanhedrin was "the only location in Jerusalem where they could operate as witnesses according to the law."[38] In addition, "the only things they could testify to was the one claim Paul had made to them—that he was on trial over a theological matter, 'the resurrection of the dead.'"[39] Hogan insists, "Before Paul can make his *peroratio*, Felix interrupts Paul."[40] However, Paul seems to conclude his speech well with a lengthier defense by reminding Felix and the plaintiffs of the three main points: Tertullus's first expression (24:18b), the Asian Jews who had provoked the Jerusalem riot (24:19), and the previous council (24:20–21).

Felix's Handling of Paul and Paul's Handling of Felix (24:22–27)

Tertullus's claim could have made Felix worried that he might not be able to escape from adjudging Paul guilty about breaking the tranquility of the city. However, fortunately to the judge reliant on the accusers, Paul not only rendered null and void the rhetor's brilliantly unprovable charge but also made the plaintiffs worried about their breakup. Ergo, Felix was able "to adjourn a court proceeding until a later time":[41] **Then Felix dispersed them because he more accurately knew the facts concerning the Way, saying, "When Lysias the tribune comes down, I will investigate your case"** (Acts 24:22). The plaintiffs failed to prove the accused guilty, and the accused protested his innocence; so the judge deferred making a decision until hearing the tribune's testimony.

38. Winter 1991: 525.
39. Witherington 1998: 713.
40. Hogan 2002: 83.
41. L&N 56.18.

In spite of Felix's promise, no further judicial enquiry seems to have been made under the procuratorship of Felix. As Walton points out, "Luke does not tell us whether Felix was able to consult Lysias or whether a consultation took place but was inconclusive."[42] Instead, some conversational meetings of Felix and Paul were introduced (Acts 24:24–26). In the meantime, Paul's custodial status was lightened: Felix **ordered the centurion for him [Paul] to be guarded, but [at the same time] to let him have some freedom/relaxation and not to prevent any of his own from serving him** (24:23). As regards to Paul's "lightened custody," Rapske points out several matters thoroughly: (1) making the centurion have charge over Paul could mean that "Paul is assigned to the personal care of a centurion rather than to a lower-ranking soldier or, for that matter, to the general care of a military prison system and its personnel"; (2) "Felix wished Paul to be healthily preserved for the longer term from the predictable vagaries of military custody in the hope of exploiting him to his own political and monetary advantage"; (3) even though Paul should have worn chains, he "would not be dependent upon his keeper(s) to sanction his every activity"; (4) "Paul was probably kept in Herod's palace," not in his own lodgings in Caesarea; (5) both Paul's "family or relatives" and "supportive or friendly co-religionists" were permitted to take care of "Paul's basic needs for physical sustenance while in prison" such as "food and clothing."[43]

Going back to the conversations between the secular leader and the spiritual one, Felix's first meeting with Paul was held some days later along with his Jewish wife Drusilla (Acts 24:24a). She was the third and last daughter of Agrippa I, who died in 44 CE (12:23); she became fatherless when she was six years old (*Ant.* 19.354).[44] Her father made her espoused to the king of Commagena, but her brother, Agrippa II (25:13–26:32), gave her in marriage to Azizus, king of Emesa, as a reply to the province he gained—the tetrarchy of Philip and Batanea, Trachonitis, Abila—from Claudius the emperor around 52 CE (*Ant.* 20.137–139). It should not have been a pleasant experience to a fourteen-year-old lady because "between October of 54 and October of 55 [her husband] Azizos died."[45] Hence, her acceptance of Felix even before Azizos's death could

42. Walton 2012: 554.

43. Rapske 1998: 168–71.

44. Josephus reports that after the death of Agrippa I, his daughters were abused by many soldiers of Caesarea and Sebaste (*Ant.* 19.356–357).

45. Brenk and de Rossi 2001: 412.

be somewhat understandable when we consider both Felix's falling in love with her and Simon the Cypriot Jew's pretending to be a *magos* and persuading Drusilla to marry Felix, the procurator of her hometown (*Ant.* 20.142).[46] Eventually, she married Felix at the age of sixteen. Josephus evaluates this marriage as a bad action and a transgression of "the laws of her forefathers," and gave a report of the disappearance of Drusilla and her son "at the conflagration of the mountain Vesuvius, in the days of Titus Caesar [79–81 CE]" (*Ant.* 20.143–144). If Agrippa III, the son of Felix and Drusilla, died when he was "around 25 years old" in 79 CE,[47] at this time (57 CE) he would have been two or three years old; and Drusilla would have been nineteen years old.

Paul met this couple who had married three years ago and might have had a happy time with their newborn baby; Felix's origin was unfit for a procurator but he was appointed as one; he married a princess and had a son; Drusilla was loved by a competent man, was married to him, and bore him a son. The only problem was that they married illegally. To them, Paul talked about not only **faith in Christ Jesus** but also **righteousness, self-control, and the coming judgment** (Acts 24:24b–25a). Even in chains Paul testified to the gospel even for "the powers-that-be"[48] and provoked repentance by mentioning "the fulfillment of obligations placed on individuals by God," "a person's mastery of his or her pleasures and desires," and "the day of judgment, when God will either reward or condemn people for their behavior."[49] Schnabel says that Luke paints Paul "as an intelligent and courageous missionary, who speaks to the highest representative of the Roman Empire in terms that are understandable for a Roman trained in popular philosophy while speaking without ideological compromise about the day of judgment and about the need to come to faith in Jesus as Israel's Messiah."[50] In this private meeting as well as in the previous official gathering, Paul did not flatter people but did his best to tell the truth.

Paul's testimony should have made Felix frightened; yet he did not accept the invitation to charge for the blessed life. **Go away for now, and when I find time, I will send for you** (Acts 24:25b), Felix replied. Luke

46. According to Josephus, Simon said "that if she would not refuse him [Felix], he would make her a happy woman."

47. See Brenk and de Rossi 2001: 413.

48. See Walton 2012: 555–56.

49. Schnabel 2012: 966.

50. Schnabel 2012: 966.

does not report on Drusilla's reaction to this whole matter, but we may expect that Paul's teaching might have come as a great shock to her all the same; unfortunately, we can presume that she was not positive toward Paul's invitation. Felix's following attitude to Paul supports this couple's refusal to believe the gospel: **At the same time he was also hoping that money would be given to him by Paul; therefore, frequently sending for him [Paul], he [Felix] conferred with him** (24:26). Felix would have needed enormous assets to please his young wife in keeping her opulent lifestyle. In his "mercenary interest," Peterson reads "his fallibility as a human being and as an administrator of Roman justice."[51]

Two years had passed, and Felix's successor, Porcius Festus, arrived; even so, Paul's status did not change. **Because he wanted to do the Jews a favor, Felix left Paul imprisoned** (Acts 24:27). It is most likely that the couple did not believe in the gospel and Paul did not bribe Felix to be released. Felix spent not a short time hearing the gospel from the proficient speaker; however, two years had passed and there was no fruit to pick. In 59 CE, "probably during the summer,"[52] Festus arrived in Judea as procurator. Josephus reports that "when Porcius Festus was sent as successor to Felix by Nero, the principal of the Jewish inhabitants of Caesarea went up to Rome to accuse Felix"; however, Nero did not punish Felix on account of Pallas, Felix's brother (*Ant.* 20.182). Paul's case should also have driven the Jews to accuse Felix, so he could only leave Paul in prison.

The new procurator was different from Felix in many aspects. First, he belonged to the well-known *gens Porcia*; in contrast, Felix had been a slave and became a freedman.[53] Second, his procuratorship ended in his death probably in 61 or 62 CE so ruled about two to three years while Felix kept his procuratorship for seven years.[54] Additionally, he seems to be a man of great self-respect in that he tried to keep the status quo with drastic measures,[55] when Felix used to put something off not to stir up trouble.

51. Peterson 2009: 641–42.

52. Witherington 1998: 716.

53. Bruce 1990: 484.

54. See *Ant.* 20.197 and Witherington 1998: 717.

55. Josephus reports two events: one is related to the *sicarii* (*Ant.* 20.186–88); the other to the wall erected by the Jews to prevent Agrippa II from watching the inner court of the temple (*Ant.* 20.189–96).

ACTS 25
Festus's Treatment of Paul

Two years passed after Paul was examined via the *Praetorium* of Felix. And despite these years, Paul's trial continued. Felix left Paul behind, and Festus took charge of the procuratorship of Judea, Samaria, Galilee, and Perea in 59 CE. In this chapter, Luke describes in detail what Festus had done and said, which might have reminded the first reader, Theophilus (Acts 1:1), about what kinds of characteristics higher-ranking Romans have, in comparison with Lysias and Felix who had got Roman citizenship after birth through money or family connections. Festus's speech appears in 25:4–5, 9, 12, 14–21, 24–27, sixteen verses, about 60 percentages of this chapter.

All the events in ch. 25 seem to have happened during the summer of 59 CE,[1] and since 57 CE, approximately the middle of May (cf. Acts 21:8), the background regions were still Jerusalem and Caesarea. With regard to the political situation at the moment of this leadership change, Josephus informs us of two crucial events (*Ant.* 20.183–85):

> Two of the principal Syrians in Caesarea persuaded Burrhus, who was Nero's tutor, and secretary for his Greek letters, by giving him a great sum of money, to annul that equality of the Jewish privileges of citizens which they as yet enjoyed.[2] So Burrhus, by his solicitations, obtained leave of the emperor that an epistle should be written to that purpose. This epistle became the occasion of the following miseries that befell our nation; for when the Jews of Caesarea were informed of the contents of this epistle to the Syrians, they were more disorderly than before, until a war was kindled.

1. See also Schnabel 2012: 973.

2. According to Josephus, this claim of Syrians was provoked by the Jews' declaration of their superiority over the Syrians; "the Jews claimed the preeminence, because Herod their king was the builder of Caesarea, and because he was by birth a Jew"; "the Syrians did not deny what was alleged about Herod; but they said that Caesarea was formerly called Strato's Tower, and that then there was not one Jewish inhabitant" (*Ant.* 20.173; Josephus 1999: 654).

> Upon Festus's coming into Judea, it happened that Judea
> was afflicted by the robbers, while all the villages were set on
> fire, and plundered by them.[3]

Both the rearrangement of Jewish status and the lack of stability
in Judea might need to be heeded in relation to Paul's trial in Caesarea
under Festus.

Before the Tribunal of Festus (25:1–12)

Three days after his arrival in the province, Festus **went up to Jerusalem
from Caesarea** (Acts 25:1). He neither lingered nor moved in a hurry.
Having a three days' rest, he moved on to face the daunting task of meeting the Jewish leadership:[4] **So the high priests and the leading men of
the Jews brought formal charges against Paul to him and requested
him to do them a favor against Paul in order that he [Festus] may
summon him [Paul] to Jerusalem, setting[5] an ambush to remove him
[Paul] on the way** (25:2–3). Bruce understands "the high priests and the
leading men of the Jews" as "another way of referring to the Sanhedrin."[6]
Right before Festus's appointment as procurator, the high priesthood was
given to Ishmael, son of Phiabi II by Agrippa II (around 58–59 CE).[7]
Ishmael and the other prominent council members requested Festus to
bring Paul back to Jerusalem.

Festus could not help refusing their request. He must have known
about the tribune's letter that informed Felix of the Jews' ambush against
Paul (cf. Acts 23:26–30). Festus's refusal was on the grounds of very reasonable excuses, **that Paul was being kept in custody at Caesarea and
that he himself was about to leave shortly** (25:4). With this flat refusal,
Festus suggested a legal process: **Therefore, let those who are influential**

3. Josephus 1999: 654–55.

4. Schnabel 2012: 986 evaluates Festus's "inaugural visit in Jerusalem" as performed "rapidly." However, since he went to Jerusalem after staying three days in
Caesarea, "somewhat rapidly" or "swiftly" would be a better expression to describe his
movement. So Witherington 1998: 718 says well that "Porcius Festus seems to have
been a person who acted with some dispatch."

5. "Setting an ambush" is translated as "planning an ambush" in recent versions,
e.g., NRSV, NET, ESV. However, *poiountes* has the same present participle as *aitou-
menoi* (requesting), so it seems that the Jews requested a favor while preparing an
ambush (see NASV and NIV).

6. Bruce 1990: 486.

7. See *Ant.* 20.179, Bruce 1990: 95, and Schnabel 2012: 986.

among you go down and bring charges against him if there is anything unreasonable (25:5). This suggestion reveals his firm conviction that Paul must not have done anything wrong. If Paul had not done anything wrong, they would not have needed to come down to Caesarea to bring a charge against him.

The new procurator stayed no more than eight or ten days among the Jews in Jerusalem (Acts 25:6a). Luke, who knew how many days Festus remained in Caesarea (25:1), did not know the accurate days when he stayed in Jerusalem; this may infer that Luke was in Caesarea at this time. The difference between eight and ten days hints at how Luke calculated Festus's travel time. It is likely that Festus came back to Caesarea from Jerusalem in fourteen days, so Luke could have thought that Festus used four or six days to move to Jerusalem and back to Caesarea, thus, concluding that Festus stayed eight or ten days in Jerusalem.

After looking around the main city in his post, Festus **went down to Caesarea, and the next day he sat on the judgment seat and ordered Paul to be brought** (Acts 25:6b). "The judgment seat" (*bēma*) does not occur in relation to Felix but is frequently employed concerning Festus (25:6, 10, 17).[8] This judgment seat was used for Paul to go to Rome (25:10). In addition, this term may reflect Festus's own pride as a judge (25:6, 17). How would he deal with the suit that both the tribune and the previous procurator wanted to escape from?

Paul arrived (Acts 25:7a) and his second trial started with the plaintiffs' accusation: **the Jews who had come down from Jerusalem stood around him, bringing many and serious charges that they could not prove** (25:7b). In comparison with the plaintiffs before Felix in 24:1b, namely Ananias the high priest, the elders, and Tertullus, the accusers before Festus are simply introduced as "the Jews," who also differ from "the high priests and the leading men of the Jews" in the next chapter (25:2a). These "Jews" may not connote the top leaders such as the high priests. Further, any legal representative like Tertullus seems not to have been joined to the plaintiffs. As regards their accusation, we may guess, as Schnabel does, that "they presumably allege again that Paul is a public enemy of the Jewish people who causes riots as a ringleader of the Nazarenes, and that Paul has attempted to desecrate the temple (cf.

8. In the NT, this word occurs twelve times (Matt 27:19; John 19:13; Acts 7:5; 12:21; 18:12, 16, 17; 25:6, 10, 17; Rom 14:10; 2 Cor 5:10). As regards Gallio, it is also used three times (Acts 18:12, 16, 17) but only via the narrator. However, Festus mentions this word by himself (25:17).

24:5–6)."⁹ Neither did they request Festus to call for Lysias the tribune as Felix had promised (cf. 24:22) nor did they press hard by questioning the judge why the trial had been delayed for two years. Rather, "the Jews" only accused Paul of the same unverifiable claims. Hence, we may conjecture that the Jews raised their voices before Festus just politically without having any prospects of legal victory against Paul due to circumstances in Felix's *Paretorium*.

After the plaintiffs' claim, Paul defended himself very briefly: **I committed no sin against the Jewish law or against the Temple or against Caesar** (Acts 25:8). Paul proved his innocence very clearly in the previous trial, so he delivered a brief summary of his testimony in 24:10–21. He did not sin against anything or anyone that the accusers alluded to: he worshiped God according to the law (24:14); he came to Jerusalem to worship in the temple (24:11) and, even when he was caught, he was already ritually purified in the temple (24:18); decisively, he did not have to do with any riots (24:12, 18). Therefore, Paul was able to proclaim his innocence with boldness again.

Festus should have been cognizant of Paul's innocence as well as the Jews' posture toward Paul's trial. Consequently, Festus put forward a political proposal to Paul: **wishing to do the Jews a favor, he asked Paul, "Are you willing to go up to Jerusalem and be tried there concerning these things before me?"** (Acts 25:9). The same "favor" (*charin*) "on the part of humans," something that "one does for another within a reciprocity system," occurred three times in Acts; one is related to Felix (24:27), and the rest to Festus (25:3, 9).¹⁰ Two weeks ago Festus refused to do something as a favor (25:3–4), but he changed speedily to allot favor to the politically influential group even though he did point out actually, by finishing his proposal with "before me," that he himself would be responsible for the future trial in Jerusalem.

A politician Festus unavoidably remained—sacrificing principles to find favor with the public. Paul had experienced this kind of politician for two years, enough time to suspect the present procurator's motive in proposing another trial in Jerusalem. It was clear that Paul was innocent: the tribune reported it (Acts 23:29), Felix confirmed it via a conventional trial (24:2–22), and Festus should have had knowledge of it (25:5, 7–9, 10b). Why was another trial necessary? Paul could not spend more time

9. Schnabel 2012: 988.
10. BDAG 1079.

being dragged into impractical legal procedures because he heard that he should testify in Rome as well (23:11).

Eventually Paul was bound for Rome by appealing to the emperor, Nero (54–68 CE), who rose to power five years ago. First of all, he made clear under which judicial system he stood: **I am standing before Caesar's judgment seat, where I should be tried** (Acts 25:10a). He was caught by the tribune, so he was taken according to the Roman judicial system. Second, Paul protested his innocence again: **I have done nothing wrong to the Jews, as you [Festus] also know well** (25:10b). He had already been evaluated by Lysias the tribune, Felix in detail, and Festus in brief. Third, Paul's stance on the principles of verdicts was declared: **Therefore if, on the one hand, I harm [anyone or anything] and have done anything that deserves death, I do not refuse to die; on the other hand, if not one of their charges against me is true, no one can show them favor** (25:11a). Paul did not ask Festus any favor. If he did sin against any Jews or Romans or any laws, he was ready for any punishment, even for the death penalty; apart from that, no concessions will be made to the Jews. He employed the verb *charizw* ("say or do something agreeable to a person, show him favour or kindness, oblige, gratify")[11] that has *charis* ("favor") as the root. This verb should have made Festus realize that Paul became aware of the reason why a further trial in Jerusalem was suggested. Lastly, Paul appealed to Caesar (25:11b), which can be seen as "the climax of Paul's trial in province of Judea, in that his appeal to the emperor removes him from the jurisdiction of the governor of Judea and from any jurisdiction of the Jews."[12]

At first Festus might have been heavy-hearted not only because his suggestion was dismissed but also because his intention was unintentionally exposed. However, sooner or later, he should have felt somewhat reassured since he would now have a reason to escape from this black hole.[13] In addition, as Barrett explains well, Festus "could not disallow the appeal, under the *Lex Iulia de vi publica* (passed in the time of Augustus)."[14] **Subsequently, after conferring with the jury [or his council],[15] Festus**

11. LSJ 1978.

12. Schnabel 2012: 991.

13. Bruce 1988: 454 says: "Festus heard Paul's words with much relief. By appealing to Caesar, Paul enabled him to escape from a responsibility with which he felt unable to cope."

14. As regards the Roman law, see Barrett 1998: 1131.

15. Bruce 1988: 454 explains this council as "a body consisting of higher officials

replied, **"You have appealed to Caesar; to Caesar you will go"** (Acts 25:12). In his official opinion, Festus did not take any responsibility by only employing the second-person pronoun. He seems to say, "You did appeal, so you would go; I did not mean this to happen." He was a very cunning man.

Festus's Introducing Paul to Agrippa II (25:13–27)

After several days had passed (Acts 25:13a), Festus could now tackle Paul's case a bit further by a lucky chance: **King Agrippa and Bernice arrived at Caesarea to pay their respects to Festus** (25:13b). Not to be mistaken with this Herod Agrippa II (27–c. 93/100 CE), the son of Herod Agrippa I, who killed James and put Peter in prison (12:1–3), he reigned at this time (in the summer of 59 CE) not only over "Batanaea, Gaulanitis, Trachonitis, and Abila" (since 53 CE) but also "the regions of Tiberias and Tarichaea, west of the sea of Galilee, together with Julias in Peraea and 14 neighboring villages" (since 56 CE):[16] the former part was handed over by Claudius and the latter part was passed down by Nero the contemporary emperor (*Ant.* 20.159). This new king had his sister Bernice (also Berenice; born in 28 CE), the eldest daughter of Herod Agrippa I, under his roof during this period; she lived with her brother after the death of her husband Herod, king of Chalcis in 48 CE.[17] These two renowned Herodian family members must have felt that they should show off their nobility to the new governor (cf. 25:23). In regard to the relationship between Agrippa II and Bernice, Josephus writes,

> As for Bernice, she lived a widow a long while after the death of Herod [king of Chalcis], who was both her husband and her uncle; but when the report went that she had criminal sexual intercourse with her brother [Agrippa, junior], she persuaded Polemo, who was king of Cilicia, to be circumcised, and to

---

of his administration and younger men who accompanied him in order to gain some experience of provincial government."

16. Bruce 1990: 490. See also *Ant.* 20.138, 159.

17. *ED* 167: "Bernice first married Marcus Julius Alexander who died in 41. She was then married to her uncle Herod, king of Chalcis." Josephus reports that "when Marcus, Alexander's son, was dead, who had married her when she was a virgin, Agrippa gave her in marriage to his brother Herod, and begged for him of Claudius the kingdom of Chalcis."

> marry her, as supposing that by this means she should prove
> those slanders upon her to be false.[18]

Hence, in a sense Agrippa and Bernice can be seen as a married couple like Felix and Drusilla, Bernice's younger sister (cf. 24:24).[19]

Agrippa and Bernice stayed many days in Caesarea (Acts 25:14a). Festus waited and finally **laid before the king the things related to Paul** (25:14b) possibly because "in his report to the emperor he would be able to assert that Agrippa, someone respected by Nero, had concurred in the way he handled matters."[20] Witherington summarizes well the main points of the relations between Agrippa and Festus: (1) "Agrippa was a supporter of Rome and interested in Roman affairs"; (2) "he also had been appointed by Claudius curator of the temple in Jerusalem, giving him the power to appoint the high priest, possession of the priestly vestments worn on Yom Kippur [the Day of Atonement], and the task of looking after the temple treasury"; (3) "It would be natural for Festus, for a variety of reasons, including Agrippa's power over the temple and priestly apparatus and his ties with Rome, to view Agrippa [II] as a higher Jewish authority than the ones he had previously been dealing with, indeed to regard Agrippa [II] as the king of the Jews."[21]

Festus's remark on Paul's case seems to have been a legal report on the situation, ultimately made for the emperor. "It may be," Witherington presumes, "since it seems unlikely that Luke would have access to the private discussions of Festus and Agrippa and Bernice, that here Luke followed the historical convention of making the persons say what they were likely to have said on the occasion."[22] However, in order to keep another account of Paul's case via a meeting with Agrippa, as Witherington also guesses as above, Festus could have delivered a prepared report to the Herodian king. According to Barrett, the sentence, **Festus laid before the king the things against Paul** (Acts 25:14b), has two legal terms: one is "laid," "most naturally taken in the technical legal sense of *refer, remit*"; and the other is "the things related to Paul," namely, "Paul's case," which

18. *Ant.* 20.145. Due to her incestuous relationship with her brother, she is evaluated as "one of the shameless women of the Bible" (*ISBE* 1:440).

19. In regard to *elthontos* in 25:23, Culy and Parsons 2003: 485 state: "The singular participle focuses attention on the arrival of Agrippa, who happened to be accompanied by his wife [should be his sister]."

20. Witherington 1998: 728.

21. Witherington 1998: 727.

22. Witherington 1998: 728.

"has a definitely legal sound."[23] Hence, Festus's remark should be regarded not as a private conversation but as a legal report; and Luke should have gained access to Festus's report on Paul for Agrippa II.

Festus's report began with mentioning a man "left behind" the previous procurator: **There is a man left as a detainee[24] by Felix, concerning whom, when I was in Jerusalem, the high priests and the elders of the Jews conveyed a formal report about a judicial matter,[25] asking for a guilty verdict against him** (Acts 25:14b–15). "A guilty verdict against him" seems a bit of a stronger expression of the Jews' charges in comparison with "formal charges against Paul" in 25:2. Still the heavier their charge was, the more delicate was the matter, thus making Festus's answer more worthy. He said, **"I answered them that it was not the custom of the Romans to hand over anyone as a favor before the accused had met his accusers face to face and had received an opportunity to make a defense against the indictment"** (25:16). According to Luke, however, Festus had already pointed out the fact **that Paul was being kept in custody at Caesarea and that he himself was about to leave shortly** (25:4). His emphasis on the Roman custom and the accused's legal rights could be a lie. In addition, by employing the verb *charizō*, which Paul had used to reveal Festus's bad intention (25:11), Festus eventually described himself as one who hated an illegal favor and followed the Roman custom.

After indicating both the Jews' strong accusation against a man and his own way of managing the accusation decently, Festus described Paul's trial directly in Acts 25:17–21. First of all, he recounted the judicial situation: **So after they came together to this place, I did not delay at all, but the next day I sat on the judgment seat and ordered the man to be brought** (25:17). This sentence also manifests the only aspect Festus had done well, namely the fact that he dealt with the matter without delay at the following day. Additionally, his high status is pointed out by "the judgment seat" and his ordering. He had authority to sit on the high seat on the tribunal and to order a detainee to be brought.

Second, Festus told Agrippa II of a mismatch of the accusers' accusation and his own expectation: **When the accusers stood up, they brought no charge of any of the evil deeds I had expected** (Acts 25:18). Calvin raises doubts about Festus's judgment, saying, "I marvel why

23. Barrett 1998: 1136 (italics his).

24. *Desmios* is generally translated as "a prisoner" but here translated as "a detainee" to indicate that Paul had been bound for political reasons.

25. BDAG 326.

Festus doth say, that there was no such crime objected to Paul as he supposed, seeing he was accused of sedition."[26] However, Festus must have read Lysias's letter and Felix's report and, via the trial opened before him, he should have confirmed that there was no witness or effective claims to the charges against Paul. So Festus's analysis itself would have been correct. To be precise, Luke seems to show what kind of traits Festus had by writing this sentence: Festus compared his normal expectation with the accusers' atypical charge, and this comparison underlines the unconventional charge of the Jews.

Festus continued by comparing the accusers with Paul: **Rather they [the accusers] had several points of disagreement with him [Paul] about their religion**[27] **and about a certain Jesus who was dead, whom Paul claimed to be alive** (Acts 25:19). According to Festus, they fought about a religious matter and the state of Jesus: either dead or alive. However, Paul's defense in 25:8 is related not only to religious matters, namely, the Jewish law and the temple, but also to Caesar. Hence, it would be incorrect to categorize Paul's case as merely a religious one. In addition, Festus revealed the name "Jesus" even though Felix's report did not include the name (cf. 24:5, 14, 21), which could show that Festus understood the core of Paul's case and that he wanted to come to the point directly.

This third point led Festus to the fourth one, his own response to Paul's trial: **Because I was at a loss how to investigate these matters, I asked if he was willing to go to Jerusalem and be tried there on these matters** (Acts 25:20). Since the "matters" that caused Festus to be perplexed were religious, it might not have decreased his dignity. Rather, Festus seems to have blamed the plaintiffs and held them responsible for accusing Paul of a religious matter before a Roman court. Moreover, Festus said that his perplexity had made him suggest a further trial in Jerusalem to Paul; however, Luke says that Festus had done so **wishing to do the Jews a favor** (25:9); so Festus's excuse was not thoroughly honest.

Lastly, Festus finished his explanation with Paul's appeal to the emperor: **when Paul appealed to be kept in custody for the decision of His Majesty the Reverend,**[28] **I ordered him to be kept under guard**

26. Calvin 2009: 365.

27. Schnabel 2012: 997 says that *deisidaimonia* in this verse means "not 'superstition' (which would have been an insult to the Jewish king) but 'religion' in terms of a particular system of cultic beliefs and practices."

28. *Sebastos*, meaning "venerable, reverend, august" (LSJ 1587), is translated as

until I could send him to Caesar (Acts 25:21). As a matter of fact, Paul did not appeal "to be kept in custody for the decision of the emperor" but just appealed to Caesar both because he was standing before Caesar's judgment seat and because he was innocent (25:10–11). Hence, Festus's report clearly shows not only that he himself tried "to describe his role in the affair in the best possible light,"[29] but also that it was false just as Luke interprets it. Moreover, Festus identified the present emperor not only with Caesar but also with *Sebastos*, "the equivalent of Lat. *Augustus* (transliterated, not translated, in Lk. 2:1 because in the case of the first Augustus the word was treated as a personal name and not simply as a title of majesty)."[30] This identification could be correct because "Nero's full name was Nero Claudius Caesar Augustus Germanicus."[31] However, since Paul called the emperor Caesar (25:10–11), the title *Sebastos* should disclose Festus's profound reverence for the present Caesar.

After hearing Festus's report, **Agrippa said to Festus, "I would also like to hear the man myself"** (Acts 25:22a). Since Agrippa II would have had enough authority and time to hear of Paul and the result of his case, he might have wanted to avoid having a disconcerting hearing. His remark in 26:28 shows he had already known that Paul's case had to do with the matter of "becoming a Christian." Nevertheless, it should be hard to reject the new procurator's first request, so he expressed his wish "for some time to hear Paul."[32] The bait was swallowed and Festus immediately replied, **"Tomorrow, you will hear him"** (25:22b). The shrewd man did not let the opportunity slip through his fingers.

Agrippa's unavoidable wish was accomplished the very next day: **So the next day Agrippa and Bernice came with great pomp and entered**[33] **the audience hall,**[34] **together with the senior military officers [chil-**

"His Majesty the Reverend" because this term was used to show great reverence for the emperor.

29. Schnabel 2012: 995.

30. Bruce 1990: 493. This title was given to "Gaius Julius Caesar Octavianus on January 16 in 27 BC when he became *Princeps*" by the senate in Rome (Schnabel 2012: 998).

31. Schnabel 2012: 998.

32. Schnabel 2012: 998.

33. As regards *eiselqhontōn*, Culy and Parsons 2003: 485 say, "The plural participle shifts the attention to the group as a whole."

34. *Akroatērion* literally means "place of hearing [audience]" because "τήριον means 'place'" (Robertson 2010 [1934]: 154). This room "would have been a large space designed for any kind of public hearing or lecture" (Peterson 2009: 655).

iarchs] and the prominent men of the city; when Festus gave the order, Paul was brought in (Acts 25:23). Agrippa II might have had an inclination for displaying his own dignity rather than to hearing Paul. The king mobilized all the military and the social leaders of Caesarea. There might have been five military tribunes according to Josephus.[35] These military leaders should have been Festus's staff, and the social leaders should have been ruled by Festus; nonetheless, both groups were headed by Agrippa II and his sister. The word "pomp" (*fantasia*), which occurs only here in the NT, seems to reveal the siblings' mind.

With this brief description of the court, Luke again reports Festus's long prologue to Paul's trial in front of Agrippa II in Acts 25:24–27. There were no Jewish plaintiffs present, so Festus's remark played an important role in this court. In addition, it can be seen as similar to the Sanhedrin council before the tribune (23:1–11) in that this trial was not a requisite for the standard Roman legal procedure. First of all, Festus summarized the Jews' request very briefly from the Jerusalem riot (21:27–36) to his own tribunal (25:2–7): **King Agrippa, and all the men who are present here with us, you see this man whom the entire Jewish populace pleaded to me both in Jerusalem and here, shouting that he ought not to live any longer** (25:24). Festus classified the audience into two groups, Agrippa II and the rest, and he put himself at the same Agrippa II by calling himself and the king "us." Then, the Jews' consistent plea was condensed into a shout, **He ought not to live any longer!** This alludes to the mob's scream, **Away with him!** (21:36).

Subsequently, Festus pointed out his own and Paul's final decision: **By the way, I did not take anything that would make him deserve death, and when he appealed to His Majesty the Reverend, I decided to send him** (Acts 25:25). As a judge, he did not find anything that would make Paul deserve death.[36] Nevertheless, this verdict was not pronounced in court because he first suggested that Paul be examined again in Jerusalem (25:9). Festus's final judgment before Agrippa II alludes to Paul's testimony (25:11a) and the tribune's final opinion revealed in his letter to Felix, namely, **I found he was accused with reference to issues about their law, but having no charge worthy of death or imprisonment** (23:29). In Festus's remark on Paul (25:25), moreover, Paul's appeal to Caesar is sandwiched between Festus's resolution and his positive response to

35. See *Ant.* 19.365; so also Bruce 1988: 459n33 and Bock 2007: 712.

36. A similar expression is found in Luke 23:15: Pilate said, "Look, nothing deserving death has been done by him."

Paul's appeal. Analyzing his remark grammatically, "I did not take" and "I decided" are the two main verbs that stood for Festus's resolution and his response to Paul's appeal. On top of that, the genitive absolute construction (aorist middle participle) was used to state Paul's appeal to Caesar. Hence, we can infer that Festus was trying to conceal from Agrippa II the very fact that his final verdict was not given on Paul's case.

Third, Festus provided two reasons for the present meeting: **But I have nothing definite to write to my lord about him, so I have brought him before you and especially before you, King Agrippa, in order that I might have something to write after this investigative hearing was taken; for it seems to me unreasonable, in sending a prisoner, not to make clear the charges against him** (Acts 25:26–27). One reason is related to all the uncertainty as to writing to the emperor "the *littera dimissoria*, which the lower court had to present to the higher court,"[37] and the other to his own custom reflecting **the custom of the Romans** in 25:16. At this time, Festus also sandwiched the fact that he brought Paul between the two reasons behind it; so looking at the top and bottom parts of the sandwich (25:25 and 25:26–27), Paul's appeal to the emperor (25:25b) parallels Festus's bringing Paul in front of the important leaders (25:26b), and Festus's resolution and his positive response to Paul's appeal (25:25a, 25c) are parallel to the two reasons attributed to this urgent meeting (25:26a, 27). Eventually, Festus seems to make Paul responsible for the current meeting while discreetly portraying himself as a reasonable judge. Furthermore, he quickly and implicitly finished the edges; he showed his respect for the emperor by calling him "my lord."

As a very crafty politician, Festus had much success in having a formal meeting to deal with Paul's case by introducing Paul to Agrippa II. Moreover, Festus delegated in secret the responsibility for writing a good *littera dimissoria* to his fellow king (cf. "us" in 25:24) by connecting Paul's appeal with the court in the sight of Agrippa II. Now, the task of finding a charge against Paul could partly be transferred from the procurator to the king.

37. Schnabel 2012: 1001. According to him, the *littera dimissoria* "had to contain the following information: a notice that an appeal had been lodged; the name of the person lodging the appeal; the sentence that is being contested; the name and identity of the parties involved." See also Barrett 1998: 1147.

ACTS 26
Paul before Agrippa II

This chapter is composed of Paul's testimony before Agrippa II (Acts 26:1–23) and a tripartite conversation between Festus, Paul, and Agrippa II (26:24–32). Witherington thinks Paul finished his speech at 26:29, regarding Festus's and Agrippa II's saying in 26:24 and 28 as interruptions: he suggests "the rhetorical structure of the speech is as follows: (1) *exordium* (vv. 2–3), (2) *narratio* (vv. 4–21), (3) *propositio* (vv. 22–23); (4) the formal proofs are omitted here, . . . a brief (5) *refutatio* (vv. 25–26), followed by the (6) *peroratio* (vv. 27, 29)."[1] However, Luke clearly says that Festus talked about Paul's insanity "when/after Paul defended himself with these [sayings]" (26:24). Hence, we see that his speech ended in 26:23 and was followed by a conversation between the three.

Paul's speech and the dialogue among Festus, Paul, and Agrippa II could be the pivot on which the significance of the "Paul's passion and four trials' section" (Acts 21–26) revolves. To begin with, Paul's testimony can be compared with his previous defense, which had been given two years ago (22:1–21), and in relation to it, questions, such as "What kind of differences could be found between his two speeches, 22:1–21 and 26:1–23?" and "What could the differences mean?" could be raised. The answers to questions such as these would be the main points of Paul's repeated conversion stories that we can obtain by analyzing Paul's testimony. Of course, his final speech itself is meaningful because it is the final legal report on his trial.

Second, the conversation (Acts 26:24–32) might show a clear result of Paul's proclamation of the gospel to the political leaders. Festus can be seen as being every inch a Roman officer representing Lysias, the tribune, and Felix, the procurator, and Agrippa II may stand in for the Jews and the Herodian families. Festus regarded Paul as insane (26:24), and Agrippa II evaluated Paul's testimony as utterly trivial (26:28); nevertheless,

1. Witherington 1998: 737–38.

Paul blessed them both to become such as he was, except for the chains on him (26:29).

The place of Paul's trial, Herod's *praetorium* (Acts 23:35), had not been changed for two years from ch. 24, but this time Paul was heard in the audience hall.[2] Hence, as Bruce says, these "proceedings were neither judicial nor in any other way official,"[3] but they should not have been private, or rather, they should have been something worthy of public report. The time is the same as that of ch. 25, viz., the summer of 59 CE.

Paul's Testimony before Agrippa II (26:1–23)

After Festus made an introductory statement about Paul's case, Agrippa II invited Paul to say something to defend his point of view: **Agrippa said to Paul, "It is permissible for you to speak for yourself"** (Acts 26:1a). Even though this hearing was not held as an official trial, Agrippa II was careful not to use the first singular pronoun, just as Festus was (25:9b, 12b), so the second singular personal pronoun and the second singular reflexive pronoun are each employed once. In addition, as Denton[4] points out, "Agrippa uses the impersonal form[5] so as not to derogate from the honour due to the Roman governor."

Paul's testimony follows: Then Paul stretched out his hand and made his defense (Acts 26:1b). Tajra reads Paul's stretching out his hand as the "freedom of movement" which "would indicate that the apostle was only very lightly chained to a soldier at the moment he began his speech."[6] As for Denton, he saw "the chains with which he was bound" in Paul's stretching hand.[7] Bruce understands this stretching as "a respectful salutation to the king" rather than "an appeal for a quiet hearing" such as 13:16 and 21:40.[8] Further, he evaluates this testimony as follows:

> Here, in the calm and dignified setting of the governor's audience chamber, Paul delivered the speech which, above all his other speeches in Acts, may worthily claim to be called his

2. See comments on 25:23.
3. Bruce 1988: 461.
4. Denton 1876: 318.
5. *Epitrepetai* means "it is permissible."
6. Tajra 1989: 164.
7. Denton 1876: 318–19.
8. Bruce 1990: 496.

Apologia pro vita sua.[9] In it he undertakes to show that neither his manner of life nor his teaching should arouse hostility, especially on the part of Jews. The construction of the speech is more careful than usual, the grammar more classical, and the style more literary,[10] as befitted the distinguished audience.

The main points of Paul's final and longest defense, according to Tajra, are "the customary *captatio benevolentiae*" (Acts 26:2–3), "his belonging to the Jewish nation" (26:4–5), "his belief in the resurrection" (26:6–8), "his early persecution of the Church" (26:9–12), "the events on the road to Damascus and the heavenly vision that he had" (26:13–18), and "a fundamental theological point in his discourse" (26:19–23); and Tajra finally points out to Paul's faithfulness to his mission (26:19b–20), his arrest "as a consequence of fulfilling this divine-ordained mission" (26:21), "divine succour" to Paul (26:22), and "a mighty proclamation of the resurrection and Messiahship of Jesus" (26:23).[11] He finds the central topic at the end of the speech.

By the way, Cheng outlines Paul's speech before Agrippa (Acts 26:6–23) like this:

The cause of the Jews' accusation of Paul (26:6–8)

A hope of God's promise to the Jewish forefathers (v. 6)

A hope regarding the resurrection of the dead (vv. 7–8)

Paul's persecution of Jesus' followers (26:9–12)

In Jerusalem (vv. 9–11a)

In gentile cities (vv. 11b–12)

Paul's encounter with Jesus (26:13–18)

Jesus' appearance (vv. 13–15)

Jesus' commission (vv. 16–18)

Paul as a witness of Jesus (26:19–22a)

Paul's mission in Jewish and gentile cities (vv. 19–20)

---

9. *Apologia pro vita sua*, literally meaning "a defense of his life," indicates "a personal and doctrinal self-vindication" (Schaff 1980 [1910]: 763).

10. Regarding Paul's classical and literary style, see Witherington 1998: 737. He quotes nine elements of style which are pointed out by Long 1982: 237–39: "(1) the classical use of the perfect ηγημαι as a present in v. 2, (2) the literary elegance of the *exordium* . . . , (3) the use of the classical ισασι (v. 4) and ακριβεστατην (v. 5), (4) the addition of the Greek proverb (v. 14), (5) genitive of the articular infinitive (v. 18), (6) litotes (v. 19), (7) Attic use of πειρασθαι (v. 21), (8) use of the classical phrasing ουδεν . . . λεγων (v. 22), and (9) the classical παθητος meaning 'must suffer' (v. 23)."

11. Tajra 1989: 164–68.

The Jews' persecution and God's help (vv. 21–22a)
The essence of Paul's proclamation (26:22b–23)
In conformity to the Prophets and Moses (v. 22b)
In reference to Jesus' suffering, resurrection, and mission (v. 23)[12]

She sees the middle of the speech, namely, "Paul's encounter with Jesus" (26:13–18), as its pivotal part, along with "Paul's persecution of Jesus' followers" (26:9–12) and "Paul as a witness of Jesus" (26:19–22a).

Tajra has read the importance of Acts 26:19–23, and Cheng that of 26:9–22a. Both seem to make some interesting points in their structures: Tajra seems to read the significance of *probatio's* conclusion (26:19–20), of *refutatio* (26:21), and of *peroratio* (26:22–23); and Cheng appears to pinpoint the function of Paul's life as *probatio* (26:8–20) and *refutatio* (26:21). Hence, Paul's testimony can be outlined according to Quintilian's five parts of forensic speech[13] as follows:

Exordium (26:2–5): In common with Agrippa II and the Jews
captatio benevolentiae (26:2–3)
Jewish awareness of Paul's life (26:4–5)
Narratio (26:6–7): Hope, the reason for Paul's trial
Probatio (26:8–20): Jesus' resurrection as the realization of the hope
An introductory question about God's power over the dead (26:8)
Paul's previous condition (26:9–11)
Paul's encounter with Jesus (26:12–18)
Paul's response to Jesus' resurrection (26:19–20)
Refutatio (26:21): Inconsistency of some Jews
Peroratio (26:22–23): Paul's life and hope as the reason of his trials

Now, let us see each section. In *exordium* (Acts 26:2–5) Paul talked about some elements that were shared between himself and Agrippa II, and between himself and the Jews. The first part related to Agrippa II has the form of *captatio benevolentiae* (26:2–3), and the second part deals with Jewish awareness of Paul's life (26:4–5). First of all, Paul made clear that he spoke of all the accusations raised by the Jews (26:2a). Then, he revealed his satisfaction to Agrippa II: **King Agrippa, I consider myself fortunate because I am going to make my defense today before you,**

12. Cheng 2011: 128.

13. For Quintilian's five parts of forensic speech, see comments on Tertullus's claim and Paul's testimony in ch. 24.

especially because you are an expert at all the customs and disputes of the Jews; hence, I beg you to listen to me patiently (26:2b–3). As Paul politely accepted Felix's status as a judge (24:10b), so Paul acknowledged that Agrippa II was suitable for listening to his case. Denton considers this acknowledgment as authentic in that "Agrippa had now resided six years in Palestine since his return from Rome" and that "he had, as part of his functions, the superintendence of the temple and the appointment and removal of the high priests, so that his office compelled him to be *expert in all customs and questions which are among the Jews.*"[14]

In relation to Jewish awareness of his own life, Paul pointed out that he had lived the Pharisaic way of life: **All the Jews know my manner of life from my youth, spent from the beginning among my own nation and in Jerusalem, and they have already known, if they are willing to testify, that according to the strictest party of our religion I have lived as a Pharisee** (Acts 26:4–5). "My own nation" could "refer to the Jews in Tarsus,"[15] and "the strictest party of our religion," the Pharisees.[16] In comparison with the first singular subject and verb in 22:3–5, the main subject and verb of 26:4–5 are more generalized as *isasi pantes [hoi] Ioudaioi* ("all the Jews know").[17] Further, Paul did not mention Gamaliel (cf. 22:3) but tagged himself as a Pharisee (26:5). If "Pharisaism" is understood as "the fundamental and most influential religious movement within Palestinian Judaism between 150 BC and AD 70," as Deines insists,[18] Paul presented more generalized information about himself as evidence. Furthermore, Paul did not identify himself as a Zealot (cf. 22:3) but just as a young Jew among his own nation and in Jerusalem (26:4).

In *narratio*, Paul illustrated "hope" as the reason for Paul's trial: **And now on account of the hope of the promise made by God to our**

14. Denton 1876: 319 (italics his).

15. See Schnabel 2012: 1002n54.

16. In relation to the time of Alexandra the Hasmonian Queen (76–67 BCE), Josephus says that the Pharisees "are a certain sect of the Jews that appear more religious than others, and seem to interpret the laws more accurately" (*J.W.* 1.110).

17. As regards 26:4–5, see Park 2011: 161.

18. Carson, O'Brien, and Seifrid 2001: 503.

ancestors,[19] I stand here on trial;[20] and our twelve tribes have hoped to attain the promise, worshipping God earnestly night and day; Concerning this hope the Jews are accusing me, O King! (26:6–7). What did Paul's hope refer to? Schnabel thinks that this hope refers to "the resurrection of the dead."[21] Witherington says that Paul alludes to "the gathering of the twelve tribes at the eschaton which is being associated with the resurrection."[22] Bruce defines this hope as "the hope that God would keep the promise which he made to the fathers of the nation long ago."[23]

However, Denton even a long time ago suggested a simple and powerful solution to understand this hope, by saying that Paul's hope referred to the Christ.[24] His idea consolidates the others' suggestion. The hope relates to "the resurrection of the dead," but particularly to Jesus' resurrection. The twelve tribes will be gathered via their resurrections, but they cannot be gathered without the Christ's resurrection as the firstfruits of resurrection. God has fulfilled His promise by raising Jesus from the dead, but Israel's hope consists not only of this fulfillment, but also of the fulfillment of God's promise on themselves. Moreover, identifying hope with Christ fits in with Paul's main proof of innocence in his speech (Acts 26:8–20), viz., "the resurrected Jesus." This hope is finally summarized in his conclusion: **If the Christ is subject to suffering, [and] if [he becomes] the first to rise from the dead, he will proclaim light both to the people and to the other nations** (26:23). Even in his epistles, Paul designates Jesus Christ as "hope," for instance, "the hope of glory" (Col 1:27), and "our hope" (1 Tim 1:1). Hence, it seems that "resurrection," "gathering," and "the fulfillment of God's promise" are compressed into "the Christ," namely his resurrection, God's fulfilling His promise of Christ, and the result of the Christ's ministry. Before Felix two years ago,

19. ἐπ᾽ ἐλπίδι τῆς εἰς τοὺς πατέρας ἡμῶν ἐπαγγελίας γενομένης ὑπὸ τοῦ θεοῦ can be translated as "the hope of the promise [given] to our ancestors and fulfilled by God," in considering the position of γενομένης. As a matter of fact, Paul at this time believed that this hope was realized via Jesus Christ.

20. In 22:7 Paul's stance is described by *epesa* (I fell), but in 26:6 by *hestēka krinomenos* (I stand to be judged). Before Agrippa II Paul clarified his position as "the accused."

21. Schnabel 2012: 1003.

22. Witherington 1998: 740.

23. Bruce 1988: 463.

24. Denton 1876: 320–21 says: "The promised hope, that is, Christ, whom not only the Pharisees, but every member of the twelve tribes, the whole house of Israel, looked forward to."

Paul talked about "a hope in God," namely, **a resurrection of both the righteous and the unrighteous** (Acts 24:15), but now before Agrippa II he delivered the core of the hope, the resurrected Jesus. "Resurrection," along with "encountering the resurrected Jesus," was Paul's main theme in his gospel and testimony in Acts (13:30–37; 17:3, 18, 31; 22:6–10, 17–21; 23:6; 24:15, 21), so it is quite natural that the resurrected Jesus took the foremost place in Paul's final testimony.

Then Paul, in *probatio*, Paul expounded on how he encountered Jesus Christ certainly because the hope of Israel was realized via Jesus' resurrection (Acts 26:8–20). Paul's proof is composed of "an introductory question about God's power over the dead" (26:8), "Paul's previous condition" (26:9–11), "Paul's encounter with Jesus" (26:12–18), and "Paul's response to Jesus' resurrection" (26:19–20).

Before propounding the resurrected Christ, first of all, Paul started with an introductory question about God's power over the dead: **Why is it thought unbelievable to you that God raises the dead?** (Acts 26:8). Witherington renders this query in a general sense by putting it in his own words: "once one admits there is an all-powerful God, why should anyone find the idea of resurrection incredible."[25] However, the following verse shows that Paul's mentioning "God's power over the dead" should have obviously related to Jesus' resurrection: **Certainly, I myself thought to myself that it was needful to do many things hostile to the name of Jesus the Nazarene** (26:9).

The audience, especially Festus and Agrippa II, knew that the Jews had several points of disagreement **about a certain Jesus who was dead, whom Paul claimed to be alive** (Acts 25:19), so they should have read Jesus' resurrection in Paul's query about belief in God's power over the dead. Also, Paul's confession might have made the audience comfortable because Paul admitted to his own disbelief in Jesus' resurrection. Moreover, Paul confessed that his disbelief had moved him to persecute believers: **And that is what I did in Jerusalem: Not only did I lock up many of the saints in prisons by the authority I received from the chief priests, but I also cast down a pebble against them when they were destroyed; in addition, I punished them often in all the synagogues and tried to force them to blaspheme; eventually because I was so furiously enraged at them, I pursued them even as far as the outermost cities** (26:10–11).

25. Witherington 1998: 741.

A pebble was "used in voting: a black one for conviction, a white one for acquittal":[26] however, "it cannot be taken to prove that Paul was a member of the Sanhedrin."[27] Paul's disbelief in Jesus' resurrection was developed to its extreme, into outrage and persecution. This maximal disbelief reaching the point of persecuting believers with indignation, in the final analysis, could produce palpable proof of Jesus' resurrection.

The main part of Paul's *probatio* is made up of his encounter with Jesus (Acts 26:12–18).[28] This story needs to be compared with chs. 9 and 22 in terms of (1) Paul's journey to Damascus (9:1b–3a; 22:5b–6a; 26:12), (2) the brightness of the light (9:3; 22:6; 26:13), (3) the scope of the light (9:3; 22:6; 26:13), (4) the response to the light (9:4; 22:7; 26:14), (5) the discourse between Jesus and Paul (9:4b–6; 22:7b–8, 10, 17–21; 26:14b–18), (6) Paul's companions (9:7; 22:9; 26:14a), Paul's blindness and fasting (9:8–9; 22:11), and Paul's recovery (9:18–19a), (7) the communication between Jesus and Ananias (9:10–16), Paul's mission (9:15–16; 22:14–15, 21; 26:16–18), and Ananias's mission (9:17; 22:12–16). All will be covered.

First and foremost, Paul's journey to Damascus appears in Acts 9:1b–3a; 22:5b–6a; and 26:12, and Jesus' sudden appearance and Paul's response are described in 9:3b–4a; 22:6b–7a; and 26:13–14a. A very interesting difference can be found through the main verbs. In 9:1b–4a, the main verbs are *ētēsato* (he asked, 9:2), *egeneto* (it happened, 9:3), *periēstrapsen* ([a light] flashed, 9:3), and *ēkousen* (he heard, 9:4). In 22:5b–7a, the main verbs are *eporeuomēn* (I went, 22:5), *egeneto* (it happened, 22:6), *epesa* (I fell, 22:7) and *ēkousa* (I heard, 22:7). In 26:12–14a, *eidon* (I saw, 26:13) and *ēkousa* (I heard, 26:14) are the main verbs. The narrator focuses on Paul's act of asking, the process of the event, and Paul's cognition in ch. 9. In 22:5b–7a, Paul emphasized his actions, namely, his departure and falling, along with the process of the event and his own cognition. However, in 26:12–14a, Paul put stress mainly on his own cognition. Further, the phrase, "in the Hebrew language" in 26:14, could be explaining why his companions could not have understood Jesus' speech (22:9b).

Second, the brightness of the light is expressed uniquely; **a light from heaven** (Acts 9:3), **a great light from heaven** (22:6) and **a light from heaven, brighter than the sun** (26:13) are employed. In 9:3 "light"

26. BDAG 1098.
27. Bruce 1990: 500.
28. In relation to 26:12–18, see Park 2011: 147, 161–66.

is the subject of the main verb, but the "light" in 22:6 is the subject of the infinitive and in 26:13 is the subject of the participle. In 22:6, the infinitive is connected with *egeneto*, so it is near to the main verb. Further, in 22:6 Paul said that **it happened that a great light shone around me [him]**, but in 26:13 he said that **I saw a light shine around me and my companions**; the former has the third-person perspective because a great light is emphasized, but the latter is described from the first-person point of view. Moreover, the "brighter than the sun" in 26:13 could emphasize the smallness of the first-person witness. So it can be said that "the brighter light" does not make Paul greater than the light. Rather, "Wow! I saw a great, great light. Before it, I was very small!" could be what Paul wanted to say. The verb (*periastraptō*, "to flash around")[29] used with the light 9:3 and 22:6 is different from that (*perilampō*, "to shine around")[30] in 26:13. The shining was expressed to be more generous and magnificent later compared to the former sudden flashing.

Third, the scope of the light is different among the three accounts, viz., **around him** (Acts 9:3), **around me** (22:6), **around me and my companions** (26:13). The scope of the light is connected with the brightness of the light above. This is not just an increasing sequence. It should be comprehended in terms of a larger context. In 26:13 Paul is described as one among the many who met Jesus.

Fourth, the response to the light also varies: **He fell to the ground** (Acts 9:4); **I fell to the ground** (22:7); **we had all fallen to the ground** (26:14). Each response to the light is also linked to the brightness and scope of the light. In 26:14 Paul did not specify his falling. He stressed that "we all" had fallen down. Paul again connotes that he was not special. He emphasizes again, "I was one of them."

The fifth part covers the communication between Jesus and Paul in Acts 9:4b–6; 22:7b–8, 10, 17–21; and 26:14b–18.[31] The communication between Jesus and Ananias is only depicted in 9:10–16, but this can be compared with 22:17–21.[32] Churchill insists that "the sequence, then, consists of an implied question with no answer (Acts 9), an explicit ques-

29. This word occurs only in these two verses in the NT. In the LXX it is used only in 4 Macc 4:10.

30. This word is employed in Luke 2:9 and here both in the NT and in the LXX.

31. "The Nazarene" in 22:8 does not appear in 9:5 and 26:15.

32. According to Park 2002: 90–91, 96–97, Ananias change in 9:10–16 can be dealt with Paul's change in 22:17–21 at the same point of view, viz., disciples' change according to the Lord Jesus.

tion with no answer (Acts 22), and Jesus' answer to the here unasked question (Acts 26)."[33] To be precise, in chs. 9 and 26 Saul's main query was **Who you are**, and in ch. 22 **What I should I do**, a more developed and I-emphasized question; if we consider 22:17–21, where Paul's later experience is told, this question has been answered, that is, **Go, for I will send you far away to the Gentiles** (26:21). In fact, when we consider the conversation between Jesus and Paul in 22:17–21, even in ch. 22 we can read Jesus' direct calling of Paul for mission. Hence, we can say that, even though Paul asked both questions, Paul focused on Jesus' identity rather than on Paul's mission before Agrippa II. In addition, we can find a distinction in terms of the mission description. When the mission is described in 26:16b–18, Jesus is the subject. The two main subjects and verbs are *ōpfthēn* (**I appeared**, 26:16b) and *egō apostellō* (**I myself am sending**, 26:17): this shows that Paul became more Jesus-centered than two years ago.

Sixth, with reference to "Paul's companions" (Acts 9:7; 22:9; 26:14a), "his blindness and fast" (9:8–9; 22:11), and "his recovery" (9:18–19a), Paul did not mention his blindness, fast, and recovery before Agrippa II but did about his companions. In ch. 9, it is said, **he [Paul] understood the voice** [the accusative] **speaking to him** (9:4), and then the companions were **hearing the voice** [the genitive] (9:7). The narrator seems to denote that Paul heard the contents the voice said, but the companions heard the voice only. In ch. 22, it is said **I listened to the speaking voice toward me** (22:7), and then **they did not hear the sound of the one speaking to me.** Paul seems to stress his obedience first and then how the others did not take notice of the contents of the voice speaking. As for Acts 26, Paul only talked about his own understanding of the contents of the speaking voice by saying, **I heard a voice speaking toward me in the Hebrew language**, not about the companions' hearing. Paul did use *ethos* less in ch. 26 than two years ago, and interestingly, he did not distinguish between himself and his companions.

Moulton thinks that the difference between Acts 9:7 and 22:9 can be understood in terms of "the maintenance of an old and well-known distinction between the acc. and the gen. with ἀκούω,"[34] but Bruce says that Moulton's suggestion "may indeed explain the discrepancy between the present text [9:7] and 22:9, but the 'distinction' does not accord with Lu-

---

33. Churchill 2008: 12.
34. Moulton 1998: 66.

kan usage."[35] Bruce calls the difference between 9:7 and 22:9 "the apparent contradiction,"[36] but these three passages could be explained in terms of Paul's change in attitude. The narrator points out Paul's understanding and the companions' simple hearing (9:7). Then, Paul first emphasized that his companions were not able to understand the contents the voice uttered (22:9), but afterward he focused just on his own understanding (26:14a) after identifying himself with his companions (26:13).

Lastly, concerning Paul's and Ananias's mission, Paul's mission appears in all three passages (Acts 9:15–16; 22:14–15, 21; 26:16–18) but Ananias's mission appears only in 9:17 and 22:12–16. In 9:15–16 and 9:17 Jesus speaks to Ananias, in 22:14–15, 12–16 Ananias talks to Paul, and in 22:21 and 26:16–18 Jesus to Paul. In 22:12 Ananias is introduced as the one **who was a devout man according to the law and well spoken of by all the Jews living there**, where Paul used *ethos*; however, using *ethos* by employing Ananias is avoided by Paul in ch. 26. This phenomenon can be read in Peter's answer to the circumcised in 11:13–14; Peter did not mention Cornelius's name, fame, piety, prayer, alms, etc., at all despite the positive effects it could bring in defending himself. In addition, in 22:15 Paul talked about *hōn heōrakas kai ēkousas* (**of what you have seen and heard**), in which what Paul has seen and heard is pointed out, but, as Bruce says,[37] Paul emphasized the heavenly origin before Agrippa II; it can also be compared with Peter's speech in 11:5, 9 where "from heaven" is added.

Therefore, we can conclude that, in comparison with Lucan testimony in ch. 9 and Paul's previous testimony in ch. 22, in his final speech Paul (1) used less *ethos*, (2) paid attention to the community rather than to himself, (3) put the spotlight on the fulfillment of Jesus' mission, not on his, and (4) employed more heavenly origins than human ones, viz., Paul's and Ananias's.

Back to the bigger picture, Paul's *probatio* ends up with his response to Jesus' resurrection (Acts 26:19–20): **Therefore, King Agrippa, I was not disobedient to the heavenly vision, but I declared both to those in Damascus first and to the Jerusalemites, ultimately [through] all the province both of Judea and of the Gentiles, so as [for them] to**

35. Bruce 1990: 236.

36. Bruce 1990: 456.

37. Bruce 1990: 457: "In 26:16 Paul reports as part of the 'heavenly vision' the substance of the communication here received from Ananias. Cf. 9:12, where Paul in a vision foresees the visit of Ananias."

repent and turn to God with performing deeds worthy of repentance (26:19–20). Paul, spurred on by disbelief in Jesus' resurrection, went on to hate and persecute Christians. However, after he was encountered by the resurrected Messiah, he obeyed the heavenly vision, viz., Jesus Christ, in Damascus and Jerusalem first, and then in Judea and to the ends of the earth; in other words, he proclaimed the gospel to people in Damascus and in Jerusalem, and then to people in Judea and the gentiles. Paul's description is different from 1:8 in two points: He started with Damascus rather than Jerusalem; and he focused on the people around him as well as the places he had been. His mission in Damascus is introduced in 9:19–25 (for Jerusalem see 9:26–30; 18:22; 21:17—23:11; for Judea see 11:29–30; 12:25; 21:8–16; 24:1–27; and for the gentiles see 13:1—21:7).

After finishing a long *probatio*, Paul added a short *refutatio*: **For these reasons, some[38] Jews seized me, when I was in the Temple, and were trying to slay me** (Acts 26:21). Even though Paul undertook his mission because of the realized hope of the whole of Israel, namely, the resurrected Messiah, some Jews seized and tried to slay him; hence, they were the ones inconsistent with what they believed in. Paul had proofs not only to show his innocence but also to refute the Jews' accusation.

Finally, Paul concluded the speech by reminding what the prophets had prophesied about the Christ: **Having therefore met help from God by chance, I put up with [a lot] up to this day, testifying to both small and great, and saying nothing except what the prophets and Moses said was going to happen: on the condition that[39] the Christ is subject to suffering, and on the condition that he is the first to rise from the dead, he will proclaim light both to the people [the Jews] and to the Gentiles** (Acts 26:22–23). This is Paul's *peroratio* that shows the reason of his trial: (1) with the help of God, Paul was able to stand there; (2) he testified without any kind of discrimination, such as social or racial; (3) he declared only what was written in the Scriptures, particularly the "hope" of the whole Israel, namely, the Christ's suffering, his resurrection, and his proclamation of light to all the nations.

Throughout Paul's final speech, "light" (*pfōs*) is stated three times: at first, in relation to the heavenly "light" shining around Paul and his companions (Acts 26:13); second, in order to convey the result of conversion in the phrase, **from darkness to light and from the power of Satan**

---

38. There is no article here; cf. 26:4.
39. The expression, "on the condition that," reflects the if-clause (*ei*).

to God (26:18); and lastly, in connection with the Christ's proclamation (26:23). On the subject of the risen Messiah's proclamation of light to all the nations, Peterson says, "This is consistent with the notion first implied in Acts 1:1–2—that the risen Lord continues to work through his disciples to fulfil his saving plan—and conveyed in various other ways throughout the narrative."[40] Hence, Paul's mission was "scripturally based and God-given, a privileged share in the Messiah's own mission of salvation to Israel and the nations."[41]

To sum up, Paul before Agrippa II stated the reason for his trial very clearly and successfully in rhetoric. In his composition, "hope" and "light" performed an important role; the former refers to the risen Jesus, and the latter to his systematic method of ministry. In addition, his speech is composed of heavenly and earthly elements: from heaven, "light" (Acts 26:13), "vision" (26:19) and "help" (26:22) fell to Paul; on earth, there were the hearers' "falling to the ground" (26:14), "obedience" (26:19), and "continuous testimony" (26:22). Furthermore, not only had Paul proved his innocence (26:8–20) but also had rejected the Jews' accusation (26:4–5, 21). Most of all, Paul was able to trace many witnesses: about the life history before his encountering Jesus, all the Jews (26:4); for his persecution, the high priests (26:10, 12); regarding the event of encountering the heavenly vision, his traveling companions (26:13); about his further ministry, people in Damascus and Jerusalem and all the Jews and gentiles (26:20); and all the prophets and Moses concerning his "hope" (26:22). Hence, Paul's testimony can be regarded as perfectly excellent.

Conversation between Festus, Paul, and Agrippa II (26:24–32)

When Paul's long and final testimony was declared, Festus said in response with a loud voice, **You are insane, Paul! Your much advanced learning**[42] **is driving you insane!** (Acts 26:24). In advance of Agrippa II, Festus, who was very political (see ch. 25) and regarded *ethos* as crucial (see 25:16), used offensive and informal expressions, that is, "insane" and "mad." Indeed, he must have been astounded by Paul's logical and rhetorical handling of religious items such as hope, resurrection, and the

---

40. Peterson 2009: 672: he mentions 3:16; 4:9–12, 29–31; 9:5–6, 10–16, 31; 11:21; and 16:6–10, along with 1:1–2.

41. Peterson 2009: 672.

42. For "much advanced learning," see Witherington 1998: 749.

resurrected Christ; to his success, Paul did make quite an impact on the highly esteemed Roman governor.

In spite of Festus's rude utterance, Paul said, **I am not insane, your Excellency, but I am speaking true and prudent**[43] **words** (Acts 26:25). He called Festus **Most Excellency** (*kratistos*). This title appears only four times in the NT: one is employed for Theophilus by Luke (Luke 1:3); two for Felix by Lysias the tribune (Acts 23:26) and Tertullus (24:3); and one for Festus by Paul (26:25). Luke might have grouped Theophilus with Felix and Festus every time he used this title; Theophilus would also have noticed this connection. Moreover, this can be the last identification between Theophilus the first reader and the character with whom the reader could probably identify. Hence, to the first reader this conversation must have been very crucial. In the presence of this kind of character, Paul denied his insanity but stressed quite the opposite, his sobriety. According to Witherington, "the contrast between 'mania' and sobriety was a well-known one in Greek literature (cf. Xenophon, *Mem.* 1.1.16; 3.9.6–7)" and "sobriety or sanity was seen as an ideal in Greek Philosophy (see Plato, *Protag.* 323B; *Republic* 430E–431B; Diogenes Laertius, *Lives* 3.91; Justin, *Dial.* 39.4)."[44]

Paul found an evidence of his sobriety in his speech appropriate to Agrippa II: **For the king, to whom I am speaking freely, knows about these things because I cannot believe that any of these things has escaped his notice; for this was not accomplished in a corner** (Acts 26:26). In respect to who the target listener of this verse was, Witherington thinks that Paul directed this argument to Agrippa II, not to Festus "perhaps sensing that Festus was out of his depth and not going to be persuaded."[45] However, v. 26 starts with a causal conjunction (*gar*) and Agrippa II is referred to in the third-person. Via this speech to Festus, Paul must have explained why he was not insane but spoke a sober truth. Religious ingredients were added to his testimony because the main listener (Agrippa II) had known and understood all those elements quite well. Moreover, Paul offered a list of eyewitnesses to all the events. As Bruce says, "The events which fulfilled the ancient promises were well

---

43. Witherington 1998: 749 sees *alētheias kai sōphrosunēs* as "an example of hendiadys" and suggests to translate it as "the sober truth."

44. Witherington 1998: 749.

45. Witherington 1998: 749.

known and public: this was no hole-and-corner esoteric mystery";[46] Festus could not have presumed that Paul was mad.

After replying to Festus's response, Paul turned to King Agrippa II, the main listener, and said: **Do you believe, King Agrippa, the prophets? I know that you believe** (Acts 26:27). Paul's arguments were based on what the prophets and Moses said as well as on the eye-witnesses. Since Agrippa II could be seen as a Jewish king, Paul with certainty asked a rhetorical question and said that Agrippa II should have believed what had been written by the prophets. In Paul's query, Peterson brilliantly reads a shift of Agrippa II's role "from being an authority who can help Paul to being one who needs help himself to recognize the fulfillment of Israel's hopes in Jesus and his resurrection."[47] Moreover, Marshall finds a "logical trap" in Paul's question because "if he [Agrippa II] confessed belief in the prophets, the obvious follow-up would be, 'surely then you accept that Jesus is the Messiah?'" and "to deny that he believed in the prophets would be unthinkable for a loyal Jew."[48]

Hence, even though it would have been hard for the king to deny it all, he **said to Paul, "With such a trivial thing you are persuading me to become a Christian"**[49] (Acts 26:28). Relating to what the "thing" in "with a trivial thing" refers to, Peterson prefers to view the trivial "thing" as "time" rather than "argument";[50] however, the king would have meant Paul's "argument" is trivial because the "great" (*megas*) in the next verse "would hardly be used of time."[51] So the expression, "with a trivial thing," would mean "with so few (or brief) arguments."[52] Agrippa II knew that

46. Bruce 1988: 471.

47. Peterson 2009: 674.

48. Marshall 1980B: 419–20.

49. As an alternative translation of "to become a Christian," "to play the Christian" is suggested; but Barrett 1998: 1171 thinks it as based on "one over-literal rendering of a Hebrew verb." For "Christian" (*Christianos* in Greek), see comments on 11:26. As for Roman and Jewish writers' usage of this term, see "Tacitus, *Ann.* 15.44; Pliny, *Ep.* 10.96–97; Lucian, *Alex.* 25.38; cf. Josephus, *Ant.* 18.64" (Witherington 1998: 751). For Josephus's note on Jesus and Christians, see Evans 2008 [2005]: 178–80. Also, see comments on 11:26.

50. Peterson 2009: 676.

51. Barrett 1998: 1170. By the way, he thinks that "there is no great difference between time and argument: a brief argument would occupy a short time, a short time would not permit a long argument." However, Paul's arguments in his final testimony were not short in length, but it should not have taken a long time.

52. See Witherington 1998: 751. Barrett 1998: 1143 translates it as "with little trouble."

Paul's full "argument" had to do with "becoming a Christian," but he
ignored Paul's testimony as seeming frivolous, although it was founded
upon both the Scriptures and many eyewitnesses, as he knew beforehand.

Then Paul set his face to all the audience and conveyed his wishes
to them: **I pray to God that, whether with so few or so many arguments, not only you but also all those who are listening to me today
become such as I am, except for these chains** (Acts 26:29). Paul should
have thought that his testimony had many arguments sufficient enough
to prove his assertion. Nevertheless, he made it clear that his primary
concern was not the number of arguments but benefits offered to the audience. Paul's condition, which **such as I am** includes, should refer to his
hopefulness (26:6–7) and his obedience to the heavenly vision (26:19–20)
rather than his Roman citizenship, his rhetorical ability, and his much
advanced learning (26:24); furthermore his chains were excluded from
his wish list for the audience.

Paul's prayer made the audience hall meeting come to an end: **The
king got up, and [with him] the governor and Bernice and those sitting with them, and they were leaving** (Acts 26:30–31a). These circumstances can be compared with their previous "pomp" (25:23); Agrippa II,
Bernice, the senior military officers, and the prominent men of the city
entered into the hall in an awesome and magnificent way, but now left the
hall in an uninspiring and humdrum manner. Some hearts could have
been swayed at that time, which Luke kept silent about, but the writer
registered their superficial reply: **They said to one another, "This man is
not doing anything deserving death or imprisonment"** (26:31b). This
not only reflects Festus's verdict that **I did not take anything that would
make him deserve death** (25:25a) but also reduces the weight of Paul's
case by adding "imprisonment." The gathered did not talk about what
Paul emphasized, namely, hope, vision, and obedience.

Chapter 26 closes with Luke's note on the final remark of the Herodian king given to Festus: **This man could have been released unless
he had appealed to Caesar** (Acts 26:32). Originally Festus wanted to get
some charges against Paul in order to write them to his "lord," Nero the
emperor (25:26–27), so Agrippa II should have given Festus something
to pass on. So the Majesty did—there were no charges; thus his "release"
was recommended. The curtain closed and the first reader should have
deeply absorbed "the certainty of what he [Theophilos] learned" (Luke
1:4) as well as Paul's innocence.

Fusing the Horizons: The Sense of Community

In a garden, plants of numerous species are planted, especially herbs and flowers. While each plant is beautiful, the beauty of the garden blossoms at its fullest when all of them bloom together. The breathtaking sight is irresistible. How we feel about beautiful gardens must be related to how Jesus dealt with disciples. Jesus did not send his disciples alone: but two by two (Luke 10:1), twelve (9:1–6), and seventy (10:1–20). The apostles were twelve in number (6:13–16) and the deacons, seven (Acts 6:5). We can also discover lots of twosomes with names: Peter and John (3:1, 3, 4, 11; 4:13, 19; 8:14), Barnabas and Saul (11:30; 12:25; 13:2, 7), Paul and Silas (15:40; 16:19, 25, 29; 17:4, 10), and Silas and Timothy (17:14, 15; 18:5). This community spirit or "togetherness" is found in the "we-passages" as well;[53] Luke and Paul, only the two, traveled together from Philippi to Troas (20:5–6). Additionally, the travel from Caesarae to Rome was also made by the two, but this time three in total, with Aristarchus (27:2).

The disciples in Acts did not work in isolation. They prayed together with Jesus' mother and brothers (Acts 1:14). The promise vindicated by Peter was open to the audience and their children, **and to all who are far away, as many as the Lord our God will call to Himself** (2:39). Jesus the powerful and gracious name was shared with the crippled beggar (3:6), the Samaritans (8:5–25), an Ethiopian eunuch (8:26–39), Saul the persecutor (9:17–19), and Cornelius the Roman centurion (10:34–48). Some of the Cypriots and the Cyreneans shared the gospel with the Greeks in Antioch (11:20). The Antiochian Christians shared their materials with the Jewish Christians in Judea (11:29–30). Afterward, under the guidance of the Holy Spirit, the mission teams of the Antioch church shared the gospel with all the other nations (13:1—20:2). Lastly, Paul promulgated the gospel even with the enraged Jews (22:1–21), Roman officers and the Herodian family (24:10—26:29), the barbarians in Malta (28:8–9), and ultimately anyone in Rome (28:30–31).

In addition, Acts shows how the disciples shared their community spirit with others very broadly. When Cornelius the centurion, **falling at his feet, worshipped him [Peter], Peter raised him and said, "Stand up! I myself am**

53. Luke, the author of this Acts of the Apostles, accompanied Paul from Troas to Philippi (16:10–17), from Philippi to Jerusalem (20:5—21:17), and finally from Caesarea to Rome (27:1—28:16): these are called "we-passages."

a mere mortal" (Acts 10:25b–26). By asserting the absolute truth of him being mortal as any other human being,[54] Peter did not coop the centurion up in the boundaries of the gentiles, but put him and himself together within the boundary of human beings. This application of the community spirit to the gentile went further to his holistic perspective on God's impartiality:[55] **Opening his mouth, Peter said, "In truth I perceive that God does not show any favoritism"** (10:34). Eventually, Peter shared the gospel with the people gathered together and the Holy Spirit came upon them.

Paul and Barnabas in Lystra identified themselves with the audience by saying, **Men, why are you doing these things? We too are human beings, with the same nature as you** (Acts 14:15b). This identification is the same as Peter's before Cornelius in 10:26, and contrasts with that of Zeus and Hermes in the legend: they said, "We are gods" (*Metam.* 8.689).[56] Here Paul used *homoiopathēs,* meaning "having the same suffering."[57] This attitude can be found in Paul's testimony in Acts 26:13b–14a: Paul said that the light from heaven shone on him and those who journeyed with him, and that all of them [originally "we"] had fallen to the ground. By using the first plural subject, Paul not only identified himself with those who traveled with him, but also employed them as his witnesses.

In the further chapters, the first plural pronoun is used very freely, especially from Acts 27:3. The five main verbs in 27:3–8 have the first plural pronoun as the subject, and the pronoun is used as objects twice (27:6, 7). Paul used the first plural pronoun to share the community spirit with the passengers (27:10),[58] just as he did in his last testimony (26:14). In relation to the first plural subject in 27:16, further, we can read the unity that bonds between the passengers on board.[59] Moreover, Luke provides the number of those who ate the broken bread by using the first plural subject in 27:37; here the unity between the passengers can be deciphered again.[60] Furthermore, Luke consistently uses the first plural pronoun and verbs with first plural suffixes referring not only to Paul and his companions but also to

54. See comments on 10:26.

55. See comments on 10:34.

56. See comments on 14:15b.

57. This word appears twice in the NT: one appears here and the other does in relation to Elijah in Jas 5:17.

58. See comments on 27:10.

59. See comments on 27:16.

60. See comments on 27:37.

the other passengers in 28:1–16. It may indicate that there was a real sense of community among them, at least within Luke toward others.[61]

Consequently, Acts shows how the disciples shared and did not fear to share their community spirit with others very broadly, even to different groups. The "we-passages" especially can be conceived as signs of togetherness in each Christian community. The first plural subject and pronoun in the Lord's prayer also could be regarded as a sign of Christian togetherness.

---

61. See comments on 28:1.

ACTS 27
Paul's Journey to Malta

Paul and his companions had a further journey with prisoners, expecting that the Lord's plan will be fulfilled (Acts 23:11). Paul was not released yet, instead handed over to a centurion. Paul's friends had the freedom to go wherever they wanted to go; nevertheless, they traveled with Paul. A new leader (Julius the centurion), new companions (prisoners, sailors, etc.), new ships (a ship from Adramyttium, a ship from Alexandria), new circumstances (adverse winds, storms, etc.), and things changing continually wait for them. On the other hand, some still remained unchanged, for example, the faithful companions Aristachus and Luke, hope in God, the Word from God, and the Eucharist.

This chapter is parallel to Jesus' death on the cross described around Luke 23.[1] A centurion played an important role both in Jesus' death on the cross (23:47) and in Paul's journey to Rome (Acts 27:1, 3, 6, 11, 31, 43). Remarkably, Jesus did not appear on the scene but we can spot him in the Eucharist, which was feasted on when at risk of shipwrecking (27:35; cf. Luke 22:19–20). Particularly, the resurrected Jesus echoes the theme of "hope." In the first half of the journey, "hope" faded away (Acts 27:1–20). The difficulties of this journey are conveyed by the Greek word *molis* ("scarcely")[2] that appears in 27:7, 8, 16.[3] This section ends up with the sentence, "finally all hope that we would be saved was faded away" (27:20b). Before that, a coal-black darkness was recognized (27:20a; cf. Luke 23:44). In its second half the "hope" thrived, where the word *molis* does not appear; this section finishes with the sentence, **all were rescued safely to land** (Acts 27:44b). The Eucharist was feasted on for salvation (27:34). Hence, the hope and the Eucharist, both of which resemble the resurrected Jesus, combine to shape salvation.

1. Goulder 1964: 61; so also see Walton 2000: 38.

2. It pertains to "being hard to accomplish" (BDAG 657).

3. In the NT, this word appears six times (Acts 14:18; 27:7, 8, 16; Rom 5:7; 1 Pet 4:18).

All the events of this chapter must have happened throughout the summer and fall of 59 CE. First, the trials arranged by Festus occurred in the summer of 59 CE.[4] Second, this voyage should have been undertaken at least before "the beginning of the autumn"; according to Philo, it was "the last season during which nautical men can safely take voyages, and during which in consequence they all return from the foreign marts in every quarter to their own native ports and harbours of refuge, especially all who exercise a prudent care not to be compelled to pass the winter in a foreign country."[5] Third, their voyage to Fair Havens was very slow, so the Jewish fast day (Day of Atonement, Yom Kippur; October 5, 59 CE) had already passed before they arrived in Fair Havens (Acts 27:9). Lastly, it took fifteen days to move from Fair Havens to Malta. Along these lines, all the events of this chapter seem to have occurred in three months, viz., August, September, and October of 59 CE.

Hope Growing Faint (27:1–20)

Festus and Agrippa II decided to send Paul to Rome in order to be judged by Caesar: **When it was decided for us to sail to Italy, they handed over[6] Paul and some other prisoners to a centurion of the Augustan Cohort named Julius** (Acts 27:1). Codex Bezae has a different reading, "and the next day, he [Festus] called a certain centurion named Julius and handed over to him Paul with other prisoners,"[7] but it would be more reasonable to think that Agrippa II and Festus decided together to send Paul to Caesar, not only because the last communication was performed between the two (26:32), making the referent of the third singular pronoun in 27:1 of Codex Bezae vague, but also because Festus would not have dared carrying alone the heavy burden of sending Paul to the emperor without clarifying the charges against him (cf. 25:27). According to the expression, "us," it can be conjectured that Luke the narrator was decided to be accompanied, possibly "as ship's doctor"[8] or as Paul's personal doctor; Aristarchus is mentioned as Paul's companion, too (20:4). The procurator

4. See also Schnabel 2012: 973.

5. *Legat.* 15.

6. This verb (*paradidōmi*) is also employed to refer to Pilate's verdict on Jesus in Luke 23:25.

7. Rius-Camps and Read-Heimerdinger 2009: 338. This reading has not been dealt with by the NA and the UBS editions.

8. Bruce 1990: 511 (cf. 28:9–10).

may decide Paul's boarding and the Caesarean church may send helpers (Luke and Aristarchus) as before (cf. 21:12–16).

The task of convoying Paul was given to a centurion of the Augustan (*Sebastos*) Cohort. Here the title **His Majesty the Reverend** (*Sebastos*), previously employed by Festus in Acts 25:21, 25, occurs again.[9] This cohort is regarded as "*Cohors Ia Augusta*," which "was largely made up of Syrian mercenaries, was stationed in Syria during most of the first century A.D., and was perhaps in Batanea [Bashan in the Transjordan] during the reign of Herod Agrippa II."[10] According to the centurion's function, Bruce suggests that Julius[11] could have been "a member of the corps of *frumentarii*—centurions who served as liaison officers between Rome and the armies in the imperial provinces, and who might be given as an additional duty the escorting of prisoners from the provinces to Rome."[12] Therefore, Julius the centurion can be regarded as a Syrian mercenary whose role was to communicate between Rome and Syria, while escorting prisoners from Syria to Rome.

Paul's companions traveled from Caesarea to the middle of the storm in the Mediterranean Sea: starting from Caesarea (Acts 27:2), stopping by Sidon (27:3), passing by Cyprus, Cilicia, and Pamphylia (27:4), stopping by Myra (27:5), passing by Cnidus and Salmone (27:7), stopping by Fair Havens (27:8); again starting from Fair Havens hoping to spend the winter in Phoenix (27:12), passing by Cauda (27:16), and finally drifting away into the middle of the storm, worrying about running aground on the Syrtis (27:17–20).

This section includes a series of reversals: rowing from Caesarea to Sidon (Acts 27:2–3), taking a hard voyage from Sidon to Myra (27:4–5), happily finding a ship sailing for Italy (27:6), taking a harder voyage for a long time from Myra to Fair Havens (27:7–8), being well advised by Paul (27:9–10), consenting to follow bad advice from the sailors (27:11–12), having a good sign, the gentle south wind (27:13), encountering a fierce wind like that of a typhoon, the northeast wind (27:14–15), rescuing the lifeboat (27:16–17), and being violently battered by the storm (27:18–20). In spite of some good fortunes the situation deteriorated further, and

9. This word appears only three times in the NT, all in Acts.

10. Fitzmyer 1998: 769; so also see Witherington 1998: 758–59 and Peterson 2009: 681.

11. Via his name, Bruce 1990: 512 suggests that "he was a Roman citizen whose father or grandfather had been enfranchised under Julius Caesar or Augustus."

12. Bruce 1990: 511.

finally passengers reached the conclusion that there remained no hope of being saved. These contents can be structured in terms of "chances of good fortune" and "hardships" as follows:

> Chance 1: Going well from Caesarea to Sidon (27:2–3)
>
> Hardship 1: Taking a hard voyage from Sidon to Myra (27:4–5)
>
> Chance 2: Happily finding a ship sailing for Italy (27:6)
>
> Hardship 2: Taking a harder voyage for a long time from Myra to Fair Havens (27:7–8)
>
> Chance 3: Being well advised by Paul (27:9–10)
>
> Hardship 3: Consenting to follow bad advice from the sailors (27:11–12)
>
> Chance 4: Having a good sign, the gentle south wind (27:13)
>
> Hardship 4: Encountering a wind like a typhoon, the northeast wind (27:14–15)
>
> Chance 5: Rescuing the lifeboat (27:16–17)
>
> Hardship 5: Being violently battered by the storm (27:18–20)

The journey of Luke and Paul[13] started out well: Going on board a ship from Adramyttium that was about to sail to various places on the coast of the province of Asia, we put out to sea, accompanied by Aristarchus, a Macedonian from Thessalonica; then the next day we took up moorings at Sidon; in addition, Julius, treating Paul benevolently, allowed him to go to his friends to be cared for (Acts 27:2–3). Luke mentions Aristarchus, with whom they had come together two and half years ago, as another companion (20:4): he could not help accompanying Paul to Rome; even afterward, he seems to have remained beside Paul according to Col 4:10 and Phlm 24.[14] They met a ship from Adramyttium, "an ancient city of Mysia [Acts 16:7, 8] in the Rom[an] province of Asia."[15] That port was about 96 kilometers away from Assos (20:13, 14) to the east. The ship should have been "a trading ship"[16] rather than "a grain ship, bound for Italy";[17] otherwise, it was unnecessary for Julius to find a ship bound for Italy in Myra (cf. 27:6). It only took a day to sail from Caesarea to Sidon, around 120 kilometers. This good commencement seems to have

---

13. On account of the first plural pronoun, "we," Luke is set at the head.

14. See also Schnabel 2012: 1034.

15. *ISBE* 1:62.

16. Schnabel 2012: 1034.

17. Bruce 1988: 477.

made Julius more generous; he showed kindness toward Paul; additionally, Julius might have taken Paul as his lucky charm.

Right after a fortunate start, however, an arduous voyage followed
from Sidon to Myra: **Putting out to sea from there, we**[18] **sailed under
the lee of Cyprus because of the opposite winds; ultimately sailing
across the high sea off Cilicia and Pamphylia, we came down to Myra
in Lycia** (Acts 27:4–5). This route was different from the course taken by
Paul when he returned to Caesarea from his third missionary journey
(21:3). At that time, the ship passed Cyprus the island on her left-hand
side, drawing a straight line from Patara to Tyre (620 km from Patara).
At this time, they made a journey from Sidon to Myra: Sidon was about
35 kilometers away from Tyra to the northeast, and Myra was about 45
kilometers away from Patara to the east. So, as before, passing Cyprus on
her left-hand side would make a line from Sidon to Myra (around 580
km by sea). Nevertheless, the opposing winds led the ship to go by the
eastern side of Cyprus and the southern sea off Cilicia and Pamphylia
(over 770 km by sea).

The first hardship should have put their journey behind schedule.
Notwithstanding, the centurion might have expected that they could
make it on time: **Since the centurion found there a ship from Alexandria sailing for Italy, he put us aboard it** (Acts 27:6). Julius's expectation
was based on his finding of a grain ship (cf. 27:38)[19] bound for Italy; according to Ogilvie, this ship "was evidently one of the ordinary corn- and
passenger-carrying merchantmen from Alexandria, of about 250 tons";[20]
thus this grain ship should not have planned to spend the winter in
Crete even though an unexpected accident occurred. Grain ships could
have been found there, not only because "Egypt was the chief granary of
Rome, and the regular and adequate supply of grain from Egypt was of
the greatest importance for the stability of the state and the power of the
emperor,"[21] but also because Myra "was nearly due north of Alexandria

18. From this verse, the first plural could refer to "all the passengers on board."

19. The sailors kept grain until the last stage and then jettisoned it (27:18, 19, 38).

20. Ogilvie 1958: 312. Keener 2012–2015: 3618–19 summarizes various sizes of
ships at that time as follows: "Some of the largest ships—and this must be one of them
(27:37)—could carry more than 250 tons; ships carrying government cargos often ran
to 340 tons, and some grain vessels to 1,200 tons. Grain ships bound for Rome carried
a minimum of 68 tons in this period, and the massive *Isis* carried at least 1,000 tons."

21. Bruce 1990: 513. According to Casson 1968 [1959]: 233–34, a third of Rome's
requirements of grain, 150,000 tons, was "shipped yearly from Egypt to Rome."

and was a regular stopping-off spot for the grain ships that sailed from Alexandria to Rome."[22] However, Patara was a better seaport city than Myra[23] and the time was near the end of navigation. Hence, it would have been very time saving to find a ship bound for Italy. Moreover, the centurion could have had "authority" over the grain ship as "a *frumentarius.*"[24] The owner of the ship (cf. 27:11) also could have been joyful over military escort and extra fares.

The centurion found the solution to his problem. And the sailor was paid to travel safely, protected by trained soldiers. As for Paul, he still had his companions with him and God to rely on. Everything seemed to go well; however, there came another huge hardship. They had to change course: **But sailing slowly for many days and arriving off Cnidus with difficulty—since the wind did not allow us to go farther—we sailed under the lee of Crete off Salmone** (Acts 27:7). A normal course of the ship would have been Puteoli or Ostia via Sicily.[25] However, in spite of Paul on board, or on account of him aboard ship, the ship voyaged at a snail's pace. It took many days to reach Cnidus [now Cape Crio], which is located at the eastern point of "a long, narrow peninsula, practically dividing the Aegean from the Mediterranean."[26] Paul's companions had passed through this sea about two and half years ago (21:1). At that time it took only two days to sail from Cos to Patara (around 230 nautical km), but this time many days to sail from Myra to Cnidus (around 240 nautical km).[27] Moreover, they were "unable to enter the harbour of the city of Cnidus, where they might have found shelter."[28] In the end they arrived at Salmone (160 nautical km from Cnidus), "a promontory on the easternmost point of the island of Crete,"[29] so there they could take "the northern shore of Crete" or its western and southern shoreline. However,

---

22. Witherington 1998: 761.

23. See comments on 21:1.

24. Bruce 1990: 513.

25. Bruce 1990: 513 says: "From Myra a northerly wind would take the ship to Sicily; thence a change of wind to the west would bring it to Puteoli or Ostia."

26. *ISBE.*

27. Denton 1876: 340 calculates the geographical distance from Myra to Cnidus as 130 miles (210 km) and says that the distance can be "attained in one day" if "with a fair wind."

28. Denton 1876: 340.

29. *ABD* 906.

they could not have taken "the northern shore of Crete"[30] because the wind did not permit them to go to the east.

Their hardship continued until they made it to a port: **Eventually sailing along the coast of Crete with difficulty, we came to a place called Fair Havens that was near the city of Lasea** (Acts 27:8). Fair Havens was 176 nautical kilometers away from Salmone by ship. Hence, they voyaged in difficulty for around 576 nautical kilometers from Myra to Fair Havens without maintenance. They had struggled for a long time to survive in poor conditions, so at this time they probably could not afford to think about the issue of spending the winter at a good harbor; besides, it is possible that the sailor was not familiar with the port (cf. 28:1). Fair Havens "opens toward the east and is sheltered on the southwest by two small islands";[31] however, it was not a good place for a winter anchorage, not only because "it stands open to nearly half the compass" but also because it "would therefore no longer provide such good protection against a northwest wind."[32] The bay had Lasea as its neighboring town; however, the town was 8 kilometers away from the bay. Most of all, it would not have been big enough for 276 people (27:37) to find shelters and purchase goods throughout the winter season.

While the ship was maintained, Paul offered good advice: **Since considerable time had passed and the voyage was sufficiently unsafe because the fast** [Day of Atonement, Yom Kippur; October 5, 59 CE] **was already over, Paul advised them, "Men, I can see the voyage is going to end in disaster and great loss not only of the cargo and the ship, but also of our lives"** (Acts 27:10). All the passengers are clearly included in the first plural pronoun "our." In this chapter, the first plural pronoun is used very freely, especially from 27:3: the five main verbs in 27:3–8 have the first plural pronoun as the subject; and that pronoun is used as object twice (27:6, 7). Luke the narrator seems to follow Paul's usage of the first plural pronoun in his last testimony (26:14); and Paul himself did, too (27:10). Paul warned the passengers, who he grouped into one, not to sail further from that time onward because great losses were expected.

---

30. According to Denton 1876: 340, "Had the wind permitted, the natural course of the vessel would have been along the northern shore of Crete, where there are good harbours for refuge if necessary, and thence through the Archipelago to the shores of Italy."

31. *ISBER* 2:270.

32. Bruce 1990: 514.

Luke and Aristarchus should have believed what Paul said, but how about the others? And at this stage, how about Theophilus? In spite of being well advised by Paul, Julius, the navigator, the ship owner, the sailor, and most of the passengers did not follow Paul's wise suggestion: **But the centurion was more convinced by the navigator and the ship owner than by what Paul said; because the bay was not suitable to spend the winter in, the majority decided to put out to sea, hoping that somehow they, by reaching Phoenix, could spend the winter at the harbor of Crete open to the southwest and northwest**[33] (Acts 27:11–12). Julius could have been disappointed in Paul or his God due to hardships continuing despite his kind attitude to Paul (cf. 27:3). Both the navigator and the ship owner could have trusted in their own experiences. The rest—that is, the soldiers, the sailors, and the passengers—were reluctant to reject the navigator's decision on the basis of a personal opinion. Experience would have been more persuasive than the words of a missionary who was not a sailor.

The ship would now steer its way to Phoenix. Regarding the geographical issues of this destination, Ogilvie argues convincingly about which bay is related to Paul's journey. First of all, he offers proof that "favours the west bay" over the east bay, that is still in operation, as follows:

1. Ptolemy, in his list, puts the harbour of Phoenix to the west of the town.

2. The west bay, as well as the little chapel at its head, retains to this day the name of Phineka. This should be the survival of an old name, for it is hard to see why the name should have been falsified in such a desolate area.

3. The description of its aspect in Acts XXVII. 12 is βλέποντα κατὰ λίβα καὶ κατὰ χῶρον. As C. Lattey, F. F. Bruce, and E. Haenchen have all recently argued, this can only mean "facing west." That the Libs is the south-west wind and the Caurus the north-west wind is made abundantly clear by passages such as Seneca (*N.Q.* 5.16.5) and Pliny (*N.H.* 2.47.46), despite Lattey's attempt to prove from a doubtful passage of Galen (406) that the Caurus is really the same as the Libs.

33. "Northwest" is parallel to *chōros*, which is regarded as the Greek transliteration of "a Latin wind-direction name," viz., *caurus* (Hemer 1975: 102).

Second, he considers the two inlets as one facing northwest and the other facing southwest.[34] Third, he suggests "earthquakes" or "the action of the sea" as a reasonable explanation for why the west bay is now deserted.[35] Lastly, his article shows clearly that Phoenix itself was "a town of some size"[36] capable of providing a number of people with shelters and goods.

A wind seemed to open up an opportunity for quick and safe travel: **When a south wind blew gently, they thought they could carry out the purpose, so they weighed [anchor] and sailed as close as possible along the coast of Crete** (Acts 27:13). Phoenix was only 48 nautical kilometers away from Fair Havens, so they should have thought that it would take less than a day to get there. Nevertheless, they sailed very carefully, close to the land as much as possible; Paul's warning must have echoed in their heads (cf. 27:10). However, they probably were not anxious over any deviation in that they did not hoist the lifeboat aboard (cf. 27:16–17).

However, they realized very shortly that their conclusion was wrong: **Before long, a wind like a typhoon called *Euroaquilo* blew against**[37] **it [the island]** (Acts 27:14). Smith attests that *Euroaquilo* "must be between Eurus [East] and Aquilo [Northeast], or E.N.E. [east-north-east]."[38] In addition, Hemer argues that *Euroaquilo* referred to "ENE" as a Greek transliteration of a Latin term for the twelve-point scheme.[39] With this east-north-east wind, their fourth hardship began: **Since the ship was caught [in *Euroaquilo*] and could not head into the wind, we were driven along by giving way** [to it] (27:15).

All the passengers must have been disappointed about the catastrophic consequences. Facing a bleak yet inviting prospect, they still had hope of being saved, of course up until they met the storm (Acts 27:18). They still had a chance; they had control over the lifeboat: **But running under the lee of a small island called Cauda, we were able with difficulty to take control of the lifeboat** (27:16). Cauda was around 60 nautical kilometers away from Fair Havens; according to Keener, "the island was

34. Ogilvie 1958: 313.

35. Ogilvie 1958: 313.

36. Ogilvie 1958: 311.

37. *Kata* with genitive could mean "down from, throughout" or "against" or "from" (Wallace 1996: 376). In this sentence, "down from" (e.g., ESV, NET, NRSV) or "across" (e.g., NLT) or "against" (e.g., KJV) would be applied.

38. Smith 1978 [1880]: 103; also see his dissertation, pp. 271–76.

39. Hemer 1975: 103–4.

inhabited in this period, although this would have made no difference for the voyagers unable to land there."[40] As Smith's map shows,[41] the ship probably passed Cape Matala, turned to the northwest, met *Euraquilo*, and then was driven to the west-south-west direction, namely the opposite of the east-north-east. Beside the island they had the opportunity to make the lifeboat[42] secure with united force.[43] This lifeboat refers to "a small boat which was normally kept aboard a larger ship and used by sailors in placing anchors, repairing the ship, or saving lives in the case of storms." In relation to the first plural subject and their efforts to save the lifeboat, we can read unity between all passengers.

With the help of the passengers, the crew was able to prepare for further sails: **Hoisting [the lifeboat] aboard, they [the crew] used auxiliary equipment to undergird the ship** (Acts 27:17a). They must have done this "to strengthen the hull with cables passed around it transversely lest it should disintegrate under the violence of wind and wave."[44] Nevertheless, they feared falling into the Syrtis (27:17b). "Syrtis" was used as "a geographical name, very commonly mentioned in first-century literature as a notorious navigational hazard."[45] If a ship would run aground in the Syrtis, it could be hard for the passengers to go ashore because of the size of the Syrtis: "the Lesser Syrtis" was about 296 kilometers around, and "the Greater Syrtis" about 925 kilometers around.[46] They could have been driven to the latter one near to them; it is the African Greater Syrtis off the northern coast of Lybia,[47] namely, "Syrtis Major (now called the Gulf

---

40. Keener 2012–2015: 3612.

41. Smith 1978 [1880]: 96.

42. L&N §6.45.

43. Bruce 1988: 485 points out that "able-bodied passengers were pressed into service."

44. Bruce 1990: 519.

45. Hemer 1975: 104–5. As regards the danger of the Syrtis, see Hemer 1975: 105 and Keener 2012–2015: 3613–15.

46. Keener 2012–2015: 3613 summarizes their sizes as follows: "According to ancient estimates, the Lesser Syrtis was estimated to be about 1,600 stadia around, with the islands of Meninx and Cercina at its mouth. The Greater Syrtis was much larger, sometimes estimated at 5,000 stadia around and 1,800 across or, more conservatively, 4,000 and 1,500 stadia respectively." If we multiply 1,600 and 5,000 by 185 meters (= 1 *stadion*), we get 296 and 925 kilometers, respectively.

47. See Bruce 1990: 520; Keener 2012–2015: 3613; Schnabel 2012: 1040.

of Sidra or Sirte)."[48] All they could do was themselves be driven with **a floating anchor** (27:17c).[49]

Finally, they were welcomed by the violence of the storm that led the ship into Malta, which was "the last tribulations": **But the next day, since we were violently battered by the storm, they began jettisoning [the cargo]** (Acts 27:18). Oops! They should have learned the seriousness of taking the wrong path. Their situation became worse and worse. First, on the second day after leaving Fair Havens, they started discarding cargo; grains were probably excluded from this. Bruce thinks "presumably the cargo (of wheat)";[50] however, it would have been too early to dispose of the grains when the danger of destruction was not yet inevitable, particularly in the eyes of Julius the centurion; possibly the same for products such as Aegean wines loaded at Myra.[51] On the next (the third) day "they threw the ship's gear overboard with their own hands" (27:19). "The ship's gear" probably included "the furniture of the ship—beds, movables of all kinds, cooking utensils, and the spare rigging."[52] Lastly, their hope was nowhere to be seen: **But since neither sun nor stars showed light for many days, eventually no mild storm lay on us, at last disappeared all hope of our being saved** (27:20). The "darkness over the whole land" and "the failure of the sun" in Luke 23:44b–45a seem to echo in this scene; at that moment, "the curtain of the Temple was torn into two" (Luke 23:45b).

Hope Uncovered (27:21–44)

This section starts with **total abstinence from food** (Acts 27:21a), which can be categorized as the first "risk" to the passengers' lives. Then Paul's

48. *ED* 1267.

49. Bruce 1990: 520 provides "setting sail," "sending down the top hamper," and "dropping a floating anchor," for interpreting *chalasantes to skeuos*, and suggests the last one as the best option.

50. Bruce 1990: 520.

51. According to Ecker 2013: 67, "the storerooms of Herod's palaces were stocked with Aegean wines, mainly from the islands of Chios and Kos." In addition, the cargo may include "cultivated plants of Egypt" in ancient times: namely, "the maize (durrah), wheat, barley and lentil; the vine, currant, date palm, dum palm, fig, olive and pomegranate; the onion, garlic, cucumber, melon and radish; the *sont* acacia, sycamore and tamarisk; the flax, henna and clover; and for ornament, the lotus, convolvulus and many others" (*ISBE* 2:907).

52. See Smith 1978 [1880]: 116n1.

speech (27:21b–26) and the ship's approach to some land (27:27–29) follow; this should have helped them recover from despair, so I would like to call this the first "opportunity" for the community. Then, the crew's bad intention ensues (27:30); this can be seen as the second risk. Then, Paul's exposure (27:31), the soldiers' action (27:32) and the special meal on board (27:33–38) are next on the list; these could have aided in a recovery from division within the newly formed community in the ship, the second opportunity. Now they prepared for making an emergency landing and sailing into a bay (27:38–40), thus the third opportunity. However, they faced the third and fourth risks straight in a row; there was a patch of crosscurrents (27:41), and the soldiers intended to kill the prisoners (27:42). This fourth danger was passed through the centurion's contribution, so everyone was saved (27:43–44); and the chapter ends with the last opportunity.

Therefore, the whole can be structured in terms of risk and opportunity as follows:

Risk 1: Total abstinence from food (27:21a)

Opportunity 1: Paul's speech (27:21b–26), the ship's approach to some land (27:27–29)

Risk 2: The crew's bad intention (27:30)

Opportunity 2: Paul's exposé (27:31), soldiers' action (27:32), the special meal (27:33–37)

Opportunity 3: Preparing to make an emergency landing, and sailing into a bay (27:38–40)

Risk 3: Meeting a patch of crosscurrents (27:41)

Risk 4: The soldiers' bad intention (27:42)

Opportunity 4: The centurion's contribution and the deliverance of all (27:43–44)

Despite the five chances, the passengers on the ship of Alexandria ran into five hardships and had no hope to cling on to, "the hope zero state." Moreover, they had to be in **total abstinence from food** (Acts 27:21a). Bruce suggests "difficulty of cooking, spoiling of food by sea water, [and] sea sickness" as reasons for their abstinence from food.[53] So naturally, they would have lost their taste for food due to these situations and their minds,[54] particularly their mood of despair. In this dreary place,

53. Bruce 1990: 521.

54. Keener 2012–2015: 3629 considers "seasickness" and "mortal anxiety (see esp. 27:36)" as the reasons for total abstinence from food.

Paul stood forth in the midst of them and said, "O Men, you should, listening to me, not have put out to sea from Crete so as to get this damage and loss" (27:21b). Luke could not specify the day because "they had no means of keeping a reckoning or calculating their whereabouts";[55] even so, we can figure out that Paul said so at one point between the third day and the fourteenth night (cf. 27:19, 27).

Paul's second advice was given to those who had run out of hope: **Cheer up!** (Acts 27:22a, 25). Before mentioning this, he reminded them of his first advice: **Men, you should have listened to me so as neither to put out to sea from Crete nor to get this injury and damage** (27:21b). People did not follow his previous recommendation, so they lost some of their cargos (27:18), the ship's gear (28:19), even their hope (27:20) and appetite (27:21). Paul seems to express deep regret at their[56] loss, "injury and damage."[57] However, they had every reason to cheer up because "a loss" will not be lost: **for there will be no loss of life among you, except the ship** (27:22b). Then, he provided the travelers with concrete evidence that was not issued to them previously (cf. 27:10): **For this night[58] an angel of God to whom I belong and whom I serve stood by me and said, "Do not be afraid, Paul! You must stand before Caesar, and behold, God has granted you all those who sail with you"** (27:23–24). Jesus the Lord himself (9:5; 18:9; 23:11) and a man (16:9) had appeared to Paul, and this time an angel of God was sent to him; God uses various agents for revelation. According to the angel's message, all the passengers' lives depended on Paul's desire. The fact that all were saved (27:44) reveals that Paul wanted God to save all of them in spite of some bad motives (27:30, 42).

Paul repeated his main point and added another reason for it, that is, his own belief in God: So cheer up, men, for I believe in God that it will happen just as he told me (Acts 27:25). As they were in his last testimony before Agrippa II (26:8–20), so his own personal and supernatural experiences were provided as the cause for accepting his suggestion. Finally Paul added one condition, we must cast ashore on some island (27:26), which would be the third reason for the passengers to believe him when

55. Bruce 1988: 487.

56. Paul doesn't seem to be included in "their."

57. Witherington 1998: 768 says, "He [Paul] is portrayed as a passionate person who cares deeply about the lives of his fellow travelers."

58. "This night" should be a better understanding of *tautē tē nukti* than "last night" (see Keener 2012–2015: 3630n791).

it does come true. That condition should have been "a slender hope"[59] to those who were worried about running aground on the Syrtis (27:17). At that time, "an island was sometimes a storm-tossed ship's final hope."[60]

The foretold hope bore fruit on the fourteenth night of their sailing from Fair Heavens (Acts 27:13).[61] That night they were **driven across the Adriatic Sea** (27:27a). The Adriatic Sea referred to "the sea S. [South] and W. [West] of Greece,"[62] namely, "the section of the Mediterranean bounded by Sicily, the foot of Italy, Crete and the Peloponnese,"[63] not to the modern "Adriatic gulf" between the peninsulas of Italy and Greece. **About midnight the sailors thought that some land was approaching** (27:27b). They might have seen "'the curl of the sea' upon the rocks" at Koura, the extreme point of St. Paul's bay, and could have "heard the breakers."[64] They checked the depth of their whereabouts by taking soundings and **found it to be twenty fathoms deep**, about 36 meters; **sailing a little farther they took soundings again and found fifteen fathoms deep**, about 27 meters (27:28). They should have rejoiced to realize that their assumption was correct.

However, they were quick to fall into anxiety: **eventually [on account of] fearing that we would dash against rough places, throwing out four anchors from the stern, they wished for day to come about** (Acts 27:29). Their anxiety is understandable when considering an accident that happened to "the 'Lively' frigate" on August 10, 1810.

> The ship was, unfortunately, and against the opinion of the Lieutenant of the watch (Lieutenant, now Admiral Lord Fitzhardinge), brought to with her head in-shore. Soon afterward the quarter-master on the look-out gave the alarm of rocks to leeward. This was upon the point of Koura, the very spot where a ship driving from the east into St. Paul's Bay must have seen and heard the breakers, and the only spot where she could have done so. Upon perceiving the danger, the order "ready about and *clear the anchor*" was immediately

59. Bruce 1990: 522.

60. Keener 2012–2015: 3634.

61. According to Smith 1978 [1880]: 127, with the storm it "would take exactly thirteen days, one hour, and twenty-one minutes" to sail 476.6 miles [762.56 km] from Cauda to the point of Koura.

62. Hemer 1975: 107.

63. Hemer 1985: 102n41.

64. Smith 1978 [1880]: 123–24.

given by Lieutenant Berkeley; and as they were bracing round the maintop-sail to fill upon the ship, the man at the lead *sounded, and found twenty-five fathoms.* Before, however, she had sufficient way upon her, the helm was put down; but the ship missed stays, that is they could not get her head round on the opposite tack. *The anchor was then let go*; but before the ship brought up, she fell off broadside on the rocks, and a gale coming on she went to pieces.[65]

Hence it was very wise for the sailors to let go four anchors from the stern; otherwise, it should have gone to pieces like the frigate above. Smith reports that the master of the frigate "was reduced in rank for bringing the ship to with her head in-shore."[66]

Even if the ship was able to approach land, the sailors could not be certain of their safety, possibly because "they might have expected the soldiers to seize the boat for themselves in the morning."[67] Now the second risk; they **tried to escape from the ship and were lowering the lifeboat into the sea, pretending that they were going to let go anchors from the bow** (Acts 27:30). Thirteen days ago beside Cauda, the small island, the passengers had helped the sailors get the lifeboat under control (27:16). Even so, the sailors took care only of their own lives. What a disgusting and irresponsible attitude! Then Paul, who had declared God's salvation (27:21–26), did not leave it to the sailors to carry out their worst end. He exposed their intentions **to the centurion and the soldiers, "Unless these men stay with the ship, you cannot be saved"** (27:31). At this time the soldiers, surely including the centurion, consented with Paul (cf. 27:11) and **cut the ropes of the lifeboat and let it fall away** (27:32). This was the only way of making the sailors stay in the ship.

No one could have taken the lifeboat. That night passed without any further incidents. Everyone should have waited for daybreak (Acts 27:29). However, as dawn was breaking, Paul broke in the third time: **waiting until today, the fourteenth day, you have been hungry, eating nothing; therefore I urge you to take some food, for this is essential for your salvation; for not one of you will separate one hair from the head** (27:33–34). The last sentence alludes to Jesus' saying in Luke 21:18, "not a hair of your head will perish":[68] "Both sentences stress that there will be

65. Smith 1978 [1880]: 123–24 (italics his).

66. Smith 1978 [1880]: 123n1.

67. Keener 2012–2015: 3641.

68. Witherington 1998: 772 mentions 1 Sam 14:45; 2 Sam 14:11; 1 Kgs 1:52; Luke

no separation resulting in malfunction—this will not happen even to a hair."[69]

Paul's saying should have made everyone, including the sailors, feel safe, so that everyone ate and became merrier: **saying these [things] and taking bread he [Paul] gave thanks to God in front of them all, and breaking it he began to eat; so everyone became cheerful and took food themselves** (Acts 27:35–36). This meal should not have been a kind of Eucharist, rather "like the account of the feeding of the five thousand."[70] Nevertheless, Paul's companions, Luke and Aristarchus (27:2), could have remembered the Holy Communion at Troas in which they had participated right after Eutychus's death (cf. 20:4, 6). Both meals were prepared right after a hard time and a happy moment, namely, after encountering Eutychus's death and resuscitation, and after meeting a storm and an island. The Lord's succor could be detected in both cases (cf. 20:10; 27:23–24); hence, some of them could have eaten the bread thinking of the Lord's body. Luke provides the number of those who ate the broken bread: **we were in all two hundred seventy-six persons on the ship** (27:37). The unification of the passengers can be read again in Luke's employing the first plural subject: those who had rescued the lifeboat (27:16) ate together. Paul's exposure (27:31), the soldiers' action (27:32), and the special meal (27:33–37) can be understood as opportunity knocking after their state of zero hope.

The third opportunity rightly followed. First, **having eaten food fully they lightened the ship by throwing the wheat into the sea** (Acts 27:38). Peterson identifies "they" as "the unbelieving soldiers and sailors who were in charge of the situation."[71] They threw the wheat that should have been transported to Italy, which could be caused not only by "the precarious conditions at this point"[72] but also by Paul's saying that **there will be no loss of life among you, except the ship** (27:12). If the ship would be destroyed or sunk at sea, the wheat could not be saved by any means. Second, **when day came, they did not recognize the land but observed a bay with a beach, where they planned to bring forward the ship if they could** (27:39). If they could drive the ship on shore, they

---

12:7; and 21:18 as the related texts.

69. Park 2007A: 121.

70. Witherington 1998: 773.

71. Peterson 2009: 694.

72. Schnabel 2012: 1047.

would survive. Third, **they steered toward the beach after taking away the anchors, at the same time loosening the ropes of rudders, and with hoisting the mainsail to the wind** (27:40). Schnabel describes these actions as follows:

> (1) Some of the crew cast off the anchors; i.e., they cut the ropes that held the four anchors that had been lowered from the stern (v. 29), letting the anchors drop into the sea, as they were no longer needed. (2) Other members of the crew untie the pennants of the two side-rudders or steering oars, lowering the rudders into the water. (3) They hoist the foresail to the wind.[73]

At this moment came the third peril: **they fell upon a place of two seas and ran the ship aground; the bow stuck fast and stayed unmovable, and the stern was being broken up by the violence of the waves** (Acts 27:41). They handled well three devices, viz., anchors, rudders, and the mainsail, but they stumbled upon three obstacles, viz., a place of two seas,[74] immovability, and the violence of the waves. These obstacles seem to have made the soldiers uneasy, being worried about failing to take control of the prisoners. **Then the soldiers planned to kill the prisoners, lest anyone would escape by swimming away** (27:42). This was the fourth and the last risk caused by the soldiers' selfish calculation; they should have thought of their fate of death and of Paul's help related to hope, sailors, and meals (27:21b–26, 31, 33–37).

The last threat was solved when the centurion blocked the soldiers' malicious impulse: **But the centurion, wanting to rescue Paul's life, prevented them from [carrying out their] intent; then he ordered those who could swim to jump overboard first and get to land and [ordered] some of the rest [to rely on] boards and others [to rely on] pieces from the ship** (Acts 27:43–44a). His order "would have been aimed at the soldiers and the prisoners"[75] but should have been worthy of being followed by all the passengers. What was the result? **In this way all were sheltered to land** (27:44b).

Ultimately Paul's prophecy in Acts 27:34 came true; for that, he should have continuously aimed at and prayed for all the passengers to be

73. Schnabel 2012: 1047.

74. This term could indicate "a sandbar, shoal, promontory, or some other ridge dividing the water" (Keener 2012–2015: 3652).

75. Schnabel 2012: 1049.

saved after God had granted him all those who were sailing with him (cf. 27:24). Julius's last remark can be compared with the centurion's under the cross, "Certainly this man was innocent!" (Luke 23:47). Just as the former centurion admitted Jesus' innocence, Julius seems to have considered Paul as a trustful prophet of God. Via Julius's contribution and the deliverance of all, the overall stormy journey had a silver lining.

ACTS 28
Paul's Ministry in Malta and Rome

Paul and all the passengers swam ashore in Malta. The island is "a little over 27 km. (17 mi.) long, 14 km. (9 mi.) wide, and with a shoreline of 137 km. (85 mi.)" and "has often had strategic importance as a base from which to control the Mediterranean narrows" on account of its location between the south of Sicily (93 km from Malta) and the north of Cape Bon, Tunisia (290 km from Malta).[1] Even though the ship had floated on the Adriatic Sea (Acts 27:27) to the west-south-west direction because of *Euraquilo*, the east-north-east wind (27:14), it arrived on an island which lay on the east of Crete; this means that the wind changed from the east-north-east direction to the west-north-west direction at one point.

In Malta, Paul and his companions stayed for three months (Acts 28:11), probably from early November in 59 CE to early February in 60 CE (or late October in 59 CE to late January in 60 CE).[2] In the early spring they departed for Rome, and it took only seven days for them to set sail from Malta to Puteoli (350 nautical km from Rhegium),[3] via Syracuse (120 nautical km from Malta) and Rhegium (130 nautical km from Syracuse); thus, 600 nautical kilometers in total. Then possibly in late February they finally reached Rome (229 km away from Puteoli),[4] one of

---

1. *ISBER* 3:231.

2. See Schnabel 2012: 1054.

3. According to *ISBER* 4:181, the distance between Rhegium and Puteoli is 290 kilometers. Schnabel 2012: 1055 calculates it as 325 kilometers, but this seems to be calculated in a straight line. A cruising distance can be approximately 350 kilometers; so also Keener 2012–2015: 3701.

4. *ISBER* 3:1060: "At that time the ordinary route to Rome, along the Via Appia from Capua, was 155 Roman miles (about 229 km., 142 mi.). Later Domitian reduced the distance by laying out the Via Domitia along the coast."

"the ends of the earth" (1:8),[5] and the biggest city at that time, having "a population of no less than a million."[6]

Hence, Paul's first ministry in Rome could have occurred in March in 60 CE (Acts 28:17–28); he then seems to have waited until March in 62 CE to be judged by Nero.

Paul's Ministry in Malta (28:1–10)

All of the survivors could have swum about half a mile (800 m) if the ship was stuck in the sand and clay between the isle of Salmonetta and the point of Koura.[7] Some swam by themselves while some relied on boards and others on fragments of the ship (Acts 27:43–44). They should have been exhausted since they had already been extremely tired owing to their fourteen-day voyage in stormy weather (cf. 27:27, 33).

Exhausted and wet, **we [the survivors] learned that the island was called Malta** (Acts 28:1). Luke consistently uses the first plural pronoun and verbs with first plural suffixes referring not only to Paul and his companions but also to other passengers in 28:1–16.[8] This could indicate that there was a true sense of community among them, or at least that Luke had it toward others.

Malta was "no small island," which nowadays "supports a population of more than 400,000,"[9] but not a "big" island in comparison with Crete, where they originally planned to winter.[10] There was **an Alexandrian ship that had wintered at the island** (Acts 28:11), so they should not have been solitary guests there.

They landed on a better place than Fair Havens for wintering (Acts 27:12) but were empty-handed. They lost everything except life.

---

5. According to van Unnik 1973: 386–401, the ends of the earth in 1:8 refers to the whole world. Hence, Rome can be one of the ends.

6. Keener 2012–2015: 3721 says that its population can be composed "of about 670,000 free citizens and, in addition, an estimated slave population of 30 percent, resident free foreigners, and citizens of status either too high or too low to be figured into the grain dole."

7. See the map in Smith 1978 [1880]: 128.

8. See 28:1, 2 (2x), 7, 10, 11, 12, 13 (2x), 14 (2x), 15 (2x), 16.

9. Keener 2012–2015: 3663. On the contrary, Malta is "a small island only 18 miles long and 8 miles wide" to Witherington 1998: 775.

10. Crete has 8,336 square kilometers and Malta 316 square kilometers.

In addition, they met rain "which had set in"[11] and coldness but also extraordinary kindness and a fire: **the barbarians granted us kindness hard to meet; for, kindling a bonfire, they welcomed us all on account of rain, which had set in, and of coldness** (28:2). This Greek term *barbaros* "was presumably onomatopoeic" and referred to "one who did not speak Greek and whose words there sounded (to a Greek) like a meaningless ba-ba-ba."[12] It may refer to their "neither hellenized nor romanized" status.[13] Hence, it can be said that the escaped passengers, in exhaustion and drenched to the skin, encountered rain, coldness, and even gibberish. Their joy of salvation could have vanished anytime now. However, bonfires welcomed them warmly; the inhabitants were exceptionally merciful.

At this hour, Paul did not rest but toiled even though he must have been an old man and had already spent a lot of time and effort mainly on the community's salvation: **Paul gathered a bundle of sticks and put it on the bonfire** (Acts 28:3a). Warming 276 people requires a very large fire, and enormous amounts of firewood must have been provided constantly. Paul did not sit down and warm himself at the fire but worked at keeping the fire alive. This was his lifestyle throughout his life: serving others with all his strength humbly.

When Paul was serving the community with his hands, **a viper, coming out because of the heat, fastened [itself] on his hand** (Acts 28:3b). Its fastening is often seen as the "wrapping" of a constrictor.[14] However, a snake that was wrapping around a hand cannot be described as **hanging** as the local people perceived (28:4). Moreover, it is surely impossible for even a constrictor to kill a man by crushing his hand by being wrapped around it. Hence, it would be better to understand that this fastening denotes "biting."[15] The question that "although there are serpents in Malta, they are not venomous, as the term ἔχιδνα (viper) implies" can

11. Bruce 1990: 531.

12. Barrett 1998: 1220. Onomatopoeia can be defined as "the use of words that are derived from natural sounds, such as buzz or oink (ὀνοματοποιία, 'making a name')" (DeMoss 2001: 90).

13. *ISBER* 3:231.

14. See Witherington 1998: 778 thinks this viper as "belonging to the species *Coronella asutriaca*."

15. Many commentators see this fastening as "biting": see Bruce 1988: 498; Barrett 1998: 1222; Bock 2007: 742–43; Peterson 2009: 699; Schnabel 2012: 1050; Keener 2012–2015: 3669; etc. As regards "snakebite," see Keener 2012–2015: 3670–73.

be explained, as Smith does, in terms of the influence of civilization.[16] In other words, in Paul's time there were vipers in Malta that are not present now due to civilization.

An evaluation of the local people followed Paul's snakebite: **the barbarians saw the wild animal hanging[17] from his [Paul's] hand, they said to one another, "Doubtless this man is a murderer whom, having been escaped from the sea, Justice[18] has not allowed him to live!"** (Acts 28:4). Their thought implies "that Paul's escape from the sea would have been popularly attested as a clear sign of his innocence, but that for a brief moment doubt had been cast over his worthiness,"[19] and this judgment is based, as Miles and Trompf argue, on "the belief that the misfortunes which befall the wicked are in reality punishments meted out by the gods for their crimes," which "was deeply ingrained in Greek thought well before the Hellenistic Age."[20] A similar idea can be found in Josephus's *War* 7.34a: "For wicked actions do not escape the divine anger, nor is *justice* too weak to punish offenders, but in time overtakes those that transgress its laws, and inflicts its punishments upon the wicked in a manner."

In spite of being bitten by a viper, Paul **shook the creature off into the fire and suffered no harm** (Acts 28:5). He might not have hated it owing to the fact that his putting the bundle of sticks into the bonfire caused the viper to bite him. Nevertheless, he could not help shaking it off into the fire to prevent it from harming others.[21] The fact that he suffered no harm might not be a sign of the viper's lack of harmfulness in that the inhabitants **expected that he was going to swell up or suddenly drop dead** (28:6a). What they expected did not happen "even though they had waited a long time" (28:6b), and **having seen nothing unusual happen to him, they changed their minds and said he was a god** (28:6c).

16. Smith 1978 [1880]: 151 says that "I would merely observe that no person who has studied the changes which the operations of man have produced on the Fauna (animals) of any country, will be surprised that a particular species of reptiles should have disappeared from that of Malta." So also Hemer 1975: 109n5.

17. In Luke-Acts, this term (*kremannumi*) is related to Jesus besides this verse (Luke 23:39; Acts 5:30; 10:39); also in Gal 3:13 (see Park 2007A: 150–51).

18. This term, *hē dikē*, is "personified as a deity" (Bruce 1990: 532).

19. Miles and Trompf 1967: 266.

20. Miles and Trompf 1967: 260.

21. In 28:3, Pervo 2009: 674 reads "the theme of the survivor or escapee who was subsequently killed by a viper."

To sum up, the kind inhabitants were under three misapprehensions about Paul: (1) Paul is a murderer (28:4); (2) Paul will swell up or be dead (28:6a); (3) Paul is a god (28:6c). It has been continually claimed in Paul's trials that the first mistake of the inhabitants, "Paul is a murderer," is wrong,[22] so it seems that Luke describes those who considered Paul a murderer as barbarians. The third one was denied even by Paul himself (14:15), so no one should grant him divinity; otherwise, that person should be reckoned a barbarian. While the other two are straightforward matters, the second is rather a delicate point; Paul could have been harmed and killed (cf. 14:19; 16:23; 21:32), but it should be remembered that he was still under divine care as an apostle (cf. 14:20; 16:26; 23:11; 27:23–24). Hence, anticipating Paul to be harmed apart from God's permission would be impossible and wrong. Due to these barbarians' erroneous impressions, it would be better to read "an identification marker of the audience" rather than "a characteristic mark of Greek authorship"[23] in the Greek term *barbaros*.

Waiting for others' physical injury and/or death without giving any help should not be considered good or even ethical. No mercy was shown to Paul by the barbarians, but the apostle healed them. Paul's healing ministry started with Publius's father. **By the way in the region around that place were fields belonging to the first [citizen] of the island, named Publius, who welcomed us and entertained us hospitably as guests for three days** (Acts 28:7). The "first" can be the title of a Roman official, such as "the praetorian legate (the administrator of Malta)" or "a procurator" governing Malta.[24] Even though Julius "the centurion could 'impress' locals to provide lodging for his soldiers and prisoners,"[25] it must have been a very gracious act of the chief officer to give a cordial reception to that large a community of survivors for three days. The context could testify that the event of Paul's snakebite caused Publius to receive them more generously than usual.

Publius's hospitality became a kind of "entertaining angels unawares" (Heb 13:2b) because **Publius's father lay sick of a fever and of dysentery** (Acts 28:8a). The fever was "gastric fever" "caused by a microbe in goat's

---

22. See comments on 23:6, 29; 24:10–21; 25:7–8, 11, 18, 25; and 26:2–23.
23. Bruce 1990: 531.
24. See Keener 1993: 3682.
25. Keener 1993: 3683.

milk."[26] Dysentery accompanied "pain and colic inside, ulcerated intes-
tines, with the passing of phlegm and bloody stools."[27] His disease could
have lingered since that year's summer because "dysentery and fever were
most common in summer after a particularly rainy spring."[28] However,
the sentence construction does not exclude the possibility that he became
sick while Paul was there;[29] in fact, it actually rained there (28:2). So it
seems that, even though Publius invited the survivors without expecting
his father to be healed, it happened that his father became sick and was
healed: **after coming in and praying, Paul healed him by placing his
hands on him** (28:8b).

Paul's remedy for fever and dysentery encouraged the sick to come
foward to Paul: **After this had happened, the rest in the island who were
sick also came and were healed** (Acts 28:9). This situation overlaps with
Jesus' healing Peter's mother-in-law and the sick people in Capernaum
(Luke 4:38–40) although there are different elements in terms of the
healer's identity and source of power.[30]

The inhabitants, who had shown their ignorance about the one true
God in evaluating what happened to Paul, did not forget to recompense
the guests for their recovery from all kinds of diseases: **They also hon-
ored us with many precious things, and they gave all the necessities to
those who were sailing** (Acts 28:10). These barbarians look more fitting
than the Jews in Capernaum who were rebuked by Jesus for their unchanged character (Luke 10:15; Mat 11:23). In addition, people in Malta,
including the chief officer, Publius, also have better character than the
four chief executives relevant to Paul's trials, namely Lysias the tribune,
Felix, Festus, and Agrippa II, who did not deal with Paul's case fairly in
spite of their clear perception that Paul is innocent.

26. Bruce 1990: 533.

27. Keener 2012–2015: 3688.

28. Keener 2012–2015: 3688.

29. Robertson 2010 [1934]: 1085 says: "The acc. and inf. occurs with ἐγένετο (Ac.
9:32) and the dative also in the sense of it 'befell' or 'happened to' one, as in Ac. 20:16."
This verse (28:8) has the construction of ἐγένετο + the accusative and infinitive. So
also see Barrett 1998: xlvi.

30. See Witherington 1998: 780.

Paul's Entry to Rome (28:11–16)

Paul and his companions stayed in Malta for three months, probably from early November in 59 CE to early February in 60 CE (Acts 28:11a). Luke does not report what happened in that period, but it can be surmised by going through what Paul previously had done after his healing ministries. In Lystra, right after the lame man's healing, Paul declared who God is and what He does (14:8–17), and that circumstance is summarized in a single phrase in the previous verse, **they proclaimed the good news** (14:7). At a later time, Paul returned to Lystra, strengthened the disciples, and appointed elders (14:21–23). In Thessalonica, he made disciples within three weeks (17:1–10). Only considering these records, we can correctly conjecture that during the winter months Paul proclaimed the gospel in Malta, made disciples, and appointed elders to equip the church. Would not Paul have done so in Malta during his stay? The residents of Malta honoring and giving necessities to all the passengers of the wrecked ship (28:10) could be a reflection of their faith.

After wintering and evangelizing in Malta, they departed from the benevolent barbarians possibly on February 8:[31] **After three months we put out to sea in an Alexandrian ship that had wintered at the island, having the Twins as its figurehead** (Acts 28:11). These "Twins" of Zeus refer to "Castor and Pollux" "often identified with the constellation Gemini and therefore in a position to rescue those in peril on the sea."[32] This ship also could have been a grain ship bound for Italy, just like the wrecked ship, but this one had safely arrived at the island. Its figurehead could be standing for what that world relied on, so Paul, Luke, and Aristarchus should have resolved not to be relaxed but to "stand alert, stand firm in the faith, show courage, [and] be strong" (1 Cor 16:13) for further ministry in Rome.

It seems to take only one day for the Alexandrian ship to draw down to Syracuse (120 nautical km from Malta), "the capital of the Roman province of Sicily" from 212 BCE:[33] **We drew down to Syracuse and stayed there three days** (Acts 28:12). If they departed on February

---

31. "Pliny (*NH* [*Natural History*] 2.122) says that the seas are re-opened to navigation in spring, which commences when the west winds (*fauonii*) begin to blow on February 8" (Bruce 1990: 534).

32. *ISBER* 4:930 under the title of "Twin Brothers." For ancient mythology of the Twins, see Keener 2012–2015: 3697.

33. *ISBER* 4:686.

8, their stay in Syracuse would be from February 9 to 11. The "wind falling" is explained to be the reason behind their stopover;[34] however, since there was no mention of any matter with the wind, unlike the next verse, loading grain[35] and taking people on board seem more plausible reasons (cf. 21:3).

The further voyage went smoothly: **Taking away from there, we arrived at Rhegium, and after one day a south wind sprang up and on the second day we came to Puteoli** (Acts 28:13). Rhegium (130 nautical km from Syracuse) was "located along the SW [southwest] coast of the 'toe' of Italy . . . opposite the Sicilian city of Messina."[36] They might have arrived on February 12 and departed for Puteoli on February 14. Puteoli, 350 nautical kilometers away from Rhegium, enjoyed its importance as Syracuse "due to the harbor's safety and the inhospitable character of the coast nearer Rome" and its population that climbed up to "nearly 100,000" "under Claudius and Nero."[37] Their sea voyage to Puteoli ended possibly on February 16; it lasted almost a half year because they departed from Caesarea in the summer of 59 CE. According to Casson, the general voyage from Alexandria to Rome "took at least fifty days and on occasions as much as seventy."[38] It took about three times more than usual.

In Puteoli they **found brothers and were invited to stay with them seven days** (Acts 28:14a). Paul again won Julius's favor even though, as Schnabel says, Julius and his soldiers might need "to replenish their equipment, damaged or lost in the shipwreck" or "to prepare for the overland journey ahead where billeting facilities would become increasingly scarce as the party drew closer to Rome."[39] Nevertheless, it should have been very atypical for a prisoner to be hosted for a week. Hence, as Wright describes, Julius and the soldiers "must by now have realized that

---

34. Bruce 1990: 535.

35. Sicily was an important supplier of grain for Rome at that time, along with Alexandria and North Africa (see Casson 1968 [1959]: 234).

36. *ABD* 709.

37. *ISBER* 3:1060.

38. Casson 1968 [1959]: 234; on the contrary, the voyage from Rome [exactly Ostia or Pozzuoli] to Alexandria took just "ten days to two weeks" on account of the wind direction.

39. Schnabel 2012: 1055.

they were either dreaming or taking part in a very strange journey with an exceedingly strange prisoner."[40]

Then Luke mentions the arrival at their final destination, Rome: **And in this way we came to Rome** (Acts 28:14b). A chain of unexpected events could be included "in this way." Schnabel suggests that this sentence "does not mark the party's arrival in Rome, which does not take place until v. 16" and translates it as, "Here is the way we arrived in Rome."[41] However, personally Bruce's elucidation seems to make sense: "Luke first states the fact of their arrival in Rome [28:14], and then goes back to relate what happened on the way there [28:15]."[42]

The chain of unexpected events reached its climax in Acts 28:15: From there [Rome] the brothers, hearing about us, came as far as the Forum of Appius and Three Taverns to meet us; and seeing them, Paul thanked God and took courage. The Forum of Appius[43] was "a station at the forty-third milestone on the Appian Road" so it was 63.5 kilometers away from Rome, "a single day's journey for energetic travelers";[44] but it would have been one-and-a-half or two days' journey for travelers in general.[45] The Three Taverns was also "a station on the Appian Way" so it was 48 kilometers away from Rome,[46] which would be one day's or one-and-a-half days' journey. If Paul and his companions departed from Puteoli on February 23 after that one week, tarrying (28:14), they would have turned up at the Forum of Appius (117.5 km from Puteoli) on February 26 and at the Three Taverns (15.5 km from the Forum of Appius) on the next day, February 27. Even so, the Christians in Rome came out to meet Paul as far as the Forum of Appius (63.5 km from Rome) and the Three Taverns (48 km from Rome). If a brother in Puteoli was sent to inform the brothers in Rome of Paul's arrival on February 26, he could have arrived there on February 22; the informed brothers in Rome should have departed within two days after being aware of Paul's itinerary in order to get as far as the Forum of Appius before February 26, thus

40. Wright 2008: 239–40.

41. Schnabel 2012: 1055.

42. Bruce 1990: 535–36.

43. It is known that "the Forum of Appius was 'crammed with boatmen and stingy tavern-keepers'" (*ABD* 2:853).

44. *ISBER* 1:214.

45. "It was a 1-day journey from Rome for ambitious travelers, although Horace preferred a 'lazy' 2-day trip (Hor. Sat. 1.5)" (*ABD* 2:853).

46. *ISBER* 4:843.

within four days to reach the Three Taverns before February 27. Bruce understands these greeting journeys as "the official welcome extended to a newly arrived dignitary by a deputation which went out from the city to greet him and escort him for the rest of his way."[47]

When Paul met the brothers in Rome on his way to Rome, he became very encouraged and could not thank God enough. Paul first planned to go to Rome four and a half years ago (Acts 19:21; the fall in 55 CE), then he finished writing the Epistle to the Romans three years ago (20:3; possibly in February in 57 CE). Too many days had passed in short notice because of abrupt, unanticipated reasons, viz., long delays in trials and wintering on account of the storm, two years in Caesarea and probably three months in Malta. Nevertheless, we may suppose that the brothers in Rome earned the opportunity and the time to discard "the law of sin and death" and apply "the law of the Spirit of life" (Rom 8:2). As for Paul, it could have been the time for him to prepare for his ministry in Rome, meeting and staying with the Roman officers.

Under these circumstances, the Roman brothers came out to meet Paul as far as the Forum of Appius and the Three Taverns. Hence, Paul must have been encouraged, since their coming revealed that his epistle had been accepted quite positively. As Paul did, we sometimes need to spend our time conscientiously to grow mature and be prepared for fulfilling God's will.

Arriving in Rome the prisoner was respected: **And when we came into Rome, Paul was allowed to stay by himself, with the soldier who guarded him** (Acts 28:16). Paul's privilege of staying by himself with a soldier might have resulted from what Julius reported on, who Paul was and what happened on the way. According to our calculation, Paul arrived in Rome February 29 in 60 CE.[48]

Fusing the Horizons: Divine Preparations

Paul wrote the Epistle to the Romans probably in February in 57 CE. He wrote it with a strong desire for going to Rome, seeing the Christians there, and imparting some spiritual gifts to them (Rom 1:10–11). However, he spent three years anticipating coming face to face with them. Differently

47. Bruce 1990: 536.
48. That year (60 CE) was a leap year.

put, the Roman Christians waited for Paul for three years; long delays in trials and wintering on account of the storm made them meet quite later than expected. If Paul had not survived in the storm, there would not have been any encounters between them. Thankfully, after passing through all the hardships, Paul encountered the Roman Christians on the way to Rome because they came out to meet him, even as far as the Forum of Appius and the Three Taverns. That meeting gave Paul such a great pleasure and impression that he **thanked God and took courage** (28:15). Here we can read the theme of "God's preparation."

In Acts, the term meaning "preparation" occurs only once: when Peter was praying, people were preparing [the meal] (*paraskeuazō*) (Acts 10:10). Then, the context talks about how God prepared a different kind of meal. He arranged a large eating sheet containing **all kinds of four-footed animals and reptiles of the earth and wild birds** (10:11–12). If we interpret this story in regard to preparation, we can find both human and God's preparation. The human and earthly one was for Peter's physical hunger, but God's and the heavenly one was for Peter's spiritual mission. For the salvation of the gentiles, an angel (10:3–7a), the sheet (10:11–12), and even Peter the apostle (10:13–20) were on His agenda. Peter neither intended to be prepared for the gentile mission nor did he know God's intention in advance. Rather, God guided the situation and went ahead of them for the gentile mission.

This kind of preparation can also be detected in Saul's conversion. His conversion was not prepared by Paul, neither being planned nor expected beforehand (Acts 9:1–3), and Ananias was at first not prepared to meet Paul (9:13–14). However, divine preparations for Paul worked efficaciously: Jesus met and communicated with Paul on his way to Damascus (9:4–6); God showed a vision to Paul to see **a man named Ananias come in and place his hands on him so that he may recover his sight** (9:12); and finally, Jesus persuaded Ananias to visit Paul. Lydia's conversion was also prepared by the Lord, who **opened her heart to pay attention to what Paul was saying** (16:14b). A holistic expression on salvation is written as follows: **As many as were appointed to eternal life believed** (13:48b). We should put God as the subject who performed that appointment; hence, we can say that people were converted on the basis of divine preparations.

These divine preparations for ministries and conversions are based on Jesus the resurrected, God's fundamental preparation for the salvation of all the nations (e.g., Acts 2:39; 3:25). Peter introduced Jesus the resurrected as **a man exhibited by God** (2:22) and **handed over by the predetermined will**

and foreknowledge of God (2:23), as **the appointed Christ** (3:20), and as the unique name given to people for salvation (4:12). Disciples identified Jesus in their prayer with the holy servant anointed by God (4:27). Paul described Jesus the resurrected as the Savior brought to Israel as promised by God (13:23b) and as the Judge designated to pass sentence upon the world (17:31). In this way, Jesus the resurrected is presented as God's foundational preparation in Acts.

Not only Jesus but also his ministers are portrayed as prepared by God. Peter called those, who had eaten with Jesus after his resurrection, **the witnesses God had already chosen** (10:41). Jesus designated Paul as his own chosen instrument (9:15). Barnabas and Saul were labeled "separated" for the work to which the Holy Spirit called them (13:2b).

To sum up, in Acts we can trace lots of divine preparations in the characters' footsteps: first, Jesus the resurrected is God's primary and fundamental preparation for the salvation of all the nations; second, divine preparations are very deeply related with gospel ministers, their ministries, and all kinds of conversions by all means. This makes divine characters, the so-called Trinity, very essential to all the events; we find particularly that God the Father does not appear directly in Acts but directs it.

Paul's Ministry in Rome (28:17–31)

In his last section, Luke tells of Paul's ministry in Rome that occurred from the spring of 60 CE to the spring of 62 CE. During this period, Colossians, Philemon, Ephesians, and Philippians were written.

Paul, who arrived in Rome as a prisoner but with a wonderful reception, did not hesitate to resume his ministry: **After three days Paul called the Jewish leaders together** (Acts 28:17a), probably on March 3 in 60 CE. In spite of his long journey, Paul began his ministry in Rome after merely three days just as Festus did (25:1). The leaders Paul called for could refer to the (possibly eleven) heads of the synagogues in Rome.[49] Modern estimates of the population of "Roman Jews at the time of Paul's arrival" vary between 20,000 and 50,000.[50]

---

49. Barrett 1998: 1238. So also Schnabel 2012: 1066.

50. Keener 2012–2015: 3734.

Paul's reason for calling the leaders of the Jewish community is explicated in his speech (Acts 28:17b–20), namely, to communicate with them. He began by summarizing the process of his trials: **Brothers, having done nothing against our people or the customs of our ancestors, I was handed over as a prisoner from Jerusalem into the hands of the Romans; and they, after examining me, wanted to release me because there was no reason for death in me** (28:17b–18). The first phrase is a précis of his defense (cf. 25:8). The second one is a summary of a series of events starting with the tribune's arresting Paul and going on to being examined by two procurators and one king. He was "handed over to the Gentiles" like Jesus[51] but not from the Jews but "from Jerusalem"; possibly because the Jews did not want to hand Paul over to the Romans; they wanted to kill him. As a result, it seems that Jerusalem, as a place, was being blamed for handing Paul over to the Romans. The third one is related to their reaching a unanimous verdict of not guilty (cf. 23:29; 25:18, 25; 26:32).

Second, he revealed the reason why he came there: **But since the Jews objected [to my release], I was forced to appeal to Caesar—not because of my having some charge to bring against my own nation** (Acts 28:19). Paul was brought to Rome due to his appeal to Caesar; however, it did not mean that he accused the Jews of any kind of culpability; he could not help appealing to the emperor since the Jews did not stop indicting for a range of crimes that Paul did not commit at all.

Last but not least, Paul talked about the reason for calling the Jewish leaders along with the real cause of his trials: **So for this reason I urged you to see and speak with me, for I am bound with this chain because of the hope of Israel** (Acts 28:20). His final remark reminds us about his present status, a prisoner, as stated, for the sake of the hope of Israel. The "hope of Israel" was literally articulated as "the risen Jesus" in his final defense before Agrippa II (26:2–23). Hence, he conducted himself to be "a prisoner of Christ Jesus" (Phlm 1); he was "bound for Christ Jesus": Paul was bound for the hope of Israel; the risen Jesus is the Hope of Israel; so the reason Paul was bound was Jesus the Christ. As a matter of fact, he received a prophetic commandment from Jesus that he should come to Rome (Acts 23:11); thus, his Lord was the cause and effect of his binding and arrival in Rome.

51. The theme of "Isaiah's Suffering Servant" flowing in the phrase is noted in Keener 2012–2015: 3739–40.

The leaders of the Jewish community in Rome responded: **We have received no letters from Judea about you, nor have any of the brothers come and reported or said anything bad about you** (Acts 28:21). The plausibility of this answer is spelled out by Witherington:

> Two things must be remembered: (1) Paul had been in Rome only three days, hardly enough time for Jewish authorities to have heard other oral reports about Paul's case from visiting Jews; (2) Paul in all likelihood arrived in Rome in February of AD 60, before most ships would have been expected to arrive to Puteoli, for it was the very beginning of the navigable season. Furthermore, we noted that all along the ship Paul was on was trying to rush to get to its destination before winter truly set in. It is hardly very plausible that another ship had gotten to Italy before Paul's in view of when both would have set out from Caesarea.[52]

Nevertheless, their response did not signal that they did not have any possibilities of contradiction: **But we count it worthy to hear from you what you think, for regarding this sect we know that it is contradicted everywhere** (28:22). They had already known of a bad reputation of the sect to which Paul belonged. What they did not have was a formal letter or an ambassadorial messenger which delivered any judgment against Paul.

Hence, they reached an agreement that the Jews in Rome should gather to hear Paul speak: **Having set a day with him, they came to his lodging in even greater numbers** (Acts 28:23a). Maybe on a Sabbath in March in 60 CE, the Jews in Rome, possibly hundreds or thousands, assembled in Paul's guest-chamber, which shows the degree of their interest in Paul's case. And Paul expounded on his belief for a whole day: **To them he explained [his belief] with testifying about the Kingdom of God and convincing them of things concerning Jesus, from both the law of Moses and the prophets, from morning until evening** (28:23b). He repeated what Jesus taught his disciples after his resurrection (1:3). In addition, he talked about Jesus by adducing evidence from the Scriptures; it should have been like 26:23, **on the condition that the Christ is subject to suffering, and on the condition that he is the first to rise from the dead, he will proclaim light both to the people [the Jews] and to the Gentiles.**

52. Witherington 1998: 799.

As usual, Paul's proclamation of the gospel was accepted by some but refused by others (Acts 28:24). So the Jews **scattered without reaching a consensus** on Paul's speech (28:25a). At that moment **Paul made one last statement** (28:25b) by quoting Isa 6:9–10 in the same words as the LXX (Acts 28:26–27). Paul designated this word as **the Holy Spirit's speech announced to their ancestors through Isaiah the prophet** (28:25c): this understanding of the authorship of the Bible runs through Acts (cf. 1:16; 15:28). Marshall summarizes the differences between the MT and the LXX; the text in the MT is initially revealed and then the "change" in the LXX is analyzed just as the following: (1) The ironic imperatives "hear continually, but do not understand" and "see continually, but do not perceive" are changed to emphatic future indicatives expressing what will happen. (2) The command to the prophet to make the people's heart dull and so on is changed to a statement that the people themselves have already done so. (3) The passive "be healed" is changed to the future indicative "I will heal them," expressing more clearly that the healing is the work of God.[53]

Among these, the third one does not seem to be relevant because a literal translation of the last sentence in Isa 6:10 of the MT could actually be "and he/He will heal him." So regarding the third one it can be said that the LXX uses the first-person singular subject ("I") rather than the third-person singular subject ("he"), and the third-person plural object ("them") rather than the third-person singular object ("him"). The text of the LXX seems to be adjusted to suit the line of thought. Likewise, the expression in the MT is also suitable for the context. The third-person singular subject could refer to God's agent, namely, the Isaianic Servant of the Lord, and the third-person singular object refers to "the people" that appears in the present and previous verses in Hebrew in a singular form (also in the singular form even in Greek; *ton laon* and *tou laou*). Hence, by considering the first and the second differences of the MT and the LXX pointed out above, we may conclude that Paul construed 6:9–10 as "emphatic future indicatives expressing what will happen" and "a statement that the people themselves have already done so"; he then later applied the word to the Jews in Rome.

After Paul analyzed the audience in terms of Isa 6:9–10, he laid bare his confidence that **this salvation from God has been sent to the Gentiles**, and that **they will listen, too** (Acts 28:28). His confidence came from experience (13:12, 48; 14:21; 16:33–34; 17:4, 12, 34; 18:8;

53. Marshall 2007: 600.

19:10, 17–19) and was often reported to the Antioch church, the people in Phoenicia and Samaria, and the apostles and the elders (14:27; 15:3, 12); in addition, the barbarians in Malta proved a couple of months ago that his confidence was reliable (28:9–10). Following his custom, Paul proclaimed the gospel to the Jews first; so now he would do the same to the gentiles in Rome.

Paul did proclaim the gospel to the gentiles for two years: **He abided in his own rented quarters two whole years and welcomed all who came to him, proclaiming the Kingdom of God and teaching the things concerning the Lord Jesus Christ with complete boldness and without restriction** (Acts 28:30–31).[54] Paul did not discriminate in favor of the gentiles; he proclaimed the same theme (the kingdom of God) in terms of the same perspective (things concerning Jesus) (cf. 28:23). He fulfilled the requirements in the disciples' prayer by proclaiming the gospel "with complete boldness" (cf. 4:29).[55] Moreover, he welcomed all who came near to him. He should have dealt with everyone well because in the meantime he met people of all kinds.

Furthermore, his ministry had been done "with no one venturing or able to hinder or prevent"[56] even though he was bound and abided in his own rented quarters. A house in Rome was very expensive: "A house could cost up to 875,000 denarii (3.5 million sesterces), which few could afford; rent for the cheapest (upper-story) apartments (rooms) might run from 100 or 125 denarii (400–500 sesterces) annually, and much more for nicer apartments."[57] Paul did not live in any brother's house. He may have used 200 or 250 denarii, an annual salary of an average person, to rent a place for two years, which was too small an amount of money in comparison with him being so great a servant of the kingdom of God. Rome was the richest and biggest in that world. Still Paul's status in the eyes of the unbelievers did not pose any problem for his ministry in Rome. Dominant and influential was God's kingdom, and is forevermore.

54. See comments on 12:24.

55. The phrase, "with complete boldness," appears only in Acts 4:29 and 28:31 in the NT.

56. Barrett 1998: 1253.

57. Keener 2012–2015: 3730. Sesterce was a Roman coin worth about one fourth of a denarius.

Bibliography

Abogunrin, Samuel O. 2003. "Jesus' Sevenfold Programmatic Declaration at Nazareth: An Exegesis of Luke 4.15–30 from an African Perspective." *BT* 1: 225–49.

Ådna, Jostein. 2000. "James' Position at the Summit Meeting of the Apostles and the Elders in Jerusalem (Acts 15)." In *The Mission of the Early Church to Jews and Gentiles*, edited by Jostein Ådna and Hans Kvalbein, 125–61. Tübingen: Mohr Siebeck.

———. 2011. "The Missionary Speeches in the Acts of the Apostles and Their Missiological Implications." *SM* 99: 242–46.

Alexander, J. A. 1984. *A Commentary on the Acts of the Apostles*. Carlisle, PA: Banner of Truth Trust.

Alexander, L. C. A. 1993A. "Acts and Ancient Intellectual Biography." In *The Book of Acts in Its Ancient Literature Setting*, edited by Bruce W. Winter and Andrew D. Clarke, 31–63. Book of Acts in Its First Century Setting 1. Grand Rapids: Eerdmans.

———. 1993B. *The Preface to Luke's Gospel: Literary Convention and Social Context in Luke 1.1–4 and Acts 1.1*. SNTSMS 78. Cambridge: Cambridge University Press.

———. 2005. *Acts in Its Ancient Literary Context: A Classicist Looks at the Acts of the Apostles*. LNTS 298. London: T. & T. Clark.

Alsup, John E. 1985. "Prayer, Consciousness, and the Early Church: A Look at Acts 2:41–47 for Today." *ASB* 101: 31–37.

Anderson, Kevin L. 2006. *"But God Raised Him from the Dead": The Theology of Jesus' Resurrection in Luke-Acts*. Paternoster Biblical Monographs. Milton Keynes: Paternoster.

Ascough, Richard S. 1998. "Civic Pride at Philippi: The Text-Critical Problem of Acts 16.12." *NTS* 44: 93–103.

Barclay, W. 1953 [1955]. *The Acts of the Apostles*. Edinburgh: St. Andrew.

Barrett, C. K. 1979. "Light on the Holy Spirit from Simon Magus (Acts 8:4–25)." In *Les Actes des Apôtres: Traditions, rédaction, théologie*, edited by J. Kremer, 281–95. Louvain: Louvain University Press.

———. 1994–1998. *A Critical and Exegetical Commentary on the Acts of the Apostles*. 2 vols. ICC. Edinburgh: T. & T. Clark.

Barreto, E. D. 2011. "Negotiating Difference: Theology and Ethnicity in the Acts of the Apostles." *WW* 31: 129–37.

Bauckham, Richard. 1995. "James and the Jerusalem Church." In *The Book of Acts in Its First-Century Setting*, vol. 4, *Palestinian Setting*, edited by R. Bauckham, 415–80. Grand Rapids: Eerdmans.

———. 1996. "James and the Gentiles (Acts 15.13–21)." In *History, Literature, and Society in the Book of Acts*, edited by Ben Witherington, 154–84. Cambridge: Cambridge University Press.

———. 2005. "James, Peter, and the Gentiles." In *The Missions of James, Peter, and Paul: Tensions in Early Christianity*, edited by Bruce Chilton and Craig Evans, 91–142. Leiden: Brill.

Bauer, Walter, et al. 2000. *A Greek-English Lexicon of the New Testament and Other Early Christian Literature*. 3rd ed. Chicago: University of Chicago Press.

Bayer, Hans F. 1998. "The Preaching of Peter in Acts." In *Witness to the Gospel: The Theology of Acts*, edited by I. H. Marshall and D. Peterson, 257–74. Grand Rapids: Eerdmans.

Ben-Dov, Jonathan. 2008. "Writing as Oracle and as Law: New Contexts for the Book-Find of King Josiah." *JBL* 127: 223–39.

Bennema, C. 2011. "Spirit and Mission in the Bible: Toward a Dialogue between Biblical Studies and Missiology." *TJ* 32: 237–58.

Beza, Marcu. 1934. *Lands of Many Religions: Palestine, Syria, Cyprus and Mount Sinai*. London: Dent.

Bligh, John. 1966. *Galatians in Greek: A Structural Analysis of St. Paul's Epistle to the Galatians with Notes on the Greek*. Detroit: University of Detroit Press.

Bloesch, D. G. 2000. *The Holy Spirit: Works and Gifts*. Downers Grove, IL: InterVarsity.

Bock, Darrell L. 1987. *Proclamation from Prophecy and Pattern: Lucan Old Testament Christology*. JSNTSup 12. Sheffield: JSOT Press.

———. 1998. "Scripture and the Realization of God's Promises." In *Witness to the Gospel: The Theology of Acts*, edited by I. H. Marshall and D. Peterson, 41–62. Grand Rapids: Eerdmans.

———. 2007. *Acts*. BECNT. Grand Rapids: Baker Academic.

Bockmuehl, Markus. 2000. *Jewish Law in Gentile Churches: Halakhah and the Beginning of Christian Public Ethics*. Edinburgh: Clark.

———. 2011. "The Son of David and His Mother." *JTS* 62: 476–93.

Boice, James Montgomery. 2007. *Psalms II: Psalms 42—106*. Grand Rapids: Baker.

Breitman, B. Eve. 1996. "Jewish Models of Self and Other: *Tzedakah* and *Gemilut ⊠asadim*." *Reconstructionist* 61: 18–26.

Brenk, Frederick E., and Filippo Canali de Rossi. 2001. "The 'Notorious' Felix, Procurator of Judaea, and His Many Wives (Acts 23–24)." *Bib* 82: 410–17.

Bristol, Lyle O. 1949. "Primitive Christian Preaching and the Epistle to the Hebrews." *JBL* 68: 89–97.

Bromiley, G. W., ed. 1979–1988. *The International Standard Bible Encyclopedia*. 4 vols. Grand Rapids: Eerdmans.

Broneer, Oscar. 1951. "Corinth: Center of St. Paul's Missionary Work in Greece." *BA* 14: 78–96.

———. 1958. "Athens: 'City of Idol Worship.'" *BA* 21: 2–28.

Brown, H. Stephen. 1996. "Paul's Hearing at Caesarea: A Preliminary Comparison with Legal Literature of the Roman Period." *SBLSP* 1996: 319–32.

Brown, Schuyler. 1977. "'Water-Baptism' and 'Spirit-Baptism' in Luke-Acts." *ATR* 59: 135–51.

Bruce, F. F. 1972. *The New Testament History*. Garden City, NY: Doubleday.

———. 1978. "The Full Name of the Procurator Felix." *JSNT* 1: 33–36.

———. 1980. *New Testament History*. New York: Doubleday.

———. 1982. *The Epistle of Paul to the Galatians: A Commentary on the Greek Text*. NIGTC. Exeter: Paternoster.

———. 1988. *The Book of the Acts*. Rev. ed. NICNT. Grand Rapids: Eerdmans.

———. 1990. *The Acts of the Apostles: The Greek Text with Introduction and Commentary*. 3rd ed. Grand Rapids: Eerdmans.

Bryan, David J. 2002. "The Herodians: A Case of Disputed Identity; A Review Article of Nikos Kokkinos, the Herodian Dynasty." *TynBul* 53: 223–38.

Calvin, John. 2009. *Commentary upon the Acts of the Apostles.* Vol. 2. Grand Rapids: Baker.

Camp, Ashby L. 1997. "Reexamination the Rule of Concord in Acts 2:38." *RQ* 39: 37–42.

Campbell, Douglas A. 2000. "Paul in Pamphylia (Acts 13.13–14a; 14.24b–26): A Critical Note." *NTS* 46: 595–602.

———. 2005. "Possible Inscriptional Attestation to Sergius Paul[l]us (Acts 13:6–12), and the Implications for Pauline Chronology." *JTS*, n.s., 56: 1–29.

Capper, Brian J. 1983. "The Interpretation of Acts 5:4." *JSNT* 19: 117–31.

———. 1995. "The Palestinian Cultural Context of Earliest Christian Community of Goods." In *The Book of Acts in Its Palestinian Setting,* edited by Richard Bauckham, 323–56. Book of Acts in Its First Century Setting 4. Grand Rapids: Eerdmans.

———. 1998. "Reciprocity and the Ethic of Acts." In *Witness to the Gospel: The Theology of Acts,* edited by I. H. Marshall and D. Peterson, 499–518. Grand Rapids: Eerdmans.

Carson, D. A., et al., eds. 2001. *Justification and Variegated Nomism.* Vol. 1, *The Complexities of Second Temple Judaism.* A Fresh Appraisal of Paul and Second Temple Judaism. Tübingen: Mohr Siebeck Academic.

Casson, Lionel. 1968. *The Ancient Mariners: Mediterranean in Ancient Times.* New York: Macmillan.

Chance, J. B. 1978. *Jerusalem, the Temple, and the New Age in Luke-Acts.* Macon, GA: Mercer University Press.

———. 2007. *Acts.* Macon, GA: Smyth & Helwys.

Charles, J. Daryl. 1995. "Engaging the (Neo)Pagan Mind: Paul's Encounter with Athenian Culture as a Model for Cultural Apologetics (Acts 17:16–34)." *TrinJ* 16, n.s.: 47–62.

Chase, Frederic Henry. 1902. *The Credibility of the Book of the Acts of the Apostles: Being the Lulsean Lectures for 1900–1901.* London: Macmillan.

Cheng, Ling. 2011. *The Characterisation of God in Acts.* Milton Keynes: Paternoster.

Cho, Youngmo. 2003. "Spirit and Kingdom in Luke-Acts: Proclamation as the Primary Role of the Spirit in Relation to the Kingdom of God in Luke-Acts." *AJPS* 6: 173–97.

———. 2005. *Spirit and Kingdom in the Writings of Luke and Paul: An Attempt to Reconcile These Concepts.* Paternoster Biblical Monographs. Milton Keynes: Paternoster.

———. 2011. "A Rejoinder to Carsten Timothy Lotz." *EQ* 83: 73–83.

———. 2012. "A Spiritual Warfare between Philip and Simon the Magician [in Korean]." *Pentecostal Theological Series* 4: 19–40.

———. 2014. "The Tasks of the Pentecostal Church through a Study of the Double-Faced Stories in the Early Church [in Korean]." *Korea Academic Society for Pentecostal Studies* 17: 21–36.

———. 2016. "The Apostles and the Apostolate, and the Holy Spirit according to Luke [in Korean]." *Pentecostal Theological Series* 6: 23–43.

Churchill, Timothy W. R. 2008. "Sequence and Initiative: The Damascus Road Encounter in the Book of Acts." Acts Seminar in the BNTC. Durham University Press.

Clark, Albert C. 1933. *The Acts of the Apostles: A Critical Edition with Introduction and Notes on Selected Passages.* Oxford: Clarendon.

Clark, Andrew C. 1998. "The Role of the Apostles." In *Witness to the Gospel: The Theology of Acts,* edited by I. H. Marshall and D. Peterson, 169–90. Grand Rapids: Eerdmans.

Clermont-Ganneau, C. 1871. "Discovery of a Tablet from Herod's Temple." *PEQ* 3: 132–33.

Clow, Kate. 2013. *The St. Paul Trail.* 2nd ed. Buxton, UK: Upcountry (Turkey).

Conzelmann, H. 1987. *Acts of the Apostles: A Commentary on the Acts of the Apostles.* Translated by J. Limburg et al. Philadelphia: Fortress.

Cooper, Alan, and Bernard R. Goldstein. 2003. "The Development of the Priestly Calendars (I): The Daily Sacrifice and the Sabbath." *HUCA* 74: 1–20.

Croy, N. Clayton. 1997. "Hellenistic Philosophies and the Preaching of the Resurrection (Acts 17:18, 32)." *NovT* 39: 21–39.

Crump, D. 1992. *Jesus the Intercessor.* WUNT 2.49. Tübingen: Mohr.

Cullman, Oscar. 1956. "Rudolf Bultmann's Concept of Myth and the New Testament." *Concordia Theological Monthly* 27: 13–24.

Culy, Martin M., and Mikeal C. Parsons. 2003. *Acts: A Handbook on the Greek Text.* Waco, TX: Baylor University Press.

Currid, John D., and David P. Barrett. 2010. *Crossway ESV Bible Atlas.* Wheaton, IL: Crossway.

Dahle, Lars. 2002. "Acts 17:16–34: An Apologetic Model Then and Now?" *TynBul* 53: 313–16.

Davis, J. A. 1984. *Wisdom and Spirit: An Investigation of 1 Corinthians 1.18—3.20 against the Background of Jewish Sapiential Tradition in the Greco-Roman Period.* Lanham, MD: University Press of America.

DeMoss, Matthew S. 2001. *Pocket Dictionary: For the Study of New Testament Greek.* Downers Grove, IL: InterVarsity.

Denton, W. 1876. *A Commentary on the Acts of the Apostles II.* London: Bell.

Detwiler, David F. 1995. "Paul's Approach to the Great Commission in Acts 14:21–23." *BSac* 152: 33–41.

De Vos, C. S. 1995. "The Significance of the Change from ΟΙΚΟΣ to ΟΙΚΙΑ in Luke's Account of the Philippian Gaoler (Acts 16.30–4)." *NTS* 41: 292–96.

———. 1999. "Finding a Charge That Fits: The Accusation against Paul and Silas at Philippi (Acts 16.19–21)." *JSNT* 74: 51–63.

Dickerson, P. L. 1997. "The Sources of the Account of the Mission to Samaria in Acts 8:5–25." *NovT* 39: 210–34.

Dillon, R. J. 1990. "The Acts of the Apostles." In *The New Jerome Biblical Commentary,* edited by R. E. Brown et al., 722–67. Englewood Cliffs, NJ: Prentice Hall.

Douglas, J. D., et al., eds. 1996. *New Bible Dictionary.* 3rd ed. Leicester, UK: InterVarsity.

Duncan, George S. 1929. *St. Paul's Ephesian Ministry: A Reconstruction with Special Reference to the Ephesian Origin of the Imprisonment Epistles.* London: Hodder and Stoughton.

Dunn, James D. G. 1970. *Baptism in the Holy Spirit: A Re-examination of the New Testament Teaching on the Gift of the Spirit in Relation to Pentecostalism Today.* London: SCM.

———. 1993. *The Epistle to the Galatians.* BNTC. Peabody, MA: Hendrickson.

———. 1996. *The Acts of the Apostles.* Peterborough, UK: Epworth.

————. 1998. "ΚΥΡΙΟΣ in Acts." In *The Christ and the Spirit*, vol. 1, *Christology*, 241–53. Grand Rapids: Eerdmans.

Dupont, J. 1985. "La structure oratoire du discours d'Étienne (Actes 7)." *Bib* 66: 153–67.

Easton, M. G., ed. 1897. *Illustrated Bible Dictionary*. 3rd ed. London: Nelson.

Ecker, Avner. 2013. "Dining with Herod." In *Herod the Great: The King's Final Journey*, edited by Silvia Rozenberg and David Mevorah, 66–79. Jerusalem: Israel Museum.

Elbert, Paul. 2013. "Acts 2:38 in Light of the Syntax of Imperative-Future Passive and Imperative-Present Participle Combinations." *CBQ* 75: 94–107.

Ellington, John. 2003. "Who's Who in Acts 16–17? Problems of Pronoun Reference." *Bible Translator* 54: 407–15.

Epp, Eldon Jay. 1966. *The Theological Tendency of Codex Beaze Cantabrigiensis in Acts*. SNTSMS 3. Cambridge: Cambridge University Press.

ESV Study Bible. 2008. Wheaton, IL: Crossway Bibles.

Evans, Craig A. 2008. *Ancient Texts for New Testament Studies: A Guide to the Background Literature*. Peabody, MA: Hendrickson.

Everts, J. M. 1992. "Conversion and Call of Paul." In *DPL*, 156–63.

Everts, Jenny. 1994. "Tongues or Languages? Contextual Consistency in the Translation of Acts 2." *JPT* 4: 71–80.

Fairchild, Mark R. 1999. "Paul's Pre-Christian Zealot Associations: A Re-examination of Gal 1.14 and Acts 22.3." *NTS* 45: 514–32.

Fantham, Elaine. 2004. *Ovid's Metamorphoses*. Oxford: Oxford University Press.

Farmer, William R. 1999. "James the Lord's Brother, according to Paul." In *James the Just and Christian Origins*, edited by Bruce Chilton and Craig A. Evans, 133–53. NovTSup. Leiden: Brill.

Ferguson, Everett. 1960. "Laying on of Hands in Acts 6:6 and 13:3." *RQ* 4: 250–52.

————. 1993. *Backgrounds of Early Christianity*. 2nd ed. Grand Rapids: Eerdmans.

Fernando, Ajith. 1998. *Acts*. NIVAC. Grand Rapids: Zondervan.

Fine, S. 1998. "This Is the Torah That Moses Set before the Children of Israel: Scripture and Authority in Rabbinic Judaism." *RevExp* 95: 523–32.

Fitzmyer, J. A. 1998. *Commentary on the Acts of the Apostles: A New Translation with Introduction and Commentary*. AB 31. London: Doubleday.

France, R. T. 2002. *The Gospel of Mark: A Commentary on the Greek Text*. NIGTC. Grand Rapids: Eerdmans.

Fuller, George C. 1994. "The Life of Jesus, after the Ascension (Luke 24:50–53; Acts1:9–11)." *WTJ* 56: 391–98.

Gaventa, B. R. 1986. *From Darkness to Light: Aspects of Conversion in the New Testament*. Philadelphia: Fortress.

————. 2004. "Theology and Ecclesiology in the Miletus Speech: Reflections on Content and Context." *NTS* 50: 36–52.

Geagan, Daniel J. 1967. *The Athenian Constitution after Sulla*. Hesperia: Supplement. Princeton: American School of Classical Studies at Athens.

Gempf, Conrad. 1994. "Acts." In *New Bible Commentary*, edited by G. J. Wenham et al., 1066–107. Leicester, UK: InterVarsity.

Gilbert, Gary. 2002. "The List of Nations in Acts 2: Roman Propaganda and the Lukan Response." *JBL* 121: 497–529.

Gill, David W. J. 1994A. "Achaia." In *The Book of Acts in Its Graeco-Roman Setting*, edited by David W. J. Gill and Conrad Gempf, 433–53. Book of Acts in Its First Century Setting 2. Grand Rapids: Eerdmans.

——. 1994B. "Macedonia." In *The Book of Acts in Its Graeco-Roman Setting*, edited by David W. J. Gill and Conrad Gempf, 397–417. Book of Acts in Its First Century Setting 2. Grand Rapids: Eerdmans.

——. 1999. "Dionysios and Damaris: A Note on Acts 17:34." *CBQ* 61: 483–90.

Glahn, Sandra L. 2015. "The Identity of Artemis in First-Century Ephesus." *BSac* 172: 316–34.

Glare, P. G. W., ed. 1996. *Greek-English Lexicon: Revised Supplement*. Oxford: Clarendon.

Gonzalez, Justo. 2001. *Acts: The Gospel of the Spirit*. New York: Orbis.

Goodspeed, E. J. 1950. "Gaius Titius Justus." *JBL* 69: 382–83.

Gorby, Pascal-Emmanuel. 2015. "Could Paganism Make a Comeback? It's Not as Crazy as It Sounds." October 23, 2015. http://theweek.com/articles/584634/could-paganism-make-comeback-not-crazy-sounds.

Goulder, M. D. 1964. *Type and History in Acts*. London: SPCK.

Gray, Patrick. 2005. "Athenian Curiosity (Acts 17:21)." *NovT* 47: 108–16.

Gundry, R. H. 1966. "'Ecstatic Utterance' (N. E. B)?" *JTS* 17: 299–307.

Haak, C. J. 2009. "The Missional Approach: Reconsidering Elenctics (Part 2)." *CTJ* 44: 288–305.

Haenchen, Ernst. 1971. *The Acts of the Apostles: A Commentary*. Translated by R. McL. Wilson. 14th German ed. Philadelphia: Westminster.

Hamm, Dennis. 1984. "Acts 3:12–26: Peter's Speech and the Healing of the Man Born Lame." *PRS* 11: 199–217.

——. 2003A. "4:23–31: A Neglected Biblical Paradigm of Christian Worship." *Wor* 77: 225–37.

——. 2003B. "The Tamid Service in Luke-Acts: The Cultic Background behind Luke's Theology of Worship (Luke 1:5–25; 18:9–14; 24:50–53; Acts 3:1; 10:3, 30)." *CBQ* 65: 215–31.

Hansen, G. Walter. 1994. "Galatia." In *The Book of Acts in Its Graeco-Roman Setting*, edited by David W. J. Gill, 377–95. Book of Acts in Its First Century Setting 2. Grand Rapids: Eerdmans.

Hanson, K. C., and Douglas E. Oakman. 1998. *Palestine in the Time of Jesus*. Minneapolis: Fortress.

Hardin, Justin K. 2006. "Decrees and Drachmas at Thessalonica: An Illegal Assembly in Jason's House (Acts 17.1–10a)." *NTS* 52: 29–49.

Harrison, Everett F. 1986 [1975]. *Interpreting Acts: The Expanding Church*. Grand Rapids: Zondervan.

Hawthorne, G. F., and R. P. Martin, eds. 1993. *Dictionary of Paul and His Letters*. Downers Grove, IL: InterVarsity.

Head, Peter. 1993. "Acts and the Problem of Its Texts." In *The Book of Acts in Its Ancient Literary Setting*, edited by Bruce W. Winter and Andrew D. Clarke, 415–44. Book of Acts in Its First Century Setting 1. Grand Rapids: Eerdmans.

Hellerman, Joseph H. 2003. "The Humiliation of Christ in the Social World of Roman Philippi, Part 2." *Bsac* 160: 421–33.

Hemer, Colin J. 1975. "Euraquilo and Melita." *JTS*, n.s., 26: 100–111.

——. 1985. "First Person Narrative in Acts 27—28." *TynBul* 36: 79–109.

——. 1987. "The Name of Felix Again." *JSNT* 31: 45–49.

Hemer, Colin J., and Conrad Gempf. 1989. *The Book of Acts in the Setting of Hellenistic History*. WUNT 49. Tübingen: Mohr.

Hengel, Martin. 1974. *Property and Riches in the Early Church: Aspects of a Social History of Christianity*. Philadelphia: Fortress.

————. 1995. "The Geography of Palestine in Acts." In *The Book of Acts in Its Palestinian Setting*, edited by Richard Bauckham, 27–78. Book of Acts in Its First Century Setting 4. Grand Rapids: Eerdmans.

————. 2000. "Ioudaia in the Geographical List of Acts 2:9–11 and Syria as 'Great Judea.'" *BBR* 10: 161–80.

Hengel, M., and M. Schwemer. 1997. *Paul between Damascus and Antioch: The Unknown Years*. Louisville: Westminster.

Hess, Richard S. 2002. "Leviticus 10:1: Strange Fire and an Odd Name." *BBR* 12: 187–98.

Hill, D. 1967. *Greek Words and Hebrew Meanings: Studies in the Semantics of Soteriological Terms*. SNTSMS 5. Cambridge: Cambridge University Press.

————. 1979. *New Testament Prophecy*. London: Marshall, Morgan & Scott.

Hill, George. 1940. *A History of Cyprus*. Vol. 1, *To the Conquest by Richard Lion Heart*. Cambridge: Cambridge University Press.

Himes, Paul A. 2011. "Peter and the Prophetic Word: The Theology of Prophecy Traced through Peter's Sermons and Epistles." *BBR* 21: 227–43.

Hinson, E. Glenn. 2007. "Persistence in Prayer in Luke-Acts." *RevExp* 104: 721–36.

Hogan, Derek. 2002. "Paul's Defense: A Comparison of the Forensic Speeches in Acts, *Callirhoe*, and *Leucippe and Clitophon*." *PRSt* 29: 73–87.

Holmås, Geir Otto. 2005. "'My House Shall Be a House of Prayer': Regarding the Temple as a Place of Prayer in Acts within the Context of Luke's Apologetic Objective." *JSNT* 27: 393–416.

Honeycutt, R. L. 1977. "Aaron, the Priesthood, and the Golden Calf." *RevExp* 74: 523–36.

Hooker, Morna D. 2013. "Artemis of Ephesus." *JTS*, n.s., 64: 37–46.

Hultgren, Arland J. 1976. "Paul's Pre-Christian Persecutions of the Church: Their Purpose, Locale, and Nature." *JBL* 95: 97–111.

————. 2010. "Paul as Theologian: His Vocation and Its Significance for His Theology." *WW* 30: 357–70.

Hume, David. 1748 [1995]. *An Enquiry concerning Human Understanding*. Edited by Charles W. Hendel. Dover Philosophical Classics. New York: Dover.

Ilife, J. H. 1938. "The ΘΑΝΑΤΟΣ Inscription from Herod's Temple." *QDAP* 6: 1–3.

Instone-Brewer, David. 2009. "Infanticide and the Apostolic Decree of Acts 15." *JETS* 52: 301–21.

Jeremias, J. 1969. *Jerusalem in the Time of Jesus: An Investigation into Economic and Social Conditions in the Time of Jesus*. London: SCM.

Jervell, Jacob. 1972. *Luke and the People of God*. Minneapolis: Augsburg.

————. 1996. *The Theology of the Acts of the Apostles*. Cambridge: Cambridge University Press.

Jewett, Robert. 1979. *Dating Paul's Life*. London: SCM.

Johnson, Luke T. 1977. *The Literary Function of Possessions in Luke-Acts*. SBLDS 39. Missoula: Scholars.

————. 1982. "The Use of Leviticus 19 in the Letter of James." *JBL* 101: 391–401.

————. 1992. *The Acts of the Apostles*. SP. Collegeville, PA: Liturgical.

————. 1998. *Religious Experience in Earliest Christianity: A Missing Dimension in New Testament Study*. Minneapolis: Fortress.

Josephus. 1999. *The New Complete Works of Josephus*. Translated by William Whiston. Rev. ed. Grand Rapids: Kregel.

Judge, E. A. 1971. "The Decrees of Caesar at Thessalonica." *RTR* 30: 1–7.

Kaiser, W. C. 1994. "The Book of Leviticus." In *The New Interpreter's Bible*, vol. 1. Nashville: Abingdon.

Kaveny, M. Cathleen. 2005. "The Order of Widows: What the Early Church Can Teach Us about Older Women and Health Care." *CB* 11: 11–34.

Kazen, Thomas. 2008. "The Christology of Early Christian Practice." *JBL* 127: 591–614.

Keener, Craig. 1993. *Bible Background Commentary: New Testament*. Downers Grove, IL: InterVarsity.

———. 2001. *Gift Giver: The Holy Spirit for Today*. Grand Rapids: Baker.

———. 2012–2015. *Acts: An Exegetical Commentary*. Vols. 1–4. Grand Rapids: Baker Academic.

Kelhoffer, J. A. 2009. "The Gradual Disclosure of Paul's Violence against Christians in the Acts of the Apostles as an Apology for the Standing of the Lukan Paul." *BR* 54: 25–35.

Kendrick, Klaude. 1961. *The Promise Fulfilled: A History of the Modern Pentecostal Movement*. Springfield, MO: Gospel Publishing.

Kern, P. H. 2003. "Paul's Conversion and Luke's Portrayal of Character in Acts 8–10." *TynBul* 54: 63–80.

Kilgallen, John. 2002. "'With Many Other Words' (Acts 2.40): Theological Assumptions of Peter's Pentecost Speech." *Bib* 83: 71–87.

———. 2003. "Hostility to Paul in Pisidian Antioch (Acts 13,45)—Why?" *Biblica* 84: 1–15.

Kim, Jin-Myung. 2007. "An Exegetical Study for the Canonical Unfoldings of Leviticus 19." ThD diss., Seoul, Presbyterian College and Theological Seminary.

———. 2011. *Holiness & Perfection: A Canonical Unfolding of Leviticus 19*. Alte Testament Im Dialog. New York: Peter Lang.

Kim, Jung Woo. 1989. "Psalm 89: Its Biblical-Theological Contribution to the Presence of Law within the Unconditional Covenant." PhD diss., Westminster Theological Seminary.

Kistemaker, Simon J. 1990. *New Testament Commentary: Exposition of the Acts of the Apostles*. Grand Rapids: Baker.

Kittel, Gerhard, and Gerhard Friedrich, eds. 1964–1976. *Theological Dictionary of the New Testament*, translated by G. W. Bromiley. 10 vols. Grand Rapids: Eerdmans.

Klawans, Jonathan. 1995. "Notion of Gentile Impurity in Ancient Judaism." *AJS Review* 20: 285–312.

———. 2000. *Impurity and Sin in Ancient Judaism*. Oxford: Oxford University Press.

Knox, W. L. 1948. *Acts of the Apostles*. Cambridge: Cambridge University Press.

Kokkinos, Nikos. 1998. *The Herodian Dynasty: Origins, Role in Society and Eclipse*. JSPSup 30. Sheffield: Sheffield Academic.

Kraus, Hans-Joachim. 1993. *Psalms 60–150: A Continental Commentary*, translated by Hilton C. Oswald. Minneapolis: Fortress.

Krentz, Edgar. 2010. "Peter: Confessor, Denier, Proclaimer, Validator of Proclamation: A Study in Diversity." *CTM* 37: 320–33.

Kruse, Colin G. 1987. *2 Corinthians: An Introduction and Commentary*. TNTC. Nottingham: InterVarsity.

Lake, Kirsopp, and Henry J. Cadbury, eds. 1933A. *The Beginnings of Christianity*. Part 1, *The Acts of the Apostles*. Vol. 5, *Additional Notes to the Commentary*. London: Macmillan.

————. 1933B. *The Beginnings of Christianity*. Part 1, *The Acts of the Apostles*. Vol. 4, *English Translation and Commentary*. London: Macmillan.

Lane, William L. 1991. *Hebrew 1–8*. WBC 47A. Dallas: Word.

Laytner, Anson. 1996. "Christianity and Judaism: Old History, New Beginnings." *JES* 33: 187–203.

Lenski, R. C. H. 1944 [1961]. *The Interpretation of the Acts of the Apostles*. Minneapolis: Augsburg.

Lessing, R. 2004. "What Really Happened at Sinai?" *CJ* 30: 288–89.

Levinsohn, Stephen H. 2000. *Discourse Features of New Testament Greek: A Coursebook on the Information Structure of New Testament Greek*. 2nd ed. Dallas: SIL International.

Liddell, H. G., et al. 1940. *A Greek-English Lexicon*. 9th ed. with revised supplement. Oxford: Oxford University Press.

Lierman, J. D. 2002. "The New Testament Moses in the Context of Ancient Judaism." *TynBul* 53: 317–20.

Litwak, Kenneth D. 2004. "Israel's Prophets Meet Athens' Philosophers: Scriptural Echoes in Acts 17,22–31." *Biblica* 85: 199–216.

Llewelyn, Stephen R., and Dionysia van Beek. 2011. "Reading the Temple Warning as a Greek Visitor." *JSJ* 42: 1–22.

Lockyer, Herbert, et al., eds. 1986. *Illustrated Dictionary of the Bible*. Nashville: Nelson.

Lohse, E. 1976. *The New Testament Environment*. Translated by John E. Steely. Nashville: Abingdon.

Long, W. R. 1982. "The Trial of Paul in the Book of Acts: History, Literary, and Theological Considerations." PhD diss., Brown University.

Longenecker, Richard N. 1981. *The Acts of the Apostles*. Expository Bible Commentary 9. Grand Rapids: Zondervan.

————. 1997. "A Realized Hope, a New Commitment, and a Developed Proclamation: Paul and Jesus." In *the Road from Damascus: The Impact of Paul's Conversion on His Life, Thought, and Ministry*, edited by R. N. Longenecker, 18–41. Grand Rapids: Eerdmans.

————. 1999 [1979]. *Biblical Exegesis in the Apostolic Period*. Grand Rapids: Eerdmans.

Louw, J. P., and E. A. Nida, eds. 1989. *Greek-English Lexicon of the New Testament: Based on Semantic Domains*. 2nd ed. New York: United Bible Societies.

Lüdemann, G. 1987. "The Acts of the Apostles and the Beginnings of Simonian Gnosis." *NTS* 33: 420–26.

Macchia, S. 1999. *Becoming a Healthy Church: Ten Characteristics*. Grand Rapids: Baker.

Maddox, R. 1982. *The Purpose of Luke-Acts*. Edinburgh: T. & T. Clark.

Malcolm, Lois. 2002. "Conversion, Conversation, and Acts 15." *WW* 22: 246–54.

Malina, Bruce J., and Jerome H. Neyrey. 1991. "Conflict in Luke-Acts: Labelling and Deviance Theory." In *The Social World of Luke-Acts: Models for Interpretation*, edited by Jerome H. Neyrey, 97–122. Peabody, MA: Hendrickson.

Malina, Bruce J., and John J. Pilch. 2008. *Social-Science Commentary on the Book of Acts*. Minneapolis: Fortress.

Malone, Andrew S. 2011. "Distinguishing the Angel of the Lord." *BBR* 21: 297–314.

Manson, T. W. 1962. *Studies in the Gospels and Epistles: With a Memoir of T. W. Manson by H. H. Rowley*. Edited by Matthew Black. Manchester: Manchester University Press.

Mare, W. Harold. 1996. "Prophet and Teacher in the New Testament Period." *BETS* 9: 139–48.

Marguerat, D. 2002. *The First Christian Historian: Writing the Acts of the Apostles.* SNTSMS 121. Cambridge: Cambridge University Press.

———. 2011. *Lukas, der Erste Christliche Historiker: Eine Studie zur Apostel-geschichte.* ATANT 92. Zürich: TVZ.

Marshall, I. Howard. 1970. *Luke: Historian and Theologian.* Grand Rapids: Zondervan.

———. 1980A. *The Acts of the Apostles: An Introduction and Commentary.* Grand Rapids: Eerdmans.

———. 1980B. *Acts.* TNTC. Nottingham: InterVarsity.

———. 2007. "Acts." In *Commentary on the New Testament Use of the Old Testament,* edited by G. K. Beale and D. A. Carson, 513–606. Grand Rapids: Baker Academic.

Martin, Luther H. 1995. "Gods or Ambassadors of God? Barnabas and Paul in Lystra." *NTS* 41: 152–56.

Martin, Thomas W. 2006. "What Makes Glory Glorious? Reading Luke's Account of the Transfiguration over against Triumphalism." *JSNT* 29: 3–26.

Marx, Werner G. 1980. "A New Theophilus." *EQ* 52: 17–26.

Mason, S. 1992. *Josephus and the NT.* Peabody, MA: Hendrickson.

———. 1995. "Chief Priests, Sadducees, Pharisees and Sanhedrin." In *The Book of Acts in Its Palestine Settings* 4, edited by R. Bauckham, 115–77. Grand Rapids: Eerdmans.

Matera, Frank J. 1987. "Acts 10:34–43." *Int* 41: 62–66.

Matson, David L., and Warren S. Brown. 2006. "Tuning the Faith: The Cornelius Story in Resonance Perspective." *PRS* 33: 449–65.

McDonough, Sean M. 2006. "Small Change: Saul to Paul, Again." *JBL* 125: 390–91.

McGee, Gary B. 1988. "The Azusa Street Revival and Twentieth-Century Missions." *IBMR* 12: 58–61.

McIntosh, John. 2002. "'For It Seemed Good to the Holy Spirit' (Acts 15:28): How Did the Members of the Jerusalem Council Know This?" *RTR* 61: 131–47.

McQueen, Larry R. 1995. *Joel and the Spirit: The Cry of a Prophetic Hermeneutics.* JPTSS 8. Sheffield: Sheffield Academic.

Meeks, W. A. 1977. "Simon Magus in Recent Research." *RSR* 3: 137–72.

Menzies, Robert P. 1991. *The Development of the Early Christian Pneumatology: With Special Reference to Luke-Acts.* JSNTSup 54. Sheffield: JSOT.

———. 1994. *Empowered for Witness: The Spirit in Luke-Acts.* JPTSS 6. Sheffield: Sheffield Academic.

Metzger, Bruce M. 1971. *A Textual Commentary on the Greek New Testament.* 2nd ed. Stuttgart: Deutsche Bibelgesellschaft / United Bible Societies.

———. 2000. *A Textual Commentary on the Greek New Testament: A Companion Volume to the United Bible Societies' Greek New Testament.* 4th ed. Stuttgart: Deutsche Bibelgesellschaft.

———. 2003. *The New Testament: Its Background, Growth & Contents.* 3rd ed. New York: Abingdon.

Miles, Gary B., and Garry Trompf. 1967. "Luke and Antiphon: The Theology of Acts 27–28 in the Light of Pagan Beliefs about Divine Retribution, Pollution, and Shipwreck." *HTR* 69: 259–67.

Miller, Chris A. 2002. "Did Peter's Vision in Acts 10 Pertain to Men or the Menu?" *BSac* 159: 302–17.

Miller, John B. F. 2010. "Exploring the Function of Symbolic Dream-Visions in the Literature of Antiquity with Another Look at 1QapGen19 and Acts 10." *PRS* 37: 441–55.

Mitchell, A. C. 1992. "The Social Function of Friendship in Acts 2:44–47 and 4:32–37." *JBL* 111: 255–72.

Mitchell, S. 1993. *Anatolia: Land, Men, and Gods in Asia Minor*. Vol. 2, *The Rise of the Church*. Oxford: Clarendon.

Miura, Yuzuru. 2008. *David in Luke-Acts: His Portrayal in the Light of Early Judaism*. WUNT. Tübingen: Mohr Siebeck.

Moessner, David P. 1986. "The Christ Must Suffer: New Light on the Jesus-Peter, Stephen, Paul Parallels in Luke-Acts." *NovT* 28: 220–56.

Montague, G. T. 1976. *The Holy Spirit: Growth of a Biblical Tradition*. New York: Paulist.

Moo, Douglas. 1996. *The Epistle to the Romans*. NICNT. Grand Rapids: Eerdmans.

Moore, G. E. 1927. *Judaism in the First Centuries of the Christian Era: The Age of Tannaim*. Cambridge, MA: Harvard University Press.

Morton, H. V. 1937. *In the Steps of St. Paul*. New York: Dodd, Mead.

Moulton, J. H. 1998. *A Grammar of New Testament Greek*. Vol. 1, *Prolegomena*. Edinburgh: T. & T. Clark.

Muers, Rachel. 2003. "Idolatry and Future Generations: The Persistence of Molech." *Modern Theology* 19: 547–61.

Mundhenk, Norman A. 2002. "A Note on Acts 17.24." *BT* 53: 441–42.

Murphy-O'Connor, Jerome. 1984. "The Corinth That Saint Paul Saw." *BA* 47: 147–59.

———. 2002. *St. Paul's Corinth: Texts and Archaeology*. Collegeville, PA: Liturgical.

———. 2008. *St. Paul's Ephesus: Texts and Archaeology*. Collegeville, PA: Liturgical.

Myrou, Augustine. 1999. "Sosthenes: The Former Crispus (?)." *GOTR* 44: 207–12.

Nagel, Norman E. 2005. "The Twelve and the Seven in Acts 6 and the Needy." *CJ* 31: 113–26.

NET notes. 2005. *NET Bible*. www.bible.org. Biblical Studies Press.

Neudorfer, Heinz-Werner. 1998. "The Speech of Stephen." In *Witness to the Gospel: The Theology of Acts,* edited by I. Marshall and D. Peterson, 275–94. Grand Rapids: Eerdmans.

Norwood, M. Thomas. 1979. "Serious Stewardship: A Second Look at the Ananias and Sapphira Narrative." *JP* 3: 4–8.

Ogilvie, R. M. 1958. "Phoenix." *JTS*, n.s., 9: 308–14.

Olley, John W. 1979. *"Righteousness" in the Septuagint of Isaiah: A Contextual Study*. SBLSCS. Missoula, MO: Scholars.

Orr, James, et al., eds. 1939. *The International Standard Bible Encyclopedia*. 5 vols. Grand Rapids: Eerdmans.

Overman, J. Andrew. 1996. *Church and Community in Crisis: The Gospel according to Matthew*. Valley Forge, PA: Trinity.

Oxley, Simon. 2004. "Certainties Transformed." *Ecumenical Review* 56: 322–26.

Pao, David W. 2000. *Acts and the Isaianic New Exodus*. Grand Rapids: Baker Academic.

———. 2011. "Waiters or Preachers: Acts 6:1–7 and the Lukan Table Fellowship Motif." *JBL* 130: 127–44.

Park, Hyung Dae. 2002. "Lordship Claim for Jesus in Acts." ThM thesis, Trinity Evangelical Divinity School, Deerfield, IL.

———. 2007A. *Finding Herem? A Study of Luke-Acts in the Light of Herem*. LNTS 357. London: T. & T. Clark.

———. 2007B. "Function of Repetition in the Story of Cornelius [in Korean]." *Biblical Studies for the Church* 5: 181–224.

———. 2010A. "Drawing Ethical Principles from the Process of the Jerusalem Council: A New Approach to Acts 15:4–29." *TynBul* 61: 271–91.

———. 2010B. "A Treatise on the Change of the Jerusalem Church in Acts [in Korean]." *Presbyterian Theological Quarterly* 77: 107–32.

———. 2011. "Combined Approach to the Repetitions in the Stories of the Conversions of Cornelius and Paul in Acts." *S&I* 5: 146–68.

———. 2012. "God's Holiness, Justice and Love Found in the NT Prayers [in Korean]." *Hermeneia Today* 54: 137–52.

———. 2013A. "Christianity's Inclusiveness and Absoluteness in Acts [in Korean]." *Hermeneia Today* 56: 65–76.

———. 2013B. "Holy Spirit's Speech in the Second Temple Jewish Literature and the Acts of the Apostles [in Korean]." *Bible & Theology* 68: 315–48.

———. 2016. "'All Things to All Men' Speech Principles: A Study on Paul's Four Main Speeches in Acts 13–20." *Chongshin Theological Journal* 24: 49–100.

———. 2017. "Tertullus versus Paul in Felix's Praetorium." *Korean Evangelical New Testament Studies* 16.2: 70–99.

Parker, Floyd. 2003. "The Term 'Angel' and 'Spirit' in Acts 23,8." *Bib* 84: 344–65.

Peace, Richard. 1999. *Conversion in the New Testament: Paul and the Twelve*. Grand Rapids: Eerdmans.

Penney, J. M. 1977. *The Missionary Emphasis of Lukan Pneumatology*. JPTSS 12. Sheffield: Sheffield Academic.

Perkins, Pheme. 1988. *Reading the New Testament: An Introduction*. London: Geoffrey Chapman.

Pervo, R. I. 1987. *Profit with Delight: The Literary Genre of the Acts of the Apostles*. Philadelphia: Fortress.

———. 2009. *Acts: A Commentary*. Hermeneia. Minneapolis: Fortress.

Peterson, David G. 2009. *The Acts of the Apostles*. Grand Rapids: Eerdmans.

Phillips, John. 1986. *Exploring Acts*. Vol. 1, *Acts 1–12*. Chicago: Moody.

Phillips, Tom. 2014. "China on Course to Become 'World's Most Christian Nation' within 15 Years." *Telegraph,* April 19, 2014. http://www.telegraph.co.uk/news/worldnews/asia/china/10776023/China-on-course-to-become-worlds-most-Christian-nation-within-15-years.html.

Polhill, J. B. 1992. *Acts*. NAC. Nashville: Broadman.

Polythree, Vern S. 1991. *The Shadow in the Law of Moses*. Phillipsburg, NJ: P&R.

Porter, Stanley E. 1994. "Excursus: The 'We' Passages." In *The Book of Acts in Its Graeco-Roman Setting*, edited by David W. J. Gill, 545–74. Book of Acts in Its First Century Setting 2. Grand Rapids: Eerdmans.

———. 2016. *When Paul Met Jesus: How an Idea Got Lost in History*. New York: Cambridge University Press.

Powell, Mark A. 1991. *What Are They Saying about Acts?* New York: Paulist.

Pritz, Ray. 2009. *The Works of Their Hands: Man-Made Things in the Bible*. London: UBS.

Proctor, John. 1996. "Proselytes and Pressure Cookers: The Meaning and Application of Acts 15:20." *International Review of Mission* 85: 469–83.

Rackham, R. B. 1925. *The Acts of the Apostles*. London: Methuen.

Rainey, Anson F., and R. Steven Notley. 2006. *The Sacred Bridge: Carta's Atlas of the Biblical World*. Jerusalem: Carta.

Ramsay, William M. 1900. "Some Recent Editions of the Acts of the Apostles." *Expositor* 6: 321–35.

———. 1910. *Pictures of the Apostolic Church: Its Life and Teaching*. London: Hodder and Stoughton.

———. 1975. *St. Paul the Traveller and the Roman Citizen*. Grand Rapids: Baker.

Rapske, Brian. 1994. *The Book of Acts and Paul in Roman Custody*. Book of Acts in Its First Century Setting 3. Grand Rapids: Eerdmans.

———. 1998. "Opposition to the Plan of God and Persecution." In *Witness to the Gospel: The Theology of Acts*, edited by I. Howard Marshall, 235–56. Grand Rapids: Eerdmans.

Ravens, David. 1995. *Luke and the Restoration of Israel*. JSNTSup 119. Sheffield: Sheffield Academic.

Rayburn, Robert Gibson. 1986. "Three Offices: Minister, Elder, Deacon." *Presb* 12: 105–14.

Reeve, William, and Jeremy Collier. 1890. *The Apology of Tertullian and the Meditations of the Emperor Marcus Aurelius Antoninus*. London: Griffith, Farran.

Regev, Eyal. 2005. "The Ritual Baths Near the Temple Mount and Extra-Purification Before Entering the Temple Courts." *IEJ* 55: 194–204.

Reymond, Robert. 2000. *Paul Missionary Theologian: A Survey of Missionary Labors and Theology*. Ross-shire, UK: Christian Focus.

Ridderbos, Herman. 1966. *Paul: An Outline of His Theology*. Grand Rapids: Eerdmans.

Riesner, R. 1995. "Synagogues in Jerusalem." In *The Book of Acts in Its Palestine Setting*, edited by R. Bauckham, 179–209. Book of Acts in Its First Century Setting 4. Grand Rapids: Eerdmans.

———. 1998. *Paul's Early Period: Chronology, Mission Strategy, Theology*. Grand Rapids: Eerdmans.

Rius-Camps, Josep, and Jenny Read-Heimerdinger. 2004. *The Message of Acts in Codex Bezae I: A Comparison with the Alexandrian Tradition (Acts 1:1–5:42)*. LNTS 257. London: T. & T. Clark.

———. 2006. *The Message of Acts in Codex Bezae II: A Comparison with the Alexandrian Tradition (Acts 6:1—12:25)*. LNTS 302. London: T. & T. Clark.

———. 2007. *The Message of Acts in Codex Bezae: A Comparison with the Alexandrian Tradition*. Vol. 3, *Acts 13:1—18:23*. LNTS 365. London: T. & T. Clark.

———. 2009. *The Message of Acts in Codex Bezae: A Comparison with the Alexandrian Tradition*. Vol. 4, *Acts 18:24—28:31: Rome Via Ephesus and Jerusalem*. LNTS 415. London: T. & T. Clark.

Robertson, A. T. 2010. *A Grammar of the Greek New Testament in the Light of Historical Research*. Nashville: Broadman.

Roloff, J. 1981. *Die Apostelgeschichte*. Göttingen: Vandenhoeck & Ruprecht.

Rosner, Brian S. 1998. "The Progress of the Word." In *Witness to the Gospel: The Theology of Acts*, edited by I. H. Marshall and D. Peterson, 215–33. Grand Rapids: Eerdmans.

Rothschild, Clare K. 2012. "Pisidian Antioch in Acts 13: The Denouement of the South Galatian Hypothesis." *NovT* 54: 334–53.

Rowe, C. Kavin. 2012. "The Ecclesiology of Acts." *Int* 66: 259–69.

Satterthwaite, Philip E. 1993. "Acts against the Background of Classical Rhetoric." In *The Book of Acts in Its Ancient Literary Setting*, edited by Bruce W. Winter and Andrew D. Clarke, 337–79. Book of Acts in Its First Century Setting 1. Grand Rapids: Eerdmans.

Savelle, Charles H. 2004. "A Reexamination of the Prohibitions in Acts 15." *BSac* 161: 449–68.

Schaff, Philip. 1980. *History of the Christian Church*. Vol. 1, *Apostolic Christianity AD 1–100*. Grand Rapids: Eerdmans.

Schams, Christine. 1998. *Jewish Scribes in the Second-Temple Period*, JSOTSup 291. Sheffield: Sheffield Academic.

Schnabel, Eckhard J. 2004. *Early Christian Mission*. Vol. 2, *Paul & the Early Church*. Downers Grove, IL: InterVarsity.

———. 2012. *Acts*. Exegetical Commentary on the New Testament. Grand Rapids: Zondervan.

Schnelle, Udo. 2005. *Apostle Paul: His Life and Theology*. Translated by M. Eugene Boring. Grand Rapids: Baker Academic.

Schürer, E. 1979. *The History of Jewish People in the Age of Jesus Christ*. Vol. 2. Revised and edited by G. Vermes et al. Edinburgh: T. & T. Clark.

Seccombe, David P. 1982. *Possessions and the Poor in Luke-Acts*. Linz: SNTU.

Sell, Phillip W. 2010. "The Seven in Acts 6 as a Ministry Team." *BSac* 167: 58–67.

Sherwin-White, A. N. 1978. *Roman Society and Roman Law in the New Testament*. Grand Rapids: Baker.

Sleeman, Matthew. 2011. "The Vision of Acts: World Right Way Up." *JSNT* 33: 327–33.

Slingerland, Dixon. 1991. "Acts 18:1–18, the Gallio Inscription, and Absolute Pauline Chronology." *JBL* 110: 439–49.

Smith, James. 1978. *The Voyage and Shipwreck of St. Paul with Dissertations on the Life and Writings of St. Luke, and the Ships and Navigation of the Ancients*. 4th ed. Minneapolis: James Family.

Snodgrass, Klyne. 1994. "The Use of the Old Testament in the New." In *The Right Doctrine from the Wrong Text? Essays on the Use of the Old Testament in the New*, edited by G. K. Beale, 29–51. Grand Rapids: Baker.

Soards, M. L. 1994. *The Speeches in Acts: Their Contents, Context and Concerns*. Louisville: Westminster John Knox.

Spencer, F. Scott. 1992. *The Portrait of Philip in Acts: A Study of Roles and Relations*. JSNTSS 67. Sheffield: Sheffield Academic.

Squires, J. T. 1993. *The Plan of God in Luke-Acts*. SNTSMS 76. Cambridge: Cambridge University Press.

———. 1998. "The Plan of God in the Acts of the Apostles." In *Witness to the Gospel: The Theology of Acts*, edited by I. H. Marshall and D. Peterson, 19–39. Grand Rapids: Eerdmans.

Stendahl, K. 1976. *Paul among Jews and Gentiles with Other Essays*. Philadelphia: Fortress.

Stenschke, Christoph W. 2011. "The Biography of Jesus in the Missionary Speeches of Acts." *SM* 99: 267–94.

Sterling, G. E. 1992. *Historiography and Self-Definition: Josephus, Luke-Acts and Apologetic Historiography*. Leiden: Brill.

Stol, M. 1999. "Kaiwan." In *Dictionary of Deities and Demons in the Bible*, edited by K. van der Toorn et al., 478. Grand Rapids: Eerdmans.

Stott, John R. W. 1990. *The Message of Acts: To the Ends of the Earth.* BST. Downers Grove, IL: InterVarsity.

———. 1990. *The Spirit, the Church and the World: The Message of Acts.* Downers Grove, IL: InterVarsity.

Strelan, Richard. 2000. "Recognizing the God (Acts 14.8–10)." *NTS* 46: 488–503.

———. 2003. "Acts 19:12: Paul's 'Aprons' Again." *JTS*, n.s., 54: 154–57.

———. 2004. "Who Was Bar Jesus (Acts 13,6–12)?" *Bib* 85: 65–81.

Strong, David K., and Cynthia A. Strong. 2007. "The Globalizing Hermeneutic of the Jerusalem Council." In *Globalizing Theology: Belief and Practice in an Era of World Christianity*, edited by Craig Ott and Harold A. Netland, 127–39. Nottingham: InterVarsity.

Swanson, Reuben J., ed. 1998. *New Testament Greek Manuscripts: Variant Readings Arranged in Horizontal Lines against Codex Vaticanus, the Acts of the Apostles.* Sheffield: Sheffield Academic.

Sylva, Dennis. 1987. "The Meaning and Function of Acts 7:46–50." *JBL* 106: 261–75.

Tajra, Harry W. 1989. *The Trial of St. Paul.* WUNT II. Tübingen: Mohr.

Talbert, Charles H. 1974. *Literary Patterns, Theological Themes, and the Genre of Luke-Acts.* SBLMS 20. Missoula: Scholar.

———. 2005. *Reading Acts: A Literary and Theological Commentary on the Acts of the Apostles.* Rev. ed. Reading the New Testament. Macon, GA: Smyth.

Tan, Kim Huat. 2008. "The Shema and Early Christianity." *TynBul* 59: 181–206.

Tannehill, Robert C. 1994. *The Narrative Unity of Luke-Acts: A Literary Interpretation.* Vol. 2, *The Acts of the Apostles.* Minneapolis: Fortress.

Taylor, Justin. 2001. "The Jerusalem Decrees (Acts 15.20, 29 and 21.25) and the Incident at Antioch (Gal 2.11–14)." *NTS* 46: 372–80.

Tenney, Merrill C. 1961. *New Testament Survey.* Grand Rapids: Eerdmans.

Thayer, Joseph Henry, trans, ed. 1970 [1962]. *Greek-English Lexicon of the New Testament: Being Grimm's Wilke's Clavis Novi Testamenti.* Grand Rapids: Zondervan.

Thomas, H. W. Derek. 2011. *Acts: Reformed Expository Commentary.* Phillipsburg, NJ: P&R.

Thompson, Richard P. 2006. *Keeping the Church in Its Place: The Church as Narrative Character in Acts.* New York: T. & T. Clark.

Thornton, T. C. G. 1977–1978. "To the End of the Earth: Acts 1:8." *ExpTim* 89: 374–75.

Thurston, Bonnie. 2003. "Paul on the Damascus Road: The Study of the New Testament and the Study of Christian Spirituality." *LTQ* 38: 227–40.

Trebilco, Paul. 1994. "Asia." In *The Book of Acts in Its Graeco-Roman Setting*, edited by David W. J. Gill, 291–362. Book of Acts in Its First Century Setting 2. Grand Rapids: Eerdmans.

———. 2004. *The Early Christians in Ephesus from Paul to Ignatius.* Grand Rapids: Eerdmans.

Trites, Allison A. 1988. "Church Growth in the Book of Acts." *BSac* 145: 162–73.

Trudinger, L. Paul. 1975. "ΕΤΕΡΟΝ ΔΕ ΤΩΝ ΑΠΟΣΤΟΛΩΝ ΟΥΚ ΕΙΔΟΝ, ΕΙ ΜΗ ΙΑΚΩΒΟΝ: A Note on Galatians i 19." *NovT* 17: 199–202.

Trull, Gregory V. 2004. "Peter's Interpretation of Psalm 16:18–20 in Acts 2:25–32." *BSac* 161: 432–48.

Turner, Max. 1996A. *Power from on High: The Spirit in Israel's Restoration and Witness in Luke-Acts.* JPTSS 9. Sheffield: Sheffield Academic.

———. 1996B. *The Holy Spirit and Spiritual Gifts: Then and Now.* Carlisle: Paternoster.

———. 1998. "The 'Spirit of Prophecy' as the Power of Israel's Restoration and Witness." In *Witness to the Gospel: The Theology of Acts*, edited by I. H. Marshall and D. Peterson, 327–48. Eerdmans: Grand Rapids.

Tyson, Joseph B. 1983. "Acts 6:1–7 and Dietary Regulations in Early Christianity." *PRS* 10: 145–61.

Unger, Merrill F. 1960. "Archaeology and Paul's Tour of Cyprus." *Bsac* 117: 229–33.

Van der Horst, Pieter W. 1992. "A New Altar of a Godfearer?" *JJS* 43: 32–37.

Van der Toorn, K., et al., eds. 1999. *Dictionary of Deities and Demons in the Bible.* Grand Rapids: Eerdmans.

Van Unnik, W. C. 1973. "Der Ausdruck ΕΩΣ ΕΣΧΑΤΟΥ ΤΗΣ ΓΗΣ (Apostelgeschichte I 8) und Sein Alttestamentlicher Hintergrund." In *Sparsa Collecta: The Collected Essays of W. C. van Unnik*, 386–401. Leiden: Brill.

Walaskay, Paul W. 1988. "Acts 3:1–10." *Int* 42: 171–75.

Wall, Robert W. 2000. "The Function of LXX Habakkuk 1:5 in the Book of Acts." *BBR* 10: 247–58.

Wallace, Daniel B. 1996. *Greek Grammar: Beyond the Basics.* Grand Rapids: Zondervan.

Walton, Steve. 2000. *Leadership and Lifestyle: The Portrait of Paul in the Miletus Speech and I Thessalonians.* SNTSMS. Cambridge: Cambridge University Press.

———. 2012. "What Does 'Mission' in Acts Mean in Relation to the 'Powers That Be'?" *JETS* 55: 537–56.

Walz, Clark A. 2004. "The Cursing Paul: Magical Contests in Acts 13 and the New Testament Apocrypha." In *Mission in Acts: Ancient Narratives in Contemporary Context*, edited by Robert L. Gallagher and Paul Hertig, 167–82. Maryknoll, NY: Orbis.

Warfield, Benjamin. 1918 [1972]. *Counterfeit Miracles.* New York: Scriber.

Wenham, David, and A. D. A. Moses. 1994. "'There Are Some Standing Here . . .': Did They Become the 'Reputed Pillars' of the Jerusalem Church? Some Reflections on Mark 9:1, Galatians 2:9 and the Transfiguration." *NovT* 36: 146–63.

Wenham, John W. 1991. "Identification of Luke." *EQ* 63: 3–44.

Wilckens, Ulrich. 1974. *Die Missionsreden der Apostelgeschichte.* Neukirchen-Vluyn.

Winefield, Moshe. 2000. "The Counsel of the 'Elders' to Rehoboam and Its Implications." In *Reconsidering Israel and Judah: Recent Studies on the Deuteronomistic History*, edited by Gary N. Knoppers and J. Gordon McConville, 516–39. Winona Lake, IN: Eisenbrauns.

Winter, Bruce W. 1991. "The Importance of the *Captatio Benevolentiae* in the Speeches of Tertullus and Paul in Acts 24:1–21." *JTS*, n.s., 42: 505–31.

———. 1993. "Official Proceedings and the Forensic Speeches in Acts 24–26." In *The Book of Acts in Its Ancient Literary Setting*, edited by Bruce W. Winter and Andrew D. Clarke, 305–36. Book of Acts in Its First Century Setting 1. Grand Rapids: Eerdmans.

———. 1994. "Acts and Food Shortages." In *The Book of Acts in Its Graeco-Roman Setting*, edited by David W. Gill and Conrad Gempf, 59–78. Book of Acts in Its First Century Setting 2. Grand Rapids: Eerdmans.

———. 1996. "On Introducing Gods to Athens: An Alternative Reading of Acts 17:18–20." *TynBul* 47: 71–90.

———. 2006. "Rehabilitating Gallio and His Judgement in Acts 18:14–15." *TynBul* 57: 291–308.

Witherington, Ben, III. 1998. *The Acts of the Apostles: A Socio-Rhetorical Commentary*. Grand Rapids: Eerdmans.

Wright, N. T. 1992. *The New Testament and the People of God*. Minneapolis: Fortress.

———. 2008. *Acts for Everyone: Parts 1–2*. London: SPCK.

Yamauchi, E. 1973. *Pre-Christian Gnosticism: A Survey of the Proposed Evidences*. London: Tyndale.

Young, Brad. 1996. *Jesus the Jewish Theologian*. Peabody, MA: Hendrickson.

Youngblood, F. Ronald. 1995. *Nelson's New Illustrated Bible Dictionary*. Oxford: Nelson.

Zerwick, Maximilian. 1963. *Biblical Greek*. English ed., adapted from the 4th Latin ed. Translated by Joseph Smith. Roma: Editrice Pontificio Istituto Biblico.

Ziesler, John A. 1979. "The Name of Jesus in the Acts of the Apostles." *JSNT* 4: 28–41.

Zwiep, Arie W. 2004. *Judas and the Choice of Matthias: A Study on Context and Concern of Acts 1:15–26*. WUNT. Tübingen: Mohr-Siebeck.

Index